GENDER IN HISTORY

Series editors:
Lynn Abrams, Cordelia Beattie, Julie Hardwick and Penny Summerfield

The expansion of research into the history of women and gender since the 1970s has changed the face of history. Using the insights of feminist theory and of historians of women, gender historians have explored the configuration in the past of gender identities and relations between the sexes. They have also investigated the history of sexuality and family relations, and analysed ideas and ideals of masculinity and femininity. Yet gender history has not abandoned the original, inspirational project of women's history: to recover and reveal the lived experience of women in the past and the present.

The series Gender in History provides a forum for these developments. Its historical coverage extends from the medieval to the modern periods, and its geographical scope encompasses not only Europe and North America but all corners of the globe. The series aims to investigate the social and cultural constructions of gender in historical sources, as well as the gendering of historical discourse itself. It embraces both detailed case studies of specific regions or periods, and broader treatments of major themes. Gender in History titles are designed to meet the needs of both scholars and students working in this dynamic area of historical research.

Women art workers and the Arts and Crafts movement

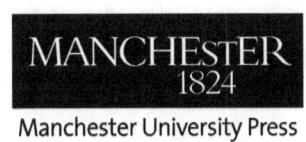

MANCHESTER
1824

Manchester University Press

WOMEN ART WORKERS AND THE ARTS AND CRAFTS MOVEMENT

⇥ Zoë Thomas ⇤

Manchester University Press

The right of Zoë Thomas to be identified as the author of this work has been asserted by her in accordance with the Copyright, Designs and Patents Act 1988.

Published by Manchester University Press
Oxford Road, Manchester M13 9PL

www.manchesteruniversitypress.co.uk

British Library Cataloguing-in-Publication Data
A catalogue record for this book is available from the British Library

ISBN 978 1 5261 4043 2 hardback
ISBN 978 1 5261 6027 0 paperback

First published 2020
The publisher has no responsibility for the persistence or accuracy of URLs for any external or third-party internet websites referred to in this book, and does not guarantee that any content on such websites is, or will remain, accurate or appropriate.

Typeset
by Toppan Best-set Premedia Limited

Contents

Figures

Acknowledgements

Firstly, I would like to thank Yoke-Sum Wong. Without her encouragement and interest I would probably never have applied to do a doctorate or become a historian. Secondly, I am grateful to the institutions who have generously supported me along the way: the Arts and Humanities Research Council; Royal Holloway, University of London; the Friendly Hand Trust; the Huntington Library; the North American Conference on British Studies; the Paul Mellon Centre for Studies in British Art; the Royal Historical Society; the Fran Trust Foundation; the Oxford Dictionary of National Biography; Wolfson College, Oxford; Gladstone Library; and most recently the University of Birmingham. Throughout this process, Manchester University Press has been a joy to work with. Special thanks to my editor Emma Brennan, who has been supportive at every step, and to Jessica Cuthbert-Smith for being the dream copy-editor.

The descendants and holders of papers belonging to Women's Guild of Arts members have enthralled me with their personal memories, letters, diaries, photographs, sketchbooks, and even tours around their 'Arts and Crafts' homes. Thanks to Wendy Duwell, Sue Field, Sarah Humphries, Phil Johnson, S. R. Kaplan, Chris Moore, Jane Nissen, David Robinson, Arthur Rope, and Richard and Susan Wallington. Archivists, curators, librarians, volunteers, and local historians have been generous in their help. Particular thanks to Rowan Bain, Lorna Beckett, Hannah Carroll, Beverley Cook, Helen Elletson, Leigh Milsom Fowler, Rebecca Green, Monica Grose-Hodge, Gillian Murphy, Judy Willcocks, and Christopher Woodham. Many thanks to David Birch, Master of the Art Workers' Guild in 2016, for inviting me to speak about my research at 6 Queen Square and to the Brothers for their kind words, interest, and support that evening and throughout the time I have been writing this book.

A number of academics, researchers, and friends have helped me over the years by sharing sources, ideas, and advice: Liz Arthur, Sarah Barber, Geoffrey Beare, Caitriona Beaumont, Grace Brockington, Charlotte Brown, Annette Carruthers, Phil Child, Tessa Chynoweth, Gerald Cinamon, Barry Clark, Irene Cockroft, Alan Crawford, Katy Deepwell, Emma Ferry, Kenneth Florey, Matthew Francis, Elaine Fulton, David Gange, Helen Glew, Freya Gowrley, Ian Hamerton, Louise Hardiman, Janice Helland, Tom Hulme, Sarah Kenny, Ben Mechen, Chris Moores, Tara Morton, Stella Moss, Laika Nevalainen, Kate Nichols, Melinda Parsons, James Pugh, Sadiah Qureshi, Derek Sayer, Beth Spacey, Peter Stansky, Alex Windscheffel, and Susan Woodall. Discussions with Laura Carter, Heidi Egginton,

Miranda Garrett, Lyndsey Jenkins, and Lucy Ella Rose have shaped this book. Their generosity in discussing research and sharing ideas has been inspiring. To all of my students at the University of Birmingham, and particularly those who have taken my Special Subject 'British Women and Internationalism since 1850': thank you for contributing to our classes and for sharing your thoughts with me, particularly about the Lyceum Club.

A very generous set of friends and scholars have read the book proposal, chapters, and even the whole book at various stages. I am so grateful to the following for pushing me to think harder and more deeply about *Women Art Workers* and for taking so much time to engage in my work: firstly, the anonymous reviewers of the manuscript, but also Deborah Cherry, Peter Cormack, Christina de Bellaigue, Kathryn Gleadle, Jane Hamlett, Janice Helland, Matt Houlbrook, Leslie Howsam, Peter Mandler, Joseph McBrinn, Mo Moulton, Otto Saumarez-Smith, Lynne Walker, and William Whyte.

Thank you to my family and to Hannah Hillen, my 'partner in crime' since we were at primary school. My greatest thank you goes to Simon Thomas Parsons for reading every single thing I have written over the last six years with boundless enthusiasm and support, for providing incisive critiques, ideas, and edits on drafts, for keeping me company on research trips, for teaching me so much about medieval history, and for reminding me that there are exciting adventures to be had outside of the archive.

Introduction
The Arts and Crafts movement, work cultures, and the politics of gender

In London today there survive countless buildings which function as important architectural symbols of late nineteenth- and early twentieth-century artistic culture. There is the Art Workers' Guild's purpose-built Hall at 6 Queen Square, Bloomsbury, which, to this day, houses meetings for 'craftspeople and architects working at the highest levels of excellence in their professions'.[1] The Hall has a rich history: it is the place where the most prestigious men associated with the Arts and Crafts movement met, in reaction to the domineering presence of the Royal Academy, to forge new bonds of brotherly comradeship and concoct radical ideas about how to reform society through the arts. The walls are lined with paintings and sculptures depicting eminent past members such as architect W. R. Lethaby, and artists Selwyn Image, Walter Crane, and C. R. Ashbee. In West London, there is St Paul's Studios, a row of purpose-built red-brick studios with colossal glass windows, a testament to the extensive growth of such buildings in this artistic area of the city in the late nineteenth century. This street was designed in 1891 for use by 'bachelor' artists; today these famed sites provide homes for millionaires. Elsewhere in Hammersmith there is Kelmscott House, once home to socialist designer and poet William Morris; the William Morris Society are now encamped in the coach house and basement rooms, ensuring his name is not forgotten. A short stroll down the river, at 7 Hammersmith Terrace, is the engraver and printer Emery Walker's home. It is open to the public, and visitors can view historical rooms with Morris & Co. wallpaper and furniture by Philip Webb, and can even peer into a drawer containing a lock of William Morris's hair. In books, walking tours, and exhibition catalogues, these buildings – the Hall, St Paul's Studios, Morris's and Walker's homes, alongside buildings such as the painter Frederic Leighton's Kensington studio home (now the Leighton House Museum, resplendent with English Heritage blue plaque) – are all used as cultural anchor points through which to construct a history framed around the centrality of exceptional male figures to the modern art scene.

But these buildings hide secrets. During this era, a vast network of artistic women working in the capital and across the country were active participants in this culture. Women art workers formed their own exclusive guild – the Women's Guild of Arts – and met at the same Hall for over fifty years. They organised lectures, exhibitions, demonstrations, and parties at their businesses, workshops, homes, exhibition venues, and studios, which included various properties at St Paul's Studios, and several houses on the banks of the river in Hammersmith. At these premises, art was designed and made – from bookcases, to stained-glass windows, necklaces, and chess sets – which was sent to customers around the world. Women art workers played a critical role in disseminating the Arts and Crafts ethos of the social importance of the arts across new local, national, and international spheres of influence, and simultaneously altering that same ethos to be more receptive to public interest in domestic consumerism. By the dawn of the twentieth century they had grown in confidence in promoting their own vision of the movement. This focused less on an idealistic rhetoric of demolishing class hierarchies and more on a pragmatic cultivation of the public obsession with obtaining 'artistic' and 'historic' objects for the home. But this was not a rejection of the political: this new conception of the Arts and Crafts redirected the radical potential of art work into contemporary women-centred causes.

Women Art Workers foregrounds these buildings, spaces, and the relationships that played out within these sites. In so doing, it offers unprecedented insight into how women, working across the arts, constructed creative lives and sought to overturn imbalances of cultural, social, political, and gendered power. These women were agents of change who shaped a range of skilled work cultures (artistic, professional, intellectual, entrepreneurial, commercial) at a critical juncture and encouraged new ideas to spread across society about gender relations, organisational cultures, family life, and the meaning of equality. Challenging the long-standing assumption that the movement simply revolved around celebrated male designers like William Morris and his circle, this book offers a new social and cultural history of the English Arts and Crafts movement which reveals the breadth of the imprint of women art workers upon the making of the modern world.

A new history of the Arts and Crafts movement

Across the nineteenth century, fear about the damaging effects of industrialisation, urbanisation, and mass consumption on social conditions and culture became increasingly prevalent. In an era of growing international competitiveness, many felt that England's decorative art tradition represented the state of its society to a watchful global audience. By the 1870s and 1880s concerns became more urgent. An army of architects, artists, and writers grew convinced of the need to take inspiration from the medieval past and to design and create art which could temper the ills of the modern world. Art critic John Ruskin was one particularly influential figure, who lamented the deterioration of different processes of design and making, so that objects could be quickly and cheaply produced by unskilled labourers. He positioned the arts as offering participants the chance to cultivate a greater sense of personal authenticity in a rapidly changing world.

Authenticity was ill-defined and devoid of fixed meaning, but in these artistic circles was loosely articulated as eschewing commercial trends, embracing the natural world, respecting materials, and working collaboratively, across the production process. There was a concentration of interest in overturning the hierarchy in the arts which had – since the Renaissance – prioritised the 'High Arts' of architecture, painting, and sculpture above the so-called 'minor' decorative arts. This growth of interest in finding artistic alternatives to industrial manufacturing was matched by a flood of consumer desire to purchase suitably artistic and historic objects for the home, as the middle classes expanded and sought to show off their new cultured statuses to the rest of society.[2]

The 1880s constituted a formative decade in the making of the move-ment.[3] The Art Workers' Guild and the Home Arts and Industries Associa-tion were established in 1884, followed by the Arts and Crafts Exhibition Society, which was established in 1887 and held its first exhibition in 1888. The Home Arts and Industries Association functioned as an umbrella organisation for craft-based industries across the country. Framed around educating working-class individuals of the benefits of the crafts, it has attracted a reputation as the amateur outer sphere of the movement, even though it played a critical role in encouraging greater societal engagement with handcrafted cultures.[4] The formation of the Exhibition Society, the point at which the phrase 'Arts and Crafts' was coined, provided important new exhibition opportunities for the women and men whose work was deemed of high enough quality. By contrast, the Art Workers' Guild, which remained male-only until 1964, cultivated an intensely private club-like environment for distinguished male architects and designers. Together these three groups are heralded as forming the tripartite insti-tutional representation of the English Arts and Crafts movement.

Histories of the movement routinely construct narratives framed around biographies of celebrated figures such as William Morris and C. R. Ashbee, and their altruistic, politicised, and creative attempts to overturn traditional class hierarchies by forging cross-class bonds between different men, in particular between labourers and architects and designers.[5]

Ashbee formed his Guild of Handicraft in the East End in 1888 to put into practice his desire to provide opportunities for working-class men to take joy in processes of making in the workshop, instead of toiling away in capitalist factories. Yet despite radical intentions, often because of the costs involved, these men spent much of their time producing work for upper-middle-class and upper-class customers, facilitating the very process they sought to reverse.[6] Morris and Ashbee were both members of the Art Workers' Guild, a group which exemplifies the class hierarchies which permeated the movement. One had to be an architect or designer (not simply a maker) to gain entry, many members were already friends, and the relationships formalised there fortified a pervasive model of elite artistic masculinity well into the twentieth century.

The Art Workers' Guild is often used as a barometer for measuring the cultural significance of different artists to the movement. Art historian Alan Crawford, amongst others, has positioned the Guild as having the atmosphere 'of a slightly Bohemian gentleman's club, smoky and exclusive. It was the most important single organisation in the Movement, and in some ways its heart.'[7] Those who did not gain access in its heyday tend to be viewed as suspicious dilettante outliers, or simply ignored, part of the ongoing tendency to position privileged male individuals and male-only institutions as uniformly appreciated symbols of expertise and disseminators of cultural knowledge. Figures such as Morris clearly were influential – those around him repeatedly venerated his role as 'artistic godfather' – but this ongoing fixation with such individuals has distorted the understanding of the movement's long-term social and cultural impact.

In contrast to the interest in class relations, scholarship using gender as a critical lens of inquiry to understand the Arts and Crafts has been notably limited. The single monograph on women in the movement remains Anthea Callen's 1979 *Angel in the Studio*, part of a mass of valuable second-wave feminist scholarship which sought to uncover the 'hidden' lives of women across history. Callen, drawing predominantly from periodicals, journals, and advice literature relating to the years 1860–1900, alongside texts often written by members of the Art Workers' Guild, concluded that the movement ultimately perpetuated prevalent patriarchal hierarchies and failed to alter wider social conceptions of the relationship between middle-class women and work.[8] Lynne Walker provided an important counter to this in an 1989 book chapter, suggesting that 'instead of further alienating women, the Arts and Crafts Movement provided women with alternative roles, institutions, and structures which they then used as active agents in their own history'.[9] Despite the emergence of scholarship convincingly emphasising the significance of women in the Scottish, Irish, Canadian, and North American Arts and Crafts movements, and a wealth of feminist scholarship which has unveiled the centrality of women's artistic outputs in the making of the modern art world more widely, histories of the English movement have continued to ignore the contributions of women, or relegate them to a single page.[10]

A small cluster of books and exhibitions have provided a productive biographical lens onto the lives and works of individual 'exceptional' Arts and Crafts women – whose relevance can be ascertained through their close association by marriage or kin to celebrated men, such as embroidery designer and jeweller May Morris, daughter of William Morris.[11] These accounts offer important insights, but they can be emblematic of older art historical approaches to the canon, tending to be framed around notions of individual exceptionality. Currently, we are reliant on these narratives to understand women's involvement in the movement, but such an approach sits uneasily within this specific historical context. Those involved in the Arts and Crafts, in their ideals at least, often sought to break down such hierarchical notions of individual exceptionality, channelling great energies into forming informal and formal collaborations to augment their commitment to the Arts and Crafts.

In this book, I offer a new history of the Arts and Crafts movement which moves beyond the tendency to construct a narrative through the perspectives of one or two celebrated individual designers, to instead position the extensive network of women working at the highest echelons of the English Arts and Crafts movement at the centre of the analysis for the first time. My 'cast' comprises many women who are today practically unknown, alongside a small number of better-known figures. They include, among others: stained-glass designer Mary Lowndes; metalworker E. C. (Ellen Caroline) Woodward and her sister the illustrator Alice B. (Bolingbroke) Woodward; painter and enameller Edith B. (Brearey) Dawson (née Robinson); muralist Mary Sargant Florence (née Sargant); sculptor Feodora Gleichen; painter and folklorist Estella Canziani; textile designer and jeweller May Morris; illustrator and toy designer M. V. (Mary Vermuyden) Wheelhouse; 'artistic' goldsmith Charlotte Newman (née Gibbs); woodworker Julia Bowley (née Hilliam); weaver Annie Garnett; and illustrator and designer Pamela Colman Smith.

The central thread connecting these women is that they were all founding or early members of the Women's Guild of Arts. Established in 1907 because women were refused entry on the basis of their sex to the Art Workers' Guild, it became the most prestigious group in the country for women 'designers and workers, principally, though not exclusively, in the applied arts'.[12] Like their male peers, members of the Women's Guild of Arts were predominantly middle and upper middle class and from professional, trading, and artistic families. Until at least the late 1920s the Guild fluctuated around sixty full members, in comparison to the Art Workers' Guild, which had approximately 240 members. Yet the Women's Guild has since been overlooked in all major histories of the Arts and Crafts movement. Throughout, my focus is the interconnected social worlds of approximately thirty of these women, positioning them amidst the cultural milieu of the era, revealing women art workers to have been central players in the Arts and Crafts movement, and arguing that any history which does not consider their activities is fundamentally flawed.

The Women's Guild of Arts functions as a powerful riposte to the repeated assertions that there were few women designers in the English movement. Even Stella Tillyard, who stressed the significance of the wider hinterland of the movement, emphasising that women were active at 'all … levels', stated there 'were few major [female] designers' (mentioning none by name) and 'For the most part professional craftswomen simply made what men had designed.' She also contended there 'were few female groups which were both professional and visionary'.[13] The Women's Guild of Arts, however, alongside other groups such as the Lyceum Club, was certainly visionary in its outlook. All members were designers to some extent, they just tended to place less significance on emphasising this specific component, largely because they regularly worked across numerous stages of the production process, putting into practice their desire to overturn hierarchies between design and making. As numerous chapters demonstrate, many of these women were still held up as major designers, although there were of course varying opportunities and restrictions from field to field, be it metalwork, sculpture, or textiles.

The Arts and Crafts movement is challenging to define: designers and makers of 'Arts and Crafts objects' and buildings did not conform to any neat, identifiable approach, incorporating a variety of influences, and ranging in scale from churches to doorknockers. Elizabeth Cumming and Wendy Kaplan have discussed how 'the very word "style", as applied to historicist revivalism, was anathema to them'.[14] As the movement grew in popularity, companies shrewdly latched onto the power of the 'Arts and Crafts' to sell their 'artistic' stock, but an 'Arts and Crafts object' should not be assumed to have been designed or crafted by a person who held Arts and Crafts ideas.[15] There were myriad interconnections between different artistic spheres: art nouveau, aestheticism, or modernism(s).

The Women's Guild of Arts forces us to confront such tensions head on, as it accepted members who worked across many fields and with hybrid influences. A good example of this tendency is member Pamela Colman Smith, who not only designed the famous Rider-Waite deck of divinatory tarot cards, but also designed sets and costumes for the Lyceum Theatre, told stories about Jamaican folklore, established the Green Sheaf press, had synesthetic sensibilities (painting visions which came to her whilst listening to music), and immersed herself in Arts and Crafts networks. Like many of her peers, Colman Smith had little interest in neatly conforming to one movement or approach, and ultimately sought to construct an immersive new lifestyle, oriented around finding inspiration by moving between a variety of stimulating artistic milieus. Such an approach situated women like Colman Smith at the cutting edge of social and cultural change when they were alive, but has subsequently led to a lacuna in scholarship, partially for the reason that these lives and works do not neatly fit amidst the movement-oriented and disciplinary divides which continue to dominate curatorial decisions and formal scholarship. Despite the difficulties of adopting a conceptual demarcation of the Arts and Crafts movement, Guild members rhetorically expressed their dedication to such an ideal. Indeed, the Guild was specifically founded to promote the centrality of women working in the movement.

Reconceptualising the movement to incorporate the centrality of this network of women shatters the traditional periodisation of the Arts and Crafts. At the exact point when women's artistic engagement was rapidly expanding – the Women's Guild of Arts was founded in 1907 – the movement was being dismissed as losing societal relevance by men such as C. R. Ashbee and Eric Gill. Both had anxieties about the state of modern society and strongly believed art workers needed to play a greater social and political role beyond working for (in the words of Ashbee) 'a narrow and tiresome little aristocracy'.[16] But their arguments were also bound up with a chauvinistic apprehension about the movement's transformation to include greater access for women, who were clamouring to express their views and use the movement for their own needs. For men such as Ashbee and Gill, this move beyond the specific model of artistic radicalism and authenticity envisaged by the small coterie of middle-class men they knew, and the movement's wider societal accessibility, impact, and even populism, by the early twentieth century, inevitably meant a 'watering down' of its core ideals.

The scholarship which has since positioned the Arts and Crafts in relation to such rhetoric has replicated this problem: flattening women's contributions and portraying the movement as the unresolved ideology (or even 'failure') of a cluster of visionary male 'Victorian' architects and designers, a periodisation which neatly follows the ebb and flow of the life of William Morris (who died in 1896) and fits with the supposed subsequent sweeping dominance of modernism. Nevertheless, this narrative of decline has slowly begun to be counteracted. Tillyard argued that modernism was so ground-breaking in Edwardian England, not because it disbanded the past in a revolutionary manner, but because it grew out of the nineteenth-century roots of the Arts and Crafts movement. Michael Saler went further, arguing that transport administrator Frank Pick, used as a representative of one of 'Morris's followers' in the interwar era, managed to convince 'many within the worlds of government, industry, education and art' at this later date that 'the cause of art was indeed that of the people'. Others have pointed to the alternative Arts and Crafts communities established across the country well into the 1930s.[17] Ultimately, the early twentieth century was not a moment which saw steady decline of interest in the Arts and Crafts in favour of stripped-back 'modernist' approaches, at either a 'High Art' or a 'middle-brow' level, in England.[18]

Despite this, even recent histories of modern design tend to position the movement as having 'lost some of its radical edge by the early twentieth century'.[19] Yet for the multiple generations of women involved, the political potential of the Arts and Crafts was not so much the opportunity to radically overturn class hierarchies, but instead the chance it offered to disrupt gendered marginalisation in the art world and in society.[20] Several artistic women combined their artistic and political energies in the suffrage campaigns.[21] Ultimately, the movement nurtured a space in which a wider cross-section of people, made up predominantly of middle- and upper-middle-class figures, could pursue harmonious, collaborative, and creative lives in a modern capitalist world. They created a more fecund landscape in which a younger generation of artistic women could – and did – take centre stage by the 1920s and 1930s.[22] By putting forward these beliefs, women art workers became central players in the formation of a progressive and creative cultural milieu in England, which still interconnected with, and fortified, a wider set of pervasive conservative and hierarchical trends.[23] The permeable 'conservative/radical' nature of the movement is explored in multiple chapters, for instance by revealing the outpouring of nationalistic patriotism and promulgation of stereotyped ideas about 'English culture' at many Arts and Crafts exhibitions during the First World War.

Furthermore, in practice, women art workers, shaped by their own gendered positions in society, developed a special relationship to 'popular' culture which elite male designers often scorned, opening up the Arts and Crafts to a more expansive variety of incomes, social backgrounds, and interests. Customers and patrons ranged from fellow artists, suffrage campaigners and supporters of the women's movement, antiquarians, the Royal Family, American collectors, and, with increasing regularity, those with smaller incomes.[24] Very few people could afford an 'Arts and Crafts house', but growing numbers could afford a brooch, bound book, or piece of pottery. Although the Art Workers' Guild was dominated by architects, the Women's Guild of Arts did not have a single member who chose to be identified as an architect. As such, women art workers were at the vanguard of directing artistic taste and promoting a consumer-friendly model of 'moral' commercialism, framed around handcrafted art for the home (although it is important to note such women also designed and produced all sorts of 'big' works not intended for domestic settings: church furniture, murals, panels, memorials, and sculptures). A wide network of alternative, fashionable cultural spaces were established: workshops, studios, homes, exhibitions, and businesses. Where possible, their independently run premises were situated in artistic areas of the city like Chelsea or in fashionable side streets snaking off Oxford Street, but women art workers also established businesses across the country, in areas such as the Lake District and the Cotswolds. They offered new sites where the public could engage in art away from the museums and grand galleries, or even the new department stores, where it is commonly understood the middle classes viewed, discussed, and bought *objets d'art* across this era.

Outside of the austere context of the Arts and Crafts Exhibition Society – always conceptualised as the public face of the movement – a more informal and interactive Arts and Crafts culture was being constructed, in which women participants were centrally involved. Members of the public thronged to watch women art workers engaging in artistry at their exhibitions and workshops; the press published exhortative pieces by female artists encouraging readers to educate themselves about historical traditions and craft techniques; and the shelves of bookshops and family homes were filled with manuals written by women equipping dilettantes and designers alike with the knowledge they needed to pursue craft projects.[25] Several of these books continue to be used today by practitioners and hobbyists alike. Drawing on this democratisation of artistic culture, women art workers fashioned roles as authoritative educators and cultural arbiters, tapping into a prevalent contemporary nostalgia for a supposedly more harmonious, pre-industrial world.[26] It was this flourishing of cultural activity which shaped the public conception of 'Arts and Crafts' and fed the success of an artistic movement which captivated the minds and hearts of larger numbers of people than any other art movement before or since in England.

Skilled work cultures: the artistic, professional, intellectual, and entrepreneurial

Reconceptualising the Arts and Crafts movement with women positioned centre stage has ramifications for the broader understanding of work and 'professional' status across this period. Through their work and lifestyles, the example of art workers forces a reconsideration of explanatory mechanisms such as the established master narrative of professionalisation which has dominated scholarly understanding since the 1980s.[27] It is well established that the meaning of the term 'professional' crystallised after the eighteenth century, becoming closely associated with a cluster of occupations which demanded training, qualifications, and assertion of expertise, and expanding beyond law, the clergy, and medicine to incorporate fields from science to education to art.[28] But scholarship routinely focuses on more traditionally recognised fields of work, guarded by institutional membership, educational standing, and legal mechanisms, when defining professional status – an approach which rarely addresses the fluidity and rhetorical self-fashioning inherent in many 'professional project[s]' (to use sociologist Anne Witz's term) which different figures engaged in.[29] This is particularly the case for those working outside of these traditionally recognised fields, such as art, where professional status becomes harder to define.

Work cultures take us to the heart of how societies have historically constructed ideals of masculinity and femininity, the attempts to engrain gender and class hierarchies within formal structures and institutions, and how different individuals and groups have contested and rejected these binaries and sought to establish new modes of living and working. In recent years, scholars of women and work have shown how professionalisation repeatedly led to women being marginalised or excluded. In science, a growth in female participation brought about reactionary fears of a 'crisis of impending feminization'.[30] Similarly, the increasingly hierarchical process of formal architectural training made it difficult for women to become architects by the nineteenth century, in contrast to the eighteenth.[31] Professionalisation often imposed a dual block for women. Firstly, they tended to lack institutional capital, through inability to possess key educational qualifications. Inequality could be enshrined in the law: for instance, women could not officially become lawyers until after the 1919 Sex Disqualification (Removal) Act. Secondly, barred entry to certain masculine social groups, women frequently lacked the necessary social capital to advance professionally.[32] Concurrently, informal processes of gender discrimination continued to prevail, which stressed the centrality of the maternal, the marital, and the domestic in women's lives.

The arts mirrored these trends. The term 'professional' was deployed to delineate status in the nineteenth century, particularly in the fine arts. Artists grew ever more protective about monopolising access to customers, whilst entry to societies was increasingly restricted, as was the regulation of exhibition displays. Numerous artistic prospects were closed to women: life study was often restricted or segregated, as were opportunities to attend specific classes.[33] Although women – with financial means – attended in ever greater numbers private art schools and co-educational art schools such as the Royal Academy Schools (women were allowed entry from 1860), and the Slade School of Art (established 1871), male figures dominated the teaching staff well into the twentieth century.[34]

In response to the growth in numbers of women becoming artists, the term 'amateur' began to be understood as having disparaging, gendered connotations, persistently associated with women's pursuits, despite the 'gentleman amateur' historically having been a respectable term for learned men.[35] In his 1908 *Craftsmanship in Competitive Industry*, C. R. Ashbee proclaimed that the 'two forms of competition' continually 'strangling the crafts and wasting human life' were 'the machine' but also the 'lady amateur' who was 'perpetually tingling to sell her work before she half knows how to make it'.[36] Yet, strikingly, there has been little scholarship focused directly on the performative model of artistic masculinity being crafted in the movement, even though certain men repeatedly portrayed Arts and Crafts activities and objects as only *becoming* 'authentic', 'serious', and 'artistic' through close contact between working-class male makers and the guiding intellect of visionary middle-class male designers.[37] Although Ashbee and many of his peers continually prioritised processes of making over finished products, asserting that a return to historic processes of production held the key to restoring integrity and satisfaction to modern society, when women joyfully engaged in such processes they were more likely to be labelled as 'amateurs' and subsequently marginalised. Work by women was not seen as having an intrinsic *authenticity* which, it was felt, best arose out of an exchange between those working-class male makers and the guiding intellect of visionary middle-class designers. Ashbee's own company ultimately failed financially and had to be closed – in noticeable contrast to the commercial successes of many of the women's businesses discussed in Chapter 4 – and even though Ashbee's biographer admits that high skill and a sense of materials were only 'present unevenly' in the work of the Guild of Handicraft, we are still deeply invested in Ashbee's journey and contributions to English culture.[38]

Feminist art historical scholarship has devoted considerable energies on trying to delineate what it meant to be a professional woman artist during this era, with much focus on the fine arts. Most recently, Nicola Moorby and Maria Quirk claimed that the 'mark of the professional artist … was the sale of work.'[39] The art market expanded rapidly during this period, and a craving for financial independence – or sheer survival – and the status wrought by commanding large sums of money meant interactions with the market was an undeniably important factor for many artists. But we should be cautious of restricting artistic professionalisation through prioritisation of a single means of assessment. Framing those women who made a regular income as 'the professionals' immediately discounts several prestigious women at the Women's Guild of Arts. Training provides no easier answers: although many members did receive some form of art training, having an art education by no means created neat categories of professionals versus non-professionals.[40] In personal papers and newspaper columns alike, people heatedly debated the 'professional' statuses of artistic women, often using contradictory methods of categorisation: alternating between stressing the importance of training, payment, membership of elite groups, regular exhibition habits, the ability of an admired artwork to convey professional status, or a variety of the above. Prioritising one specific strand does not take into account the range of strategies 'successful' women working across the arts had to navigate in order to be taken seriously, and it misreads the contested ways artistic roles continued to be discussed. Ultimately, there is no single test one can apply to determine if an artist is 'professional', nor was there one in the late nineteenth or early twentieth centuries.

Writer Constance Smedley, who encouraged new professional networks to blossom between women by establishing Lyceum Clubs across the world, reflected in her 1929 memoir *Crusaders* about the relationship between the 'professions' and literary and artistic work at the dawn of the twentieth century. Smedley stressed that, unlike those 'headed for safer ground' in 'professions that involved a definite training at a University or Technical College', the arts were 'pursuits in an unfenced borderland'. She hinted at the problems which beset women in these fields: 'in 1902 that shadow was always hanging about the working world and professional bypaths were always on the edge of the abyss. One slip, and you were gone forever.'[41] Yet despite all of this – the institutional restrictions, the suggestions of amateurism, and the ominous pitfalls Smedley alludes to – it was this inherent elasticity, this ability to pursue a range of different 'unfenced borderland[s]', which made art such an attractive option for women, offering them opportunities to assert new roles largely outside of the formal restrictions they faced in other professions. This was particularly the case in the Arts and Crafts, where women could swiftly gain authority through learning about and adapting historic methods and techniques in fields less regulated and hierarchical than the fine arts.

Weaving throughout these tactics was a vocational ethos characteristic of the arts and the liberal work ethic of the era.[42] For Arts and Crafts protagonists, there was no easy divide between living and working. A quasi-religious, fervent belief in the possibilities of forming a new world, where all the arts could be harmoniously enjoyed, fed into all they did. Friendships became artistic networks, homes were turned into studios, and romantic partners were selected because of their artistic commitments. Such attempts to negotiate these new roles actually constituted a complete reimagining of their entire lives. This culture was particularly permeable to women, for whom gendered expectations demanded the integration of their domestic and professional lives.

In part, demonstrating allegiance to the movement involved performatively divesting oneself of overt traces of 'professionalism'. Many men associated with the Arts and Crafts movement had little interest in portraying themselves in such a way, and in fact made concerted attempts to distance themselves linguistically from the professions due to its implications of overt regulation, uniformity, and 'the establishment'.[43] In noticeable contrast, Arts and Crafts women were more likely to accept being labelled as 'professionals', and indeed were often described specifically as such by sympathetic social commentators, in a gendered framing rarely used to describe their male peers.[44] Whenever possible, however, they preferred to use descriptive terms such as 'workers', 'designers', 'artists', 'craft workers', and 'art workers' (often prefixing all these terms with 'serious') over 'professional' to describe their occupational choices. Throughout this book, I draw interchangeably from this extensive rhetorical discourse – and take a similar approach to terms such as applied art, craft, decorative, and handicraft – in a manner appropriate to their flexible and inconsistent usage at the time. Of these, 'art worker' and 'Arts and Crafts' tended to be the most encompassing and frequently employed in the documentary record. I do, however, still use 'professional'. The specific processes Arts and Crafts women (and men) engaged in to assert cultural expertise often emulated and interconnected with professionalising currents, such as obsessively regulating access to certain groups and exhibitions. Situating Arts and Crafts networks in relation to wider debates about professionalisation also evokes a discursive world Women's Guild of Arts members would have recognised. Press reports about Mary Lowndes's Englishwoman Exhibition of Arts and Handicrafts, for instance, consistently asserted that 'Only the best professional work is accepted.'[45] At times, different art workers used this term to signal serious intent, and this was especially the case for women.

Facing heightened suspicions due to their gender, women art workers needed to ensure they were perceived to be offering an alternative to the efflorescence of amateur 'dabblers'. Keen to remove notions of amateurism, they often embedded themselves amidst the women's movement, where they were admired as important representatives of pioneering professional women. Both the suffrage campaigns and the women's movement facilitated the expansion of new women-centred, politicised spaces for the performance of professionalisation, socialisation, and an avid consumer market. The neologism 'professional' – and 'business woman' – was a specific focal point of these empowerment strategies.[46] This can clearly be seen at the International Congress of Women conference in 1899, held in London, in the section on 'Women in Professions'. In the subfield of the handicrafts, architect W. R. Lethaby began with a paper discussing the 'Special Aptitude of Women for Handicrafts'. Subsequently, four leading women agreed to represent their respective fields: May Morris provided a paper on needlework, Charlotte Newman on metalwork, Mary Lowndes on stained glass, and Julia Hilliam on woodwork. In her paper, Hilliam asked, 'Do we realise what an influence we have on the taste of the future, as our work lives after us?'[47] She also appeared aggrieved (similarly to C. R. Ashbee) about the many women now making '"nice little things for the house and bazaars, but they are only amateurs," and how we wish there were only half the number'.[48] This tendency to differentiate themselves as influential figures in society, who were making history, intersected with a wish to ensure they were defined as 'art workers' who provided an alternative to trade companies and the mass market. Despite the condescension of Hilliam's dismissal of 'amateurs', which was common amongst her network, Hilliam and her female peers were deeply reliant upon this wider sphere of feminine, amateurish interest. It provided both a receptive market and spaces where they could more easily establish and assert their authority.

Throughout this book, I show how women repeatedly asserted expertise across fields of activity often conceptualised as having been largely separate: moving competently between artistic, professional, intellectual, and commercial spheres, lecturing, exhibiting, designing, making, and writing. Partially due to this approach – at once everywhere and nowhere – art workers have slipped through the historiographical net, having received little analysis from art historians, economic and intellectual historians, gender historians, or historians of work. Arts and Crafts women recalibrated societal and cultural understanding of women in the arts by obfuscating the boundaries between art and craft; between creativity, the professions, and entrepreneurial intent; between modern and medieval; and between public and private, domestic life. The different elements to maintaining one's status as a 'professional art worker' was especially beneficial for women. They did not have to persistently attempt to gain entry to one, tightly controlled world of work, but could instead attempt to make headway by partially participating in a range of different activities. In a similar manner to their refusal to conform to a particular 'style', they refused to commit themselves to a particular model of working.

Women art workers wholeheartedly embraced these strategies of adopting multiple roles and engaging with different registers of activity. A 'successful art worker' could be equal parts culturally authoritative intellectual, business owner, and artistic idealist. For example, Charlotte Newman sought to garner an artistic and intellectual reputation – and to raise the status of goldsmith work – by giving formal lectures for elite male-only art societies, but she also used her commercially profitable jewellery business to assert authority on her own terms, which allowed her discreetly to negotiate access to a receptive market and an international audience clamouring to buy handmade 'artistic' and 'historic' jewellery. She was portrayed as a celebrity in detailed interviews for the women's and the art press: the *Woman's Signal* extolled her virtues as 'far more than the clever businesswoman, or even the skilled worker'. Instead she had been 'for years a student of ancient history and art ... She has exalted the ordinary craft of the jeweller into a fine art.'[49] By weaving their way through these different worlds these figures appeared as cultured participants in society, even if such tactics came at least partially from positions of instability. Together, Arts and Crafts women expanded the boundaries of respectability in artistic and work cultures, establishing a series of new pathways through which women could more readily participate, by repeatedly taking advantage of the various 'unfenced borderland[s]' available to them.

Artistic equality, the women's movement, and the politics of gender

The second half of the nineteenth century marked a critical period when the women's movement on both sides of the Atlantic resolutely pushed for the expansion of opportunities for women in politics, education, civic cultures, and work. As part of this, there was a rapid growth of a women-focused print culture, from feminist advocacy papers such as the *Englishwoman's Review* to fashionable publications like *Hearth and Home*, as well as women's sections in local and national newspapers, alongside books, published lectures, and conference proceedings.[50] By the early twentieth century, the suffrage campaigns saw ever more feminist papers, such as *Votes for Women* and the *Common Cause*. All of these different publications promoted women's extensive knowledge of household management, home decoration, and fashion, priming a space where women art workers – and women art historians, critics, and interior decorators – could situate themselves as experts, ready to direct the tastes of the ever-growing sector of the public interested in buying 'artistic' and 'historic' objects.[51] Several women embedded in Arts and Crafts currents asserted that women had special aptitudes for designing and making domestic artwork. E. C. Woodward told readers of *Mrs Strang's Annual for Girls* that jewellery making was 'perhaps specially suited to women, who, being the chief wearers of jewellery, should know what they want'.[52] Women like Woodward encouraged this interest to amplify their own positions, to further the blossoming of an empowering feminised market framed around women buying art by other women, and to open up a space for the next generation of women to carve out their own successful niche in Arts and Crafts cultures.

But the ways women art workers sought to position themselves sat, at times, uneasily with the prominent essentialised rhetoric about womanhood that was dominating the women's movement and the suffrage campaigns. Threaded throughout the women's and feminist press was a socially maternalistic view which went beyond framing women as having particular interest in art and fashions for the home. Instead considerable energies were used to position women – and middle-class white women in particular – as having a heightened moral compass, an emotional way of seeing the world, and a yearning for motherhood. Many used this widespread belief to justify the need for women's public participation in specific national and international political cultures.[53] Pamela Sharpe has labelled this the deliberate creation of a 'facade' of gendered femininity and domesticity which has masked the full extent of women's involvement in public life.[54] Teaching and nursing were frequently suggested as viable occupations for women because they were viewed as especially nurturing, compassionate positions. The applied arts, in particular needlework and jewellery, viewed as repetitive and requiring 'nimble fingers', were much promoted: middle-class women were already expected to have dabbled in the arts as part of their wider performance of classed femininity. Well into the 1930s, the physical appearance of artistic women in the press continued to be described as feminine, their studios and showrooms as domesticated and pretty, their crafts as dainty and delicate. Editors and journalists still often showed great support for women artists, portraying them as celebrity-like figures, featuring them in interviews, reviewing their exhibitions, and whetting a supportive public appetite for their work. This gendered language featured in all of the leading art journals, alongside local and national newspapers. The work of women art workers was discussed with surprising regularity in prestigious art journals like the *Studio* and the *Art Workers' Quarterly*. Although portraying specific women as esteemed figures, and their work as highly skilled, descriptions were usually brief in contrast to those of their male peers and were frequently – although by no means always – disparagingly gendered in tone, diminishing the aesthetic and intellectual contributions of women to the culture of the time.

When we turn to consider how Arts and Crafts women sought to articulate their views on questions of art, work, equality, and gender relations we find a rather different strategy being implemented. Rejecting prevalent Victorian ideas about the innate creative differences between women and men, they positioned themselves as equally capable of participating in artistic culture, as engaged in the same aesthetic, moral quest as their male peers, and as responsible for resurrecting a wider cultural lineage of design and making which stretched back through history. Women art workers consistently expressed the view that the gender of the artist was irrelevant, and stressed the equal capacity of women and men to produce work of excellent standards. After Lethaby had given his paper on women's 'Special Aptitude' for handicrafts at the International Congress of Women conference, Mary Lowndes indirectly responded to him in her paper that it is 'unprofitable, to talk about any art with relation to the sex of the person who pursues it'.[55] This egalitarian framing was put forward by many women across the professions, as well as in certain feminist circles: Hertha Ayrton refused to be stereotyped as a '*woman* in science', instead arguing that her work should be 'studied from the scientific, not the sex, point of view'.[56] Lectures, manuals, articles, even advertisements and calling cards, relating to the working lives of women art workers are all noticeable in their eschewal of a gendered or a feminised framing. This approach is exemplified in Edith B. Dawson's commissioned 1906 book *Enamels* for Methuen. Aside from her name there is little hint of her gender. Dawson focused instead on positioning herself as a serious pioneer, instructing others that if the craft is done 'with capable hand and brain ... we may yet have a school of enamellers equal to, perhaps even better than any that the world has seen'.[57] Others, such as E. C. Woodward and M. V. Wheelhouse, used initials to disguise their gender.

Although collectively women art workers tended to argue against professional distinctions on the basis of sex, individually they espoused a variety of views about women's status in society more widely. Rarely explicitly against women getting the vote, they did veer between the apathetic and the fiercely committed, and often prioritised artistic commitments. Some, such as Mary Lowndes, used the suffrage press and their art to self-actualise new political identities, as we shall see in Chapter 5. This could contrast with their professional self-fashioning at other moments. Lowndes wrote in dismay for the *Common Cause* in 1914 – in an approach which diverges from her wish to avoid the topic at the conference in 1899 – about how 'women have not shared with men in any sort of equality' because 'Women are not free – they have never been free.' Seeking to rally her fellow campaigners, she emphatically stressed this was now 'the age of woman', the moment when women – and women artists in particular – would 'lead a world-wide revolt against the prejudice and ancient tyranny that … struggle ever to keep woman the inferior creature they proclaim her'. She went on to assert optimistically that she and her artistic peers – using several Women's Guild of Arts members as examples – were finally starting to carve out a 'sort of progress towards equality with the sex that has hitherto monopolised to so great an extent the intellectual opportunities of life'.[58]

These writings function as a reminder of the need to take care when using print culture to make snap judgements about gender, artistic culture, skilled work, and women's lives. It is important to account for the breadth of viewpoints being expressed on these pages, indicative of wider power struggles in the arts and in society. Furthermore, as Kathryn Gleadle has cogently argued: 'Statements articulated in public sites of high cultural or political capital could be much more distinctly gendered than the dynamics of interpersonal interaction or the particularities of specific social and cultural communities.'[59] By exploring these views and how they played out within different relationships, contexts, and spaces, *Women Art Workers* provides a more complete account of how artistic women and men constructed new lifestyles alongside each other. Whilst taking a detailed look at the ongoing centrality of women's relationships to the construction and maintenance of such networks, I stress that the lives of women art workers intermeshed with innumerable field-specific and classed similarities with their male peers, who often played supportive, central roles as co-workers, husbands, family members, and enthusiastic champions of their work. For example, W. R. Lethaby, who spoke at the

International Congress of Women conference and later joined the Women's Guild of Arts as Honorary Associate, showed considerable encouragement and interest in his female peers. Other men played a crucial role by offering women paid work or the chance to train at their businesses and workshops. In everyday life, artistic women across the country did not uniformly understand their identities to be defined by their gender, did not always feel the need to present their work as feminised to maintain class status, and often worked closely with their male peers, perceiving themselves as united disciples of the same movement. Metalworker Edith B. Dawson is usually briefly described in histories of the movement as having been taught by her husband, but in contemporary writings she is described as working *with* her husband Nelson, at the studio of the silversmith Alexander Fisher, 'not as pupils, but as co-workers', part of a network of artists instrumental in 'finding out a little here and a little there' because trade jewellers refused to help them.[60] To set up a dichotomous (and flattening) distinction between women and men would fail to capture the complexities of identity formation, and the fact that those active in the Arts and Crafts movement often faced comparable difficulties which would not have been experienced by those in other professions or walks of life.

Archives in attics: the problem of sources

A major challenge in writing a history about Arts and Crafts women is the lack of surviving or accessible artworks. More generally, the work of women artists in public galleries and museums constituted less than 10 per cent of collection material in twentieth-century Britain.[61] This undoubtedly creates difficulties when trying to use an object-oriented approach. The works of the women who feature in these pages have often been lost, are behind closed doors in private households, or are inaccessible at museums and galleries, institutions which face considerable funding cuts and often prioritise artworks by men, widely believed to be worth more money and to attract larger crowds. One of very few, fleetingly accessible pieces I have found by a key protagonist of this book, metalworker E. C. Woodward, was a single silver spoon listed for sale by an antique dealer.[62] During her day, Woodward was heralded as epitomising artistic excellence in design and making; was featured in prestigious art journals such as the *Studio*; acted as co-owner with Agnes Withers of the metalwork business Woodward and Withers in Notting Hill; and designed and made objects for the Royal Family, theatre companies, and churches around the world (such as a ruby-encrusted orb for St Augustine's Priory, South Africa, and a silver chalice with garnets and carbuncles for the English

Church, San Remo, Italy). Her wide-ranging skills saw her, at various moments, design and make war memorials, university trowels, and badges for the suffrage campaign. She even established the first welding school for women during the First World War.[63]

Textual archives reveal Woodward's peers had similarly rich artistic outputs, making this loss and inaccessibility frustrating. As it stands, feminist art historical scholarship has tended to prioritise women's paintings and illustrations. The fine arts often appear to offer clearer answers than craft for those seeking to understand the proto-feminist motivations of historical women.[64] Guild member Emily Ford's painting *Towards the Dawn* (1889) portrayed a woman purposefully floating upwards through clouds, face turned towards the light, and leaves one with no doubt about her belief in the need for women-centred political and social reforms.[65] It can be more difficult to assess similarly the objects designed and made by women who worked across the arts. Scholarship has instead focused on the tendency for women to work in traditionally 'feminised' fields such as embroidery and jewellery. Scrutiny of processes of production has revealed the ongoing attempts to encourage contemporary gendered hierarchies of design (male) and making (female). Furthermore, the ephemeral nature of fields such as needlework has led to women being omitted from histories, as has the lack of signatures on several pieces, and the tendency for these women to work across different crafts. Women in the Arts and Crafts movement have thus been marginalised by both their gender and their choice of artistic field, during the period they were active, and particularly in later histories of the movement. Cheryl Buckley's 1986 survey of design literature, theory, and practice led her to announce that the omission of women has been so overwhelming that 'one realises these silences are not accidental or haphazard; rather, they are the direct consequence of specific historiographical methods.'[66]

Archiving processes across the twentieth century have indelibly suffused the ways histories are told, leading to certain objects and writings being archived, catalogued, and exhibited for the benefit of posterity, whilst others have been destroyed or tossed aside. This is particularly the case for archives pertaining to the histories of women, which are notoriously fragmentary, routinely subjected to gendered processes of compilation and destruction as artworks which ostensibly are based on 'worth' and 'importance', but which implicitly preserve the marginalising phenomenon of gendered dismissal. In part because of the scarcity of surviving material, and in part because these objects only allow limited inroads into the ideological conceptualisations, and experiences, of work cultures in this period, *Women Art Workers* is not ultimately framed around artistic objects or individual biographies, although at certain moments across the following chapters life stories and specific works are naturally the subject of targeted analysis. I do not mean to suggest these complex historical objects do not offer copious critical insights, but my interest here as a social and cultural historian is in tracing the textual, visual, and material worlds in which art workers were immersed. Additionally, as Alan Crawford has suggested, for many adherents to the movement, such as C. R. Ashbee's Guild of Handicraft, the 'aims and ideals of the Guild were not achieved once a fine piece of workmanship had been produced – the object was not the object – they were achieved as the workman's experiences became more creative', which it was believed would make 'the world a better place'.[67] Ways of seeing are always shaped by the context in which different objects – and their designers and makers – are situated.

In recent years, the discovery of boxes filled with documents pertaining to the Women's Guild of Arts in a Hammersmith attic once belonging to the etcher and watercolourist Mary A. Sloane, long-term Honorary Secretary, were gifted to the William Morris Society by her great-nephew, enabling the story of the Guild finally to be told. These hitherto unexamined documents – annual reports, meeting minutes, letters, and ephemera – alongside a large collection of Sloane's personal correspondence, provide unprecedented insight into women's associational life in the Arts and Crafts movement predominantly during the years when Sloane was Honorary Secretary: c. 1909–1924. In particular, these boxes contain a wealth of evidence for the, at times fraught, private institutional debates at the height of suffrage militancy, c. 1907–1913, the curious contradiction between the institutional and personal responses of women art workers to suffrage and feminist politics, and the implications of politics on the ways women constructed working lives. Alongside this, Duke University in North Carolina recently purchased (in 2015) a second Women's Guild of Arts archive, which provides a wealth of further details, as it includes over eighty letters between members.

The personal papers consulted for this project were usually uncatalogued or accessed privately through family descendants. Although on an individual level only glimpses of the lives of women such as E. C. Woodward can be reconstructed, considering these women's lives together means I have been able to draw from a surprisingly extensive range of unstudied archival materials. These relatively privileged women have left scattered traces of their strategies of professionalisation across the many different spheres they moved between in their lifetimes. My approach has been to bring together as many visual and written sources as possible, incorporating materials from the press (local, national, and international newspapers, art journals, the women's press, and suffrage papers), institutional archives, artist manuals, exhibition catalogues, advertisements, posters, postcards, memoirs, autobiographies, biographies, diaries, letters, and calling cards. There is a rich surviving corpus of photographs which provides a further frame of analysis, reiterating the ways women sought to take charge of their self-representation as modern working women through this newly available visual mode. Census, birth, death, and marriage records aided the collection of biographical data. Archival research has taken me across England, to attics in the suburbs of Birmingham, local collections in the Lake District, Wiltshire, and Leeds, to houses once belonging to Women's Guild of Arts members across the country, and on many trips to the Art Workers' Guild and Women's Guild of Arts archives in London. I have visited and used archival materials in international depositories based in locations as far afield as San Francisco, Los Angeles, North Carolina, and Cape Town. By bringing together this wealth of materials, this book provides the first history of the cultural and social worlds professional women art workers inhabited, the language and spaces they used to assert their new roles and show off their work, and the impact these individuals, networks, and institutions had on society.

The spaces of artistic self-actualisation

At the heart of the strategies implemented by women art workers was the spatial remapping of the capital. They set up a network of sites across London through their homes, studios, workshops, businesses, guild halls, clubhouses, and exhibitions. One of the most enduring inquiries into women's and gender history over the last forty years has been the examination of the ideology of 'public and private spheres', drawing a contrast between men inhabiting the public world of work, and women coming to possess ever-increasing authority in the private world of the home.[68] Yet there has been an absence of research into how women – separately and collaboratively – sought to construct and assert new working lives by adapting the range of different spaces available to them into sites framed around material demonstration of their roles as 'serious' workers.[69]

Building on the work of art historians, historical geographers, and feminist theorists who have sought to untangle how different environments, be these built 'places' or conceptualised 'spaces', influenced political power, social experience, and cultural production, *Women Art Workers* revolves around a series of thematic chapters focused on the buildings and spaces women art workers repeatedly conceptualised as critical to the formation of their artistic, professional lives.[70] Chapter 1 peers into clubhouses and guild halls, Chapter 2 explores the exhibition spaces of the Arts and Crafts, Chapter 3 is based in artistic homes and studios, whilst Chapter 4 assesses businesses and workshops. The final chapter, Chapter 5, focuses on the impact of the suffrage campaigns and the First World War in shifting the stakes of these professional endeavours. The book concludes with an Epilogue which uses the moment women finally gained access to the Art Workers' Guild in 1964 as a heuristic device to complicate simplistic narratives of the steady 'progress' of women's opportunities in the arts across the twentieth century.

Several analytical threads run across the book: for example, many chapters discuss domesticity as it was positioned as such a central force in these women's lives. Of course, these women interacted with other spaces relevant to their working lives such as art school and the church. As revealed in Chapter 4, women business owners played an important role in opening up their specific artistic fields to the next generation, often employing and training women apprentices and staff; in order not to neatly cut away an 'educational' section of these women's lives, these activities will be viewed holistically in numerous chapters.[71] Furthermore, although religious beliefs appear to have rarely been discussed in groups such as the Women's Guild of Arts, on an individual level some artistic women were as much motivated by spiritual dedication as by a need to articulate professional status.[72] Guild members are positioned centre stage throughout this book, but along the way a wide-ranging cast of supporting characters wheel in and out of view: maids and caretakers, supportive (and unsupportive) parents, German art gallery directors, suffrage campaigners, fellow artists, and many – often anonymous – journalists, writers, and social commentators.

Structuring the chapters around the construction of professional 'space' challenges attempts to impose a neat linear history of profession-alisation and the formation of clearly defined 'professional identities'. It lays bare the ongoing fissures between ideals and praxis, unveiling how women repeatedly tried to navigate and break down binaries of public/private, medieval/modern, amateur/professional, masculine/feminine, and commercial/artistic. The spaces women art workers had access to – and did not have access to – actively shaped and reshaped social dynamics, cultural production, and attempts to claim political power. Throughout, artistic spaces are shown as important imagined and idealised *loci* (the 'artist's studio', the pseudo-medieval 'workshop', the 'guild hall') in the cultural geography of the city.

The cosmopolitan capital was a congenial place for artistic women. Propinquity and the urban environment played a central role in the performance of artistic roles and how art work was understood. The rapid expansion of the metropolis across this era offered a multitude of unique opportunities for the art workers who lived there: the exhibition scene was vibrant and increasingly diverse, and there were many buildings available to rent in culturally and historically significant areas. By focusing on London across many of the chapters that follow I do not mean to move the lens of inquiry away from the centrality of regional and international elements in the making of the movement, a topic of detailed inquiry in recent years.[73] Instead, I seek to feed into these debates by showing that for many London-based artists – and contemporary figures – these activities in the capital played a central role in shaping how such individuals conceptualised their positions, and tried to construct a hierarchy of expertise, framed around the prestige they felt to be conferred on those who lived, trained, and worked there. This was the case even whilst London-based art workers idealised the countryside, repeatedly using it for artistic inspiration and spending considerable time in rural communities. Furthermore, the capital simultaneously encouraged specific competitive and conservative attitudes to flourish, especially in the heartland of masculine artistic culture at institutions such as the Royal Academy, which contrasted with local artistic contexts elsewhere in England, such as the Northern Art Workers' Guild, which had women on the Committee in the 1890s.

Members of the Women's Guild of Arts were important interlocutors who benefited from, and shaped, different local, national, and international contexts throughout their lives. The majority were English and based in the South-East, but several others lived far from London, travelling back and forth for meetings and exhibitions: sculptor and painter Edith Bateson was in Yorkshire, embroiderer Clara Tustain in North Wales, stained-glass worker Ethel Rhind in Dublin, whilst textile worker Annie Garnett was in the Lake District. Based in London, there was a cluster of Irish members, including writer and decorative artist Alys Fane Trotter, painter Rose Barton, Associate member and embroiderer Una Taylor, and Welsh sculptor and medallist Ruby Levick. There was a surprising lack of members from Scotland, likely because of the supportive environment at the Glasgow Society of Women Artists. Some members grew up in mainland Europe, like German calligrapher Anna Simons and Austrian painter Marianne Stokes. Many travelled regularly, spreading knowledge about the movement while advertising their own independent roles: May Morris lectured in North America, Christiana Herringham journeyed to India to copy the frescoes in the Ajanta Caves, Myra K. Hughes wrote about and illustrated her experiences in Palestine for the *Studio*, whilst

Edith Harwood lived in Rome, writing and illustrating the book *Notable Pictures in Rome*. Others who moved to pursue new opportunities in the capital regularly journeyed back to the areas where they had grown up, to visit family and participate in local art exhibitions, organisations, and cultural events.

That *Women Art Workers* is constructed around the different spaces of women art workers' professionalising strategies stems directly from the fixation expressed by the women themselves; they repeatedly returned to the impact of space in negotiating acceptability, achieving professional success, and preserving 'authenticity'. Letters, photographs, memoirs, and the press all reveal the veritable obsession women art workers (and wider society) had with buildings, material environments, and the impact of this upon working lives. Through reconstructing these conceptual landscapes, we can see their world as they built it, and how they sought to disseminate ideas about careful design, gender equality, new forms of labour, and a desire to promote a shared entitlement to participate in cultural life across society.

Across the following chapters I destabilise the traditional notions of a core elite of Arts and Crafts men as figures of unrelenting authority and the sole disseminators of radical artistic ideas across this era. Instead I focus on the experiences of an extensive network of Arts and Crafts women as they sought to claim new professional, artistic positions in society, which intersected with a moment of profound social change, and facilitated these attempts to achieve status and acclaim. Such women navigated both new and traditional modes of dissemination: taking advantage of the growth of the capital, middle-class networks, print culture, public interest in the past, the cult of domesticity, and the emergence of celebrity cultures. Through this spectrum of approaches, women art workers disseminated the ethos of the movement across new local, national, and international registers, continually moving between, and disrupting, the porous and contested categories of 'radical, bohemian', 'Arts and Crafts', and 'popular culture'. I explore how gender both facilitated and hindered opportunities: in enabling the ready assertion of authority and knowledge about art for the home, but persistently associating their work with questionable dilettantism rather than radical masculine craftsmanship. Throughout, I foreground the *processes* which different women art workers engaged in to construct and maintain nascent professional roles, unveiling the making of modern artistic cultures and the ongoing centrality of gender to the ideals and practice of 'expertise' in late nineteenth- and early twentieth-century England.

Notes

1 www.artworkersguild.org, accessed 19 September 2019.

2 Deborah Cohen, *Household Gods: The British and Their Possessions* (New Haven: Yale University Press, 2006); Jane Hamlett, *Material Relations: Domestic Interiors and Middle-Class Families in England, 1850–1910* (Manchester: Manchester University Press, 2010); Judith A. Neiswander, *The Cosmopolitan Interior: Liberalism and the British Home, 1870–1914* (New Haven: Yale University Press, 2008).

3 Peter Stansky, *Redesigning the World: William Morris, the 1880s, and the Arts and Crafts* (Princeton: Princeton University Press, 1985).

4 Janice Helland, *British and Irish Home Arts and Industries, 1880–1914: Marketing Craft, Making Fashion* (Dublin: Irish Academic Press, 2007); Janice Helland, '"Good Work and Clever Design": Early Exhibitions of the Home Arts and Industries Association', *Journal of Modern Craft*, 5/3 (2012), pp. 275–293.

5 Pamela Todd, *William Morris and the Arts and Crafts Home* (London: Thames and Hudson, 2012); Fiona MacCarthy, *William Morris: A Life for Our Time* (London: Faber and Faber, 1995); Alan Crawford, *C. R. Ashbee: Architect, Designer and Romantic Socialist* (New Haven: Yale University Press, 1985).

6 Michael S. Kimmel, 'Review: The Arts and Crafts Movement: Handmade Socialism or Elite Consumerism?', *Contemporary Sociology*, 16/3 (1987), pp. 388–390.

7 Alan Crawford, 'The Arts and Crafts Movement: A Sketch', in *By Hammer and Hand: The Arts and Crafts Movement in Birmingham* (ed.) Alan Crawford (Birmingham: Birmingham Museums and Art Gallery, 1984), pp. 5–26 (p. 8); Lara Platman, *Art Workers Guild: 125 Years* (Norwich: Unicorn, 2009); Gavin Stamp, *Beauty's Awakening: The Centenary Exhibition of the Art Workers' Guild, 1884–1984* (Brighton: Brighton Museum, 1984).

8 Anthea Callen, *Angel in the Studio: Women in the Arts and Crafts Movement, 1870–1914* (London: Astragal, 1979); Anthea Callen, 'Sexual Division of Labor in the Arts and Crafts Movement', *Woman's Art Journal*, 5/2 (1984–1985), pp. 1–6; Anthea Callen, 'Sexual Division of Labour in the Arts and Crafts Movement', in *A View from the Interior: Feminism, Women and Design* (eds) Judy Attfield and Pat Kirkham (London: Women's Press, 1989), pp. 151–164.

9 Lynne Walker, 'The Arts and Crafts Alternative', in *A View from the Interior: Feminism, Women and Design* (eds) Judy Attfield and Pat Kirkham (London: Women's Press, 1989), pp. 165–173 (p. 165).

10 Jude Burkhauser (ed.), *Glasgow Girls: Women in Art and Design, 1880–1920* (Edinburgh: Canongate, 1990); Elaine Cheasley Paterson, 'Crafting a National Identity: The Dun Emer Guild, 1902–1908', in *The Irish Revival Reappraised* (eds) Betsey Taylor FitzSimon and James H. Murphy (Dublin: Four Courts, 2004), pp. 106–118; Joseph McBrinn, '"A Populous Solitude": The Life and Art of Sophia Rosamond Praeger, 1867–1954', *Women's History Review*, 18/4 (2009), pp. 577–596; Ellen Easton McLeod, *In Good Hands: The Women of the Canadian Handicrafts Guild* (London: Routledge, 1999); Catherine W. Zipf, *Professional Pursuits: Women and the American Arts and Crafts Movement* (Knoxville: University of Tennessee Press, 2007). More generally: Deborah Cherry, *Painting Women: Victorian Women Artists* (London: Routledge, 1993); Deborah Cherry, *Beyond the Frame: Feminism and Visual Culture, Britain 1850–1900* (London:

Routledge, 2000); Pamela Gerrish Nunn, *Victorian Women Artists* (London: Women's Press, 1987); Cheryl Buckley, *Potters and Paintresses: Women Designers in the Pottery Industry, 1870–1955* (London: Women's Press, 1990); Bridget Elliott and Janice Helland (eds), *Women Artists and the Decorative Arts, 1880–1935: The Gender of Ornament* (Farnham: Ashgate, 2002); Janice Helland, *Professional Women Painters in Nineteenth-Century Scotland: Commitment, Friendship, Pleasure* (Farnham: Ashgate, 2000); Kirsten Swinth, *Painting Professionals: Women Artists and the Development of Modern American Art, 1870–1930* (Chapel Hill: University of North Carolina Press, 2001); Laura R. Prieto, *At Home in the Studio: The Professionalization of Women Artists in America* (Cambridge, MA: Harvard University Press, 2001).

11 Jan Marsh, *Jane and May Morris: A Biographical Story, 1839–1938* (London: Pandora, 1986); Anna Mason and others, *May Morris: Arts and Crafts Designer* (London: Thames and Hudson, 2017); Lynne Hulse (ed.), *May Morris: Art and Life, New Perspectives* (London: Friends of the William Morris Gallery, 2017).

12 Women's Guild of Arts Archive, William Morris Society, London (hereafter WGAA), Rules, undated. Zoë Thomas, *Founding Members of the Women's Guild of Arts (act. 1907–c. 1939)*, Oxford Dictionary of National Biography, 2018.

13 Stella Tillyard, *The Impact of Modernism, 1900–1920: Early Modernism and the Arts and Crafts Movement in Edwardian England* (London: Routledge, 1988), pp. 7–9.

14 Elizabeth Cumming and Wendy Kaplan, *The Arts and Crafts Movement* (London: Thames and Hudson, 1991), p. 9.

15 Imogen Hart, *Arts and Crafts Objects* (Manchester: Manchester University Press, 2010).

16 This quote from Ashbee's memoir is often used as evidence that he felt the movement 'failed'. Rosalind P. Blakesley, *The Arts and Crafts Movement* (London: Phaidon, 2006), p. 51. Gill promoted trade unions and the Labour Party over guilds and workshops. He asserted that 'For everyone, save a few "artist-craftsmen" who get some advertisement by exhibiting their wares at Arts and Crafts Exhibitions, the Arts and Crafts movement is now more or less discredited.' Eric Gill, 'The Failure of the Arts and Crafts Movement: A Lesson for Trade Unionists', *Socialist Review* (December 1909), pp. 289–300 (p. 289).

17 Tillyard, *The Impact of Modernism*; Michael Saler, *The Avant-Garde in Interwar England: Medieval Modernism and the London Underground* (Oxford: Oxford University Press, 2001), p. 177; Annette Carruthers, *Edward Barnsley and his Workshop: Arts and Crafts in the Twentieth Century* (Oxford: White Cockade, 1992).

18 Deborah Sugg Ryan, *Ideal Homes, 1918–1939: Domestic Design and Suburban Modernism* (Manchester: Manchester University Press, 2018); Judy Giles, *The Parlour and the Suburb: Domestic Identities, Class, Femininity and Modernity* (Oxford: Berg, 2004); Tom Crook, 'Craft and the Dialogics of Modernity: The Arts and Crafts Movement in Late-Victorian and Edwardian England', *Journal of Modern Craft*, 2/1 (2009), pp. 17–32.

19 Most recently Cheryl Buckley, *Designing Modern Britain* (London: Reaktion, 2007), p. 15.

20 This is not to deny that many women fused their artistic skills with philanthropic interests and showed considerable commitment to building inter-class relationships. Mary Seton Watts taught clay modelling classes for shoeblacks in London's East End, and several of her peers pursued similar projects. Furthermore, Tara Morton's recent

scholarship on the Suffrage Atelier has demonstrated that for some Arts and Crafts women, a critique of class hierarchies could be central to their creative work and interests. Tara Morton, '"An Arts and Crafts Society, Working for the Enfranchisement of Women": Unpicking the Political Threads of the Suffrage Atelier, 1909–1914', in *Suffrage and the Arts: Visual Culture, Politics and Enterprise* (eds) Miranda Garrett and Zoë Thomas (London: Bloomsbury, 2018), pp. 65–89.

21 Lisa Tickner, *The Spectacle of Women: Imagery of the Suffrage Campaign, 1907–1914* (London: Chatto and Windus, 1987); Miranda Garrett and Zoë Thomas (eds), *Suffrage and the Arts: Visual Culture, Politics and Enterprise* (London: Bloomsbury, 2018).

22 Tanya Harrod's path-breaking book discusses the integral role played by craftswomen in the 1920s and 1930s but the pre-history to this is crucial, as are the many individuals who continued to be embedded within Arts and Crafts networks. Tanya Harrod, *The Crafts in Britain in the Twentieth Century* (New Haven: Yale University Press, 1999). See also Jill Seddon and Suzette Worden (eds), *Women Designing: Redefining Design in Britain Between the Wars* (Brighton: University of Brighton, 1994).

23 For a productive discussion of the complexities of this 'conservative/radical dichotomy', see Amy Palmer, 'Radical Conservatism and International Nationalism: The Peasant Arts Movement and its Search for the Country Heart of England', *Journal of the Social History Society*, 15/5 (2018), pp. 663–680.

24 Sculptor E. M. Rope's panels, for instance, were often 'purposely designed to be executed at a low cost and repeated if desired, so that they could be used by others than the very rich'. 'Sculpture Panels', *Builder* (3 December 1898), p. 508.

25 Metalworker E. C. Woodward provides a quintessential example: she educated her readers about the rich historical tradition of enamelling across Asia, India, and Europe alongside practical details about hall-marking and getting licensed. E. C. Woodward, 'Jewellery and Metal Work', in *Mrs Strang's Annual for Girls* (Oxford: Oxford University Press, 1921), pp. 47–53; E. C. Woodward, 'Enamelling and Hall-Marking', in *Mrs Strang's Annual for Girls* (Oxford: Oxford University Press, 1922), pp. 82–87. More generally, manuals and books include: May Morris, *Decorative Needlework* (London: Hughes, 1893); Mary Seton Watts, *The Word in the Pattern* (London: Astolat, 1905); S. T. Prideaux, *An Historical Sketch of Bookbinding* (London: Lawrence and Bullen, 1893); S. T. Prideaux, *Bookbinders and their Craft* (London: Zaehnsdorf, 1903); S. T. Prideaux, *Modern Bookbindings: Their Design and Decoration* (London: Archibald Constable, 1906); Annie Garnett, *Notes on Hand-Spinning* (London: Dulau, 1896); Eleanor Rowe, *Hints on Wood-Carving: Recreative Classes and Modelling for Beginners* (London: City and Guilds Institute, 1891); Eleanor Rowe, *Practical Wood-Carving: A Book for the Student, Carver, Teacher, Designer, and Architect* (London: Batsford, 1907); Edith B. Dawson, *Enamels* (London: Methuen, 1906); Mary Lowndes, *Banners and Banner Making* (London: Artists' Suffrage League, 1909); Elizabeth Ellin Carter, *Artistic Leather Work* (London: E. and F. N. Spon, 1921). There were even collaborative all-women collections such as *Some Arts and Crafts* (London: Chapman and Hall, 1903). This had a chapter by Elinor Hallé on 'The Art of Enamelling' and Maria Reeks on woodcarving.

26 Paul Readman, 'The Place of the Past in English Culture, c. 1890–1914', *Past and Present*, 186/1 (2005), pp. 147–199; Rosemary Mitchell, 'A Stitch in Time? Women, Needlework, and the Making of History in Victorian Britain', *Journal of Victorian Culture*, 1/2 (1996), pp. 185–202.

27   Most famously, Harold Perkin, *The Rise of Professional Society: England since 1880* (London: Routledge, 1989).

28   David Crook, 'Some Historical Perspectives on Professionalism', in *Exploring Professionalism* (ed.) Bryan Cunningham (London: Institute of Education, 2008), pp. 10–27; Penelope J. Corfield, *Power and the Professions in Britain, 1700–1850* (London: Routledge, 1995).

29   Anne Witz, *Professions and Patriarchy* (London: Routledge, 1992), p. 5. Celia Davies, 'The Sociology of Professions and the Professions of Gender', *Sociology*, 30/4 (1996), pp. 661–678. In 2015 Gillian Sutherland emphasised the unstudied 'mass presence' of middle-class working women in their thousands: 'If we are looking for signs of real change in the labour force and in social structures, they deserve much fuller scrutiny than hitherto they have received.' Gillian Sutherland, *In Search of the New Woman: Middle-Class Women and Work in Britain, 1870–1914* (Cambridge: Cambridge University Press, 2015), p. 161.

30   Leslie Madsen-Brooks, 'A Synthesis of Expertise and Expectations: Women Museum Scientists, Club Women and Populist Natural Science in the United States, 1890–1950', *Gender and History*, 25/1 (2013), pp. 27–46 (p. 27).

31   Ethel Charles became the first woman member of the Royal Institute of British Architects, the foremost professional body for architecture, in 1898. Her sister and architectural partner Bessie Charles joined in 1900. Elizabeth Darling and Lynne Walker, *AA Women in Architecture, 1917–2017* (London: Architectural Association, 2017).

32   Krista Cowman and Louise A. Jackson, 'Introduction: Middle-Class Women and Professional Identity', *Women's History Review*, 14/2 (2005), pp. 165–180; Krista Cowman and Louise A. Jackson, 'Introduction: Women's Work, a Cultural History', in *Women and Work Culture: Britain c. 1850–1950* (eds) Krista Cowman and Louise A. Jackson (Farnham: Ashgate, 2005), pp. 1–24.

33   For a useful discussion about the persistent organisation of nineteenth-century art training around ideas of gendered difference (with Glasgow School of Art providing a notably progressive contrast), see Cherry, *Painting Women*, pp. 53–64.

34   There were of course certain exceptions. Eleanor Rowe was described as 'Twenty Years Manager of the School of Art Wood-Carving, South Kensington' on the title page of Eleanor Rowe, *Practical Wood-Carving: A Book for the Student, Carver, Teacher, Designer, and Architect* (London: Batsford, 1907).

35   Using the census to assess patterns of women's work can be problematic (such work was often not captured), but there was clear growth across this era. In 1851, there were approximately 934 women artists, whereas by 1911 there were at least 8,923. For males: in 1851, there were 9,175 and in 1911, 27,423. Data kindly supplied by Harry Smith and extracted from K. Schürer, E. Higgs, A. M. Reid, and E. M. Garrett, *Integrated Census Microdata, 1851–1911*, version 2 (2016), UK Data Service, SN: 7481.

36   C. R. Ashbee, *Craftsmanship in Competitive Industry* (Campden: Essex House Press, 1908), pp. 37–38.

37   Amelia Yeates and Serena Trowbridge (eds), *Pre-Raphaelite Masculinities: Constructions of Masculinity in Art and Literature* (Farnham: Ashgate, 2014); Laura Morowitz and William Vaughan (eds), *Artistic Brotherhoods in the Nineteenth Century* (Farnham: Ashgate, 2000); John Potvin, *Material and Visual Cultures Beyond Male Bonding, 1870–1914: Bodies, Boundaries and Intimacy* (Aldershot: Ashgate, 2008). See also Andrew Stephenson, 'Leighton and the Shifting Repertoires of "Masculine" Artistic

Identity in the Late Victorian Period', in *Frederic Leighton: Antiquity, Renaissance, Modernity* (eds) Tim Barringer and Elizabeth Prettejohn (New Haven: Yale University Press, 1999), pp. 221–247. For specific focus on craft see Freya Gowrley and Katie Faulkner, 'Making Masculinity: Craft, Gender, and Material Production in the Long Nineteenth Century', *Nineteenth-Century Gender Studies*, 14/2 (2018), pp. 1–10.

38 Alan Crawford, 'The Object is Not the Object: C. R. Ashbee and the Guild of Handicraft', in *Pioneers of Modern Craft: Twelve Essays Profiling Key Figures in the History of Twentieth-Century Craft* (ed.) Margot Coatts (Manchester: Manchester University Press, 1997), pp. 1–11 (p. 9).

39 The quote is by Nicola Moorby, 'Her Indoors: Women Artists and Depictions of the Domestic Interior', www.tate.org.uk/art/research-publications/camden-town-group/nicola-moorby-her-indoors-women-artists-and-depictions-of-the-domestic-interior-r1104359, accessed 19 September 2019. Quirk's doctorate concluded that women painters and illustrators reached professional status through paid interactions with the market. Maria Quirk, 'Reconsidering Professionalism: Women, Space and Art in England, 1880–1914' (Unpublished PhD thesis, University of Queensland, 2015).

40 Several women in the Arts and Crafts movement first met at the Slade. See Charlotte J. Weeks, 'Women at Work: The Slade Girls', *Magazine of Art* (January 1883), pp. 324–329.

41 Constance Smedley, *Crusaders: Reminiscences of Constance Smedley / Mrs Maxwell Armfield* (London: Duckworth, 1929), p. 56.

42 Peter Mandler (ed.), *Liberty and Authority in Victorian Britain* (Oxford: Oxford University Press, 2006); Joyce Senders Pedersen, 'Victorian Liberal Feminism and the "Idea" of Work', in *Women and Work Culture: Britain, c. 1850–1950* (eds) Krista Cowman and Louise A. Jackson (Farnham: Ashgate, 2005), pp. 27–47.

43 Many were architects, influenced by an 1891 Registration Bill which proposed that only those who had officially qualified through examination should have the right to use the title 'architect'. This provoked disagreement from those identifying as 'art-architects' as they felt architecture would lose its inherent creativity if the Bill was applied, unlike the 'professional-architects' who had proposed the measure. See the series of letters in *The Times* from A. W. Blomfield and others, 'Architecture – A Profession or an Art?', *The Times* (3 March 1891), p. 9. Mark Crinson and Jules Lubbock, *Architecture, Art or Profession? Three Hundred Years of Architectural Education in Britain* (Manchester: Manchester University Press, 1994), pp. 61–62.

44 Constance Smedley repeatedly described members of the Lyceum Club – which included many Arts and Crafts women – as 'professional workers'. Smedley, *Crusaders*, p. 69. Articles in the press also regularly described women working across the arts as professionals, see H. H. R., 'Art as a Profession', *Englishwoman's Review* (16 October 1893), p. 274.

45 'The "Englishwoman" Exhibition', *Common Cause* (17 September 1915), p. 295.

46 See various examples such as 'An Interview with a Successful Business Woman', *Woman's Signal* (11 March 1897), p. 154 and 'Every Girl a Business Woman', *Girl's Own Paper* (2 October 1886), p. 5.

47 Ishbel Maria Hamilton-Gordon (ed.), *Women in Professions: Being the Professional Section of the International Congress of Women, London, July 1899* (London: Fisher Unwin, 1900), p. 201.

48 Ibid., p. 199.

49 Sarah A. Tooley, 'A Lady Goldsmith', *Woman's Signal* (9 May 1895), p. 289.

50 Michelle Elizabeth Tusan, *Women Making News: Gender and Journalism in Modern Britain* (Champaign: University of Illinois Press, 2005).

51 Hilary Fraser, *Women Writing Art History in the Nineteenth Century* (Cambridge: Cambridge University Press, 2014).

52 Woodward, 'Jewellery and Metal Work', p. 47.

53 Seth Koven and Sonya Michel, 'Womanly Duties: Maternalist Politics and the Origins of Welfare States in France, Germany, Great Britain, and the United States, 1880–1920', *American Historical Review*, 95/4 (1990), pp. 1076–1108.

54 Pamela Sharpe (ed.), *Women's Work: The English Experience, 1650–1914* (Oxford: Oxford University Press, 1998), p. 10.

55 Hamilton-Gordon (ed.), *Women in Professions*, p. 195.

56 Claire Jones, 'The Laboratory: A Suitable Place For a Woman? Gender and Laboratory Culture around 1900', in *Women and Work Culture: Britain, c. 1850–1950* (eds) Krista Cowman and Louise A. Jackson (Farnham: Ashgate, 2005), pp. 177–194. This example is taken from Cowman and Jackson's 'Introduction', p. 16. Italics in original.

57 Edith B. Dawson, *Enamels* (London: Methuen, 1906), p. 198.

58 Mary Lowndes, 'Genius, and Women Painters', *Common Cause* (17 April 1914), p. 31.

59 Kathryn Gleadle, '"The Riches and Treasures of Other Countries": Women, Empire and Maritime Expertise in Early Victorian London', *Gender and History*, 25/1 (2013), pp. 7–26 (p. 19).

60 Jean Hadaway, 'Developments in the Art of Jewellery', *Journal of the Royal Society of Arts*, 56 (1908), pp. 287–297 (p. 289).

61 Katy Deepwell, *Women Artists Between the Wars: 'A Fair Field and No Favour'* (Manchester: Manchester University Press, 2010), p. 8.

62 The antique dealer, Peter Cameron, is based in Chancery Lane, London.

63 Several articles in the women's press discuss the suffrage badges Woodward produced at her workshop. See for instance 'Presentation to Miss I. O. Ford', *Common Cause* (30 May 1913), p. 120. There is a file at Bushey Museum, Hertfordshire, about E. C. Woodward which lists many of her artistic commissions.

64 There are of course notable exceptions to this which have illuminated the politics inherent in the processes of design and making. See in particular Rozsika Parker, *The Subversive Stitch: Embroidery and the Making of the Feminine* (London: Women's Press, 1984).

65 The painting is now lost but there is a photograph in Cherry, *Beyond the Frame*, p. 199.

66 Cheryl Buckley, 'Made in Patriarchy: Towards a Feminist Analysis of Women and Design', *Design Issues*, 3/2 (1986), pp. 3–14 (p. 3).

67 Crawford, 'The Object is Not the Object', p. 9.

68 In the last twenty years there has been a move to explore the intricacies of lived practices, which rarely stood up to prescribed norms. Delap and others have reasoned it makes no sense to set up 'separate spheres' as 'a theory whose only utility lies in the insights we can develop by disproving it'. They instead encourage examination of how 'the rhetoric of domesticity operated and was made meaningful in particular contexts, how contemporaries used it to make sense of their experiences, how it shaped the actions of particular individuals or groups, and how it changed over time'. Lucy

Delap, Ben Griffin, and Abigail Wills, 'Introduction', in *The Politics of Domestic Authority in Britain since 1800* (eds) Lucy Delap, Ben Griffin, and Abigail Wills (Basingstoke: Palgrave Macmillan, 2009), pp. 1–24 (pp. 11–12). 'Social borderland', coined by Anne Digby, elucidates how women could, and did, act outside of the immediate private sphere without being challenged – although they tended to need to employ a discrete demeanour. Anne Digby, 'Victorian Values and Women in Public and Private', *Proceedings of the British Academy*, 78 (1992), pp. 195–215.

69 Lynne Walker's path-breaking research provides a rare exception here. Lynne Walker, 'Vistas of Pleasure: Women Consumers of Urban Space in the West End of London, 1850–1900', in *Women in the Victorian Art World* (ed.) Clarissa Campbell Orr (Manchester: Manchester University Press, 1995), pp. 70–85; Lynne Walker, 'Home and Away: The Feminist Remapping of Public and Private Space in Victorian London', in *The Unknown City: Contesting Architecture and Social Space* (eds) Iain Borden and others (London: MIT Press, 2001), pp. 296–311.

70 Kathryne Beebe, Angela Davis, and Kathryn Gleadle, 'Introduction: Space, Place and Gendered Identities: Feminist History and the Spatial Turn', *Women's History Review*, 21/4 (2012), pp. 523–532; Gillian Rose, *Feminism and Geography: The Limits of Geographical Knowledge* (Cambridge: Polity, 1993); Doreen Massey, *Space, Place and Gender* (Cambridge: Polity, 1994); Elizabeth Darling and Lesley Whitworth (eds), *Women and the Making of Built Space in England, 1870–1950* (London: Ashgate, 2007).

71 For a useful recent discussion see Patricia Zakreski, 'Creative Industry: Design, Art Education and the Woman Professional', in *Crafting the Woman Professional in the Long Nineteenth Century: Artistry and Industry in Britain* (eds) Kyriaki Hadjiafxendi and Patricia Zakreski (Farnham: Ashgate, 2013), pp. 145–166.

72 Religion was meaningful on both a personal and professional level to women like Quaker Edith B. Dawson and Emily Ford, who was brought up a Quaker before converting to Anglicanism. Lynne Walker, 'Women and Church Art', *Studies in Victorian Architecture and Design*, 3 (2010), pp. 121–143.

73 Elizabeth Cumming and Nicola Gordon Bowe, *The Arts and Crafts Movement in Dublin and Edinburgh, 1885–1930* (Dublin: Irish Academic Press, 1998); Elizabeth Cumming, *Hand, Heart and Soul: The Arts and Crafts Movement in Scotland* (Edinburgh: Birlinn, 2006); Annette Carruthers, *The Arts and Crafts Movement in Scotland: A History* (New Haven: Yale University Press, 2013); Paul Larmour, *The Arts and Crafts Movement in Ireland* (Belfast: Friar's Bush, 1992); Vera Kreilkamp (ed.), *The Arts and Crafts Movement: Making it Irish* (Chestnut Hill: McMullen Museum, 2016); Judith A. Barter, *Apostles of Beauty: Arts and Crafts from Britain to Chicago* (New Haven: Yale University Press, 2009); Alan Crawford and Wendy Kaplan, *The Arts and Crafts Movement in Europe and America: Design for the Modern World, 1880–1920* (London: Thames and Hudson, 2004); Jennie Brunton, *The Arts and Crafts Movement in the Lake District: A Social History* (Lancaster: University of Lancaster, 2001); Barrie Armstrong and Wendy Armstrong, *The Arts and Crafts Movement in the North East of England: A Handbook* (Wetherby: Oblong Creative, 2013); Barrie Armstrong and Wendy Armstrong, *The Arts and Crafts Movement in the North West of England: A Handbook* (Wetherby: Oblong Creative, 2005); Barrie Armstrong and Wendy Armstrong, *The Arts and Crafts Movement in Yorkshire: A Handbook* (Wetherby: Oblong Creative, 2013).

1

Clubhouses and guild halls

The formation of the Women's Guild of Arts in 1907 was a revolutionary moment for women art workers in England. On a winter's
evening in December, the Guild's first official meeting took place
in a Hall at Clifford's Inn, Fleet Street, London. Mary Seton Watts chaired
the event, which was packed with guests who had come to hear speeches
from members of the nascent Guild and – intriguingly – from members
of the male-only Art Workers' Guild who had 'kindly lent' the Hall for
the evening. Stained-glass designer Mary Lowndes and the tempera painter
Christiana Herringham gave speeches to the crowd of visitors alongside
architects W. R. Lethaby and Halsey Ricardo, book illustrator Walter Crane,
and portrait painter William Rothenstein.[1] The evening, which united
key participants of the Art Workers' Guild with leading women in the
Arts and Crafts movement, appeared to mark a move away from the
formal model of single-sex organisational socialising which had dominated
the Victorian era, ostensibly ushering in a new egalitarian mixed-sex
artistic culture at the dawn of the twentieth century.

Traditionally, scholars have argued that the Arts and Crafts movement
reinforced the prevalent patriarchal ideologies of modern society. For
Anthea Callen, the Art Workers' Guild's decision not to allow women to
join *their* meetings at the Hall for over eighty years meant there were no
attempts 'at this central, influential level' to 'institutionalize alternative
patterns of male–female labor divisions'.[2] She even dismissed the Women's
Guild of Arts in one sentence as a 'minor off-shoot', founded 'too late by
then for it to fulfil the functions needed'.[3] In the pages that follow I begin
by exploring how Brothers at the Art Workers' Guild sought to claim
cultural authority from the Guild's foundation in 1884; understanding
their strategies is crucial in beginning to unpack the relational dynamics
between women and men in the movement. Ultimately, I offer an alternative
perspective to Callen's and move the debate away from positioning one

male-only group as the singular, stable core of the movement. In the second section, I provide the first comprehensive account of the interconnected Arts and Crafts networks that were formed at women's art groups such as the '91 Art Club, the Arts and Crafts Board at the Lyceum Club, and the Women's Guild of Arts, as these women sought access to professional and artistic, rather than simply class-based, modes of social interaction.

Refusing women entry to the Art Workers' Guild should be understood as an attempt to claim back elite, masculine, cultural power, at a time of significant social and cultural change, rather than being simply demonstrative of an unwavering status quo. Feminist art historians have used the Society of Women Artists (founded in the 1860s), which was known to accept 'amateurs', as indicative of the poor reputation of women's art groups in society more generally across this era.[4] Yet between the 1890s and the 1910s, a wave of new 'professional' women's art groups began to be established, and the networks and relationships that played out between these women and their various audiences were integral to the making of modern artistic culture. As it stands, this critical period has been a blind spot for scholars who have commonly argued that, after 1900 in particular, women artists 'did not organise together as women' outside of the suffrage campaigns.[5] Throughout, I do not just consider these groups in relation to contemporary male-only groups as part of a peripheral context; instead I consider this rich associational culture on its own terms. I focus on Arts and Crafts cultures (rather than the ongoing tendency to prioritise the fine arts) to explore the competing debates different members had about how best to gain artistic recognition, revealing that strategies repeatedly revolved around how best to navigate the gendered politics of space and place.

The period spanning the late nineteenth and early twentieth centuries constituted a critical moment when growing numbers of women were pushing for greater access to the 'public sphere' of skilled work and political reforms. Women's groups sought especially to establish their own alternative buildings and spaces during the years before the First World War, seeking visibility within society.[6] In the arts, focus was often centred around fostering public reputations through a rapidly expanding print culture, alongside exhibitions. But this chapter complicates the master narrative of the steady feminisation of public life as the central goal. For those identifying as 'serious' art workers, at the start of the twentieth century it was increasingly not simply the 'public sphere' they specifically aspired to gain access to but was, in fact, the 'private sphere' of the secretive, higher echelons of the male-oriented art world, represented and sustained by intellectually driven meetings at Clifford's Inn, and from 1914 at 6 Queen Square,

Bloomsbury. I consider, in the final section, the Women's Guild of Arts' infiltration of the Hall for its own meetings from 1907, arguing this constituted a key strategy of self-actualisation in women art workers' quest for formal recognition in the Arts and Crafts movement. By maintaining their stoic presence in the same building as their male peers, despite continuing to be segregated at actual meetings, they sought to rework the ideological and spatial gender divisions inherent in the Arts and Crafts movement. I explore how – after the first triumphant meeting – women art workers sought to emulate, and where possible integrate, themselves with this exclusive, secretive brotherhood, whilst simultaneously striving to sustain a women-focused, professional, and intellectual culture of their own.

Male-only institutions and the making of the modern art world

Male-only clubs and organisations were at the heart of the making of a highly masculinised, urban culture in the nineteenth and early twentieth centuries. Walter Crane dubbed it 'the age of societies'.[7] Such networks offered those men who could gain access a myriad of leisure and professional opportunities, whilst simultaneously upholding class privilege and notions of male authority. In London, many clubhouses were established in Piccadilly.[8] The Garrick Club, for instance, founded in 1831, which continues to be male-only to this day, forged new bonds between men active across public life. Members included Pre-Raphaelite painter Dante Gabriel Rossetti, *Punch* cartoonist Linley Sambourne, politician and businessman Viscount William Astor, and King Edward VII.

Amidst this world of homosocial bonding, a cluster of disillusioned male architects and art workers tried to distance themselves from 'professional society' in the final decades of the nineteenth century, concerned about the damaging effects of professionalisation – of overt regulation and uniformity – which they felt was evidenced by the hegemony of the Royal Academy on artistic culture. This was part of a wider rebellion against ostentatious displays of wealth, and the impact of capitalism and industrialisation on modern society. The formation of the Art Workers' Guild in 1884 exemplifies this discontentment and desire for change. It was not a 'guild' in the traditional, historical sense of the word, of regulating entry and training in crafts and trades whilst controlling prices and rates of pay. George Blackall Simonds, the first Master, waxed lyrical about how:

> The A.W.G. differs from all Art Societies in that it is not formed for the propagation of any one branch or style of Art. It is not a school, it

is not a club, it is not a debating society. In the Art-Workers' Guild I find something of the spirit of the studio-life of Rome.[9]

The Guild focused on dissolving the hierarchies between the arts, and in so doing encouraged a move away from overtly professional and capitalist structures, instead creating a sense of common fellowship between artistic men. The formation of this group played a central role in enabling members to have regular opportunities to meet and build networks through lectures and events. In the 1890s this included a talk about the history of English pottery, a debate on town-planning proposals, and a demonstration of copper-plate printing.[10] By the end of the nineteenth century many members had powerful jobs in the most prestigious art and design establishments across the country: Walter Crane had become director of the Manchester School of Art; F. M. Simpson, R. A. Bell and C. J. Allen had become professors and instructors at the Liverpool Municipal Craft School; whilst W. R. Lethaby and George Frampton had been appointed as inspectors and advisers to the Technical Education Board of the London County Council.[11]

Despite its posturing, the Art Workers' Guild was shaped by many prevalent middle-class, masculine, and professional currents. The refusal to allow women to join until 1964 speaks volumes of the general apathy, and indeed, the widely held expectation that artistic sociability should be male-only if it were to be truly ground-breaking. The Guild mirrored the Royal Academy, which had no women formally involved between the eighteenth century and the 1920s. Writings by Guild members portray the movement as closely revolving around their brotherhood. Master in 1888, Walter Crane, presented the Guild as the representative 'force' of the entire movement when he declared: 'There can be no doubt that the Art Workers' Guild is a force – that it represents a very real, very important movement in the Arts.' Comparing the founding of the Guild with the classic seafaring metaphor of the launching of a ship, he continued: 'Long may our good ship float upon the waters of fellowship and have an influence for good.'[12] In his own published works, C. R. Ashbee similarly stressed that he and other 'men of this movement' were involved in a 'mission' that was 'serious and ... sacred' which would lead to the 'destruction of the commercial system, to discredit it, undermine it, overthrow it'.[13]

Writings often effaced women's contributions; this build-up of regular misattributions, or questionable silences, quickly becomes noticeable to the researcher. In his memoir, Crane discussed the opening of new buildings at University College, Reading, by the Prince of Wales and the presentation of a 'silver and enamelled casket made by Mr Nelson Dawson'.[14] The casket was made by both Edith B. and Nelson Dawson.[15] Later, Crane describes the Society of Painters in Tempera, co-founded by Christiana Herringham, as 'principally' the work of John Dickson Batten, with Herringham listed in the next paragraph simply as member.[16] There are many other examples. When women are – very occasionally – mentioned in Guild texts, they are routinely discussed in relation to domestic, social occasions rather than being portrayed as actively involved in the development of the movement. In his Master's Address to the Guild in 1887, the architect J. D. Sedding even dedicated a part of his talk to a hotly debated topic for male artists and architects of the era: the problem of the 'shadow of matrimony' which 'carries off a member now and then'. Although Sedding was himself married, he warned his peers of the potential for marriage to diminish one's artistic potency, to take 'the heroic out of a man's conception of things, and [make] him slack and selfish', instead encouraging a life view that 'Art is much, but my own fireside is more!'[17] By stoking concerns in this way, influential figures such as Sedding contributed to a dominant perspective in the art world that regular opportunities for male-only bonding were crucial in restoring artistic culture to its pure and authentic expression.[18]

At the Hall, members implemented a bohemian, highly masculinised model of institution-building, instantly recognisable to other privileged men involved in club culture. They smoked pipes and drank grog, adopted an elaborate language which prioritised their central, pioneering roles as 'Brothers', had a Roll of Members, and strictly regulated entry through election processes.[19] Those designated solely as 'makers' could not join, only architects and designers, who were predominantly well-educated, often having met at Oxford or Cambridge, and usually from wealthy backgrounds, thus maintaining the class-based monopoly of formal artistic networks. Despite the engagement of members such as Ashbee in working-class cultures elsewhere in the city, class hierarchies at the Guild were never seriously challenged. In the era they were immersed in, this was the much-trodden path envisaged as necessary in creating a powerful new institution.

The desire to claim cultural power for themselves was fuelled by the anxiety Brothers felt about their own unstable new positions in society, particularly in the early years. As the painter and art critic Roger Fry discussed, 'Among professional artists there is a certain social class-feeling … a vague idea that a man can still remain a gentleman if he paints bad pictures, but must forfeit the conventional right to his Esquire if he makes good pots or serviceable furniture.'[20] For members of the Guild, seeking to remove hierarchies between different forms of artistry, great effort was needed to establish reputations as artistic gentlemen instead of tradesmen in an era obsessed with hierarchical societal structures. Despite the collaborative ethos underpinning the Arts and Crafts, male pioneers were keen to portray themselves as *the* expert figureheads, in polarised contrast to what had, by the end of the century, become a flood of national and international interest in the movement.

The Art Workers' Guild dedicated considerable energy towards establishing a permanent symbolic architectural 'home' for the movement. Originally, they rented rooms from the Century Club in Pall Mall – the heart of male club land – but then moved to the Inns of Chancery, a group of buildings associated with the legal profession in central London. They were based initially at Barnard's Inn, and then from 1894 at Clifford's Inn.[21] This region, just within the boundaries of the old City of London, was seen as 'neutral ground' for the Brothers. The 1894 annual report detailed how 'Here the men of Chelsea and Kensington have no cause to be jealous of the men of Hampstead and St John's Wood, and here the townsmen are but little better off than the men of Bedford Park and the suburbs.'[22] Alongside helping to balance a sense of geographical equilibrium between men based in competing artistic corners of the city, Clifford's Inn enabled the Brothers to assert their credibility as gatekeepers through use of a Hall which had a rich history of elite, male-only professional networking. Traditionally an Inn of Chancery, founded in 1344 to train students in jurisprudence, it was dissolved of this function by 1903. During the latter part of the nineteenth century, it began to be rented to 'professional' groups such as the Guild. The site fortuitously allowed members to express their shared dedication to medieval culture – a key tenet of the movement – as the building represented a rare fragment of the historic fabric of the city. The Hall itself was remodelled in 1767 (although few details survive about this redesign), but its historical importance was persistently commented upon by Brothers and in contemporary descriptions. In a short 1912 history, social commentator C. M. Hay-Edwards wrote: 'Many men have come and gone, and many events happened in the little world of Clifford's Inn, one of the most ancient parts of London.' Hay-Edwards carefully noted for readers: 'the old-world atmosphere that pervades these ancient nooks.'[23] The historical significance of the Hall and the area was regularly commented on by members and by wider society, reaching fever pitch in the interwar era when plans began for the building to be destroyed (Figure 1.1).

Clifford's Inn held additional appeal because the area was felt to evoke a curious feeling of privacy and quietness, away from the hustle and bustle of the modern capital, despite its central location. Secrecy was deemed of paramount importance in enabling the Brothers to claim status. J. D. Sedding discussed how 'with the instinct of true artists we shun

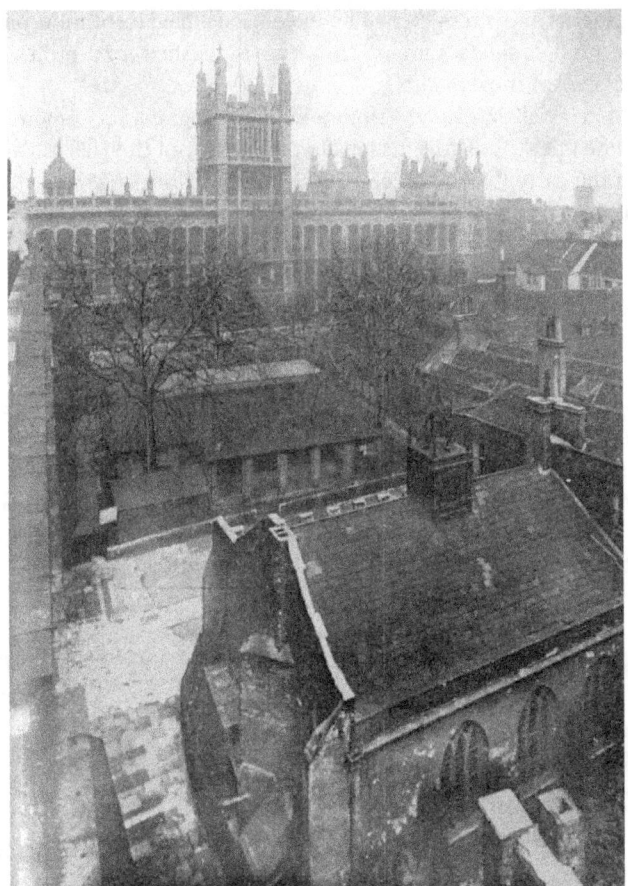

Figure 1.1 'Doomed: a wonderful aerial view of Clifford's Inn, the Hall of which, in the foreground, is to be destroyed', *Sphere* (26 February 1927), p. 355

publicity'.[24] Such an approach mirrored other cultural and intellectual clubs of the era, such as the Cambridge Apostles. Yet, in fact, the Hall stood at the crossroads to several, busy 'male' worlds: alongside its position amidst the law courts and the Royal Courts of Justice, the building was in the publishing district, close to Emery Walker's printing firm on Fleet Street, a short walk from artistic Bloomsbury, and a longer amble from male club land in Piccadilly. Several Brothers lived in rooms at nearby Gray's Inn. These clubs, offices, and bachelor households together formed a vibrant, paternalistic built environment, oriented around masculine camaraderie, and strengthened by industrious male institution-building across multiple fields, ranging from the established legal profession to progressive art movements.

Emery Walker, who took hundreds of photographs documenting the city as he knew it, turned his lens to the interior of the Hall at Clifford's Inn in the early twentieth century, capturing it for posterity before the Guild moved to new premises. These photographs provide a glimpse of how members sought to position themselves. In contrast to Piccadilly, where an ornate and sumptuous decor was the norm throughout the endless den of rooms at each club – for smoking, debating, and playing games – at this 'plain hall', simplicity was prized.[25] There were half-panelled walls, large arched windows, and a few discreetly placed busts and paintings. Rows of chairs were positioned in orderly lines, anticipating a lecture, emphasising the space was for intellectual endeavours (Figure 1.2). A large group portrait hung above the wooden fireplace in the centre of the room. Painted by John Percy Cooke, it depicts three Brothers – George Blackall Simonds, Gerald Horsley, and Mervyn Macartney – presiding over the twenty-fifth anniversary of the Guild in 1909.

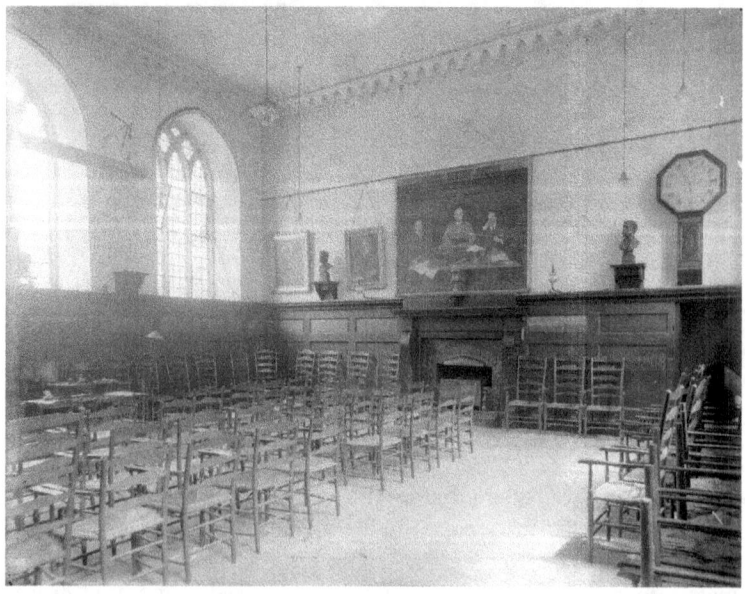

Figure 1.2 Interior of Clifford's Inn Hall, London by Sir Emery Walker, early twentieth century

The painting hints at what would later be far more extensive attempts to portray the importance of male-only collaborations in the Arts and Crafts after the Guild bought its Georgian house at 6 Queen Square, Bloomsbury, a short walk from Clifford's Inn, in 1914. The role it was felt the Hall at Queen Square would play in providing a quasi-domestic, companionable 'home' which sustained male bonds through regular ritualistic meetings is revealed in a 1915 address by Master Harold Speed, who stated he knew members would miss the 'picturesque and lovable old Hall and Inn' but encouraged them to enjoy 'the satisfaction of being our own masters in our own home, and shall doubtless accumulate, in the future, traditions and properties, in Queen Square, which will render the new home even dearer and more interesting to us than the old'.[26]

Brothers often pondered at meetings how the Guild would be portrayed by historians of the future. This was part of their wider anxiety about how to navigate – and avoid – public representation. In his 1894 speech as Master of the Guild, Heywood Sumner discussed his worries about accidentally entertaining 'unawares one of those clever gentlemen who … will turn us into copy' for the press.[27] After their 1914 move, a purpose-built Hall was carefully constructed at the back of the premises by architect and Brother Francis W. Troup. The Hall enabled them to convey, on their own terms, the authenticity of their artistic endeavours to members and visitors alike, rather than being reliant on press reports written by outsiders. Members repositioned the painting by John Percy Cooke centre stage, now alongside walls adorned with the hand-inked names of Brothers in gold paint. A pantheon of portraits and busts of past Masters enabled the Guild to promote a sense of tradition, at this point established for thirty years, reinvigorating them in their aims to foster unity between different arts and crafts (Figure 1.3). Such tradition-building continues to play a central role to this day: the current Master wears a red robe designed by C. F. A. Voysey, a chain of office by George Frampton, and sits in a chair by W. R. Lethaby, behind a table provided by W. A. S. Benson. Members participate in this complex power structure combining creative belonging, tradition, and exclusivity, by sitting on rush-seated, ladder-backed Clissett chairs based on a design by Ernest Gimson.

New mixed-sex and single-sex institutions: strategies for artistic success

Whilst this male-only Arts and Crafts world was carefully being constructed through the appropriation and construction of the built environment, the use of material tradition, and the forging of a passionate rhetoric, a

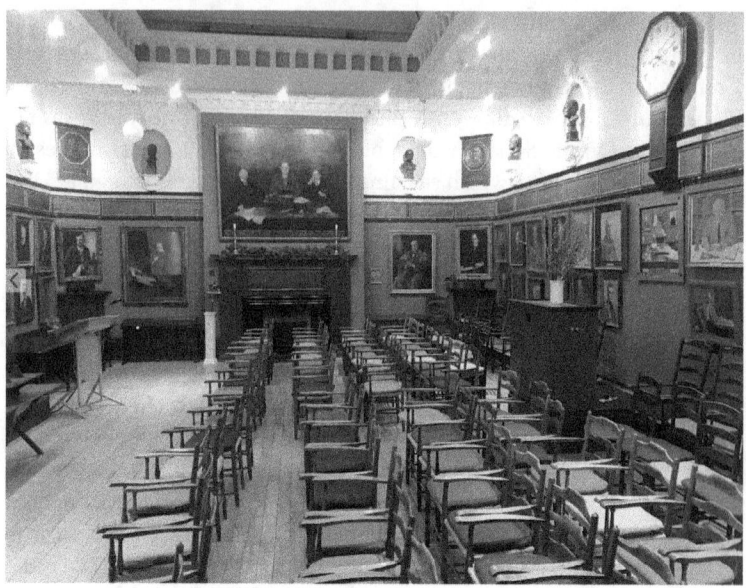

Figure 1.3 The interior of the Art Workers' Guild's Hall, 6 Queen Square, 2018

mixed-sex artistic organisational culture was emerging, which engendered a sense of change and opportunity at the turn of the century. The Northern Art Workers' Guild was founded in 1896 in Manchester, and although modelled on the Art Workers' Guild – Walter Crane was heavily involved – the Guild accepted women as members, as did the Arts and Crafts Exhibition Society (founded 1887). Women with financial means created a number of mixed-sex artistic organisations: Irish social reformer Eglantyne Jebb founded the Home Arts and Industries Association in 1884 and Christiana Herringham co-founded the Society of Painters in Tempera in 1901, of which a cluster of Women's Guild of Arts members were centrally involved: Mary Sargant Florence, Mary Batten, Emily Ford, and Estella Canziani, alongside Roger Fry and John Dickson Batten. The establishment of these mixed-sex art groups and exhibition societies, which were widely respected in their day and facilitated a wealth of new creative collaborations, further heightened the sense of disillusionment about the continuation of gender segregation elsewhere in society.

Despite the emergence of mixed-sex artistic associational collaborations, the gender of the artist continued to influence deeply how artistic work was assessed and understood, particularly within the heightened environments at elite urban lecture series and discussion groups where theatrical masculine performances played a critical role in the making of reputations. In 1894, Charlotte Newman was given the prestigious opportunity to lecture on her work for the Society of Arts. Interestingly, the event was held at Clifford's Inn, where the Society held some of its meetings – as did several other art groups – reiterating the significance of this building in the cultural milieu of the capital. Newman had worked as a goldsmith for twenty-five years and was now running her own business in central London. The second woman ever to lecture for the Society, she tackled the topic from historical, technical, and artistic perspectives, titling it 'Goldsmith's Work: Past and Present', and using lantern slides depicting works from the 'gem room' at the British Museum as visual aids. But, as a journalist at the *Woman's Signal* put forward: 'Interesting however as was the subject of the lecture and its illustrations, a deeper interest attached to the lecturer herself and her reception by her auditors. One felt at once how far, and yet how little way, public opinion had gone in the matter of full liberty for women.' Although the talk was deemed a success by the Society in its journal, the discussions afterwards reveal an acute awareness of Newman's gender, which dominated how the artist's work was understood and discussed, clearly heightened by the environment of a Hall recognised for masculine intellectual endeavours. Six men offered comments, four of whom framed an initial portion of their discussion around her gender. Each informed the audience they personally approved of women working in the arts, although the *Woman's Signal* journalist felt this was used problematically as a symbol of the Society's modernity, to congratulate itself 'on its liberality in inviting a woman of known proficiency in her art', rather than demonstrative of any real commitment to artistic equality.[28]

Most noticeably, there was an outpouring of disdain towards women who engaged in the political sphere – even though Newman's talk was not about politics. Sir George Birdwood, who worked for the India Office, ominously cautioned that all women must 'avoid the broad, downward road of politics, as they would poison'.[29] Evidently, women's emergent professionalisation in the arts was seen as indelibly linked to suffrage and the wider women's movement, engendering a disapproving backlash and dual sense of encroachment in the eyes of conservative male figures such as Birdwood. For many men at the Society of Arts, the growing efforts to gain political enfranchisement for women were seen as suggestive of potentially worrying changes to artistic culture and established intellectual traditions.

The artistic aptitude of women continued to be debated at Clifford's Inn across this era. A talk about embroidery design at a 'Members' Evening' of the Society of Designers in 1900 brought 'as large an audience as was ever crowded into the historic building', although the *Artist: An Illustrated Monthly Record of Arts, Crafts, and Industries* felt this to be because of the 'intense interest which is to-day shown in any subject which offers to provide amusement and employment to the fair sex'. After the talk, there was an extensive debate, with 'several ladies' taking part, amongst them Newman. Together the group discussed why women were so badly paid in this field, the President asserted that most of women's needlework was of a 'trifling nature', and one 'rash male individual' (whose name the paper decided not to print) was 'bold enough to say the best embroidery had been done by men'.[30]

The comments made by the *Woman's Signal* journalist – 'One felt at once how far, and yet how little way, public opinion had gone in the matter of full liberty for women' – perfectly sums up the cultural milieu at these elite environments during this era. Individual women such as Newman reached great heights of acclaim by the 1890s. These evenings were key in challenging ideas that women were inferior: Newman was spreading knowledge about her work to large audiences in intellectual settings in the capital, and these cultural events were being picked up and relayed to an even wider audience through print culture. But these events explain why women's groups were continually being formed: they provided alternative, supportive sites where women had greater agency and licence to perform their artistic roles in settings not dominated by suspicious debates about the encroachment of women on male affairs.

More generally, the 1890s were a boom time for women's clubs. There were at least thirty (in comparison to 300 men's clubs) by this point, often based in an area quickly nicknamed 'Petticoat Lane' around Dover and Albemarle Streets, between Piccadilly and Berkeley Square. This was a separate area to the male club district lining Pall Mall, Piccadilly, and St James's. A number, such as the Empress Club, were intended for very wealthy women, and many focused on leisure and shopping. Each signalled the new opportunities for middle- and upper-class women to engage in the modern pleasures of the capital as consumers and cultural participants.[31]

Amidst this, women's clubs and organisations with reformist zeal and professional aspirations began to grow. Here, members sought to position themselves away from the wider leisure culture associated with club land. One of the most progressive establishments of the 1890s was the Pioneer Club, which in its day was a symbol of the 'New Woman'. Founded in 1892 by wealthy women's rights campaigner Emily Massingberd,

'Pioneer' was in reference to the poem 'Pioneers! O Pioneers!' by American poet Walt Whitman.[32] By 1899, there were over 600 members, who could attend weekly debates on topics as varied as suffrage, temperance, homelessness, the nature of sanity, and the conflict between marriage and a career. Members were supposedly known by number rather than name to encourage equality of treatment. As Mary H. Krout enthusiastically told readers of her book *A Looker on in London*: '"99" might be a duchess or a post-office clerk.'[33] Those deemed 'professionals' were given a lower rate of subscription, to enable them to participate.[34] Clubs such as the Pioneer demonstrate the growing drive to encourage new mixed-class collaborations to blossom based around professional interests by the turn of the century, particularly between middle- and upper-class women.

Women art workers swiftly took advantage of these new networks, and also formed their own professional groups. The Glasgow Society of Women Artists was founded in 1882 and had its own clubhouse at 5 Blythswood Square from 1893, where members 'gave, or begged for,' furniture, carpets and crockery' and organised 'sewing-bees for running up curtains and cushions' to furnish the house to an appropriately domestic level.[35] The Women's International Art Club was founded in Paris, but members quickly moved the Club to London, holding the first exhibition there in 1900. By this point there were over a hundred members based in seventeen countries.[36] But for the art workers who later joined the Women's Guild of Arts the most popular group in the 1890s appears to have been the '91 Art Club. Today largely unknown to scholarship, it was founded by radical Swedish painter Anna Nordgren in 1891 and focused on both the fine and applied arts. Many future members of the Guild were involved: E. M. Rope was Vice President, Mary Lowndes and E. C. Woodward were committee members, whilst general members included Rose Barton, Edith Bateson, Mary Sargant Florence, Emily Ford, and Esther Moore.[37]

By the early twentieth century, the most important network for professional Arts and Crafts women could be found at the Lyceum Club, which was formally opened in 1904.[38] Writer Constance Smedley, who founded the Club, was, like other wealthy women such as Massingberd, deeply concerned about the working women who did not have familial and financial support or appropriate places to meet potential employers and customers. She was infuriated at the 'difference of the treatment accorded … to women who looked shabby and wretched' in contrast to those who 'looked prosperous and insouciant' in dress and surroundings.[39] As such, with the help of her father, she established the Lyceum Club, which provided a serious and prestigious centre for working women.

Smedley chose a 'title that would be understood in every country: something intellectual that would not be a "Society"'.[40] 'Lyceum' gave the Club this edge, signalling a meeting place of interdisciplinary intellectual debates, evoking ancient Athens. This perfectly suited Smedley, as the London Lyceum Club was merely the first of what she hoped would be a 'chain of Clubhouses in all countries' around the world.[41] Indeed, by the 1920s twenty-eight branches had been founded in thirteen countries and across three continents, including China and Australia.[42]

Smedley dedicated considerable time and energy to women in the Arts and Crafts; she appears clearly influenced by her background at the Birmingham School of Art, where she had 'thrilled at lectures from May Morris'.[43] Amongst her Advisory Boards, each of which focused on a different profession, she created a special Arts and Crafts Board to represent 'the great body of craftswomen banded together' in the Club. The Board included established figures such as Charlotte Newman and E. C. Woodward.[44] 'Representing Art' more generally, with the majority working in the fine arts, were celebrated women such as Feodora Gleichen, Louise Jopling, Henrietta Rae, Marianne Stokes, Jessie King, and Alice B. Woodward.[45]

At the Lyceum Club, professional status was accorded to those women 'of any nationality who have published any original work in literature, journalism, science, art, or music; or who have University qualifications; or who have rendered important public service; or who are wives of men, or daughters of men or women, distinguished' in the above fields.[46] Allowing women to join who were part of the 'right' familial circles emphasises the awareness of the decidedly un-meritocratic nature of professional society, and the practical methods the Club intended to use to mitigate this from the beginning. In Smedley's memoir, she openly discussed how wives and daughters of 'men of letters and artists and eminent professors' tended to 'belong to interesting circles' and were necessary to 'keep the Club in contact with men in the professions.'[47] Members sought to encourage structural change, away from evenings like those at Clifford's Inn Hall in the 1890s where, despite occasional invitations being proffered to individual women such as Charlotte Newman, women were viewed as curious anomalies and engaged in a peripheral world of work to their male peers.

There was considerable anxiety by this point that women's formal, and even informal, networks were encouraging an ever-more segregated world of femininity. Across women's professional networks, a wish for mixed-sex collaborations was being more frequently stressed; even the Pioneer Club invited men to visit on Wednesday afternoons.[48] Smedley proclaimed that male involvement was vital to ensure the Club would 'not be so exclusively a feminine affair'.[49] In an early article for the *Lyceum*, the Club's journal, she asserted the Club's *raison d'être* was to be:

> the first union of women which has put the quality of the work first, the help of the individual second. The idea of women banding together to help one another in the thorny wilderness of the professional world is a fine one; but the idea of the women workers of the world joining in a great endeavour to lift the onus of inferiority from women's work and to raise it by a strenuous effort and rigid self-denial to the high plane of man's achievement is finer still.[50]

There was much emphasis on the urgent need for women to move away from simply supporting fellow women because of their gender, and to instead 'put the quality of the work first', an approach which ruptured an earlier sense of community in favour of clearly designated professional alliances.[51] Many prominent women were involved – Lady Frances Balfour became President and Chair of the Executive Committee – and the Club had extensive rules, regulations, and increasing numbers of sub-committees and boards.[52] But this approach was evidently popular because within a year there were over 2,000 members, despite Smedley's proclamation of the care taken to restrict membership, with Committee Meetings where as many as sixty applications were 'rejected at a single sitting'.[53] Moreover, Smedley proudly noted that as early as 1905 discussions about the Club had apparently begun 'to drop the fatal catchword "woman"' when detailing the activities of members, instead talking of '"excellent work" rather than "excellent *women's* work"'.[54]

In stark contrast to the Art Workers' Guild's rejection of publicity and marketing, the Lyceum Club, like the majority of art groups of the era, directed considerable energy into attracting public interest. There was clearly an extensive appetite for news about the Club: alongside featuring in many interviews, Smedley had numerous articles printed across the Anglophone press. She regularly focused her attention on women art workers, enabling unprecedented insight into the collaborative strategies being implemented by women in the Arts and Crafts movement. In one article for the *World's Work*, a North American publication edited by diplomat and journalist Walter Hines Page, Smedley asserted that a 'living wage' had become the central priority at the dawn of the twentieth century. This was for two main reasons. The Board perceived professional success to be intrinsically linked with money-making, feeling if women made more money it would help combat the stereotypes persistently framing 'women's work' as inadequate. Secondly, enforcing a living wage would put a stop to the growing numbers of women with 'unlimited means and leisure' pursuing craft and underselling their work because an income was unimportant to them. Indeed, Smedley informed readers that the Board had been 'formed in sheer self-protection to fight the inroads of the leisured woman!' Although Board members were sympathetic to the 'natural desire' for these women to sell work 'like her bread-earning sister', this was negatively shaping the market and was denigrating women's reputations.[55]

Another strategy the Lyceum Club implemented was to have weekly dinners and lectures in honour of 'a special craft, or subject' to further extend women's professional and intellectual networks. Many women and men came to speak, such as Ethel and Philip Snowden, who discussed socialism and the Arts and Crafts. Different intellectual communities were targeted one by one, so that 'gradually London became like a well-known map wherein each of the five arts had its clearly defined territory'. In so doing, the clubhouse could function as a 'corporate social home for educated women, wherein women of small or large incomes could feel part of the aristocracy of intellect, and come into free and helpful contact with the men and women from all over the world'.[56] Similarly to the Pioneer Club, there was a considerable appetite for the forging of new ties between working women from different classes and backgrounds. The Lyceum Club offered practical and ideological opportunities to change the status quo, and the tensions between its various aims prefigured those faced by the Women's Guild of Arts.[57]

Women's groups, whether they were clubs for leisure, professional organisations, or suffrage societies, like those of their male peers, were firmly of the opinion that the buildings they used held considerable power in shaping how members would be understood. Mirroring the model of social maternalism often linguistically espoused by the women's movement, care was taken to ensure the femininity of the inhabitants was showcased through architectural designs and interiors, to assert the respectability, prestige, and class status of those involved, and to counteract ongoing equations of such women as masculine and 'unsexed'. Margaret Birney Vickery's work has shown that early women's university colleges were 'not built to mirror their male Oxbridge predecessors. Instead they relied on a domestic model both architectural and social'.[58] Similarly, the London headquarters for the International Woman Suffrage Alliance was an elegant eighteenth-century town house, which, Lynne Walker has written, Edwardian observers would have considered 'appropriate to the femininity of the suffrage occupants', due to the 'dainty honeysuckle ornament on the pilasters and the rich plasterwork detailing of the interiors'.[59] Women seeking cultural, social, or political change sought to signal publicly the gender and class status of the occupants, to engrain ideas about the acceptability, and respectability, of industrious feminine sites of endeavour. Yet this tactic ironically furthered a dominant perception of there being innate differences between the activities of women and men in public life.

The 1904 formation of the Lyceum Club at 128 Piccadilly marked an important departure from the trend of setting up in 'Petticoat Lane', becoming the first group of women to take over a club in male club land, previously the home of the Imperial Service Club, 'a bastion of masculine empire'.[60] In her memoir, Smedley gleefully discussed how 'We will stand on our own doorstep in Piccadilly, and look out from there on to our Clubs all over the world'.[61] Architectural historian Despina Stratigakos has argued that by 'conquering Piccadilly' the Club created public space no longer neatly segregated by gender, and instead 'made explicit, in geographical terms, the founders' intention to gain access to the nation's centers of power'.[62] Smedley claimed that the Club was the first women's club to 'emerge from a feministic atmosphere' by ensuring that the 'masculine furniture' was kept from the Imperial Service Club to create an environment in which 'men at the head of their profession feel the Lyceum was an integral part of Clubdom, contributing its own type of the intercourse they were used to, and enjoyed'.[63]

In a series of photojournalistic articles titled 'Our Ladies' Clubs' in the *Graphic*, the journalist ventured across London visiting women's clubs such as the Lyceum.[64] A brief paragraph sums up the Club's aims, but it is the six photographs which are intended as the real focus, allowing readers to journey voyeuristically through the rooms and make up their own minds about this industrious new professional world (Figure 1.4). Each photograph provides a snapshot of these different spaces: drawing room, dining room, reading and writing room, and so on. Noticeably, the photographs portraying members all include women who are reading, seeking to reinforce visibly the Club's dedication to higher learning and professional pursuits. The inclusion of servants, the grandeur and eminently respectable aesthetic, and the comforting familiar symbols of upper-middle-class domesticity – plush sofas, thick curtains, ornamental lighting – would have soothed readers suspicious about their motives. Yet alongside this, the smoking room, the most controversial of rooms at women's clubs due to the established tradition of smoking as a male pursuit, and the 'Arts and Crafts gallery' both function as signifiers of the Club's modernity and progressive nature. This array of interior spaces exemplifies how clubs such as the Lyceum began to merge established models of domestic and feminine modes of socialising, with grand, transgressive efforts to encourage new professional opportunities for women.

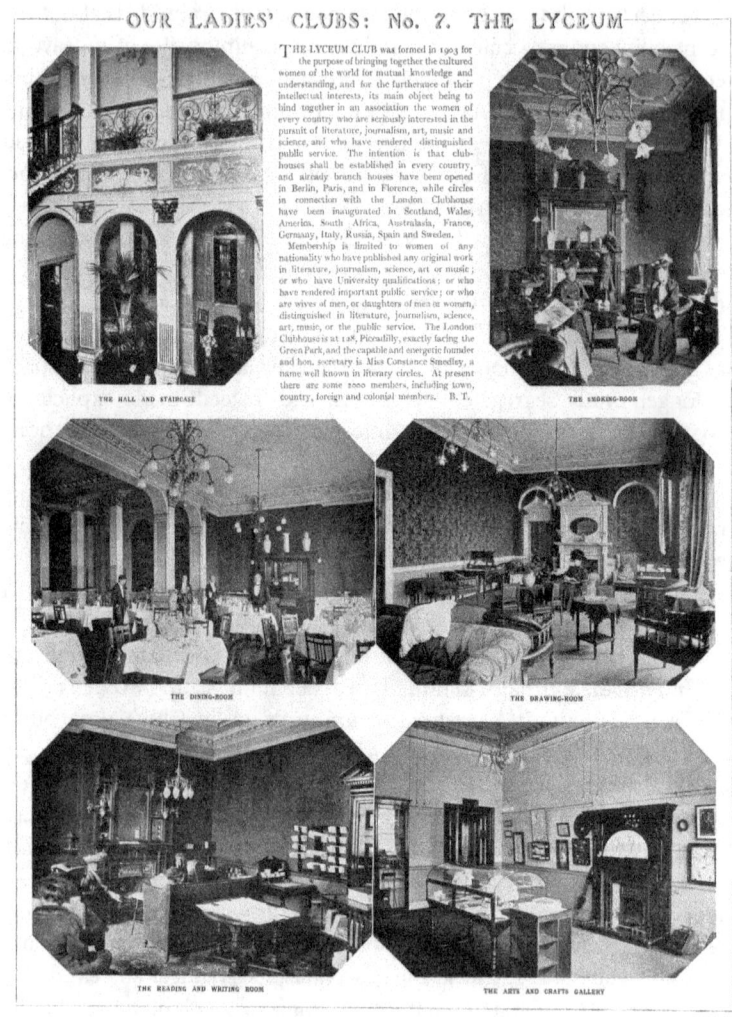

Figure 1.4 'Our Ladies' Clubs: No. 7. The Lyceum', *Graphic* (18 April 1908), p. 555

From 1907, the Women's Guild of Arts was to draw from several of the strategies implemented at the Lyceum Club, having similar ambitions about the need to target and gain access to areas traditionally established as masculine intellectual and artistic sites in the spatial mapping of the capital, to raise the cultural statuses of women. The Guild's focus was not, however, Piccadilly. Instead, it was the Hall at Clifford's Inn, Fleet Street, and later the Hall at 6 Queen Square, Bloomsbury – sites members such as Honorary Secretary May Morris felt constituted the core of the Arts and Crafts movement. The Women's Guild of Arts was solely focused on the Arts and Crafts, and its members were to gain entry to buildings where their male peers still continued to meet – albeit separately. Here privacy, unlike publicity, was viewed as of paramount importance. Let us now turn to see how this played out.

At the Guild Hall: formalising women's contributions to the Arts and Crafts movement

To this day, Clifford's Inn and 6 Queen Square are heralded as crucial centralising sites which cemented the bonds of fellowship between men, facilitating their intellectual debates, artistic experimentations, and impact on modern culture. Clifford's Inn Hall was knocked down in 1934, and although 6 Queen Square continues to thrive as the home of the Art Workers' Guild today, there is no visible trace that the Women's Guild of Arts met there for over fifty years. The historiographical perception of women's overall exclusion from the Arts and Crafts partially stems from the absence of their impact on the architectural heritage of the movement, and from the rhetoric asserted by the Art Workers' Guild in the late nineteenth and early twentieth centuries. Elizabeth Cumming and Wendy Kaplan have observed that because 'the ideal of a brotherhood of craftsmen denied the inclusion of women as full members', women who 'were art school-trained were confined to the pursuit of craft as a pastime or as philanthropy, or to crafts considered appropriate for their sex'.[65] But, as this chapter has already revealed, women were actively forming their own artistic networks and were gaining entry to mixed-sex institutional spaces. The Women's Guild of Arts was to provide many new opportunities for its members, who were by this point predominantly middle-aged and working at the top of their respective fields.

Unlike at the Lyceum Club, a living wage was never an official focal point, although there was a fund to help members who 'may at any time find their work hindered by temporary want of funds'. This approach was similar to the Art Workers' Guild, who already had a 'Guild Chest'.[66] This exemplifies the Women's Guild of Arts' attitude from the beginning: members made consistent attempts to emulate the strategies used by the Art Workers' Guild. The very title of the Guild was ostensibly shaped by a wish to linguistically connect the two Guilds, alongside a general enthusiasm for a pseudo-medieval aestheticism. Both Guilds had the same central aims – restoring the status of the 'Crafts' to that of the 'High Arts', whilst simultaneously seeking to position members as expert cultural figures – although women had additionally to combat the ongoing suspicions about the authenticity of their design skills and craftwork.

The tactics women art workers used to associate themselves with the Art Workers' Guild influenced the crafting of all official documentation. Reports were often written by May Morris, who instrumentally shaped the Guild in its early years. One in 1913 reminded members that 'The Art Workers' Guild, as you know, has been established for a great many years, and seeing the extraordinary benefit this body has been to its members, it was thought that a service might be rendered to women art-workers by the formation of an organisation on similar lines.'[67] Formal documentation always avoided inflammatory statements about why it had been necessary to form their own group, or detailed discussion about their positions as women. Instead, members stressed their shared commitment to the Arts and Crafts and deep respect for their male peers, focusing on the rewards they felt they could potentially reap by abiding by this non-controversial approach, with persistent adaption of linguistic norms and regular use of the Hall.

Negotiating access to the two Halls, firstly at Clifford's Inn and later at Queen Square, prestigious sites of masculine empowerment, was seen as a tremendously important step, even if members were segregated at actual meetings. Although the women had first met at Mary Sargant Florence's studio, amongst other places, members were keen to have a set building to hold meetings in. Whilst male groups could, and did, host meetings in the homes of members, this reflects the different gendered expectations of artistic groups. A woman was all too easily relegated into a non-professional role by virtue of her social environment. The drawing room was perceived as domestic and feminine when appropriated by women, whereas these same rooms could be conceptualised as artistic when used by men.

The Hall held the unique ability to temper what this group of women saw as their frustrating, segregated 'feminine' presence in society, to showcase instead their respectability and 'serious' focus, working companionably close to their male peers at the heart of the capital. They believed a shared character could be cultivated, anchored in, and shaped by, the artistic and cultural semiotics of the Hall. In a 1908 letter to May Morris, metalworker Edith B. Dawson discussed the influence she personally felt this building wielded, but she hinted at the unease felt by other members when writing:

> Since I heard of the offer of Clifford's Inn Hall by the Art Workers' Guild to our new Women's Guild, I have been wondering whether all of us realise how important an offer it is and what a very great mistake we shall make if we lightly refuse it. For years the Art Workers' Guild has held its meetings there and perhaps only those of us who have men-folk belonging to the guild know how attached they are to the fine old hall with its many associations, and what a dignifying and benign influence such a place of meeting would have on any gathering.

Furthermore, Dawson clearly felt the Art Workers' Guild was offering the Hall as implicit support, writing that it had been proposed:

> in a spirit of welcome and comradeship which we should not at any rate put lightly aside, and to some of us it seems a poor substitute to wander homelessly from one member's workplace to another, ever changing and having nowhere to call our own, as well as giving much more trouble to the officers of our Guild.

Concerns they would be 'homeless', reliant on meeting at each other's workplaces, demonstrates the desire to anchor their group physically, in emulation of the male Guild, within a professional meeting space. Continuing, she stressed the importance of having evening meetings, 'as we are women whose work makes daylight and day time valuable, and also the holding of the meetings in the evening would prevent the feeling of "drawing-room meeting" to which I think we may all object'. Dawson finished by writing she had 'the interest of our new Guild at heart, with the hopes and ambitions for it that all its members must feel, that we may be a united body of women art workers, looking at things broadly and responsibly'.[68] This letter provides a rare glimpse of the prominent role it was hoped the Guild would have in these women's lives. The celebrity status of founding members such as the embroiderer Jane Morris, and the fact they had finally gained entry to the Hall, must have made this seem a moment of unprecedented opportunity.

The first decades of the twentieth century were a moment of wider change at the Inns of Chancery, as slowly the area opened to professional women, representing in microcosm the shifts taking place on a national level. In his history of Clifford's Inn, C. M. Hay-Edwards acknowledged the move away from the Hall's previously male-only stance, writing that: 'Women – in all contradistinction to the ancient laws – came and went, and worked in their rooms there.' The Society of Women Journalists had begun to meet at the Inn; 'to its rooms have come most of the leading women writers of the day'.[69] That being said, other Inns of Court were still being used for legal purposes, and the area continued to be dominated by male activity even after the Sex Disqualification (Removal) Act opened the Bar to women in 1919. Ren Pepitone has illuminated how men in the legal professions effectively controlled the area across the interwar era, using dining halls, offices, and even toilets 'as both excuses and devices for marginalizing women'.[70] For Arts and Crafts women on the fringes of this environment, the continued emphasis of professional masculinity had the rather unexpected effect of directly enhancing the prestige of their own meetings: demonstrating to the world how removed they – as a group of serious art workers – now were from the domestic or suburban socialisation expected of them as middle-class women.

Like the Art Workers' Guild, the Women's Guild of Arts avoided publicity, which aligned their work with an established model of anti-commercialist, intellectual pursuits – and fortuitously enhanced their prestige.[71] Members clearly enjoyed such privacy. In one unpublished poem, 'Rhyme of the Ancient Inn', illuminator Ethel Sandell wrote about her delight at the Hall, entered through 'A little passage dim and grey'.[72] Sculptor Feodora Gleichen even used privacy and location to justify the male-only stance of the Art Workers' Guild, writing it 'would do away with the whole character of the meetings if they took place in a large Hall where both Guilds could meet; it would be like a large unwieldy public meeting!'[73] Gleichen's letter highlights a reticence felt by many members, reiterating the ongoing role played by privacy and tradition in the making of elite, intellectual cultures and the difficulties this posed for women seeking to establish themselves, who were often reliant on courting public attention through the press. The sense of achievement different individuals felt by gaining access to these prestigious, predominantly male, venues helps us understand the decision of these women to then uphold the prevalent social order once they had personally gained entry.

The Hall acted as an essential site of centralising institutionalism, but the survival and health of the Guild depended on the sociability which played out within its walls. The physical grounding of the Hall was complemented by an invisible, but just as tangible, network of sociability which bound members together in dedication to exhibiting expertise. Thirty-six women joined in the first year, including leading lights such as bookbinder S. T. Prideaux, interior decorator Agnes Garrett, and the painters Marianne Stokes, Annie Swynnerton, and Evelyn De Morgan. Although these founding members had been specially invited, the Guild quickly implemented a formal policy whereby prospective members had to be nominated by a proposer and a seconder already on the Committee. Potential members had to submit several examples of work or other proofs of competence to be inspected by members who were experts in that specific field of artistry. Much emphasis was placed on this formal process, which enabled members to assert professional status through strict control of entry, and to become gatekeepers of the movement. A two-thirds majority of those present was necessary for election. If allowed to join, members paid a small annual fee.[74]

Attempts made by 'amateurs' to join were always firmly refuted. May Morris in particular was fixated with standards and the need for absolute professionalism in the face of societal expectations to the contrary. In an early speech in 1908, alongside emphasising the importance of members attending meetings 'in a spirit of comradeship', she stressed that the Guild had begun having only 'picked artists', and could not expand quickly because of the need to ensure those involved were consistently working at the highest levels:

> Your Committee only presents to you names of candidates whose work they judge competent and sincere, so to belong to the Guild is by no means an empty honour. The process of selection may seem troublesome to candidates – as it is to the Committee and Secretary: but one of the points of our body is that it is not easy of access, and we have no wish to slacken the rules in that respect.[75]

Another speech by Morris in 1912 reiterated their roles as taste makers. She showed sympathy for the problems members faced in their roles as 'connoisseurs or expert workers', torn between 'freezing at a North Pole of splendid isolation, and that of getting a little too good-natured in admitting people who have not reached the necessary standard of work'. But she went on to warn them that if they did not implement this elitist approach and admitted women 'who would not themselves lay claim to being among the experts', then current members would be responsible for 'lower[ing] the standard of taste', would 'lose the kind of influence we wish to have, and become a mediocrity. And then we might as well break up our body'.[76] In Morris's opinion, there was simply no point in meeting if Guild events were not professional at all times.

Undoubtedly, the most important service the Guild provided during the early years was to present members with opportunities to lecture and give demonstrations on the fields in which they were experts, thus facilitating their self-actualisation as art workers and intellectuals. When Edith B. Dawson wrote to May Morris, she stressed that the Guild would be the most successful if it were 'to be like the Men's Guild, as Mr Rooke who was here last night said, it was for "no use at all" and was all the better for it. Really he knew it was a great deal of use to its members, but not in a business way."[77] The Women's Guild of Arts followed Dawson's recommendations and focused on hosting official meetings, six to seven times a year, where members spoke about their work. Despite the proclamations that these events were 'no use at all', they were critically important. They generated a sense of solidarity and strengthened the bonds between members. But most importantly, these events were framed as intellectual endeavours. By fostering this approach, the Guild built on the strategies being put forward at the Lyceum Club, facilitating the making of a collaborative, women-focused, intellectual artistic culture.

The Hall created a framework of social interaction which women claimed for transitory displays of artistic proficiency, to assert their roles as taste makers, and to conjure up new intellectual ideas for modern society where artistic creativity was woven into debates about design, work, education, and history. By framing their learning within the characteristic teaching space of the lecture hall, the space invigorated members in their pursuits. The tables and walls were temporarily adorned with craftwork. In 1908 papers were given such as: Christiana Herringham on 'Indian Architecture' and Elinor Hallé and Feodora Gleichen a joint paper on 'Relief in Sculpture', whilst in 1909 topics discussed included 'Fresco' by Mary Sargant Florence and 'Thoughts which Have Occurred to Me about Arts and Crafts during a Long Struggle with Both' by sculptor Esther Moore. In 1910 there was a discussion by Emily Ford 'and others' about 'Imagination in Education' and even a 'Debate' on 'The Scope and Power of Guilds'.[78] Members could invite guests, and by inviting visitors to the Hall, the Women's Guild of Arts gained greater opportunities to interact with other men and women as intellectual equals in a professional setting, and through these actions to challenge perceptions about the role of women in society. These events were crucial in engendering a wider sphere of sociability which encompassed mixed-sex political debates: at one Guild gathering, playwright George Bernard Shaw was described by Alys Fane Trotter as on 'a mission' to spread his socialism. As such, Trotter – who had little interest in socialism, and had been rather dismayed by the 'strong Socialist element' in Chiswick where she was living – had a 'spirited disagreement' with him.[79]

Women were not allowed to attend Art Workers' Guild meetings until 1964, but in lived practice the informal boundaries between single-sex groups were rarely impermeable. There were numerous interactions and mixed-sex bonds formed through shared commitment to the Arts and Crafts, professional ties, marriages, families, and friendships. The Women's

Guild of Arts encouraged the holding of joint lectures wherever possible; in one letter to the Art Workers' Guild, May Morris suggested having three joint meetings that year, but questioned if three 'would be overdoing it?'[80] Bookbinder Katharine Adams was one of a number of women, including May Morris, who maintained close friendships with the Brothers. She joined the Art Workers' Guild, as an unmarried woman, on trips across mainland Europe. In 1903, Art Workers' Guild Master Charles Harrison Townsend wrote to Adams asking if he could use the photographs she had taken on a recent trip to Rome for an Art Workers' Guild meeting. Sensing the hypocrisy of asking Adams if he could use her materials at a meeting she was not allowed to attend, he awkwardly added, 'I wish ladies could come on the 18th and that you could be at Clifford's Inn to hear and see.'[81] Adams evidently maintained these friendships, as in 1911 she received a letter lamenting her inability to go on holiday that year, which shows the respect her male peers held for her: 'Greetings and Love (in the most A.W.G. and respectful sense) to Miss Kate Adams from the following, her sincere friends and admirers now wobbling ... across the Bay of Biscay ... and regretting intensely that the said Miss K. Adams is not of the party.'[82]

From the early twentieth century onwards, women, more generally, were sometimes invited to social events at the Art Workers' Guild in the form of special 'Ladies' Nights'. The retiring Master in 1913, Edward Warren, suggested that 'surplus' Fridays could be used to host evenings women could attend. Warren informed his fellow Brothers that there were 'many ladies who are vicariously interested in the Guild, and many of whom are more than capable of contributing papers, or of speaking, upon matters somewhat without the ken of the average Guildsmen, but well within the range of his appreciations'.[83] Although these events were generally popular, they do not appear to have been liked by professional women. H. J. L. J. Massé reported in his 1935 history of the Art Workers' Guild that: 'It has always been difficult, if not impossible, to convince the ladies that the meetings were not concocted or faked to suit the taste that was imagined to be peculiar to them. It has been almost as difficult to induce a lady to speak on a Ladies' Night.'[84]

Yet whatever the apprehensions of individual members about the impact of women's networks on professional aspirations, and the ongoing attempts to emulate the Art Workers' Guild, it was the relationships between these women which sustained their collaborative professional world and intellectual interactions. Their male peers may have seen them as personal friends – and on an individual level as fellow experts – but on a Guild level, and at a societal level, there was a refusal to see women as artistic equals. Feeling networking was key to success, in 1909 the Women's Guild of Arts established Associate members, for women more generally 'interested in art'.[85] This tactic mirrored the Lyceum Club: allowing women who had a link to intellectual and professional circles through family connections to be allowed to participate to widen their networks. Part of being a 'serious' artist was displaying unease about commercial motivations, and Associates provided an acceptable way of broadening the scope of the Guild, and building its power in cultural and wealthy circles. The role of Associate members was stipulated in a special leaflet:

> To assist the production of good art. By helping to keep up the right spirit – in the workers – by helping to keep the good ones (tried and trained and tested ones) from being driven, by want of funds and employment, into work which wastes them, and their training … etc. The Associates are there to be shown the right quality, if they don't know it already, to be told where they can obtain good work, of good quality … and to back up the Guild.

Members ('the workers') – proven 'good' artists – were seen to need the Associates, who provided a wider sphere of community and financial support which could assist them from having to seek employment on disadvantageous terms. The leaflet discussed the difficulties of being an artist and how Associates could help them: 'from getting swamped and artists from falling out, or succumbing to the onset of the hostile forces constantly besetting their paths'.[86] Many prominent women, with a diversity of interests, joined as Associates, such as: actress Hilda Trevelyan; art collector and patron Juliet M. Morse; writer and poet Alix Egerton; and bookbinder Winifred Stopes (sister of Marie Stopes, pioneer in birth control).[87] An approving account in one report described the behaviour of the ideal Associate: 'One engagement ring I know one Associate secured as a commission for a Guild member – that is the right line for an Associate!'[88] By inviting this network of women to become involved, these women together played a critical role in disseminating the ethos of the Arts and Crafts across a wider sphere of influence than previously acknowledged in the twentieth century.

The networks of sociability and professionalisation facilitated by groups such as the Women's Guild of Arts did not solely orbit around physical meetings. The correspondence between members built an additional layer of institutional experience, intellectual exchange, and sense of intimacy, which transgressed local and national borders.[89] This was often in lieu of being physically able to attend meetings due to domestic commitments or distance to travel. Friendships and artistic networks could run for years relying on letter writing in place of physical contact. Members tried to participate whilst also negotiating busy roles as middle-class women – roles which held extensive expectations of them as wives, daughters, sisters, and mothers – alongside maintaining their own artistic workloads.[90] One letter to Mary A. Sloane from a Miss Cole lamented that 'she is unable after all to join' because her father is in 'delicate health and cannot be left in the evening'. Miss Cole's hope to maintain a connection with the Guild comes across clearly. She was 'greatly sorry for the trouble she has given Miss Sloane and hopes that some other year she will be allowed to join'.[91] A similar letter from Ethel K. Martyn discussed her concerns about taking on paid artistic work as she wanted 'to make a special effort to do more at home to help – my sister won't let me do that if I've big work on hand – so I have just written to Mr Butler ... to give it up'.[92] Although Martyn's family were supportive, her own personal feeling of responsibility, and the need to fulfil her domestic duties, made her reduce the time she dedicated to art.

The Women's Guild of Arts even commissioned their own Guild Roll to strengthen their artistic and intellectual collaborations. Taking the form of an engraved, illuminated booklet, bound in red pigskin, it listed the names of all members. Ethel Sandell and Katharine Adams were commissioned to make the Roll. Letters were exchanged reiterating the need for 'lots of room' for future members, revealing their optimism about the future. There was much deliberation about how to present the names and fields of members, indicating the extent to which these women thought about how to represent their endeavours.[93] Demonstrating the range of respective crafts being practised by members was important to the Guild, as it showed they were fulfilling their commitment to equality and collaboration across the arts.[94] It is striking that the Roll was finished the same year that the Art Workers' Guild were to inscribe their names for posterity, using gold paint, on the walls of their new home at 6 Queen Square. Although the Women's Guild of Arts were allowed access to the new Hall for their own separate meetings, their names were not to be included on the walls, and so they instead used the Roll to symbolise a shared commitment to the movement. Here, from 1914, the women's meetings took place in a building purposely designed to showcase male artistic identities through portraits, furniture, and wall decorations.[95] Poignantly, the Roll shows the determination of these women to materially represent and celebrate their collaborative efforts, but it also embodies their liminal status as a Guild, as it is now lost. Conversely, the Hall, with its architectural permanency, continues to memorialise the contributions of male figures to the movement.

From 1913, the Women's Guild of Arts, bolstered by their regular meetings at the Hall, but clearly dissatisfied by the lack of new occasions for formal mixed-sex integration, made the controversial decision to form the category of Honorary Associates. This new category included men, and they used it to ask a cluster of prominent Brothers from the Art Workers' Guild formally to join *their* Guild, to further encourage an interchange of ideas. The Women's Guild of Arts Committee also began increasingly to host lectures with male speakers – rather than having talks predominantly by expert women. The final chapter of *Women Art Workers* explores the outcry from certain members in 1913 about this shift in approach, positioning these institutional tactics amidst the wider context of the suffrage movement, and considering the impact of the First World War and the 1920s and 1930s on the aspirations of Arts and Crafts women.

This first chapter has demonstrated that although the English Arts and Crafts movement is routinely portrayed as the activities of a small radical cluster of male architects and art workers, there were significant numbers of women practitioners who gathered together their energies, particularly in the early twentieth century, to establish several formal, interconnected groups for Arts and Crafts women. Such groups, in particular the Lyceum Club with its Arts and Crafts Board and the Women's Guild of Arts, enabled women to stress more readily the integral role they, and their art, had to play in modern society. Women's formal involvement has thus been shown to have been integral to the institutional and visionary core of the movement. An examination of spaces where women met and collaborated reveals the tactics women implemented in retaliation to rigid gender divisions, permits greater understanding of the plurality of ways women enacted their artistic roles, and uncovers the range of priorities in these settings.

The activities of these groups can be seen as part of a wider shift in the phenomenon of institutional and associational sociability, where women increasingly appropriated tactics of demonstrating cultural authority which had been honed in male networks during the preceding decades. But the application of these strategies was not uncontested, and it exposed many gendered tensions within the women's groups that have been discussed. There had been mounting anxieties about separatism at women's organisations since the late nineteenth century and, from 1907, the Women's Guild of Arts, in particular, had deeply felt concerns about how best to arrange meetings so as to avoid exacerbating what members saw as their segregated feminised presence in the capital and in society. Whereas the

Lyceum Club focused on geographically remodelling the city through establishing its clubhouse at the heart of male club land in Piccadilly, the Women's Guild of Arts instead entered the private, historic buildings of Clifford's Inn Hall and 6 Queen Square as its chosen approach subtly to disrupt gendered segregation, encourage mixed-sex artistic sociability, and formally assert the role of women in the Arts and Crafts movement. There was never any simple process of institutional professionalisation: women art workers continually had to negotiate and assert their presence during their lifetimes.

Additionally, the decision made by the Women's Guild of Arts to focus on meeting at the two Halls has masked the endeavours of the Guild within the broader remit of the Art Workers' Guild, due to the deliberately private nature of these groups, the already established male presence of the Art Workers' Guild at these sites, and because of the wider failure to take women's cultural networks seriously. The Lyceum Club has fared little better in posterity, despite its prominent architectural presence in the city in its heyday and the extensive interest of the press. But during their lives, members found many new opportunities for self-assertion and leadership at the Club and at the Guild, where they performed their roles as art workers to fellow members, Associates, and visiting guests. Friendships and emotional lives were nurtured, commitment to the movement was strengthened, and a nascent intellectual artistic culture was cultivated. The following chapter moves from these halls and clubhouses to explore how Arts and Crafts women reshaped the world of exhibitions for their needs and interests – and how society responded.

Notes

1   WGAA, Handwritten Secretary Report, 1908.
2   Anthea Callen, 'Sexual Division of Labor in the Arts and Crafts Movement', *Woman's Art Journal*, 5/2 (1984–1985), pp. 1–6 (p. 6).
3   Anthea Callen, *Angel in the Studio: Women in the Arts and Crafts Movement, 1870–1914* (London: Astragal, 1979), p. 9.
4   Deborah Cherry, *Beyond the Frame: Feminism and Visual Culture, Britain 1850–1900* (London: Routledge, 2000), pp. 67–68; Pamela Gerrish Nunn, *Victorian Women Artists* (London: Women's Press, 1987), pp. 72–87.
5   Deborah Cherry, *Painting Women: Victorian Women Artists* (London: Routledge, 1993), p. 77.
6   Estelle Freedman, 'Separatism as Strategy: Female Institution Building and American Feminism, 1870–1930', *Feminist Studies*, 5/3 (1979), pp. 512–529; Martha Vicinus, *Independent Women: Work and Community for Single Women, 1850–1920* (Chicago: University of Chicago Press, 1985).

7   Julie F. Codell, 'Artists' Professional Societies: Production, Consumption, and Aesthetics', in *Towards a Modern Art World* (ed.) Brian Allen (London: Yale University Press, 1995), pp. 169–188 (p. 169).

8   Barbara J. Black, *A Room of His Own: A Literary-Cultural Study of Victorian Clubland* (Athens: Ohio University Press, 2012); Amy Milne-Smith, *London Clubland: A Cultural History of Gender and Class in Late-Victorian Britain* (London: Palgrave Macmillan, 2011).

9   Art Workers' Guild Archive, the Art Workers' Guild, London (hereafter AWGA), George Blackall Simonds, Address of the Master, 1885.

10 William Whyte, *Founding Members of the Art Workers' Guild (act. 1884–1899)*, Oxford Dictionary of National Biography, 2007.

11 AWGA, Heywood Sumner, Address of the Master, 1894.

12 AWGA, Walter Crane, Address of the Master, 1888.

13 C. R. Ashbee, *Craftsmanship in Competitive Industry* (Campden: Essex House Press, 1908), p. 10.

14 Walter Crane, *An Artist's Reminiscences* (London: Methuen, 1907), p. 442.

15 See 'Architecture and Crafts at the Royal Academy', *Architectural Review* (1 May 1899), p. 262.

16 Crane, *An Artist's Reminiscences*, p. 481.

17 AWGA, J. D. Sedding, Address of the Master, 1887.

18 This attitude was mirrored across various intellectual communities, such as those at universities, which often had a homosexual undercurrent. See Emily Rutherford, 'Impossible Love and Victorian Values: J. A. Symonds and the Intellectual History of Homosexuality', *Journal of the History of Ideas*, 75/4 (2014), pp. 605–627.

19 Eric Hobsbawm and Terence Ranger (eds), *The Invention of Tradition* (Cambridge: Cambridge University Press, 1983).

20 Christopher Reed, *Bloomsbury Rooms: Modernism, Subculture, and Domesticity* (New Haven: Yale University Press, 2004), p. 114.

21 AWGA, Annual Report, 1894.

22 AWGA, Heywood Sumner, Address of the Master, 1894.

23 C. M. Hay-Edwards, *A History of Clifford's Inn, with a Chapter on its Present Owners by Willoughby Bullock* (London: Thomas Werner Laurie, 1912), pp. xi, xii.

24 AWGA, J. D. Sedding, Address of the Master, 1887.

25 AWGA, Heywood Sumner, Address of the Master, 1894.

26 AWGA, Harold Speed, Address of the Master, 1915.

27 AWGA, Heywood Sumner, Address of the Master, 1894.

28 'Concerning Women', *Woman's Signal* (8 March 1894), p. 159.

29 'Applied Art Section, "Goldsmith's Work: Past and Present" by Mrs Philip Newman', *Journal of the Society of Arts*, 42 (1894), pp. 312–322 (p. 319).

30 'Designers' Jottings', *Artist: An Illustrated Monthly Record of Arts, Crafts, and Industries* (February–May 1900), p. 458.

31 Erika Rappaport, *Shopping for Pleasure: Women in the Making of London's West End* (Princeton: Princeton University Press, 2001).

32 David Doughan, *The Pioneer Club*, Oxford Dictionary of National Biography, 2007.

33 Mary H. Krout, *A Looker on in London* (New York: Dodd and Mead, 1899), p. 80.

34 The general annual subscription was initially two guineas per annum, entrance fee one guinea. Elizabeth Crawford, *The Women's Suffrage Movement: A Reference Guide, 1866–1928* (London: UCL Press, 2000), p. 126.

35 DeCourcy Lewthwaite Dewar, *History of the Glasgow Society of Lady Artists' Club* (Glasgow: University Press, 1950), p. 13.

36 For a short history of the Society of Women Artists, the Glasgow Society of Women Artists, and the Women's International Art Club, amongst others, see Cherry, *Painting Women*, pp. 67–77.

37 National Art Library, Victoria and Albert Museum, '91 Art Club, Clifford's Gallery Exhibition Pamphlet, 1896.

38 Grace Brockington, "'A World Fellowship": The Founding of the International Lyceum Club', *Transnational Associations*, 1 (2005), pp. 15–22.

39 Constance Smedley, *Crusaders: Reminiscences of Constance Smedley / Mrs Maxwell Armfield* (London: Duckworth, 1929), pp. 56, 60.

40 Ibid., p. 61.

41 Ibid., p. 60.

42 Despina Stratigakos, *A Women's Berlin: Building the Modern City* (Minneapolis: University of Minnesota Press, 2008), p. 25.

43 Smedley, *Crusaders*, p. 17.

44 Constance Smedley, 'A Guild of Craftswomen', *World's Work: An Illustrated Magazine of National Efficiency and Social Progress*, 9 (December 1906–May 1907), pp. 314–322 (pp. 314, 318).

45 Smedley, *Crusaders*, p. 65.

46 'Our Ladies' Clubs: No. 7. The Lyceum', *Graphic* (18 April 1908), p. 555.

47 Smedley, *Crusaders*, p. 61.

48 Krout, *A Looker on in London*, p. 81.

49 Smedley, *Crusaders*, p. 61.

50 Ibid., p. 91.

51 There was a similar shift towards professional alliances at all costs in North America. Kirsten Swinth, *Painting Professionals: Women Artists and the Development of Modern American Art, 1870–1930* (Chapel Hill: University of North Carolina Press, 2001), p. 123.

52 Smedley, *Crusaders*, p. 62.

53 Ibid., p. 70.

54 Ibid., p. 92. Italics in original.

55 Smedley, 'A Guild of Craftswomen', pp. 314–316.

56 Smedley, *Crusaders*, pp. 94–99.

57 Smedley, 'A Guild of Craftswomen', p. 318.

58 Margaret Birney Vickery, *Buildings for Bluestockings: The Architecture and Social History of Women's Colleges in Late-Victorian England* (London: Associated University Press, 1999), p. xii.

59 Lynne Walker, 'Locating the Global/Rethinking the Local: Suffrage Politics, Architecture and Space', *Women's Studies Quarterly*, 34/1/2 (2006), pp. 174–196 (p. 178).

60 Stratigakos, *A Women's Berlin*, p. 18.

61 Smedley, *Crusaders*, p. 59.

62 Stratigakos, *A Women's Berlin*, p. 24.

63 Smedley, *Crusaders*, p. 94.
64 'Our Ladies' Clubs: No. 7. The Lyceum', *Graphic* (18 April 1908), p. 555.
65 Elizabeth Cumming and Wendy Kaplan, *The Arts and Crafts Movement* (London: Thames and Hudson, 1991), p. 28.
66 WGAA, undated flyer.
67 WGAA, Printed Version, Annual Report, 1913.
68 WGAA, Edith B. Dawson to May Morris, 5 February 1908.
69 Hay-Edwards, *A History of Clifford's Inn*, p. 198.
70 Ren Pepitone, 'Gender, Space, and Ritual: Women Barristers, the Inns of Court, and the Interwar Press', *Journal of Women's History*, 28/1 (2016), pp. 60–83 (p. 61).
71 General meetings for both Guilds were advertised in the *Journal of the Royal Society of Arts* and in *The Year's Art* but in contrast to other groups' advertisements were very basic, simply stating the Guilds met at the Hall. In 1922, the Art Workers' Guild's Annual Report curtly reminded members 'all meetings, whether ordinary, special, or ladies' meetings, are absolutely private, and that it is a distinct breach of courtesy for anyone to describe or report in any daily paper or other periodical the proceedings of the Guild', AWGA, Annual Report, 1922.
72 Wiltshire Museum and Archive, Ethel Sandell papers, MSS. 3906 (i) 'Sundry Poems'.
73 WGAA, Feodora Gleichen to May Morris, February 1913.
74 In the early years, the annual subscription was ten shillings for town members and five shillings for country members. WGAA, Members, Associates, Rules, 1911.
75 WGAA, Handwritten Secretary Report, 1908.
76 WGAA, Handwritten Secretary Report, 1912.
77 WGAA, Edith B. Dawson to May Morris, 4 January, no year.
78 WGAA, Handwritten Secretary Report, 1908; meeting cards for 1909 and 1910.
79 University of Cape Town Library, Alys Fane Trotter papers, unpublished biography about Trotter titled 'Full Cycle' by Helen Holt. See Chapter 6.
80 WGAA, May Morris to H. J. L. J. Massé, 1922.
81 University of Berkeley, Bancroft Library, Katharine Adams papers, BANC MSS 2011/262. Box 1, Charles Harrison Townsend to Katharine Adams, 3 December 1903.
82 University of Berkeley, Bancroft Library, Katharine Adams papers, BANC MSS 2011/262. Box 1, Emery Walker and others to Katharine Adams, 3 October 1911.
83 AWGA, Annual Report, 1913.
84 Speakers at Ladies' Nights were often male, but there were occasionally female speakers, such as in 1939 when famed travel writer Penelope Chetwode talked about the history of the Dravidian Temples of India and their sculptors. The names listed as 'continuing the discussion' after the main talks at Ladies' Nights were usually male, although this may reflect the editorial decisions of the writer. These events appear to have been consistently popular with a general audience: in 1927, all three Ladies' Nights were said to be 'exceedingly popular, the Hall on these occasions being filled to overflowing'. AWGA, Annual Report, 1927 and 1939; H. J. L. J. Massé, *The Art Workers' Guild, 1884-1934* (London: Shakespeare Head, 1935), p. 71.
85 WGAA, Members, Associates, Rules, 1911.
86 WGAA, leaflet about Associates, undated.
87 Associates paid ten shillings a year. Unlike full members, Associates could not vote in elections. WGAA, Members, Associates, Rules, 1911.

88 WGAA, leaflet about Associates, undated.

89 Letters were received from members across the United Kingdom, and from those working in mainland Europe.

90 In her resignation speech as Honorary Secretary in 1923, Mary A. Sloane discussed with members her sheer lack of time, being unable to dedicate any more time to the Guild as she was 'exceptionally busy with one's own work – whatever it may be – models or clients or domestic catastrophes a burst boiler, or all these at once'. WGAA, Mary A. Sloane's resignation speech, December 1923.

91 WGAA, letter from 'Miss Cole', 29 October, no year.

92 WGAA, letter from Ethel K. Martyn, 10 August, no year.

93 WGAA, see the letters between Ethel Sandell and Mary A. Sloane in 1912.

94 A surviving paper copy of the Roll at the William Morris Society details all of the members who joined before 1923 and lists their respective fields, but the scribed and bound Roll has not been located. Wiltshire Museum and Archive holds the papers of Ethel Sandell which contain a sample of her lettering for the Roll and the names of the founding members. It also has a page detailing how the names of members were to be presented. Wiltshire Museum and Archive, Ethel Sandell papers, MSS 3906 Box 386.

95 Meeting minutes note M. D. Spooner and Mary A. Sloane went for an 'interview' at the new Hall with Francis W. Troup. WGAA, Committee Meeting 12 December 1913, Meeting Minutes Book 1913–1917.

2

Exhibiting the Arts and Crafts

I n November 1911, a new exhibition titled the Englishwoman Exhibition
of Arts and Handicrafts opened at Maddox Street Gallery just off
Regent Street in central London.[1] For a shilling, visitors could roam
around stalls displaying colour printing, lithography, book illustrations,
jewellery, and leatherwork, and view loaned special-interest items, such
as Buddhist robes and a lace handkerchief once belonging to Marie Louise,
Empress of France.[2] Over the next few years, the exhibition – which took
place every November, just in time to find 'Christmas gifts that show
individuality and taste' – continued to grow in size and popularity.[3] By
the interwar years, the exhibition had grown to approximately 150 stalls.
There were contributors from England, Scotland, Wales, Ireland, and
further afield. All the art on display had been assessed by a 'board of five
directors' who ensured it was of high artistic standard.[4] The exhibition
received favourable reviews in publications as diverse as the *Pall Mall
Gazette*, *Nursing Mirror*, *Country Life*, *Royal Society of Arts*, *Agricultural
Gazette*, *Daily Mail*, *Cabinet Maker*, and the *Common Cause*. It was
repeatedly described as an annual highlight of the artistic *and* social
calendar, one local newspaper even declaring in 1934 that it had become
'a sort of Royal Academy of arts and crafts and the best of its kind'.[5]

Despite its clear contemporary importance and extensive impact in
the press and in wider society, the Englishwoman Exhibition has not been
analysed in any history of the period. Its absence is particularly jarring
for histories of the Arts and Crafts, which often portray the movement
as in decline at this very point, when, in fact, societal interest was clearly
on the ascendant. The exhibition was the brainchild of Mary Lowndes,
stained-glass worker and Women's Guild of Arts member. In the early
twentieth century, at the height of her success, Lowndes turned her attention
towards establishing several alternative artistic spaces for women across
the capital. Alongside setting up the Glass House in 1906, an enterprise

which rented rooms to stained-glass designers – many female – she was the driving force in the Artists' Suffrage League (from 1907) and the *Englishwoman* paper (from 1909).[6] The Englishwoman Exhibition was Lowndes's most ambitious attempt to engage the nation in the Arts and Crafts. Hosted each year at prestigious locations across central London, the exhibition provided an immersive experience which always stressed the social value of art; functioned as an alternative to male-dominated exhibitions such as the Arts and Crafts Exhibition Society; and offered a supportive, collaborative space where (mostly female) art workers could build a reputation and generate income.

Lowndes was one of many women in the Arts and Crafts movement who sought to reshape England's exhibition culture for their own creative and professional needs. The Arts and Crafts Exhibition Society is today portrayed as having been the movement's 'public face' and 'coherent public identity' – the natural counterpart to the reclusive Art Workers' Guild, conceptualised as the private heart of the movement.[7] Yet analysing the Arts and Crafts Exhibition Society as the exclusive, sole site where Arts and Crafts practitioners displayed and sold work, and spread the ethos of the movement, is untenable: during the late nineteenth and early twentieth centuries, there was an explosion in the number and diversity of public sites where the Arts and Crafts were exhibited.

My particular intention in this chapter is to unpack the constraining term 'women's exhibitions' to unveil the wealth of events, including several national and international exhibitions, which are largely ignored by the historiography but were, in their day, highly influential and popular occasions. Women art workers, ever committed to asserting their expert statuses, were obliged to navigate and situate themselves amongst these bigger, commercial exhibitions. They offered a host of new entrepreneurial, cultural, and empowering opportunities which could not easily be turned down, situated as they were at an intersection between the women's movement and a booming leisure and commercial market. Although the relationship between women and consumption stretched back to the eighteenth century, the late nineteenth century marked a critical moment when women consumers (and women exhibitors) were increasingly targeted, strengthened by the prevalent belief that women could – and should – use their heightened moral capacities to shape the capitalist market.[8] Furthermore, I illuminate how such exhibitions reinforced and reproduced certain prevalent classed, gendered, nationalistic, and racialised stereotypes.

By the dawn of the twentieth century, fuelled increasingly by anxieties about the ongoing marginalisation and problematic representation of women within mixed-sex exhibition cultures, artistic and commercial alike, there was a bifurcation of approaches among women art workers. Some, like many members of the Women's Guild of Arts, withdrew from exhibiting together rather than subjecting themselves to the pigeonholed 'women's section'. Others, like Lowndes, created their own independent exhibitions, women-focused spaces for professional and artistic self-actualisation, arranged around political or social aims: suffrage, a living wage, or national pride. Such venues were designed to provide women with greater opportunities to formulate modern working lives and to envisage the Arts and Crafts as linked to broader socio-political questions of relevance to them.

These exhibitions take us far beyond questions of gendered marginalisation, however. Such spaces demonstrate the centrality of this network of women in encouraging widespread public engagement in quality Arts and Crafts products, and in the making of a highly creative, yet still 'popular', culture which has been little considered. Throughout, I situate my discussions around the protean nature of these exhibition spaces, at once modern and progressive, at times reproducing conservative, nationalistic, and imperialistic models of bourgeois femininity, as well as constituting important but little-studied repositories for a burgeoning women-centred consumer culture. This era marked a critical moment when the art world thought seriously about how to engage a wider public, although approaches tended to be didactic and contradictory rather than truly democratic, as growing numbers of artists and artistic groups jostled to stake their claims as arbiters of taste. Women were especially dedicated to breaking down barriers, which in part stemmed from a somewhat contradictory desire to claim new cultural power via avenues more receptive to their participation, but also due to real belief in the progressive opportunities engendered by the Arts and Crafts. Ultimately, exhibitions enabled this network of women to play a central role in the public expansion of the movement, through the dual process of connecting them with people more receptive to their assertions of expertise, and by facilitating the engagement of different audiences with Arts and Crafts objects across an ever-widening range of public spaces.

Exhibiting at the Arts and Crafts Exhibition Society

The Arts and Crafts Exhibition Society was founded in 1887 by several members of the Art Workers' Guild, and the first exhibition was held at the New Gallery, Regent Street, in October 1888. Until 1890 exhibitions were held annually, after which the Committee decided longer was needed to generate new exhibits. Triennial exhibitions were then held, although occasionally there were longer gaps. In the first catalogue, Walter Crane (then Master of the Guild), positioned the Society's exhibitions as offering the unique opportunity to overturn artistic hierarchies by displaying the Arts and Crafts together in perfect union:

> The decorative artist and the handicraftsman have hitherto had but little opportunity of displaying their work in the public eye, or rather of appealing to it upon strictly artistic grounds in the same sense as the pictorial artist; and it is a somewhat singular state of things that at a time when the Arts are perhaps more looked after, and certainly more talked about, than they have ever been before, and the beautifying of houses, to those to whom it is possible, has become in some cases almost a religion, so little is known of the actual designer and maker (as distinct from the proprietary manufacturer or middleman) of those familiar things which contribute so much to the comfort and refinement of life – of our chairs and cabinets, our chintzes and wallpapers, our lamps and pitchers.[9]

At this 'strictly artistic' exhibition, objects were displayed in glass cases as though in a museum, which contrasted to many other exhibitions across Europe during this era which took the form of model interiors, to encourage consumers to envisage the objects *in situ* in their own private homes.[10] Additionally, at early Society exhibitions, no prices were listed, to affirm the educational rather than commercial aspirations of the organisers.[11] Lectures on art were given by figures such as William Morris, Emery Walker, and Walter Crane which further acclimatised visitors to the type of exhibition they were participating in. Later, in 1913, there were debates amongst the Committee about whether they should set up a permanent profit-making saleroom, but the decision not to do so reiterates the Society's ongoing rejection of overt commercialism.[12]

Authoritatively delineating artistic intention through display and rhetoric was crucial in shaping the participants' understanding of the cultural integrity of those involved, and the worth of the objects on display. For those positioning themselves as 'serious' art worshippers, exhibitions were seen to be a hotbed of dangerous temptations where the risks of the commercial lurked, threatening to overthrow the intellectual, pure credentials of the art worker. As one journalist lamented in the *Studio* in 1893, exhibitions encouraged the 'sanguine and superfluous lover of the visible' and needed careful regulation – for artists and visitors alike. Fairs and bazaars were used in art journals and artists' writings as pejorative symbols to describe those exhibitions viewed to be failing aesthetically and morally, usually because of the attempts of exhibition organisers to use these events as 'entertainments and shops with a well understood line of business and a steady public of their own'. The much-idealised model for the dedicated artist continued to be the long-established patronage approach. The *Studio* journalist insisted to readers that 'The artist is fortunate if he can avoid them [exhibitions] altogether and secure a patron or two who will buy him secretly.'[13] In reality, this model was far from achievable for most. Indeed, the emergence of ever more exhibitions in the final decades of the century helped move the arts away from the traditional reliance on an 'old boys' network of elite contacts, instead offering artists a range of spaces in which to sell work, even if this did encourage a competitive, commercial-focused culture to flourish.

By ostensibly eschewing the commercial, and asserting visionary artistic significance, the Society created a more palatable environment for 'serious' participants and a discerning public. Such a tactic, of being seen to be motivated by altruistic rather than financial concerns, was intoxicating for the large portion of the public lamenting the ramifications of industrialisation who wanted to express their aesthetic and moral views materially by encouraging handcrafted cultures to blossom. Behind the scenes, the Committee, acutely aware of the need to attract customers and the press, still pursued commercial strategies such as sending letters to the *Pall Mall Gazette* advertising the exhibition.[14]

The Society's ability to position itself in this visionary manner was assured by the class status and gender of the organisers. One of the first things readers of the Society's catalogue were confronted with was the long list of renowned Committee members: Morris, De Morgan, Burne-Jones, amongst others. Although in the lists of the exhibition proper the catalogue was radical in labelling both designer and maker, elsewhere value and worth continued to be assigned through the already established status of the designer, and predominantly the male designer. Unlike the Art Workers' Guild, however, the Arts and Crafts Exhibition Society was mixed-sex. This was certainly progressive, but was likely due to a view that including works by women would ensure the range of works on display, scale, and popularity of the exhibition. Moreover, this approach helped the Society to gain control by encouraging art workers from around the country to participate at *their* event. There was a cluster of committed women exhibitors from the start, and by the early twentieth century there were substantial numbers, many of whom were Women's Guild of Arts members. At the Society's exhibitions these women could find a sense of common fellowship, which strengthened mixed-sex bonds, allegiance to the Arts and Crafts, and, perhaps most importantly, generated new occasions to sell work. In 1895, the painter Louise Jopling readily informed *Atalanta* that the Society's exhibitions 'have done good service in bringing designers and buyers in touch with each other'.[15]

The Society's approach was indicative of the growing number of mixed-sex exhibitions by this era, such as at the Clarion Guild of Handicraft and the Northern Art Workers' Guild. Many Women's Guild of Art members exhibited at Royal Academy exhibitions and increasing numbers of one-woman exhibitions were taking place.[16] A cluster of women art workers were independently sending work abroad, which helped them build their reputations across an additional sphere of cultural influence. Charlotte Newman received the unique award of a *médaille d'honneur* as 'collaboratrice' (whilst her manager John Brogden was admitted to the Légion d'Honneur) by the French Jury in Paris.[17] E. C. Woodward exhibited a buckle she had 'designed and executed' for the 'Original Objects of Art Workmanship' section of the 1904 Universal Exposition in St Louis, as did C. R. Ashbee and several other women such as E. M. Rope.[18]

Yet women were rarely on exhibition boards, had little curatorial control, and often received limited praise in the press, especially when reviewed at mixed-sex exhibitions where journalists tended to write long, rapturous descriptions about the works of the male 'genius'. At the Arts and Crafts Exhibition Society, although there were twenty-six women members and ninety-one men by the 1910 exhibition, May Morris was the only woman on the Committee.[19] Morris's acceptance at this higher level influenced her personal decision to exhibit predominantly at the Society – and the strategies of professionalisation she encouraged at the Women's Guild of Arts. Other women, however, continually looked for further opportunities to claim cultural status and support. This search fortuitously dovetailed with a moment when both the women's movement and a women-centred consumer culture were rapidly expanding, a topic this chapter now turns to explore.

Celebrating 'women's work': consumer pleasures and feminist concerns

The Arts and Crafts Exhibition Society seemingly offers a moment of coherence in a movement which is difficult to pin down and delineate. Many powerful contemporaries viewed the Society as central to the movement. Indeed, it was where the term 'Arts and Crafts' was formalised. Still, as Imogen Hart has argued, the exhibition needs to be positioned amidst its wider context. Prioritising the 1890s, and using the Society as the central locus of scrutiny, Hart emphasised the Society's intersections with several artistic currents, rather than simply representing one discrete movement: the Schools of Design, the Royal Academy, and the Design Reform and Aesthetic movements.[20] But by decentring the Society even further, we can see it as one of many significant exhibitions, manifestations of a cultural movement which sought to disrupt the dominance of fine art exhibitions as the premier cultural venues during this period.

In the second half of the nineteenth century a new public spectacle emerged, which aimed to represent the industrious potential of modern humankind and place different nations in competitive comparison: world fairs, expositions, and international exhibitions. Beginning with the Great Exhibition in 1851, such events have continued ever since in Europe, North America, Asia, and Latin America. As T. J. Boisseau and Abigail M. Markwyn have argued, they constituted the first modern global gatherings of mass numbers of people. Since they claimed to showcase the activities of the entire nation to the world, it was difficult to exclude women, and many had women's buildings or sections. Here, certain women found an opportunity to showcase 'a vision of themselves as constituent members of particular nations and a newly collective consciousness of themselves as a sex'.[21] The 1893 World's Columbian Exposition in Chicago, which focused on achievements in industry, art, and science since Columbus's arrival in America, had a Women's Building, designed by architect Sophia Hayden and overseen by a Board of 'Lady Managers' who filled it with women's art, literature, science, music, and home economics. These events provide a unique window onto how hierarchies around gender and other axes of identity such as class and race were constructed – and subsequently played out at these artificially constructed edifices. Boisseau and Markwyn's work has emphasised that a 'reliance on a set of racialized contrasts between "modern" and "civilized" women and colonised or "backward" women' functioned as a 'central organizing trope' for elite women organisers, which had considerable ramifications on understandings of gender, class, and racialised difference across a host of local, national, and international registers.[22]

Such exhibitions offered women art workers designated new spaces where they could assert authority beyond national borders, and play a part in the circulation of ideas about the artistic, the professional, and the feminine in mass culture. The Chicago Women's Building, which included the decoration of the building itself, offered several well-known Arts and Crafts women based in England an occasion to make an international name for themselves. E. M. Rope and Elinor Hallé worked together on bas-reliefs which filled the spandrels of the arcade in the entrance vestibule. The *Builder* informed its readers that Rope had illustrated her panels with Faith 'lighting the world with her lamp', Hope 'represented as struggling with despair', Charity in 'her aspect of sheltering love', and 'Heavenly Wisdom', Sophia of the Greeks as 'drinking from the fountain of wisdom'. Hallé focused on similar themes 'which illustrate specially womanly virtues' of 'Purity, Fortitude, Peace and Sympathy', whilst Annie Swynnerton and Anna Lea Merritt decorated the sides of the vestibule with paintings representing women in teaching, nursing, and embroidery.[23] In the British Section of Women's Work, many Arts and Crafts women showed work: amongst others, S. T. Prideaux contributed bindings, Mary Newill several cartoons for stained-glass windows, Charlotte Newman various pieces of jewellery, whilst May Morris showed a coverlet for a bed and E. C. Woodward a worked bible cover.[24] As such, the exhibition constituted a complex site for the formation of modern artistic identities, progressive in enabling women to celebrate their working roles and expertise, but also, when such work was exhibited collectively – particularly in the Women's Building – simultaneously reproduced an essentialised view of women as uniquely sympathetic, pure, and capable of providing 'sheltering love' to a mass audience.

Several exhibitions in England were inspired by international exposi-tions. The 1897 Victorian Era Exhibition and the 1900 Woman's Exhibition, both held at Earl's Court, London, provide two quintessential examples. These exhibitions appear unapologetically commercial – garish and jin-goistic, even – focused on celebrating the nation, leisure, and consumerism. The Victorian Era Exhibition consisted of a series of buildings which portrayed the supposedly rapid developments in art, history, commerce, drama, music, women's work, science, and sport since Queen Victoria's ascendancy. Entrance cost one shilling, and there were many special features such as the famed 'Gigantic Wheel', a shooting gallery, and a 'Pantomi-mograph'.[25] The section dedicated to Women's Work was so popular it led to the Woman's Exhibition three years later, organised on the same principles, with one noticeable difference: the whole venue was dedicated solely to the activities of women.

Both exhibitions were led by 'Director-General' Imrè Kiralfy, and his elite all-male committee of advisers. Imrè Kiralfy was one half of the Hungarian-born Kiralfy Brothers who staged several popular imperialistic performances and exhibitions across mainland Europe, the USA, and London; the Indian and Ceylon Exhibition at Earl's Court of 1895–1896 had four million visitors.[26] Imrè Kiralfy determinedly took advantage of the burgeoning interest in the 'New Woman' and the growing capacity of women as consumers in their own right. But although these exhibitions pertained to support women, the organisational structure openly replicated prevalent social gender hierarchies. At the 1897 exhibition, the Women's

Work section was the only area to have a sub-committee composed of women managers. This was dominated by upper-class women who were viewed as uniquely placed to ensure the rooms were tasteful.[27] The only working painter on the Fine Art Sub-Committee was Henrietta Rae, whilst Elinor Hallé represented the handicrafts.[28] As such, these exhibitions provide an important, but little-studied, window onto the sustained attempts to construct sites which celebrated a highly feminised, nationalistic, class-based, and consumer-focused ideal of 'English womanhood' at the turn of the century.

At first glance, it is hard to understand what motivated Arts and Crafts women to exhibit at events which appear antithetical to the anti-commercial ethos of the movement, especially at a moment when there was a growth of exhibitions consciously framed around 'authentic' artistry. But many of the key players in this book contributed to at least one of the Earl's Court exhibitions. Such events offered 'serious' art workers ample opportunities to fulfil their urge to 'convert' different audiences to the benefits of high-quality craftwork, by positioning themselves in noticeable contrast to the distasteful commercial elements of the exhibition. At the same time, these exhibitions offered artists new commercial and professional opportunities to display their work in spaces which had an established reputation for generating public interest, something women working at the margins of the male-oriented exhibition scene sorely needed. Featured on the front page of fashionable newspapers such as the *Graphic* and the *Illustrated London News*, the Victorian Era Exhibition was described as 'crowded with visitors from noon to night inspecting the various galleries'.[29] In contrast to many other exhibitions, women art workers were actively sought out, viewed as fitting emblems of middle-class women working as respectable pioneers in the Arts and Crafts movement which was ever growing in status. Antiquarian and bibliophile Frank Karslake was one of many to become enchanted by the bookbinding on display at the 1897 Women's Work section. He gathered together the 'names and addresses of workers, who were scattered in isolated units through the length and breadth of the land' to obtain 150 'representative specimens' for an exhibition at his bookshop at 61 Charing Cross Road. The exhibition was so popular it stayed open for four months and Karslake went on to incorporate these activities formally into the Guild of Women Book-Binders.[30]

An aura of seriousness pervaded the art division of the Women's Work section at the Victorian Era Exhibition. Artists could only exhibit if they had received a 'special invitation', to 'preclude the possibility of feeble or mediocre work finding a place in the galleries'.[31] Like the Arts and Crafts Exhibition Society, no prices were listed in the catalogue, emblematic of a desire to remove accusations of an overtly commercial approach in these rooms at least, and instead to encourage an aesthetic and moral response. Indeed, the exhibition featured the works of many women who exhibited at the Society, including portrait medals by Elinor Hallé and Feodora Gleichen, a bronze clasp by Esther Moore, an enamelled copper cup by Edith B. Dawson ('lent by H. M. The Queen'), and designs for church windows by Mary Lowndes. A central aim was to show the *range* of women's work, demonstrating the commitment of participants to raising the status of the applied arts to that of the fine arts. The exhibition included displays by the Royal Irish School of Art Needlework, the Ladies' Work Society, and photographs by the late Julia Margaret Cameron. Altogether, there were over 300 exhibits, including designs and specimens of embroideries, photography, wallpaper, woodcarvings, bookbinding, stained glass, and enamelling.[32] By confronting visitors with this rich display of – in the words of the *Lady's Realm* – 'really beautiful work produced by women in twenty or more branches of artistic handicraft', alongside a grand display of 'masterpieces' by women painters, it was hoped 'the doors of the Royal Academy will no longer be shut in the face of artists simply because they are women'.[33]

This unifying visual narrative was bolstered further by attempts to educate readers, through the catalogue and in the press, about the extensive history of women's craftwork. Such an approach further legitimised these modern-day activities by connecting exhibitors to an extremely popular and nostalgic pre-industrial version of 'English' history. Somewhat paradoxically, situating this work amidst an established backdrop of a women-focused craft tradition simultaneously offered a way to assert the 'rapid progress' of women's creativity and intellect across the nineteenth century, and their new positions as modern women, ready to take full part in society. The *Lady's Realm* journalist contemplated how:

> One is naturally drawn to compare the present with the past, and it is easy to imagine the blank despair which would have fallen upon a committee entrusted with the task of preparing an exhibition of women's work when the Queen came to the throne … We question if it would have been considered quite modest for a girl to have embroidered a pair of braces – or even a cigar case … It was but a natural outcome of a woman being upon the throne, that the general status of all women should be improved, and in consequence, the progress of women's work has been more remarkable during the Victorian Era than in any other period of the world's history.[34]

The article's illustrated frontispiece featured two women in medieval-style robes, surrounded by flowers and holding a crafted pot and a book, symbolising their literary and artistic prowess (Figure 2.1). A coin featuring Queen Victoria's profile was positioned in the middle, giving what was essentially an advertisement further weight and respectability, but also reiterating the exhibition's fashionable status, as this was a venture supported by royalty. Such emphasis, embodying tradition and modernity intertwined, in word and image, convincingly reimagined the Arts and Crafts movement with women placed centre stage.

Three years later the Woman's Exhibition took place at Earl's Court. Again costing a shilling, the *raison d'être* was to 'show the claims of the fair sex to the best advantage' through an extravagant visual spectacle of the contributions of women to the making of the modern world.[35] At the turnstiles, visitors, rather than being confronted with 'the burly male attendants one would naturally expect', found uniformed women standing guard, 'controlling the entrances' to this 'vast enterprise'. There were endless leisure pursuits, such as the 'Magic Table' of illusions, an all-female orchestra, 'the Transvaal Rifle Range', a mirror maze, and a large collection of the Queen of Romania's dolls. A congratulatory visual narrative of women's 'progress' across the nineteenth century again played a central role. Imrè Kiralfy built on the widespread belief in the special moral superiority of women, positioning this amidst an explicitly racialised framing. In the catalogue, he declared that: 'The true progress of every race is marked in the condition of woman: whatever she is the race will

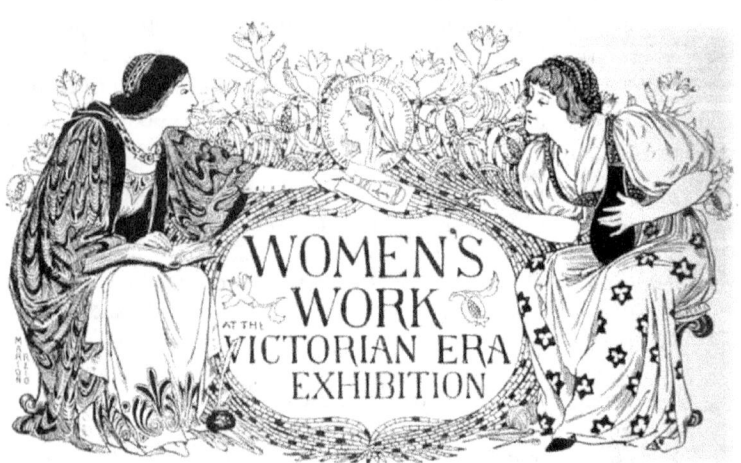

Figure 2.1 'Women's Work at the Victorian Era Exhibition', *Lady's Realm: An Illustrated Monthly Magazine* (May to October 1897), p. 58

be, for she is the civiliser, the purifier of life.'[36] At a display of 'Women of all Nations', different women dressed up to represent their countries, and the audience voted for their favourites. The 'Irish Colleens' won first prize and an award of £100, having received 32,095 votes. As Annie E. Coombes has shown, the event featured twenty-four national groups, but not one of them was African; the representation of African womanhood was limited solely to a section of the exhibit titled 'The Dinka Village'.[37]

Alongside this overtly racialised and nationalistic framing, hierarchies of gender and class were again laced throughout the organisational structure of the exhibition. The five Directors were all male, the art sections had a male curator, and the all-female Committees, which were responsible for specific sections, were dominated by aristocratic women, although there was a growing cluster of 'professional' women involved. The Artistic Committees included Elinor Hallé, Feodora Gleichen, and Mary Seton Watts, who were designated the arbiters of appropriate expertise.[38] Several more 'women workers' were positioned in 'active operation' making crafts in the 'handicraft hall', where they persuaded spectators of their aptitude for work. The *Sphere* discussed the necessity of seeing women physically working in the arts, otherwise the audience might not believe their competency: 'We need … no teaching to tell us that both as a mother and as a nurse for the sick and wounded woman is in her element. But when she comes into competition with man in the applied arts we see her in another light.'[39] As such, alongside displays of art on the walls and in glass cases, you could see woodworker Julia Hilliam, then an instructor at Reading College, and several of her peers, giving demonstrations of woodcarving, hammering away, surrounded by the evidence of her skills in designing and making: a writing table, music seat, worktables, and a carved chest.[40] At a time when there was considerable belief in women's physical and mental deficiencies, positioning Hilliam as skilfully using the tools of her craft was designed to trigger a reconceptualisation in the perspectives of viewers about – white, middle-class – women's bodily and intellectual capacities to contribute to professional society and artistic culture.

Although press commentaries foregrounded the prospects 'For the vast numbers of the public … to be amused or to while away the time' at these events, the progressive aspirations of such women clearly made an impact. Journalists discussed the exhibition's 'serious side', which sought to 'let the world see what she can do … as a worker in the outward race for life'.[41] Several satirical cartoons and articles also portrayed the exhibition as potentially subversive and demonstrative of the significant changes taking place in society. One sketch in the *Illustrated Sporting and Dramatic*

News was designed as a tongue-in-cheek commentary, but could be viewed as trying to trigger deeper fears about the behaviour of impressionable young women at the turn of the century (Figure 2.2). The piece depicts a crowd of young be-hatted ladies eagerly lined up outside the exhibition waiting to pay. At the centre stands a stern older woman wearing a monocle, a well-known symbol of the learned woman and women's rights campaigner. The women were standing behind a lone man nervously hunting out money to pay a woman server who looked imperiously down at him from her booth. The sketch was captioned with the title 'It is interesting to notice that the "inferior" sex is not entirely dispensed with at Earl's Court.'[42]

The women's press was brimming with enthusiastic discussions about the industrious women exhibiting there.[43] Yet not all commentators saw the close juxtaposition of entertainment, commerce, and skilled creative work as productive in the quest for female enfranchisement. The feminist paper the *Englishwoman's Review* expressed concern about the exhibition's overtly commercial tones, replication of gender hierarchies, and failure to take the women's movement seriously. In one anonymous article, ominously titled 'An Averted Danger', the writer bluntly discussed how:

> the connection of an Exhibition of women's work with the series of popular shows which the public have learned to associate with Earl's

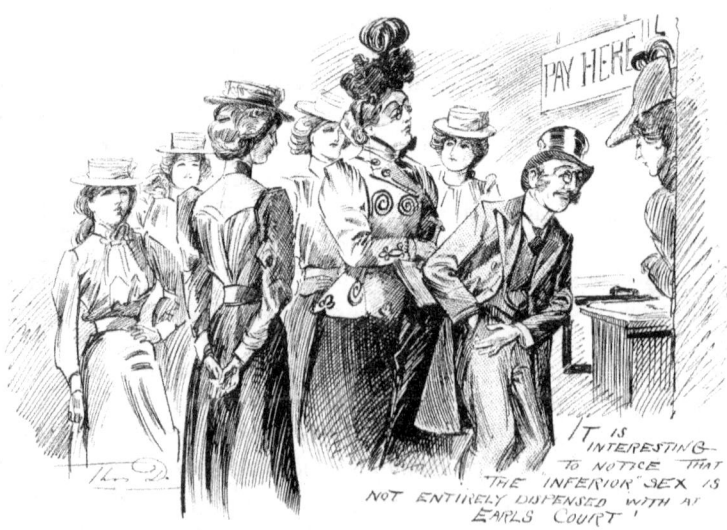

Figure 2.2 'Women's Exhibition at Earl's Court', *Illustrated Sporting and Dramatic News* (2 June 1900), p. 558

Court was distasteful to many persons, as exploiting the women's movement – a movement fraught for most of us with far-reaching and serious interests – for the sake of a commercial speculation.

The women on the Honorary Committees also supposedly had 'no voice or control over the general direction, which was in the hands of a few men directors'. Such debates even entered the international arena: members of the women's movement across Europe expressed concern at the misogynistic, male-dominated nature of an exhibition, which, at least nominally, was framed as celebratory and supportive. One anonymous Swedish woman had glimpsed, in a leading daily paper in Stockholm, a troubling advertisement for the exhibition and had written in anger to the *Englishwoman's Review*. The advertisement, which was translated in its entirety for readers, reveals it had been proposed to hold a beauty competition between women 'of all nationalities' at the exhibition, to which the Swedish correspondent responded in fury: 'A competition for the prize of beauty in the year 1900 – how humiliating, how degrading!' Furthermore, it was noted with horror that not one single woman's name was listed in the advertisement. The beauty competition appears to have been abandoned in its original guise, although, as mentioned, there were still events in which women were objectified for the gaze of attendees, such as the 'Women of all Nations' performance. 'An Averted Danger' went on to express shock that: 'a management who had sought the co-operation' of women 'distinguished by their desire to help' promote the works of other women 'could actually contemplate a concurrent scheme which ignored the essential dignity of women as human beings'.[44]

Despite this criticism, the 1900 exhibition by no means saw the end of the 'women's exhibition'. Indeed, they continued with regularity in various guises across the early to mid-twentieth century. There was a Palace of Women's Work at the 1908 Franco-British Exhibition and the *Daily Express* staged several popular interwar Woman's Exhibitions. Many women continued to exhibit there. But the populism and perceived cheap commercialism of the Earl's Court exhibitions directly influenced the collaborative strategies of display taken up by leading women art workers, and women embedded in the women's movement, in the early twentieth century. Some women directed their energies into creating a new world of exhibitions, controlled and curated by women, whilst others restricted their professional involvement solely to 'serious' mixed-sex events. Many more fluctuated in their views, moving between different strategies to find empowerment. Although these events were by no means free from class, race, or gender hierarchies, they allowed larger numbers of professional and politically active women to take charge of their representation more readily, as we shall discover in the next section.[45]

Women's Arts and Crafts exhibitions: the political and the professional

In spring 1914, the constitutional National Union of Women's Suffrage Societies staged a grand exhibition at Olympia, titled a Woman's Kingdom, as a self-contained section of the Children's Welfare Exhibition. The exhibition sought to offer both 'attractions of a lighter kind' for casual passers-by through to a 'perfect mine of information' for anyone interested in learning about suffrage, the welfare of children, and the world of women and work. Women in the arts, industry, the professions, the sciences, and business were all represented. Going far beyond any traditional definition of an 'exhibition', the organisers constructed an extensive, alternative feminised world where the needs of women workers, of all classes, played a central role. The Women Taxpayers' Agency and Legal Advice Bureau, the Day Servants' Hostel, the International Woman Suffrage Alliance, and many others, all had stands. There was much emphasis on the practical opportunities to interact with stallholders: at Stand 45 you could obtain from 'Miss Lyon' 'data as to professions open to the women in this and other lands', whilst at the next stand you could scrutinise the 'most up-to-date equipment and methods' from 'Mrs Hoster' at her 'Office and Work' stall. Nearby, 'Miss G. Griff' was on hand to be 'consulted on machinery of all kinds and electric appliances'. Elsewhere there was a crèche, a suffrage literature stall, a 'Betterment Book Room', and prototype bedrooms designed for factory girls.[46] Widely reported, the exhibition was presented as a unique spectacle: 'Never before has there been such an opportunity of obtaining in the course of a few hours a broad view of the ever widening activities of the modern woman.'[47]

Yet suffrage exhibitions clearly had their genesis in late nineteenth-century exhibitions such as those held at Earl's Court. Suffrage groups – constitutional and militant – took advantage of the established interest in commercial spectacle, fashion, and shopping when staging their own large exhibitions. These exhibitions were, however, fundamentally different. Here, women managed the committees, and the venues were used for openly political needs, as well as to assist women working in many different fields. Suffrage exhibitions were uniquely placed to show off participants as fashionable and cultured, offered pleasurable occasions to shop and socialise, generated considerable money for the cause, and perhaps even empowered visitors to become campaigners themselves. The 1909 Women's

Social and Political Union's Women's Exhibition at the Prince's Skating Rink, Knightsbridge, is widely recognised as demonstrative of the savvy visual propaganda implemented by militant suffrage activists (Figure 2.3). But there were many more suffrage exhibitions which are rich, largely untapped repositories providing extensive insight into the wide-ranging attempts made by campaigners to encourage a wider sector of the public to become politically awakened – and to learn more about women's contributions to the world of work. They included the Women's Social and Political Union's Grand Suffrage Bazaar and Exhibition in Glasgow in 1910, the National Union's Oriental Fête and Bazaar in London in 1912, and the Women's Freedom League's Green, White, and Gold fairs, as well as others, such as the smaller studio exhibitions held by the Suffrage Atelier.[48]

Certain women art workers played a central role in suffrage exhibitions, demonstrating their political support for the cause by exhibiting work or helping to organise and curate these events. They were partly motivated by a desire to engender new professional and commercial prospects for themselves, to tap into a burgeoning market of engaged consumers, and to generate a space for industrious Arts and Crafts activity, away from the jurisdiction of the Committee of the Arts and Crafts Exhibition Society.

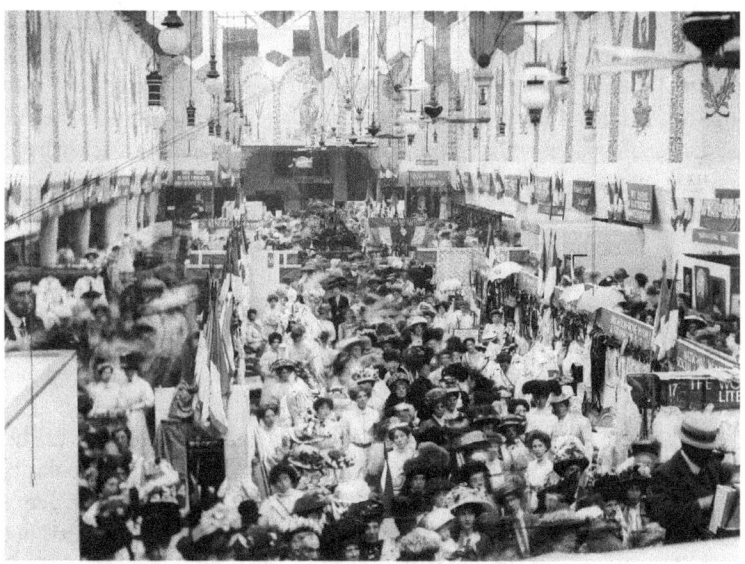

Figure 2.3 The main hall of the Women's Exhibition at Prince's Skating Rink, Knightsbridge, 1909

At the Woman's Kingdom exhibition, a substantial section was dedicated to the arts. There was a photographic salon, fine art gallery, Arts and Crafts section, and a display by the Suffrage Atelier. Käthe Kollwitz's haunting etchings *Death and Woman*, *The Unemployed*, and *The Guillotine*, which illustrated the effects of poverty and hunger on the working classes, were described by the *Common Cause* as 'brutal' and 'works of genius'. The journalist was clearly seeking to encourage a new taxonomy through which to understand the work of women such as Kollwitz, using terms usually reserved to describe male creativity. Elsewhere, E. M. Rope showed off bas-relief work, Louise Jacobs displayed lithographs, E. C. Woodward a champlevé enamel crucifix and other jewellery, whilst Mabel Esplin showed designs for stained glass.[49] Building on the Earl's Court exhibitions, artistic women could be seen in action, working in mock workshops where spectators could purchase the very objects 'watched in the process of making'.[50] Such a juxtaposition of the private, creative world of the artist and the public, commercial world of the exhibition constituted a key site where women could carve out authority in the face of male institutional and cultural hegemony.

Taking this wide-angle lens, which spans different exhibition venues and draws together these threads of activity, we can more fully grasp the frenetic engagement of women art workers in the making and remaking of the artistic – and political – cultures of their day. Yet suffrage exhibitions were, first and foremost, fundraising events designed to promote the 'cause'. Indeed, at several events the money raised was directed back into the campaigns. Although attempts were made to delineate the specific activities of women workers, the necessity of forging an inclusive environment somewhat diminished the hierarchies between amateurs and professionals in favour of prioritising the collaborative efforts of women working together in common aim. Despite the clear opportunity to exhibit skilled work, suffrage exhibitions did not, for many artistic women, sufficiently embody the cultural authority they believed was needed to make their names on the same level as their male peers. The majority of women art workers, therefore, looked for further exhibition spaces where they could demonstrate expertise and make an income.

This view was intensified by the fact that many leading Arts and Crafts figures were anxious about the movement's spread and popularity by the early twentieth century. This was partially due to the emergence of new mass-produced objects being marketed as 'Arts and Crafts', but was also because of disapproval about the apparently unsophisticated, 'amateur' ways many people, often women, who were not active in the elite echelons of the London art world, were engaging in artistic cultures across the country. The sheer number of exhibitions being described as 'Arts and Crafts' by this point is testament to the lack of a united contemporary understanding that a singular exhibition constituted the movement's public face, but also ignited a fear that has shaped alternative cultures across the modern era: the fear of 'selling out'. This view is evident in one representative 1909 article in the *Studio* which alerted readers that:

> Arts and Crafts exhibitions before Christmas are becoming more numerous each year, and it is to be hoped that by the power of competition they may be prevented from deteriorating into mere bazaars. Several commercial enterprises of the bazaar calibre have of recent years posed as art exhibitions, and one is led into fearing the rapid degeneration of the true 'Arts and Crafts' exhibition.[51]

At the Women's Guild of Arts, there was considerable reticence about staging public exhibitions. As the last chapter argued, a wish to claim 'authentic' cultural power meant members focused their energies on talks at the Guild Hall, a space symbolic of their serious intentions: discreet, historical, and metropolitan. Partial acceptance in 'male' artistic networks such as the Arts and Crafts Exhibition Society further bolstered their sense of achievement and generated a feeling of apathy towards 'women's exhibitions'. Several members had participated in the Earl's Court exhibitions but had dramatically shifted in their opinions by the time the Guild was formed, suggesting they held similar views to the outraged writer in the *Englishwoman's Review*. In one letter by woodworker Julia Bowley – who had given a 'performance' at Earl's Court – to the Guild, she warned that women's exhibitions often had a bad reputation: 'Look at the failure of the Women's Society of Arts exhibitions at least at a great many of them the work was very poor.'[52] Feodora Gleichen, who had been on the Committee for the 1900 Woman's Exhibition, even sent a call-to-arms letter to numerous members in 1908, writing of the need for:

> your co-operation in a protest against the growing practice of holding Fine Art Exhibitions for women's work only – which will certainly end in causing our work to be judged by a different standard to that of men, and eventually force us to work for lower terms. The competition for space in all public exhibitions is so severe, that the committees – always composed of men – welcome any reason for diminishing the number of exhibitors, and I am afraid that the multiplication of these women's art societies will justify them in excluding us from general exhibitions, under the pretext that we have enough of our own.
>
> It is easy to foresee the bad influence this will have on women's work, where no longer forced into comparison with the stronger work of the best artists of the time. – Already in these larger exhibitions

women are being invited to show in a section of their own, and almost entirely excluded from the General Fine Art Sections.

It is as a protest against this, that I am asking you to join with me in declining to send to the Women's Section of the Franco-British, or of the Edinburgh Exhibition, which is being conducted on the same lines.

There can surely be no doubt that the work of artists should be judged without regard to the question of sex, and it seems to me that if the best known women artists join in declining to exhibit, <u>except in the General Fine Art Section</u>, it would be a step towards regaining the so-called equality, which has hitherto been the rule in judging works of art.[53]

Gleichen's letter focused on the fine arts, but the move towards having segregated women's sections at exhibitions at all was clearly viewed as antithetical to the artistic aims of this group of women.

As such, the Guild, before the war, consistently refused to exhibit publicly together. Furthermore, they sent pointed group letters to exhibitions which asked them to segregate themselves. When the Guild was asked to exhibit in the Women's Section of the 1908 Scottish National Exhibition, Christiana Herringham and May Morris sent an adapted version of Gleichen's letter:

We regret that we are unable to accept your invitation. We object as a matter of principle to women's sections in art exhibitions. There can surely be no doubt that the work of artists should be judged without regard to questions of sex. And, moreover, there is reason to fear that the association of fine art exhibits with those that have to do with the domestic occupations of women will tend to depreciate the importance of the former. The standard of art for women will be debased and prices lowered, women being forced to work for less terms than men will accept.[54]

Rather surprisingly, considering their views on press publicity, the same letter was published in the conservative paper, the *Morning Post*. Caustic comments had been added by the editors, who questioned, 'Then why the *Women's* Guild of Arts' and asserted 'The logic of the last two sentences needs no comment.'[55] At a later meeting in 1913 the Committee rejected another invitation, this time for members to take part in an exhibition in Leipzig, Germany, as part of the Women's Section of Book-Production.[56] Feodora Gleichen continued to reiterate in private letters to May Morris that the Guild ought not to be: 'a Society for display of what has been accomplished (except in so far as showing their works to each other may conduce to mutual help)'.[57] Similarly, Edith B. Dawson informed Morris she had 'heard several members ... speak very strongly against the Guild being used as an exhibition society or for business purposes at all, and I feel so myself and promised a member I would tell you.' Dawson stated:

> [I do] not know how the foundation members felt about it or if the Guild was originally formed to become at some future time an Exhibition Society, but when I think of the very good letter that you sent, with I think Mrs. Herringham, to the Edinburgh exhibition I feel we would be making a mistake to exhibit anywhere else as a body for business. Several women workers I know wish to protest against women's art exhibitions and I do very much myself and I think your letter did too.

She went on to warn Morris that members had discussed leaving if the Guild was used in this way, 'I could give you their names, if you like, they are some of the best and really serious workers we have. There are so very many places now where we can show our work, men and women too know of these, and take advantage of them.' She then added a contemplative final note declaring she would personally not mind an exhibition so long as it:

> were to be done in the same way as the men's guild have exhibitions, in which members may become familiar with work done by other members of the guild, that I think, no one could have objection to and is quite good, but I don't think the exhibitions of the men's guild have been for business purposes <u>directly</u> at all.[58]

The views of members reveal the extent to which artistic women's strategies were influenced by acute awareness of the gendered politics of space. The ways these women navigated 'public' and 'private' spaces as a Guild has meant there is relative silence in the public historical record. Members deliberately avoided public exhibitions together – even though this could have potentially facilitated new networks to blossom with art workers and audiences in Scotland and Germany – because they were so concerned about the impact this would have on prevalent discourses around 'lady artists' and amateur displays. Still, in their lifetime, this approach did bring about individual achievements: Gleichen, for instance, who appeared so dismayed about the Women's Section of the Franco-British Exhibition, exhibited in the Fine Art Section.[59]

Although members were anxious about exhibiting *publicly* together, they did organise several small exhibitions carefully labelled as 'private' or 'for the Guild and friends' at the homes and studios of wealthy members. The hybridity of homes and studios, as discussed in the next chapter, enabled these women to strike a comfortable balance between the commercial, domestic, and artistic.[60] In June 1912, the Guild even held what was firmly described as a 'successful private exhibition' in rented rooms at Lindsey Hall, Notting Hill.[61] Intriguingly, despite the proclamations of privacy, the Royal Society of Arts reviewed the exhibition. It is unknown why a reporter attended: it suggests the exhibition had become larger than intended, or perhaps a journalist had been discreetly contacted. Ultimately, the review validated their fears, beginning as it did with the usual generic portrayal of women's ineptitude in contrast to men: 'A certain number of the exhibitions devoted exclusively to women's work are not of such a character as to prove superiority over, or even her equality with, man in the field of Arts and Crafts.' After getting this off their chest, the reviewer wrote that this 'little show' – although 'it could not be called very remarkable' – 'did at least demonstrate what really capable, competent, and workmanlike work women are doing in the various branches of applied art'. There was, however, persistent labelling of the work of members as 'dainty', a flattening term which did little to convey the skilled labour involved: May Morris showed 'a very dainty piece of boldly executed embroidery on muslin'; Grace Christies' four d'oyleys were 'dainty and instructive pieces of workmanship'; whilst Georgie Gaskin's 'daintily shown' jewellery was 'well designed and characterised by a sense of style'.[62]

The Guild's approach to exhibitions in the years before the war exemplifies the paralysis felt by many women art workers, faced with an unhappy choice between separatism leading to patronisation and amateurism, and collaboration leading to effective marginalisation and the preservation of a sexist status quo. Still, other women's art groups took a more public-minded approach, feeling the key was to organise their own public exhibitions – on their own terms – so people could see the high quality of their artwork. The '91 Art Club and the Women's International Art Club regularly exhibited at fashionable venues across central London such as the Egyptian Hall, Piccadilly, the Grafton Galleries, Mayfair, and Clifford's Gallery, Haymarket. Many prominent Arts and Crafts women exhibited with them. The press often described these exhibitions as showing very high-quality works, although newspapers were more likely to write reviews than art journals. At times, reviews were even devoid of gendered rhetoric, framing these exhibitions as at the epicentre of the fashionable art world. In 1896, *Lloyd's Weekly Newspaper* wrote that the '91 Art Club's 'entire exhibition witnesses exceptional culture and taste'. Similarly, in 1910 the *Studio* described the Women's International Art Club's exhibition as 'a great success this year. The galleries are always so well filled that detailed reference is impossible here, but the Society is greatly to be congratulated on the high standard of the work shown on the walls.'[63]

But the premier women's organisation to exhibit Arts and Crafts work in the early twentieth century was undoubtedly the Lyceum Club. Constance Smedley, the founder, did not just want to organise exhibitions in the city or even the country in which she lived. Instead, her wish was to form a 'system by which the Lyceum could be useful to professional workers all over the world'.[64] In 1904, when there was only the London Club, Smedley was determined to create a Berlin Clubhouse. To lay the groundwork for international exchange, and promote Anglo-German relations, she decided to organise a series of exhibitions in Germany where British Lyceum Club members could show their work to international audiences.[65] Taking advantage of her network of contacts who were embedded across European cultural networks, she travelled to Germany, where she secured meetings with the art world in Berlin. Her heart was set on hosting an Arts and Crafts exhibition at the fashionable new Modern Living Spaces Gallery at the Wertheim department store, and a second exhibition, on the fine arts, at Schulte's Gallery, which had an equally impressive reputation.

Smedley secured a meeting with the Wertheim brothers and their colleagues, detailing later in her memoir that these 'stern and remote gentlemen' had discussed her proposal 'hotly, vindictively, and sceptically' due to the 'disconcertingly candid and abysmally low' view of women's art work in Germany. But Smedley, well versed in the recognition male connections could afford, proposed to them: 'If all the work is judged by our greatest architects and artists and their written guarantee as to its excellence obtained, will you exhibit it then?' She then reeled off her list of male contacts, promising they would act as formal judges. The names included C. R. Ashbee, Fra Newbery, Walter Crane, and Douglas Cockerell. Apparently, this list 'not only satisfied but silenced' her audience and she 'left the room with their promise to have the Lyceum exhibit on these conditions'. She had similar success at Schulte's Gallery. Later, as promised, she gathered together several supportive letters to send to the sceptical Wertheim Committee: Walter Crane stated the works were 'remarkably good' whilst William Reynolds-Stephens declared, 'I can certainly say that the general average was equal to that of our Arts and Crafts Society's Exhibitions.'[66]

This success in gaining access to two of the premier artistic venues in Berlin is testament to the power of class privilege in enabling certain women to bypass specific gender inequalities. But it is important to account for Smedley's personal commitment, and her ability to inspire those around her. This was the case even whilst she dealt with ill-health (she suffered from heart problems and used a wheelchair throughout her life, including whilst in Germany). Her experiences in Berlin also exemplify the difficulties faced by women battling for professional equality, who continually had to navigate – and adapt – their ideals to fit different structural realities. Here, Smedley adhered to the established custom of having prominent male figures as judges to assure the world that 'professional' work was being exhibited. But she was confident that forging such collaborations with men, all united by their interest in 'serious' work, would have a 'wider appeal than that of feminism alone', as such a tactic more effectively 'aroused the sympathy and enlisted the co-operation' of male professionals. Exploiting the nationalistic tone of female 'advancement' which often featured at national and international exhibitions, Smedley felt 'even the most reactionary men' would help support the efforts of women on the international stage, because they 'did not like to feel their own womankind in the rear compared to the women of other nations'.[67] Although her memoir likely glosses over some of the difficulties she encountered so as to construct an inspirational and entertaining read, this approach did gain her the support of several members of the Art Workers' Guild (such as Ashbee, Crane, and Cockerell), who all backed her international projects.

The Wertheim exhibition took place in Berlin in late 1904 and early 1905 and also travelled to Hamburg, Düsseldorf, Bremen, and Cologne.[68] It caused a considerable stir in the English press, and several photographs were also included in a review for the prestigious German art journal *Deutsche Kunst und Dekoration*. These images reveal the gallery was noticeable in its simplicity, focused around the high-quality art on display. Small art pieces were positioned in glass cases close to the windows, whilst the furniture and wall displays made up the main section (Figures 2.4 and 2.5). Works by E. M. Rope, E. C. Woodward, Ada Ridley, and Annie Garnett all featured prominently. Of special note is a collaborative silver casket with bronze side panels and figures surmounting the lid by Rope and Woodward (Figure 2.6). This piece was photographed again in 1906 for the *Studio*, where it was described as exemplary with its 'bronzes and antique colour of the silver … well in harmony'.[69]

The artworks on display had been selected during an extensive vetting process. Although the male jury approved the final pieces at the London Club, there had been opportunities to form new networks between women working across Britain. A 'Scotch committee of ladies' secured works in Scotland, predominantly from the Glasgow School of Art, and there were similar representatives based in Birmingham.[70] Furthermore, an 'Executive Committee of artist craftswomen', led by Alice B. Woodward in London, gave advice to members before work was submitted for 'final judgement'.[71]

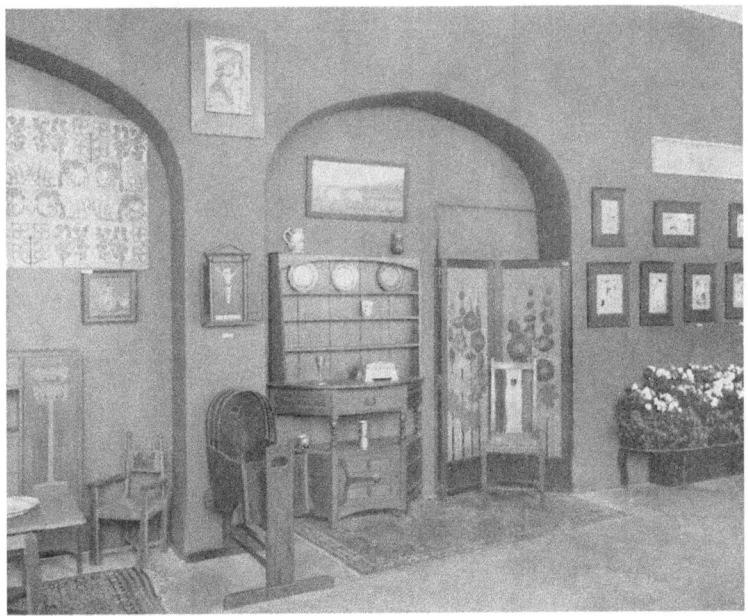

Figure 2.4 The Arts and Crafts exhibition of the Lyceum Club at the Modern Living Spaces Gallery, Wertheim department store, Berlin, 1905

After touring Germany, the exhibition opened at the London Lyceum Club between July and September 1905. The *Studio* was quick to offer praise, describing the bookbinding as 'exceptionally refined', a copper standing mirror by Evelyn Hickman as 'one of the most beautiful things of the kind that have been made', E. M. Rope's silver-bronze panel titled *Guardian Angel* as 'ambitious' and 'noticeable', and Annie Garnett's hand-woven fabrics as of the most 'exquisite colours'. Although the London exhibition was 'open only during the so-called "dead" season', there were still 'very large sales', and 'No branch of applied art was neglected in this exhibition of the work of women in the world of arts and crafts'.[72] Having claimed cultural authority by being exhibited in 'serious' art venues across Germany, and with the support of the Arts and Crafts establishment, the Lyceum exhibition managed to avoid many of the negative connotations of a 'women's art exhibition'.[73]

A permanent Arts and Crafts gallery was quickly established at the Club's headquarters, 128 Piccadilly, where free exhibitions were regularly held. In direct contrast to the Women's Guild of Arts, the Club's Board felt these public exhibitions were critical in emphasising the ongoing

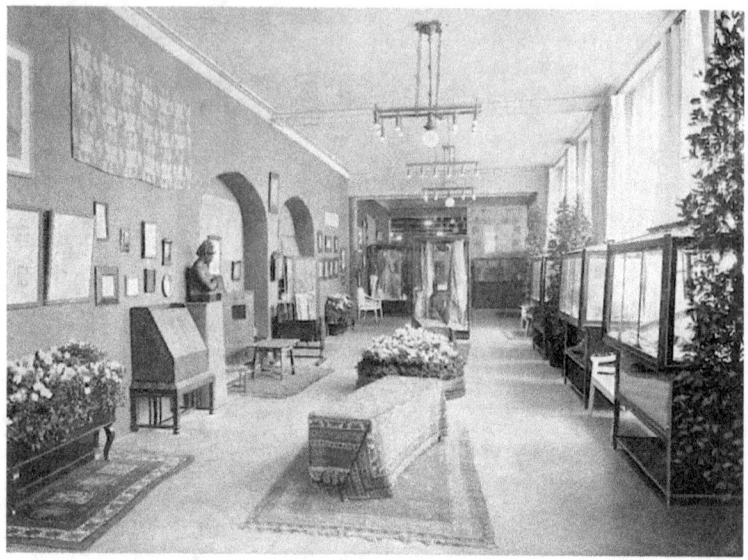

Figure 2.5 The Arts and Crafts exhibition of the Lyceum Club at the Modern Living Spaces Gallery, Wertheim department store, Berlin, 1905

commitment of members to embodying artistic values. This was largely the result of careful advertising, and a cautious negotiation of the dividing line between cultural display and commercial venture. In the view of Constance Smedley and her Board, both standards and 'absolute impartiality' were assured through retaining the judging panel of 'eminent men artists' who 'adjudicate on all work sent in, strict anonymity of the artist being maintained'.[74] The seriousness and exclusivity of the judging process, and the fact that well-established men had judged the work as worthy, was one of the primary features of these exhibitions remarked upon in the press. There was also great interest in the opportunities the Lyceum gave to 'the unknown worker', as apparently 'Names matter nothing to its selection committees.' The judges often rejected artworks which had been accepted by the New Gallery and the Royal Academy – still viewed as the ultimate barometer of success in many circles.[75] Reviews of Lyceum exhibitions in the press were extremely favourable; the *Art Workers' Quarterly* described the jewellery on display in terms which exemplify the belief the Club was doing much to further the aims of the Arts and Crafts movement, as it was 'so much better, more distinctive, and therefore more interesting than that which can be obtained from the jewellers, that no

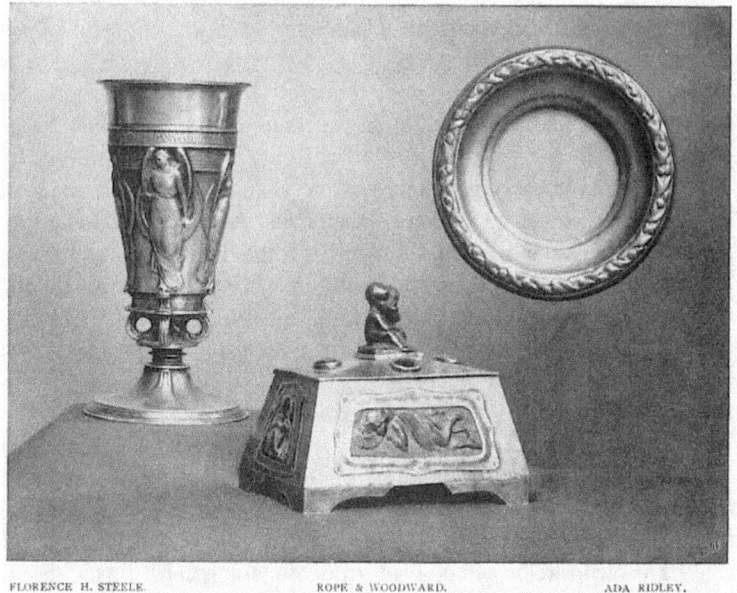

AUSSTELLUNG DES LONDONER LYCEUM-CLUB IN BERLIN.

FLORENCE H. STEELE.
SILBERBECHER.

ROPE & WOODWARD.
KASSETTE IN KUPFER-BRONZE UND EMAIL.

ADA RIDLEY.
VERGOLD. HOLZ-RAHMEN.

Figure 2.6 The Arts and Crafts exhibition of the Lyceum Club at the Modern Living Spaces Gallery, Wertheim department store, Berlin, 1905

difficulty should be experienced in finding purchasers for these beautiful works'.[76]

While the exhibitions were oriented around cultural display, the set-up of the exhibition room was such that women art workers could profit from attendees who wished to purchase work. Visitors to the gallery could be put in touch with the designers by a secretary, who was 'always' in the room ready to unlock cases, supply information, and hand out cards. The outer walls were filled with a line of permanent cases, each devoted to individual displays of 'the most representative craftswomen', bearing their names 'in clear letters'. In the centre, the 'miscellaneous work' of a much larger number of women was displayed at a 'moderate price' – although still at a price the 'Board of experts' felt constituted a 'life-supporting wage to the maker'. One exhibition in 1906 sold £700 of work, enabling the gallery to begin to function as a 'co-operative business'.[77] This permanent gallery at the heart of the capital was intended to provide a central hub for Lyceum members based 'in all corners of the country' such as Annie

Garnett in the Lake District, for whom 'it is impossible for the public to ferret out their whereabouts unaided'.[78] Displaying art produced by women such as Garnett, working in rural locations across the country, helped attract ever more social interest, as London visitors were keen to view these 'authentic' wares, shaped in their interests by the much romanticised and idealised discussions of rural industries in writings and illustrations of the era.

Although the Lyceum Gallery was successful in providing a national showroom for women art workers in the capital, the tactics used to balance cultural authority and societal respect with the demands of commerce demonstrate that engaging with exhibition space was a tightrope along which women's organisations had to walk tentatively. Smedley repeatedly positioned her desire for women to have a 'life-supporting wage' amidst a romanticised rhetoric of vocational devotion to the arts. She emphasised the Club's hope for a return to the patronage model, a crucial part of 'each Renaissance of Art', of fostering a mutually beneficial 'communion between artist, craftsworker, and patron'. Ever aware of the need to court the public, the Club's strategies were intended to create a society in which art workers and patrons would be united, of 'the pleasure in gifts or articles of furniture or personal adornment made specially' over 'things manufactured by the score' with 'no individual meaning'.[79]

With a reputation in the press and in wider society for selling high-value, high-quality work, the Lyceum nevertheless encouraged a binary classification of work between 'professional' and 'amateur' which was reliant on the arbitration of male experts. For the American journalist and women's rights campaigner Gertrude Atherton, upon visiting the Club's exhibition, her ultimate compliment was to describe the art as something of which 'Cobden Saunderson [sic] would not be ashamed'. She emphatically detailed how there was not a 'trace of the amateur in these displays. It was an exhibition of professionals, every bit of it.' Like Smedley, Atherton asserted to readers that the Club itself had the unique 'atmosphere' of a 'man's club', something she felt 'no other woman's club on earth can boast'.[80] This approach offered a modified yet still gendered way of viewing and understanding art, but it did constitute a more appealing tactic which women could use to reach a wide audience without experiencing societal opprobrium for being amateur, separatist, inferior, or lacking in feminine respectability. Politically motivated, Smedley's quest to carve out a space for female professionalism at the Lyceum Club had resulted in a prestigious venue in which women art workers could negotiate a hybrid commercial-artistic outlet for selling and displaying their work.

The Englishwoman Exhibition: the 'Royal Academy of Arts and Crafts'

In 1911, three years after Atherton's proclamations about the art on display at 'The Greatest Woman's Club in the World', Mary Lowndes decided to establish the Englishwoman Exhibition. Unlike the Lyceum's exhibitions at its Piccadilly Clubhouse, Lowndes's strategy was to commandeer large public venues in the capital. Beginning at Maddox Street Gallery, near Oxford Circus, the exhibition soon moved to the Methodist Central Hall, a vast Edwardian neo-baroque building opposite Westminster Abbey, and a much-used venue for religious services and grand suffrage events. In creating the Englishwoman Exhibition, Lowndes evidently disagreed with the Women's Guild of Arts' strategy of avoiding public exhibitions of women's work. She clearly also felt the Arts and Crafts Exhibition Society was not doing enough to engage the public on the wide-ranging societal benefits of handcrafted work – or the centrality of women in this culture.

The principal aim of the exhibition was, like the Lyceum Club, to help women build reputations and make a liveable wage; to form 'a bridge between the artist and her public' so they could ultimately 'set up their own shop', as Lowndes had done with Lowndes and Drury.[81] There was a steady stream of exhibitors from the leading women's Arts and Crafts groups in the country: E. C. Woodward regularly exhibited at the Lyceum Club and the Englishwoman Exhibition – and lectured at the Women's Guild of Arts. Each year, the exhibition was opened by different prominent, fashionable women, such as Lady Frances Balfour, President of the Central Society for Women's Suffrage, and Lady Rhondda, who established *Time and Tide* alongside the ardently feminist Six Point Group and declared that the Englishwoman Exhibition offered the best 'hunting ground for Christmas gifts' in the capital.[82] Much was made of the regular attendance of the Royal Family, who 'mixed with the ordinary people', and the time taken by the Queen to inspect exhibits and make purchases.[83] Adopting the tactic used by the Lyceum of attracting powerful supporters, there was a substantial list of patrons, including members of the artistic aristocracy such as Sir Edward Poynter, President of the Royal Academy.[84]

One of the difficulties in analysing this exhibition is navigating the outpouring of zealous reviews. The sheer number of positive press reports makes the complete absence of any history of the exhibition even more striking. From the start, the press (ranging from women-centred, feminist, local, to national papers) repeatedly discussed the professional, 'artistic' standards of the work. *Country Life* wrote that, 'In spite of the crowd of interested visitors' they had 'managed to get a very good view of the exhibits' but found it 'difficult to specialise where all is so good'.[85] The *Pall Mall Gazette* stressed that 'There are exhibitions and exhibitions, but one of the most interesting of the year is always the Englishwoman's Exhibition of Arts and Crafts.'[86] Turning to the ever-conservative *Journal of the Royal Society of Arts*, a review in 1916 commenced with the usual sweeping gendered sentiments (which appear noticeably similar to its earlier review of the Women's Guild of Arts exhibition): 'Exhibitions of Arts and Crafts devoted entirely to women's work are not, as a rule, very satisfying affairs from the point of view of art. There is, for the most part, an air of amateurishness about them which tends to make the scoffer rate women's achievements far below their real standard.' Going on, the author did state there were some 'defects', but 'on the whole' it was 'a very interesting show', had 'reached a really high level', suggesting that 'women hand-workers are advancing both in technique and in taste'.[87]

Well into the 1930s, the exhibition was described as the go-to place if you wanted to see authentic 'Arts and Crafts', which had to be distinguished from the host of 'amateur' or mass-produced products appropriating its name. As the *Scotsman* told its readers in 1928: 'The term "arts and crafts" may mean anything nowadays, but here the description more than justifies itself.'[88] Rather than a simplistic shift from Arts and Crafts to modernism by the 1920s and 1930s, the Englishwoman Exhibition constituted a key site for the cross-pollination of artistic, cultural, and social ideas. Journalists often discussed the range in interests of exhibitors. The *Manchester Guardian* informed readers that 'the dress and appearance of the stall-holders suggests the Morris-Burne-Jones period' but at other stalls, 'the bright hard colours of the wares … hints at Futurism' whilst another talked of 'The serious-looking girl artists, in their bright jazz jumpers and bobbed hair, who tend the various stalls, look deliciously quaint, and give the place an air of youth and joyous industry.'[89] Altogether, this wealth of evidence suggests the exhibition became one of the premier national sites for the display of craftwork across the early to mid-twentieth century. Furthermore, it paved the way for the emergence of other prominent, interwar craft exhibitions such as those of the Red Rose Guild, established and led by the wood engraver Margaret Pilkington.

The tactics used at the Englishwoman Exhibition were the culmination of many of the approaches used at the earlier exhibitions examined in this chapter. Lowndes ensured the exhibition became embedded within the established infrastructure of a women-centred consumer culture which had developed across the second half of the nineteenth century. The press greatly encouraged this. The *Pall Mall Gazette* was one of many to declare: 'If you believe that women should, as far as possible, patronise women, you won't omit a visit.'[90] Prominent figures in the interwar women's movement commented on the exhibition's important function in providing an established, central site where artistic women could exhibit work. Vera Brittain declared in her 1928 *Women's Work in Modern England* that with the Englishwoman Exhibition, 'never before has the craft worker had such good opportunities'.[91] The *Common Cause*, going even further, described it as keeping 'alive the spirit of craftsmanship in a commercially sordid age', a 'centre for the interchange of ideas as well as for the acquisition of orders'. It was approvingly noted that the event displayed 'the enterprise of that type of woman worker who has found or made the opportunity to use her hands and her brain and her artistic gifts all at once, under conditions of her own arrangement'. These workers 'who are far more numerous than is realised' were said to 'carry on a most valuable warfare against the mechanical goods of mass production'.[92]

Hearkening back to the historical sentimentalism of the Earl's Court exhibitions in the 1890s, the Englishwoman Exhibition evoked a nostalgic, pseudo-medieval world of industrious creativity which evidently continued to be very popular with visitors. One local newspaper waxed lyrical about how 'The old and the new are rather curiously blended at "The English-woman".'[93] Another declared, 'it may be questioned whether, since the golden days of the mediaeval guilds, beautiful things and finished workmanship have ever been so much in evidence as they are to-day'.[94] An understanding of the exhibition as an edifying experience was encouraged further by regular displays of objects of historical and cultural significance which had been loaned from museums and private collectors, such as the cot quilt of Charles II, old costumes, lace, jewellery, and 'gorgeous Buddhist robes'.[95]

The other major strand in which the Englishwoman Exhibition resembled its forebears was its utilisation of ideas of a 'national' artistic culture. The exhibition's title appears curiously at odds with Lowndes's assertion of the need for recognition without gendered commentary, seeming to embrace a nationalistic understanding of female participation in modern life, conjuring up the spectre of Kiralfy's exhibitions. Such a decision is testament to the growing nationalistic tendency beginning to permeate the Arts and Crafts, and the wider art world, which reached its heights during the First World War and in the aftermath, as we shall see in Chapter 5. The Arts and Crafts Exhibition Society's catalogues of these years had a similarly virulent nationalistic framing.[96] At a moment when patriotic choices in the buying habits of the public were increasingly being extolled, the exhibition organisers took advantage of the widespread interest in 'traditional', supposedly 'English' products. Over the years, the Englishwoman Exhibition was a complex, contradictory site for the promulgation of ideas of belonging, but also of national difference. Exhibitors from the South-East of England dominated the exhibition and although work from further afield was regularly shown it was often described simply as 'exotic'. For instance, groups such as the Orkney and Shetland Home Industry, the Midland Lace Association, and the South Indian Village Lace Industry all showed work. 'Quaint Welsh toys' were also displayed.[97] Lady Frances Balfour – who was Scottish – frequently protested against the name, feeling it ought to be 'Britishwoman'.[98] The exhibition was, in this regard, reflective of an ascendant strand of 'English' national pride which dominated the first half of the twentieth century and became closely associated with craft cultures.[99]

But for all the continuity with earlier exhibitions, such as those at Earl's Court, there were notable differences. The Englishwoman Exhibition was more consistent, held every year, and was far grander in scale than many other Arts and Crafts exhibitions. Furthermore, women-centred as it was, the Committee encouraged a mixed-sex environment and had a regular cluster of male exhibitors, such as Ivor Innes who carved the Elfin Oak in Kensington Gardens, the 'Brothers Hopkins' who showed pottery, and Sir Nevile Wilkinson, the British Army officer and dollhouse designer who became a patron and exhibitor.[100]

Lowndes and her Committee also refused to shy away from entertaining visitors and seeking commercial support. There appears to have been a pragmatic realisation that such an approach would spread the ethos of the movement to a far greater range of people – and help pay for the costs. The catalogue was intermixed with advertisements which included Bourneville Cocoa and gas companies, but where possible was oriented towards women's entrepreneurial endeavours, such as 'Miss M. Harris Smith' and her accounting courses. Alongside this, the exhibition tried to ensure that some of the art on display each year was costed at moderate prices, an approach the *Manchester Guardian* felt provided an 'exciting experience for people of modest purposes' who could now 'select a precious stone and have it mounted as a ring or brooch according to the pattern they choose. It makes an ordinary shopper feel like a Medici.'[101] There was the chance to buy smaller, inexpensive items such as Pamela Colman Smith's calendars, Christmas cards, and handcoloured prints.[102] Those with more money could buy a 'portrait in pottery in your best frock' for £18.[103] Attendees could also 'take home the catalogue to order other things as they want or can afford them.'[104]

Rather than having glass cases, the exhibition took the form of a series of rentable stalls. Using stalls was an approach troublingly suggestive of the 'amateur' charity bazaar in the eyes of many, but had the benefit of encouraging meaningful interactions between customers and art workers – who were in attendance, ready to converse with the public. Women were often *in situ* using the tools of their craft; woodcarver Ruth Bannister and wax modeller F. E. Hill even posed at their stalls for the *Sphere's* press photographer (Figure 2.7). Such entertainments were underpinned with a progressive ethos, of making conscious efforts to showcase women's artistic contributions to society. One repeated focal point was to remind spectators that women were designers as well as makers. At the 1912 exhibition, visitors to E. C. Woodward's stall could see the design of a cross being worked in enamel at her studio for the Church of St Peter Mancroft in Norwich.[105] The following year visitors were confronted in the corridor with plans of houses, cottages, and bungalows by the architect Elspeth Spencer (who had the added celebrity allure of having posted herself as a 'human letter' to the Prime Minister as a stunt in support of the suffrage campaigns).[106]

Two of Lowndes's key interests were Arts and Crafts and feminist politics, yet in contrast to suffrage exhibitions, the Englishwoman Exhibition was first and foremost conceived of as a space for Arts and Crafts excellency. One of the most striking features of the exhibition was its lack of overt socio-political commentary. Aside from press reports, and in contrast to the Arts and Crafts Exhibition Society catalogues, which included detailed

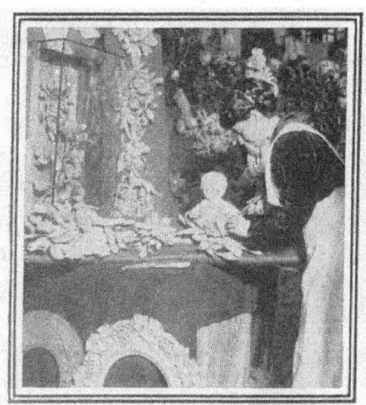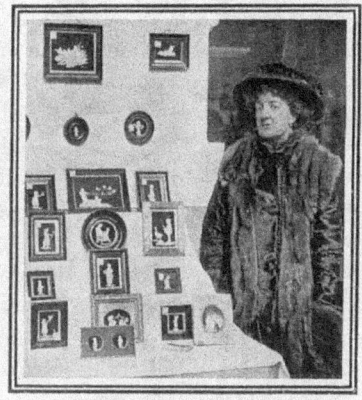

Woodcarving Exhibit at Westminster

Miss Ruth Bannister exhibits some remarkably fine and deep wood carving at the Westminster Central Hall this week

Modelled Wax at Westminster

Miss F. E. Hill exhibits some very charming wax portraits and figures at the Exhibition of Arts and Handicrafts

Figure 2.7 Two exhibitors, Ruth Bannister and F. E. Hill, posing at their stalls at the Englishwoman Exhibition, 1915

statements about the exhibition's ideological intentions, there are very few (surviving, at least) writings from those involved in running the Englishwoman Exhibition about its ethos or mission. Surviving catalogues simply list exhibitors and advertisements. A retrospective piece about Lowndes after her death discussed how:

> Many at the present time do not realise that this exhibition owes its existence to Mary Lowndes, for it was never her desire to assert her own claims to leadership in such matters. All she wished for was the permanent benefit to women facing the battle of life as she herself had faced it.[107]

This piece characterises the attitude Lowndes and many of her female Arts and Crafts peers had throughout their lives; rather than emphasising their own contributions they focused on creating a collaborative artistic world where greater numbers of people could participate. Furthermore, Lowndes never shied away from expressing her feminist views in articles for the press, but she sought to position the exhibition at the nexus of both socially conservative (in the sense of preserving an 'English' historic culture) and politically radical currents: part of the establishment whilst simultaneously reshaping the establishment, as a way to ensure the movement had significant national reach.

This equivocation did not prevent, however, this protean space from appealing to both militant and non-militant suffrage campaigners. *Votes for Women*, the organ of the Women's Social and Political Union, told readers in 1911 that 'This exhibition should appeal especially to Suffragettes' and would 'include exhibits from many well-known women workers who are in sympathy with the cause'.[108] The *Common Cause*, however (the paper for the non-militant National Union of Women's Suffrage Societies, whom Lowndes was attached to), informed readers that the exhibition's objective was to 'emphasise the truth that art is of no sex, the committee of selection welcome men's work equally with women's'.[109] Many other newspapers positioned the exhibition as a key site for the fashionable performance of modern womanhood. This was particularly the case when women gained partial emancipation. Several papers included celebratory articles by women journalists, who, after duly recording their votes for the 1922 General Election, had travelled 'through streets in which the whole world seemed to be congregating' to celebrate at the Englishwoman Exhibition.[110] It seems as if Lowndes's strategy of thrusting Arts and Crafts exhibitions before the public eye in a populist, and at times problematic, exhibition had indeed resulted in the establishment of a national institution which facilitated substantial female participation *and* had remarkable cultural and social reach: a kind of 'Royal Academy of Arts and Crafts', as the *Midland Daily Telegraph* was to describe it.

The contested space of the exhibition, threatened on the one side by the looming taboo of commercialism, and on the other by the male-dominated rarefication and monopolisation of cultural authority, provides the perfect venue for tracing how women art workers navigated, and reshaped, different social, cultural, and political worlds. By moving away from considering the Arts and Crafts Exhibition Society as the cynosure of the movement's exhibition culture, we can observe a more profound engagement between the Arts and Crafts and popular culture. In fact, the Arts and Crafts Exhibition Society was just one of many manifestations of display and sale of artworks associated with the movement; organisers firmly positioned it at the exclusive end of a spectrum of exhibitions which could encompass fairground rides and the sale of women's clothing. Taken together, these exhibitions take us to the heart of circulating anxieties about gender separatism and the influence of contemporary stereotypes of masculinity and femininity, alongside class, race, and nationalism, in mediating how art and artist were bestowed with value. These spaces illuminate the persistently interwoven nature of the progressive Arts and Crafts movement and feminist politics with the nationalistic and imperial currents of the day.

There were many commonalities in the approaches of women art workers to exhibition cultures. Focused on demonstrating 'expertise' and trying to escape the taint of the female 'amateur', they avoided maternal language or overt strategies of feminisation, instead promoting that their exhibitions were professional, collaborative sites where handcrafted creativity and design skills could be viewed. Beyond this, two relatively distinct approaches can be adumbrated. One tactic, espoused by several prominent members of the Women's Guild of Arts, sought to emulate the guarded elite culture of the artistic exhibition, free from direct mercantilism, a tactic which they shared with their male peers in the Art Workers' Guild. They spurned the idea of categories for women at mixed-sex exhibitions and stuck to their belief that there should be no division of artistic culture on the grounds of sex. Others used exhibition spaces to forge new professional and affective ties between women, or to advance political ideas, often focused around dismantling inequalities of gender. Subsequently, these women implicated themselves in the creation of feminised spaces of display. But they tried to mitigate the effects of this on their reputation, and avoid accusations of amateurism, by utilising tactics which demarcated their cultural authority: male panels of judges, the physical performance of artistry in the exhibition space, or the reassuring distance of the glass display cabinet.

The confident engagement of women such as Mary Lowndes in seeking democratically to 'open up' the exhibition world – particularly at 'women's exhibitions' – undoubtedly stoked fears about the increasing popularisation and failure of the movement. The public and press interest in her exhibition is both a barometer of its success but is also indicative of what traditional historiography has seen as the dilution of the movement. Yet it is through considering this range of exhibition spaces that we can more fully grasp how different people engaged with and sought to make sense of the Arts and Crafts movement, particularly by the early twentieth century. These different events brought together the commercial, artistic, educational, historical, and political in new ways and encouraged interactions between many different people: the general spectator, exhibitors, the women's movement, and the conservative press alike. Ultimately, the exhibitions considered in this chapter challenge dominant definitions of what con-stituted cultural influence and reach across this era. Many of the exhibitions – aside from Arts and Crafts Exhibition Society exhibitions – sit outside of the established trajectory of culturally significant art exhibitions, which are usually defined in part through the writings of an elite few and selective use of the press. The following chapter leaves behind this world of grand public exhibitions, of exhibition boards and sub-committees, to consider how women art workers navigated the politics of gendered space in the places where they had the most power: at their own homes and studios.

Notes

1   In the press, the exhibition was often referred to as the 'Englishwoman Exhibition of Arts and Crafts' or simply the 'Englishwoman' but the small number of surviving catalogues at the Women's Library, London School of Economics (hereafter WL), all refer to it as the 'Englishwoman Exhibition of Arts and Handicrafts'. Throughout this chapter I tend to refer to it as the 'Englishwoman Exhibition'.

2   'Woman's Exhibition', *Votes for Women* (15 September 1911), p. 797; 'Women's Work', *Darlington and Stockton Times, Ripon and Richmond Chronicle* (18 November 1911), p. 6.

3   '"The Englishwoman" Exhibition', *Common Cause* (14 November 1913), p. 566.

4   'A London Letter', *Yorkshire Post and Leeds Intelligencer* (17 November 1922), p. 4.

5   'Arts and Crafts', *Midland Daily Telegraph* (16 November 1934), p. 5.

6   Leila Ryan and Maria DiCenzo, 'The *Englishwoman*: "Twelve Years of Brilliant Life"', in *Feminist Media History: Suffrage, Periodicals and the Public Sphere* (eds) Maria DiCenzo, Lucy Delap, and Leila Ryan (Basingstoke: Palgrave Macmillan, 2011), pp. 120–158.

7 Imogen Hart, 'On the Arts and Crafts Exhibition Society', www.branchcollective.org/?ps_articles=imogen-hart-on-the-first-arts-and-crafts-exhibition, accessed 19 September 2019.

8 Peter J. Gurney, '"The Sublime of the Bazaar": A Moment in the Making of a Consumer Culture in Mid-Nineteenth-Century England', *Journal of Social History*, 40/2 (2006), pp. 385–405 (pp. 390–391); Erika Rappaport, *Shopping for Pleasure: Women in the Making of London's West End* (Princeton: Princeton University Press, 2001).

9 Arts and Crafts Exhibition Society, *Catalogue of the First Exhibition* (London: Chiswick Press, 1888), pp. 5–6.

10 Morna O'Neill, 'Rhetorics of Display: Arts and Crafts and Art Nouveau at the Turin Exhibition of 1902', *Journal of Design History*, 20/3 (2007), pp. 205–225 (p. 206).

11 *Catalogue of the First Exhibition*, p. 94. Prices were displayed from 1903, but this does not necessarily indicate the Society was embracing a more commercial approach. By this point it had established a respectable, artistic reputation. May Morris, who became centrally involved, continued to assert that 'the Society was founded originally to educate the public by means of exhibitions, and raise the standard of craftsmanship; the selling of articles being a secondary matter'. Peter Rose, '"It Must be Done Now": The Arts and Crafts Exhibition at Burlington House, 1916', *Journal of the Decorative Arts Society 1850–the Present*, 17 (1993), pp. 3–12 (p. 3).

12 Tanya Harrod, *The Crafts in Britain in the Twentieth Century* (New Haven: Yale University Press, 1999), p. 22.

13 'Exhibition', *Studio*, 1 (1893), p. 50.

14 Heather Haskins, 'Now You See Them, Now You Don't: The Critical Reception of Women's Work at the Arts and Crafts Exhibition Society, 1888–1916' (Unpublished PhD thesis, Concordia University, 2005), pp. 57–58.

15 Louise Jopling, 'Occupations for Gentlewomen', *Atalanta* (January 1895), p. 221.

16 Charlotte Yeldham's research has shown there was a steady increase in one-woman exhibitions across this era. There were three in the 1850s, in contrast to the 185 held between 1906 and 1910. Charlotte Yeldham, *Women Artists in Nineteenth-Century France and England* (London: Garland, 1984), p. 114.

17 'The Jewellery of Mrs Philip Newman', *Magazine of Art* (January 1902), p. 466.

18 *Official Catalogue of Exhibitors, Universal Exposition St. Louis, USA* (St Louis: Catalogue Company, 1904), pp. 220–228.

19 Arts and Crafts Exhibition Society, *Catalogue of the Ninth Exhibition* (London: Chiswick Press, 1910), p. 11.

20 Hart, 'On the Arts and Crafts Exhibition Society'.

21 T. J. Boisseau and Abigail M. Markwyn, 'Introduction', in *Gendering the Fair: Histories of Women and Gender at World's Fairs* (eds) T. J. Boisseau and Abigail M. Markwyn (Urbana: University of Illinois Press, 2010), pp. 1–16 (p. 2); Myriam Boussahba-Bravard and Rebecca Rogers (eds), *Women in International and Universal Exhibitions, 1876–1937* (London: Routledge, 2017).

22 Boisseau and Markwyn, *Gendering the Fair*, p. 14; T. J. Boisseau, 'White Queens at the Chicago World's Fair, 1893: New Womanhood in the Service of Class, Race, and Nation', *Gender and History*, 12/1 (2000), pp. 33–81.

23 'Sculptural Decorations to the "Women's Building", Chicago', *Builder* (27 May 1893), p. 409.

24 *Official Catalogue of the British Section, Royal Commission for the Chicago Exhibition, 1893* (London: William Clowes, 1893), pp. 403–462.

25 *Victorian Era Exhibition Guide* (London: Riddle and Couchman, 1897), pp. 45, 48.

26 Janice Helland, *British and Irish Home Arts and Industries, 1880–1914: Marketing Craft, Making Fashion* (Dublin: Irish Academic Press, 2007), p. 162. Imrè Kiralfy's exhibitions in London included the Empire of India Exhibition (1895) which saw the first use of the 300-foot high 'Great Wheel', amongst others such as the 1898 International Universal Exhibition. Susan Tenneriello, *Spectacle Culture and American Identity: 1815–1940* (New York: Palgrave Macmillan, 2013).

27 Lady Cowper, Chair of the Handicraft Committee, was described as having such 'refined taste and knowledge of art' she would 'guarantee ... the beauty and completeness of this department'. Marion Leslie, 'Women's Work at the Victorian Era Exhibition', *Lady's Realm: An Illustrated Monthly Magazine* (May–October 1897), p. 63.

28 *Victorian Era Exhibition Catalogue, Woman's Work Section* (London: Riddle and Couchman, 1897), pp. 11, 69.

29 'The Victorian Era Exhibition and Sanitation', *Sanitation Record* (30 July 1897), p. 124.

30 Ernest C. Fincham, *Women as Bookbinders* (London: Guild of Women Binders, 1901), p. 1. For more on bookbinding, see Marianne Tidcombe, *Women Bookbinders, 1880–1920* (New Castle: Oak Knoll, 1996).

31 Leslie, 'Women's Work', p. 62.

32 *Victorian Era Exhibition Catalogue, Woman's Work Section*, pp. 69–83.

33 Leslie, 'Women's Work', pp. 62–63.

34 Ibid., pp. 58–59.

35 'The Woman's Exhibition at Earl's Court', *Sphere* (5 May 1900), p. 490.

36 *Woman's Exhibition, 1900, Official Guide* (London: Spottiswoode, 1900), p. 11.

37 Annie E. Coombes, *Reinventing Africa: Museums, Material Culture and Popular Imagination in Late Victorian and Edwardian England* (New Haven: Yale University Press, 1994), pp. 100–101.

38 *Woman's Exhibition, 1900, Fine Art, Historical, and General Catalogue* (London: Spottiswoode, 1900).

39 'The Woman's Exhibition at Earl's Court', *Sphere*, p. 490.

40 *Woman's Exhibition, 1900, Fine Art, Historical, and General Catalogue*, p. 203.

41 'The Woman's Exhibition at Earl's Court', *Sphere*, p. 490.

42 'Women's Exhibition at Earl's Court', *Illustrated Sporting and Dramatic News* (2 June 1900), p. 558.

43 See for instance, 'The Earl's Court Exhibition', *Hearth and Home* (17 May 1900), p. 102.

44 'Art. II. – The Exhibition of Women's Work. An Averted Danger', *Englishwoman's Review* (17 April 1900), p. 84.

45 For more on the use of imperialistic ideologies, grounded in a troubling rhetoric of moral and racial superiority some women used to achieve political ends, see Antoinette Burton, *Burdens of History: British Feminists, Indian Women, and Imperial Culture, 1865–1915* (Chapel Hill: University of North Carolina Press, 1994).

46 'A Mine of Interesting Information', *Common Cause* (24 April 1914), p. 57; 'Woman's Kingdom', *Sheffield Daily Telegraph* (23 January 1914), p. 9.

47 'A Remarkable Exhibition', *Mid Sussex Times* (7 April 1914), p. 5.

48 Tara Morton, 'Changing Spaces: Art, Politics, and Identity in the Home Studios of the Suffrage Atelier', *Women's History Review*, 21/4 (2012), pp. 623–637.

49 'The Arts and Crafts Section', *Common Cause* (24 April 1914), p. 57.

50 'Woman's Kingdom', *Sheffield Daily Telegraph*, p. 9.

51 'Studio-Talk', *Studio*, 46 (1909), p. 62.

52 WGAA, Copy of letter from Julia Bowley, 1913.

53 Women's Guild of Arts Archive, Duke University, North Carolina, Feodora Gleichen to 'Madame', 6 March 1908. Underlining in original.

54 WGAA, Christiana Herringham and May Morris to the Secretary of the Women's Section of the Scottish National Exhibition, *c.* 1908.

55 'Art and Artists', *Morning Post* (17 April 1908), p. 3. Italics in original.

56 WGAA, Committee Meeting 27 November 1913, Meeting Minutes Book 1913–1917.

57 WGAA, Feodora Gleichen to May Morris, February 1913.

58 WGAA, Edith B. Dawson to May Morris, 4 January, no year. Underlining in original.

59 *Franco-British Exhibition, London, Fine Arts Catalogue* (London: Bemrose, 1908), p. 132.

60 At the end of 1915 members held 'A series of private shows of members' works' at the premises of 'Mrs Wallace Bruce', Estella Canziani, and Cecilia Roberts. Also see WGAA, Printed Version, Annual Report, 1915.

61 WGAA, Printed Version, Annual Report, 1912.

62 'The Women's Guild of Arts and Crafts', *Journal of the Royal Society of Arts* (12 July 1912), p. 827.

63 'The Picture Galleries', *Lloyd's Weekly Newspaper* (7 June 1896), p. 11; 'Studio-Talk', *Studio*, 49/203 (February 1910), p. 223.

64 Constance Smedley, *Crusaders: Reminiscences of Constance Smedley / Mrs Maxwell Armfield* (London: Duckworth, 1929), p. 78.

65 The Lyceum Club also established several International Advisory Boards where members could get advice and be put in touch with foreign openings. Smedley invited eminent figures to join these Boards such as Impressionist painter and printer Max Liebermann, designer and architect of the *Jugendstil* style Bruno Möhring, and architect, author, and diplomat Hermann Muthesius. Ibid., p. 85.

66 Ibid., pp. 79–83.

67 Ibid., p. 117.

68 'Studio-Talk', *Studio*, 36/153 (December 1905), p. 71.

69 'Studio-Talk', *Studio*, 39/163 (October 1906), p. 169.

70 'Metropolitan Gossip', *Belfast Weekly News* (8 September 1904), p. 4; 'Miss Constance Smedley and the Lyceum Club', *Birmingham Daily Gazette* (29 September 1904), p. 4.

71 Smedley, *Crusaders*, p. 82.

72 'Studio-Talk', *Studio*, 36/153 (December 1905), pp. 71–72.

73 The London Lyceum Club's experiment in Berlin was unfortunately short lived. In the light of growing political and military tensions between Britain and Germany, alongside specific tensions about the English Club's dominating presence in decisions being made at the Berlin Clubhouse, by 1908 the Berlin Club had 'severed its financial

ties with the English management'. Despina Stratigakos, *A Women's Berlin: Building the Modern City* (Minneapolis: University of Minnesota Press, 2008), pp. 17–51.

74 Smedley, *Crusaders*, p. 84.

75 'Miss Constance Smedley and the Lyceum Club', *Birmingham Daily Gazette*, p. 4.

76 'Lyceum Club Arts and Crafts Exhibition', *Art Workers' Quarterly: A Portfolio of Practical Designs for Decorative and Applied Art*, 5 (1906), p. 39.

77 'Exhibition at the Lyceum Club', *London Daily News* (28 March 1906), p. 5.

78 Constance Smedley, 'A Guild of Craftswomen', *World's Work: An Illustrated Magazine of National Efficiency and Social Progress*, 9 (December 1906–1907), pp. 314–322 (p. 322).

79 Smedley, 'A Guild of Craftswomen', p. 317.

80 Gertrude Atherton, 'The Greatest Woman's Club in the World', *Bookman: An Illustrated Magazine of Literature and Life*, 27 (March–August 1908), pp. 250–251.

81 'Coming Events', *Yorkshire Post and Leeds Intelligencer* (16 November 1923), p. 4.

82 'Useful to Know', *Country Life* (19 November 1921), p. lx.

83 'The Queen at an Exhibition', *Scotsman* (20 November 1917), p. 4.

84 WL, Englishwoman Exhibition Catalogue, 1917.

85 'The "Englishwoman" Exhibition', *Country Life* (26 November 1927), p. lvi.

86 'A Really Interesting Exhibition', *Pall Mall Gazette* (27 October 1921), p. 9.

87 'The "Englishwoman" Exhibition of Art and Handicrafts', *Journal of the Royal Society of Arts* (8 December 1916), p. 73.

88 'Woman to Date', *Scotsman* (19 November 1928), p. 12.

89 'Our London Correspondence', *Manchester Guardian* (20 November 1922), p. 6; 'Signs of Christmas', *Lancashire Evening Post* (17 November 1920), p. 2.

90 'The Talk of the Town', *Pall Mall Gazette* (10 November 1919), p. 7.

91 Vera Brittain, *Women's Work in Modern England* (London: Noel Douglas, 1928), p. 89.

92 'The Englishwoman', *Common Cause* (7 January 1921), p. 1037.

93 'Women's Work', *Darlington and Stockton Times*, p. 6.

94 '"The Englishwoman" Exhibition', *Cheltenham Examiner* (13 November 1913), p. 2.

95 'Women's Work', *Darlington and Stockton Times*, p. 6.

96 See the Introduction to the 1916 exhibition: 'They should have kept their encouragement for their own native artistry, developed national gifts, instead of establishing a parasitic dependence on outside help.' Arts and Crafts Exhibition Society, *Catalogue of the Eleventh Exhibition* (London: Chiswick Press, 1916), p. 19.

97 '"The Englishwoman" Exhibition', *Cheltenham Examiner*, p. 2.

98 'Eighth Year of the Englishwoman Exhibition', *Common Cause* (22 November 1918), p. 379.

99 As Janice Helland's research into the Home Arts and Industries Association has shown, whilst the Association's work might seem commendable, it did also signify the colonisation of the 'so-called Celtic fringe by London society'. Furthermore, the location of the 'workers in remote rural areas … marginalized the products within the more rarefied, metropolitan world of the Arts and Crafts movement.' Helland, *British and Irish Home Arts and Industries*, pp. 2–3.

100 'Court and Society', *Daily Mail* (5 November 1935), p. 10; 'Pottery at the "Englishwoman" Exhibition', *Pottery Gazette* (1 December 1917), p. 1170; 'Shadows on a Woman's Screen', *Graphic* (9 November 1929), p. 282.

101 'Our London Correspondence', *Manchester Guardian*, p. 6.
102 'The "Englishwoman's" Exhibition', *Common Cause* (14 November 1912), p. 554.
103 'Our London Correspondence', *Manchester Guardian*, p. 6.
104 'Coming Events', *Yorkshire Post*, p. 4.
105 'The "Englishwoman's" Exhibition', *Common Cause* (14 November 1912), p. 554. (Incorrectly described as Alice B. Woodward in the publication).
106 '"The Englishwoman's" Exhibition', *Common Cause* (14 November 1913), p. 566.
107 'A Dorset Woman Pioneer', *Western Gazette* (15 March 1929), p. 11.
108 'Woman's Exhibition', *Votes for Women*, p. 797.
109 'The "Englishwoman" Exhibition', *Common Cause* (5 October 1911), p. 446.
110 'A London Letter', *Yorkshire Post and Leeds Intelligencer* (17 November 1922), p. 4.

3

'At Home' in artistic houses and studios

From a distance, *The Mulberry Tree* in Beaufort Street, Chelsea, does not betray itself as the abode of an artificer in metals ... at first sight it is just a pleasant house of old-world aspect, but you are no sooner past the outer gate than a wonderful arrangement of a copper ball suspended upon a copper chain by way of door-knocker, and a repoussé name-plate, also in copper, prove that you have not come to the wrong house, but are at Mr. Nelson Dawson's home.[1]

In this 1896 article for the *Studio*, titled 'A Chat with Mr. & Mrs. Nelson Dawson on Enamelling', the journalist wrote with voyeuristic and conversational panache, seeking to encourage readers to read on and learn more about the artistic delights awaiting at the home of Edith B. and Nelson Dawson, metalwork partners and married couple. The article was one of many such interviews to appear in the press during this era. Journalists described the homes of noteworthy individuals in lingering detail as a key narrative device to introduce them to a public clamouring for ever more details about the 'personal' lives of the great and the good. The domestic interior became closely associated with the construction of self across the nineteenth century, as did the view that the middle-class home constituted the heart of English culture. For a considerable sector of the population, handcrafted art was viewed as unique in the possibilities it offered to demonstrate one's cultured and moral predilections to the outside world. The Arts and Crafts household was seen as offering an exemplary model; visitors and readers of the press expected these homes to be 'authentically' artistic. The Mulberry Tree with its 'old-world aspect' and handcrafted doorknocker and name-plate offered this in abundance. It symbolised a reprieve from a fast-paced, capitalist world before the journalist had even stepped through the doorway – or met the artists. As such, being able to provide this curated snapshot of the artistic household to the world became the key site through which to assert credibility, whilst also subtly cultivating celebrity status and consumer interest.

Histories of modern artistic culture tell, in lavish detail, of the studio homes of male artists. This chapter instead provides the first comprehensive history of the network of homes and studios belonging to Arts and Crafts women and the relationships that played out in these spaces.[2] Debates about whether the home was a site of empowerment or confinement for women is one of the most enduring questions of women's and gender history, yet there has been surprisingly limited scrutiny of the many different ways middle-class women adapted domestic spaces for 'professional' work in the modern era. For women art workers like Edith B. Dawson, although keen to meet at clubhouses and guild halls for official meetings, homes and studios played a fundamental role in the daily maintenance of artistic lives. Together these homes, which ranged from rented rooms in purpose-built urban housing for working women through to grand country houses, constituted key sites of resistance and self-expression. In the quest to find 'a room of one's own', women art workers increasingly sought access to their own studios, which functioned as the central space in their lives.[3] Although the women discussed in *Women Art Workers* were relatively privileged, the studio could still be makeshift and temporary, set up in the corner of a multi-purpose room within the home. Even when they were in different locations and spatially distinct, the studio fulfilled many of the functions of domestic space. There could be no clear delineation, in practice, between home and studio – something art workers actively encouraged as a display of authenticity and a rejection of staid *petit bourgeois* domesticity.

There were profound differences, however, between the homes of unmarried and married artists. Following the life course of women art workers, this chapter begins in the unmarried home. Firstly, exploring the experiences of young women in the family home, and then their adult lives, often in all-female households, or staying in the houses they had grown up in. Many remained unmarried, but this was by no means the overwhelming majority. Although there remains an assumption that if you wanted to work – as a middle-class woman – you needed to remain unmarried across this era, there was a sizeable group of women art workers who married, usually to fellow artists. The second section addresses the impact of marriage on artistic aspirations, through close study of couples such as the Dawsons. While marriage could create situations which interfered with women's art work and could promote models which made married women more susceptible to societal expectations of domestic behaviour, the partnership of artists could function as a productive site for artistic self-fashioning.

But considering the isolated home or studio does not, in itself, encompass the greater importance of this kind of space for the actualisation of the woman art worker. The final section explores how art workers, married and unmarried, together used their homes and studios to create an expansive network spread across the capital, and across the country. By reformulating traditional practices of domestic socialisation such as 'At Homes' to organise meetings focused around art, work, education, and political reform, these women remained respectably situated amidst an expansive domestic milieu, whilst simultaneously engaging in the very process of pursuing modern working lives. Situated between the private institutional space of the Hall, and the public-commercial space of the metropolis, this invisible superstructure of homes and studios tied together communities of artists through programmes of sociability and mutual reinforcement of artistic authority. Throughout, I consider the impact of representations of homes and studios on the cultural imagination, alongside the central role these environments played in shaping daily practices of professionalisation. Despite ongoing obstacles, artistic women used homes and studios to muddy the waters between restrictive gendered ideas about domesticity and a neatly separate public world of masculine work. By examining how different people interacted within these spaces – fellow artists, family members, customers, journalists, friends – we can better understand the central role women art workers played in directing the artistic currents of the day, by reformulating Arts and Crafts work cultures to take place within spaces where they had greater opportunities to participate.

The unmarried home and studio

The women art workers considered in this book were predominantly born between the 1850s and the 1870s and, like other women of similar social standing, spent extensive periods of time at home. This was usually the place they were educated, in contrast to brothers who were often educated away from the home.[4] It was in their late teens and twenties (if at all) that such women tended to pursue formal art training. But home education, although undoubtedly gendered, did not signify any consistent parental aspiration to diminish women's ambitions in adult life. Writing for an American publication about contemporary illustrators in 1930, Alice B. Woodward detailed how she and her siblings were 'brought up at home with governesses' as this was 'cheaper than school'. She reflected fondly that from earliest childhood she and two of her sisters (E. C. and Gertrude) had wanted to become artists and gleefully told readers that John Ruskin had once given them a drawing lesson. Like many others, they also practised drawing in the galleries at the British Museum. For young artistic women like the Woodwards, youthful attempts at professional practice at home appear to have been openly orchestrated and accepted. The sisters used stables and later rooms at their homes in South-West London for artistic projects and also rented studios nearby.[5] Their proximity in age and time spent together fostered an extensive familial world which sustained their artistic aspirations throughout their lives.

Traditional perspectives of nineteenth-century parenting – the mother as 'angel in the house' and the stern, distant father – are now known to have been stereotypes. Writing in 1890, interior decorator Agnes Garrett informed the *Women's Penny Paper* her father was a 'singularly well-educated, liberal man, of large ideas, and he brought up his children to think and act for themselves'. Amongst her siblings 'the girls had full and equal privileges with the boys in every respect'. Garrett's comments were written later in life for a publication keen to encourage readers to promote a progressive attitude in their own lives. Still, the presentation of her early years as central in forming her adult view that 'every girl should, like her brothers, be brought up to some profession or business' did become a more common perspective in several liberal families in the late nineteenth century.[6] Painter Helena Gleichen, sister of the sculptor Feodora, wrote flippantly in her memoir that although 'In those days it was a terrible thing for one's daughters to insist on having professions', her father, naval officer and sculptor Prince Victor of Hohenlohe-Langenburg, still 'encouraged us each to go ahead as if we had been boys'.[7]

In these networks, fathers regularly promoted the world of work, and even at the earliest stages of these women's lives, the home could be a place where artistic ambition was nurtured. Although Anthea Callen discusses the haunting shame felt by women who needed to receive payment for art, stressing the 'socially imposed necessity of hiding their need to earn a living', I have found little evidence of this.[8] Edith Robinson (later Dawson), daughter of a Quaker schoolmaster, was brought up in a 'sober and pious, and far from wealthy' home in Scarborough. Her painting was deemed 'somewhat frivolous' until her parents realised she could earn an income, at which point it was actively encouraged. Before marriage, in the 1880s, she made £100 annually through art lessons, selling her work in shops, and painting for commissions.[9] Alice B. Woodward similarly detailed how her father's work as Keeper of Geology at the British Museum did not pay well and his daughters needed to fund their own lives. Henry

Woodward commissioned his daughters to draw scientific illustrations for himself and his colleagues. Alice provided illustrations for palaeontologists such as Sir Richard Owen and Othniel Marsh. Upon earning £20 she started her 'student days at South Kensington', attended other classes in London, and later spent three months in Paris at the Académie Julien. She also gave classes herself, 'studying when I can afford it'.[10]

Mothers were mentioned less frequently in retrospective accounts, but could still help their daughters to construct artistic lives. Alice B. Woodward informed her publisher she tested out her illustrations on her mother because she provided 'an excellent example of the great B[ritish] P[ublic]'.[11] Where mothers were artists, daughters carefully detailed their achievements. Estella Canziani dedicated considerable room in her memoir – the title was the name of the family home, 3 Palace Green, evidently envisaged as the root of her career – to her mother, noted painter Louisa Starr. Likewise, Starr told the *Woman's Herald* she would 'dearly like her [daughter] to be an artist, as it opens out the senses to all that is beautiful in life'.[12]

Parental authority at home could nevertheless cause considerable tensions, especially when mothers and fathers had competing aspirations for their offspring. Although Feodora Gleichen's father had encouraged her to become a sculptor, upon his death her mother took a different stance with Helena, the younger daughter. Helena lamented: 'when I came along, demanding also to go to art schools to study drawing, I was told that I might go to an animal school if I wished but not to study from the nude'. Helena 'knew' her father would have 'backed her up', but had to wait several years before her mother allowed her to attend life classes.[13] Still, restrictions could provide fertile ground for rebellion, making certain young women ever more committed to pursuing art. Wilhelmina Stirling, sister of Evelyn Pickering (later De Morgan), detailed Evelyn's youthful battles with her parents. Her painting was viewed as a 'passing mania' and her mother complained, 'I want a daughter – not an artist!' The large size of the house enabled Pickering to paint secretly, an option unavailable for those in the crowded homes of the lower classes. When she moved out of the nursery and into her own rooms, she constructed a private workspace. Pasting up the doorways to mask the smell of paint, she kept the key turned in the lock and hid evidence of the paint and canvasses she had bought with pocket money. She relied on sisters and servants to pose as models and kept drapery close by to 'fling over the paraphernalia which might otherwise have revealed her occupation'. Pickering supposedly even added a false bottom to her bag so she could covertly carry around drawing materials. When Pickering's mother discovered her secret workroom, this material assemblage of artistic intent finally convinced her to provide her daughter with a drawing master. Later she allowed Evelyn to enrol at the Slade School of Art.[14]

Artistic families and homes in particular tended to offer a site where young women could embryonically visualise lives as artists, even to the extent that some women may have felt pressure to pursue artistic lives themselves. This is evident in reflective memoirs, where women such as Estella Canziani used their early engagement in artistic domestic networks to authoritatively position themselves as having been at the heart of the artistic scene. One of Canziani's earliest memories was the home studio: 'I remember my mother's beautiful, soft voice, when she walked up and down the studio with me in her arms.' As she grew up she realised 'that my mother was a very busy professional woman, always occupied by her portraits, that work of any kind must not be interrupted, except out of necessity'. Estella spent hours practising drawing on the backs of canvasses, and the studio walls began to be stacked with paintings by both mother and daughter. Before the age of twelve she did not have regular lessons due to illness, 'but the surrounding of artists and interesting people, who were in and out of the house, could not fail to be an educational influence'. This elite young woman was introduced to people who were to shape her future without even needing to leave the nurturing site of the home. Whenever John Callcott Horsley, Treasurer of the Royal Academy, visited he asked Louisa about Estella, saying, 'How is she getting on? Is she going to be an artist?'[15]

Memoirs and writings are rich in emphasis of the material environments in these artistic homes, filled with treasured objects. Helena Gleichen associated her father's studio with joyful family events, as whenever he 'made some money in the studio he used to give us all some treat or some lovely present'.[16] May Morris was fascinated with her father's study, where she ground his sticks of Chinese ink but could touch nothing else, such as the gold leaf for illuminating manuscripts. As soon as they were deemed old enough, May and her sister Jenny were taught to assist in family embroideries. The artistic reputation of their parents, Jane and William Morris, influenced the ways this work was perceived from the beginning. By also dressing their children in medieval-style robes – not a common practice – their artistic nature was authenticated even within the childhood home.[17]

These youthful experiences indicate that although women art workers were influenced by their gendered upbringings, both non-artistic and artistic homes could provide empowering bases. Class privilege repeatedly enabled these women to begin to build artistic networks from their own homes, and find rooms to work in where they could visualise adult lives as artists. Young women did tend to pursue sketching and painting projects, accepted social accomplishments for women of this class. Metal and woodwork projects, which may have caused greater anxieties about respectability, were usually pursued in adulthood. Still, payment for artistic work rarely seems to have caused discomfort, instead functioning as a sign of serious artistic intent.

Women art workers came of age during an era of acute societal concern about unmarried middle-class women. Triggered by the 1851 census, which revealed there were greater numbers of women than men in Britain, concerns continued into the twentieth century about the 'surplus' women who would never marry.[18] Conservative campaigners, novelists, and the women's movement alike were preoccupied with the 'Marriage Question' and the dangers of women leading independent lives. Traditional scholarship has repeatedly positioned unmarried women as living in the shadow of married women, doomed to 'spinsterhood'. But in recent years several historians have dismissed the projection of such a negative experience of unmarried life.[19] Many women in the Arts and Crafts movement did not marry, but there is little evidence suggesting they wanted to marry or felt pressure to do so. Remaining unmarried could be an effective option for those wanting to live with another woman (as friends or in intimate and sexual relationships) or those wanting to remain independent, particularly before the Married Women's Property Acts, when a woman's property legally became her husband's upon marriage. Groups such as the Women's Guild of Arts – where unmarried women outnumbered married – reiterates that being single was by no means necessarily a marginalised experience, especially in urban artistic environments.

Remaining unmarried did, however, have substantial impact upon the home, the key site for asserting artistic authority. At the affluent end of the spectrum, unmarried women purchased grand houses designed by respected architects, which bolstered their reputations as tastemakers spread across the South-East of England. Illustrator Maud Beddington enlisted W. A. S. Benson to design and decorate several cottages for her and her sister Beatrice in artistic Winchelsea, Sussex. Apparently, they ended up living 'in some luxury in adjoining houses' because they 'were not on speaking terms'.[20] May Morris (after her divorce) had streams of visitors keen to visit Kelmscott Manor, Oxfordshire, once home of William Morris, where she lived for many years with her companion Mary Lobb.[21] Widower Mary Sargant Florence, who also maintained a Chelsea studio, lived in a Queen Anne property called Lords Wood, best known today as having been a countryside refuge for the Bloomsbury set as a result of her daughter Alix's marriage to James Strachey. Wealthy and determined, Sargant Florence selected the beech-covered hills of Buckinghamshire near Marlow, an artists' colony, as the site for her home.[22] She decided against plastering the interior walls, instead painting them with frescoes. Inspired by Italian houses, she left many doorways without doors, covered only by curtains, and worked in a specially built studio in the back garden. Others in London had similarly privileged homes. Feodora Gleichen spent her entire life living and working at her studio at St James's Palace, as did Estella Canziani nearby at 3 Palace Green.

Such homes and studios by no means represented the typical living situations of unmarried Arts and Crafts women. The majority of women art workers experienced a range of domestic situations throughout their lives, which shaped the fields they worked in: pursuing painting and sculpture projects required far more space than jewellery making. The physical size of these spaces also influenced their ability to entertain – a key element in asserting status. At the Women's Guild of Arts, Honorary Secretary Mary A. Sloane was regularly contacted with housing enquiries. One letter wrote: 'They hope to go to London ... I suppose you do not know anyone who has a boarding house or a hotel not too expensive there. They are girls quite ignorant of these places.'[23] Families across the country relied on middle-class networks to find housing for the growing numbers of women seeking work and independence.

Many women continued to work from the family home, or boarded at the homes of family friends. Others moved into the purpose-built accommodation which began to be built in the late nineteenth century for the new generation of unmarried professional women in London areas like Bloomsbury and Kensington. Less restrictive than traditional boarding houses, these buildings still reassured the wider public that women were being partially supervised.[24] Mary Lowndes, originally from Dorset, lived in rooms at Sloane Gardens House, Ladies' Associated Dwellings Company in 1891 whilst in her early thirties, and Edith Harwood lived at York Street Chambers in 1894.[25] From this base, Harwood advertised in the *Woman's Signal* about the paid lectures she was giving on Italian pictures in the National Gallery, and wrote articles for the same paper.[26] Later, she illustrated C. R. Ashbee's *The Masque of the Edwards of England*, and published *Notable Pictures in Rome*.

Members of the Women's Guild of Arts often rented mansion flats and studios. These studios could be located a short walk from the family home, for visiting during the day, allowing women to fit their lives around established customs of respectability. Others moved into specially built studio houses. Those not born in London used, where possible, artistic success or family wealth to move strategically to known boroughs. M. V. Wheelhouse moved from Yorkshire to 3 Pomona Studios, 111 New Kings Road, where she appears to have lived with an artistic couple and a male artist in 1901.[27] Gaining access to a studio was critically important, offering physical space to work, professional validation, and the ability to assert status. The cost of maintaining studios could be expensive by contemporary standards: welfare campaigner Emily Hobhouse complained that nearly a third of the average income of a woman artist was needed to rent a studio in 1900.[28] The fact that many women did rent their own studios and flats is demonstrative of the high social standing of those who were able to make names for themselves as artists. Still, Florence Kate Kingsford lived in 'chronic poverty' before marrying curator Sydney Cockerell, and Pamela Colman Smith had to write desperate letters to publishers trying to get money she was owed.[29] A great many women used their studios to give art lessons, which helped to recoup costs and spread the ethos of the Arts and Crafts across a wider educational sphere.[30]

During this era, newspapers and the art press conducted regular interviews with male artists in their studios, which helped cement their reputations as figures of cultural significance. The *Pall Mall Gazette* interviewed painters like William Frith, whilst the *Studio* featured articles such as 'Afternoons in Studios. A Chat with Mr. George Frampton, A. R. A.'[31] Unmarried women artists were rarely asked to do extensive interviews in these papers, but they did begin to be subjected to detailed interviews in the women's press from the 1880s. Unsurprisingly, their homes and studios were positioned as a key focal point, a means to conjure the artistic personalities of these working women. Unlike their male peers, however, interviews tended to begin with a formulaic discussion of the inspiring domestic prowess of the artist and the femininity of the space, to assure readers these women were respectable and had not become 'unsexed'. Painter Fannie Moody was interviewed at her 'pretty residence' on Grosvenor Road for the *Woman's Herald* – Moody felt 'you will get a better idea of me there' – whilst readers of *Hearth and Home* were informed that pastelist Maud Coleridge kept her studio at William Street, Knightsbridge, filled with daffodils, tulips, and azaleas and positioned 'pictures of pretty women' on tall easels throughout the 'charming' room.[32] Although Irish painter Lizzie McGill strategically moved to London in the 1890s and rented a studio previously used by 'celebrated' animal painter Briton Rivière, a common strategy used by those seeking to bolster their positions, when McGill lived there – along with her servant and dog – it was depicted by the *Women's Penny Paper* as the 'prettiest' studio in Kensington.[33]

Women's studios became alluring spaces in the public imagination, and the ways they were discussed in the press often bypassed the intentions of the artists in question, instead being repeatedly framed in terms of performative femininity, fashionable high society, and a growing celebrity culture. But the women being interviewed were not passive figures in this discourse. Many clearly enjoyed presenting themselves in this way, and by asserting a degree of conformity to established models of femininity (often framed around 'prettiness') certain women – usually animal painters or portrait painters of the aristocracy – managed to market themselves, receive acclaim, and make a steady income.

Others, however, rejected this portrayal of artistic life at home and in the studio. Painter of battle scenes, Elizabeth Butler, decorated her studio with conventionally masculine adornments such as 'wild beast skins' and her 'arms and armour furbished up'.[34] Women associated with the Arts and Crafts movement rarely appeared in extended interviews in the women's press; this feminised framing likely did not suit their self-conceptualisation as 'serious' workers, while they ostensibly sought to avoid celebrity cultures. For the woman art worker, living and working in environments noticeably lacking in feminine domestic accoutrements was common. In these restrained studios and mansion flats, women practically and symbolically restructured domestic norms and fostered artistic lives on their own terms. For some at least, photography played a considerable role in asserting status. One, clearly posed, photograph of Feodora Gleichen in her studio, captures her seated away from the camera, dressed simply, skilfully using the tools of her craft and surrounded by work. The only hint of domesticity is the presence of her pet dogs (Figure 3.1).

A series of photographs in Canziani's papers turn a more informal lens on the Canziani family home. 3 Palace Green provided a regular set piece for family photographs, appearing as the model artistic retreat from the city. In one, the exterior walls have almost entirely been taken over with lush foliage, whilst in the distance a young Estella plays, probably with her mother (Figure 3.2). Another shows Estella, now an adult, cheerfully talking with her father and a visitor. She is dressed in a loose artist's smock and clutching painting materials, perhaps on her way to the garden studio (Figure 3.3). There are several snapshots of the studio itself: clearly a much-used workspace filled with paintings (Figure 3.4). The close juxtaposition of family life in the leafy idyll, the working studio, the smock of the art worker, and suggestions of upper-middle-class sociability all comingling in the same place – at once childhood home and site of artistic self-fashioning – reiterate the interwoven nature of artistic work cultures and domestic life.

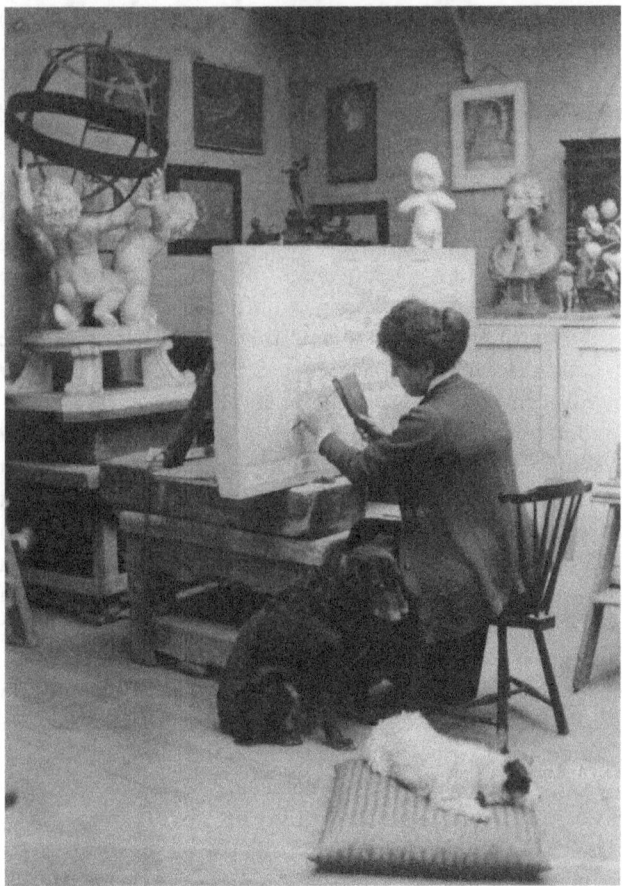

Figure 3.1 Lady Feodora Gleichen by unknown photographer, 1905 or after

But such embodiment of artistic ideals in the built environment was not exclusively the domain of the wealthy family home or palatial studio. Even a small, barely furnished workplace – particularly if located in the 'right' area – could position the artist as seriously committed. Mary Lowndes wrote a short story in 1912 about two women who rented a studio together in Chelsea, and detailed how it 'contained very little furniture ... a settee or divan, a table, and one or two chairs, which, with Tinker's rather grand easel and my very rickety one, made up, we felt, a strictly professional if unimposing interior'.[35] Pamela Colman Smith, who spent her early years touring with the Lyceum theatre group, lived at various times in England,

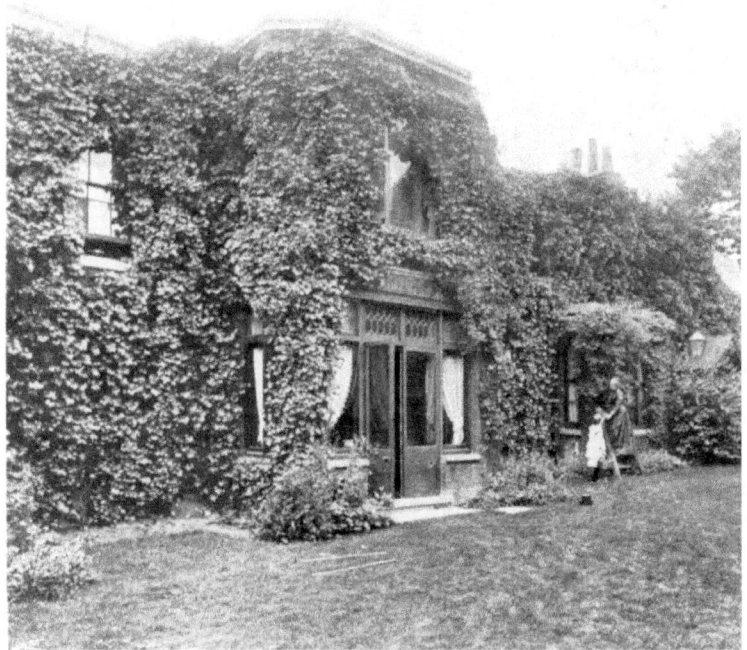

Figure 3.2 The exterior of 3 Palace Green, late nineteenth century

Jamaica, and North America. Her different flats and studios symbolised her independence and creativity, but also her financially constrained lifestyle.[36] Embroiderer Lily Yeats detailed in one letter to her father how 'Pixie is as delightful as ever and has a big-roomed flat near Victoria Station with black walls and orange curtains. She is now an ardent and pious Roman Catholic, which has added to her happiness but taken from her friends.'[37] After the First World War, Colman Smith's uncle died and left an inheritance, and she bought the lease for a property in the Lizard, Cornwall. Here she was at 'the centre of artistic interest' and started a vacation home for Catholic clergymen, which she decorated throughout in a variety of unusual colours.[38]

Despite the new freedoms offered by renting studios and flats, unmarried women were the first to be called home to look after families in times of need, a practice which significantly hindered independence and showed little sign of changing by the 1930s. There are many examples. Bookbinder

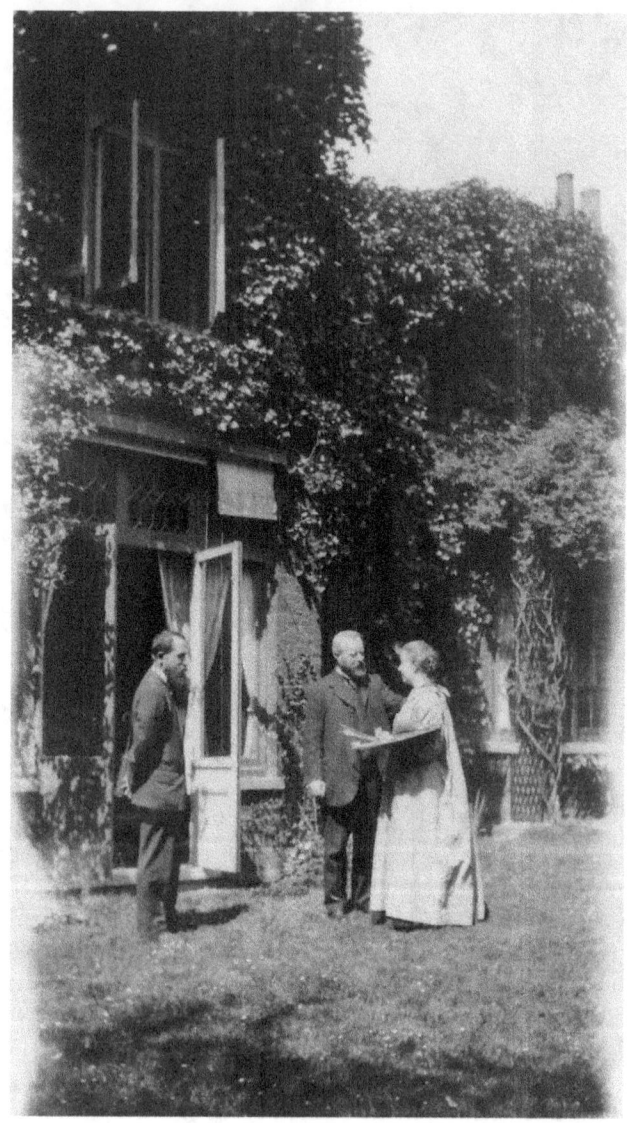

Figure 3.3 Estella Canziani wearing her painting smock working at her home studio, 3 Palace Green. Directly to her left is her father, early twentieth century

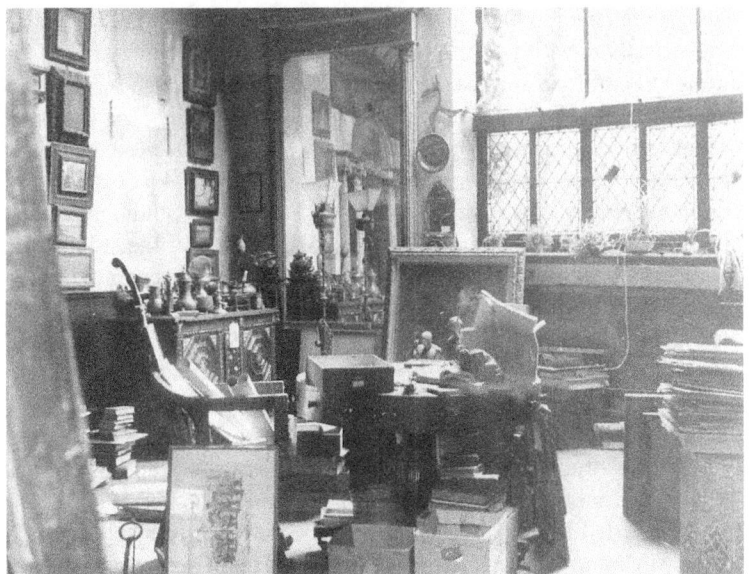

Figure 3.4 Estella Canziani and Louisa Starr's studio, date unknown

S. T. Prideaux went to Newnham College, Cambridge, in the 1870s but her father began to lose his sight and she had to return home.[39] A 1922 letter from 'Cecilia' to Mary A. Sloane discussed similar issues. Cecilia lamented her lack of time to work due to family commitments: 'I have had very little opportunity not being able to go sketching by myself – my brother is to be married next month, so my time will be rather scanty till that is over.'[40] There also continued to be concerns about unmarried women living alone. Writer Alice Dew-Smith described Prideaux as a 'poisonous cat' for supposedly spreading rumours about the propriety of the living arrangements of classical scholar Jane Ellen Harrison. Although Harrison did live with a female friend, the friend regularly made trips away, leaving Harrison alone. Due to Prideaux, Harrison felt she had to be extremely cautious about her living arrangements, even spending extended periods of time abroad herself, making it difficult for people at home to pry.[41]

Still, the pertinent point is that women were renting their own properties and carving out new domestic and working lives, despite societal concern. Women art workers undertook several measures to ensure respectability was assured, where possible employing servants and caretakers as chaperones. Helena Gleichen rented her own cottage to paint in whilst training, until her mother found out and forced her to employ a charwoman who slept there with her at night.[42] Eleanor Rowe lived and worked for a time at Pembroke Studios, Pembroke Road, which had an ornamental gatehouse where a caretaker could vet potential visitors.[43] The labour of caretakers and servants played a crucial role, removing the need for artistic women to exert energies on domestic tasks. In her book about the city, *Familiar London*, Rose Barton mentioned she had a studio caretaker, although she was dismissive of his role. She wrote that the studio was: 'handicapped with a caretaker whose only object in life was to save himself trouble. Nothing was ever dusted except by me. In vain I used to expostulate. He put on a dignified and injured look, and assured me he swep' this and swep' that the day before.'[44] This quotation is illuminating in Barton's assertion of her class authority, and is suggestive of her desire to show off her own domestic expertise. In comparison, however, Julia Alsop displayed gratitude at having a caretaker to clean her studio, writing this gave her crucial time to focus on her mezzotint engravings.[45]

Unmarried women often sidestepped societal concern and financial woes by living with sisters. In the Women's Guild of Arts alone there were many artistic sisters who lived together, or close by, throughout their lives, such as Alice and E. C. Woodward, Phyllis and Delphis Gardner, Maud and Beatrice Beddington, and Kate and Myra Bunce, amongst others. Embroiderer Una Taylor, an Honorary Associate, lived with her sister Ida, the novelist and biographer, at a 'small house' in Montpelier Square between the 1890s and the 1920s, where *The Times* detailed that they had 'received their many friends and conducted a literary salon, of which the characteristic notes were intellectual interest and Irish warm-heartedness'.[46] In one letter that Alice B. Woodward wrote to her publisher in 1920 she described how the Woodward sisters had moved from London and now all lived with their widower father in a 'colony' in artistic Bushey, Hertfordshire:

> We have a colony here sort of alms houses. We first, many years since, bought the 'Mulberry Bush' & then 'Lawn Cottage' & last year 'Tudor'. My father & some of my sisters live, and we all dine, at Tudor. One of my sisters & I live at the 'Mulberry Bush' & we furnished and let 'Lawn Cottage'. I give the address 'Tudor' as a general rule as we have paper stamps etc. & it [is our] headquarters & so many addresses are confusing. My studio which is exactly opposite is No. 19 Meadow Studios so you see I am a person of even more addresses … do come and see us I think it would interest and amuse you … I believe you would like it [the studio]. It's very big, 40ft. long & now that it is painted & cleaned & cleared out generally I confess gives me a good deal of pleasure.[47]

These alms houses functioned as a community organised around artistic needs, with different connected buildings which gave space for creativity, privacy, but also companionship. Here, Alice illustrated books and E. C. Woodward pursued metalwork projects.

Others instead found female partners or companions, routinely fellow art workers, to share their hybrid domestic workspaces with.[48] Although detailed archival traces are extremely limited pertaining to women in the Arts and Crafts, loving, intimate partnerships between women who were professional pioneers were common and accepted.[49] Mary Lowndes lived with her long-term partner and fellow stained-glass worker Barbara Forbes as 'co-occupier' with a maid at 259 King's Road, Chelsea, across the early twentieth century.[50] The short story Lowndes wrote about the two women artists – Cecilia and 'Tinker' – closely echoed the domestic situation of Lowndes and Forbes and provides a glimpse into their relationship. It too centred around a shared Chelsea studio based 'in a turning off the King's Road'. In the story, the two women's respectability was ensured because they had a caretaker, but although Cecilia lived in this space Tinker's parents expected her regularly to go home at night to sleep. Still, their shared studio provided new freedoms, and when possible they spent the nights together: 'The dark, cold studio after midnight seemed strangely empty and peaceful – at last we have it all to ourselves.'[51] Women built rich, intimate lives within spare moments at these artistic spaces, which were fostered further through joint commitment to constructing creative and emotionally fulfilling lifestyles together.

The marital home and studio

For women art workers, the question of marriage prompted deep thought. Having established lives which carved out space (often informal and hybrid) for work, privacy, and socialising, marriage symbolised great change and threatened to rupture the hard-won structures of artistic self-actualisation. But art, unlike many other fields, offered certain opportunities for women to marry *and* try to pursue a career – predominantly because the work could plausibly be carried out from home. At the Women's Guild of Arts in 1911, of fifty-nine members, at least twenty-five were, or had been, married.[52] They tended to have no children, or only one or two, who were looked after by servants. Most women art workers who married did so with artistic men (some working in the same field), often in their thirties after they had established their working lives, later than the national average of mid- to late twenties.[53] There were the painters Marianne and Adrian Stokes; gilder Mary Batten and painter and illustrator John Dickson Batten; potters Louise and Alfred Powell; painter Evelyn and potter William De Morgan; metalworkers Georgie and Arthur Gaskin; sculptor and modeller Phoebe Stabler and her husband, silversmith Harold Stabler; sculptors Gertrude and Gilbert Bayes; sculptor Ruby Levick and architect Gervase Bailey; metalworkers Edith B. and Nelson Dawson; and jeweller Charlotte Newman and her artist husband Philip H. Newman, amongst many others.

For some scholars, marriage has been best conceptualised as a largely negative and occluding force in these lives, leaving women 'veiled in mystery'.[54] Others, writing about specific women, in particular Mary Seton Watts, have argued that there continued to be potential for a married artistic woman to 'negotiate a space' to practise professionally.[55] Even though Mary Seton Watts stopped painting after marrying painter G. F. Watts, she pursued projects such as designing and making the Watts Chapel in Compton, Surrey, with local residents. Deborah Cherry, considering a wide range of painter couples, has similarly stressed the multitude of opportunities marriage could offer women.[56] This chapter builds on this approach, considering the corpus of women art workers as a whole, to allow for a fuller picture of the impact of marriage on the creation and sustenance of artistic careers.

The press was awash with debates about artistic marriages during this era. *Myra's Journal* warned readers about the perils of marrying penniless male artists.[57] On the other hand, there were also articles promoting men interested in art who had the necessary creative 'qualities which go far to convert a house into a home'.[58] By the final decades of the century, the suitability of husbands was increasingly assessed in relation to their likely conduct within the marriage, alongside more long-standing judgements about their 'breadwinning' capacities. Furthermore, in the women's press at least, articles rarely assumed the husband would be the sole worker in the household. In reaction to the growing opportunities for women to work in diverse fields, the press began to acknowledge that women's working aspirations could – and should – be adapted to fit with one's domestic duties. The *Girl's Own Paper* told readers: 'Even the literary woman and the female artist need to know something of housekeeping; it is a branch of knowledge which cannot be left out of any woman's daily life unless under the most peculiar circumstances.' Readers were assured 'It is a very wrong and false notion' that such women 'cannot make the best of wives and mothers'. Indeed, her 'extra refinement and delicacy' should enable her to 'exceed all other women in the way in which she holds both positions; while her greater breadth of mind should show her that it is no indignity to lay down her pen in order that she may make a pudding'.[59] Although these examples suggest there was space for creative and artistic work in the conceptualised perfect marriage within late nineteenth-century print culture, the implicit constraints upon this potential are evident. Women's artistic credentials were to be seen as fully integrated within their domestic duty – as markers of cultural sophistication and desirable feminine characteristics of sensitive expression – and yet were simultaneously not to be indulged to the detriment of the ability of the wife to act as curator of an idyllic domestic environment. Throughout, the pressures on women to conform to this limiting demand were pervasive.

Although social moralists hoped marriage would train women and men in the virtues deemed appropriate to their sex, artists and their families often discussed marriage in terms of companionship based upon mutual passions. When both partners had artistic interests, there was confidence the marriage would be a triumph. Upon curator Sydney Cockerell's engagement to Florence Kate Kingsford, he excitedly wrote to a friend, taking care to detail the field his fiancée worked in: 'I am engaged to be married to Miss Kingsford the painter of Hornby's Song of Songs. The ceremony will take place in some quiet country church in about ten weeks. No more book buying for me!'[60] Cockerell clearly saw Kingsford's calligraphy skills as important to their marital unity, and perceived marriage as a turning point in his own personal and professional life. In contrast, marriage between artists and non-artists could cause concern, as it was thought an artistic temperament might not be suited to married domestic life. One friend wrote to Louisa Starr that she thought she was a 'clever little woman, to have got it all your own way' – by marrying Italian civil servant Enrico Canziani – but added that she thought Enrico 'an angel, worthy to inhabit the sky with the Star [Louisa], for I think there are very few men who would do what he is doing'. Enrico's mother did not at first like him being engaged to an artist, thinking he 'might be happier with a beautiful young countess of the conventional type … and who would not have painting to interfere'.[61]

Courting was a critical stage when marriage and work were discussed to ensure compatibility. After Starr decided to marry she wrote to her fiancé listing the negotiations she was prepared to undertake. Contributing to the family finances, even if not precisely equal, from both partners, was important for her. She did not think it 'wise or right' for them to depend upon her income, although encouraged Enrico that 'we need not mind what other people think'. Going on, she stated: 'as you said you have about £500 or £600 a year, I could in one way or another add £300, or even £400'. She also removed the words 'promise to obey' from their vows.[62] Starr's example provides a critical snapshot of a developing model of middle- and upper-middle-class marriage, an institution in flux, where both partners could be expected to negotiate the continuation or otherwise of their respective profession: if not on an equal footing, then to their mutual advantage.

Paid work could significantly alter married power relations and held the potential to elevate the status of the wife within the marital relationship. Evelyn De Morgan contributed substantial financial funds from her success as a painter to her husband's pottery business.[63] Discussions about the need for both partners to contribute to the household income was a feature of letters between Edith B. and Nelson Dawson before marriage. Edith Robinson met and became engaged – even though her parents disapproved – to 'penniless painter' Nelson who had moved to Scarborough, where Edith lived, to work in an art shop owned by his uncle.[64] Nelson later moved to London and their courtship was conducted largely through letter writing. Edith sent Nelson her paintings for comment, and so they could be shown to other artists. One 1892 letter from Nelson about a painting she had sent described how 'C. J. Watson was looking at them today, Walter Sickert and thy brother yesterday'.[65] The couple had frank discussions about which artistic field was most profitable, and Nelson advised Edith to continue with flower paintings, describing these as 'likely to sell'. There appears no indication these sorts of discussions were unusual. He commended Edith on joining a life class in Scarborough, although he thought she should have regular access to undraped models and suggested she move to London for this. In 1892, the year before they married, he even invited her to London for a 'month or two' with her sister, framing this around the progression of Edith's professional career. He suggested she could:

> work in the evening life class at South Kensington and I should be only too pleased to help you with your work in the studio in the day time. It would do you any amount of good (professionally) and besides I think studio life at the schools would be a decided novelty to you and rather enjoyable probably, it has a refreshing independence about it. Several women-painters have studios here and there are some empty lodgings.[66]

Nelson complied with contemporary behavioural norms by suggesting Edith brought a companion and reassured her there would be other women partaking in these activities, but beyond this there appears little anxiety. Clearly, engagement and marriage held potential to offer women new opportunities to embed themselves in the metropolitan art world.

Upon marriage, Arts and Crafts couples often set up in collaborative partnership together. Homes and studios became key venues for work, and also spaces for intimacy and family life. Louise and Alfred Powell worked together, sharing a studio and employing two assistants in London, and also had the provisions of a studio at Wedgwood's Etruria factory.[67] Embroiderer Eve Simmonds lived and worked with her husband William on the top floor of Louise and Alfred Powell's house in Hampstead *c*. 1915. Here they prepared work for Arts and Crafts Exhibition Society exhibitions and made puppets for puppet shows in drawing rooms across the West End.[68] After marrying in 1893, the Dawsons' first home together marked a substantial shift for both. Since they barely had any money, Edith moved into Nelson's bachelor rooms at Wentworth Studios, built in 1885, at the heart of Chelsea. The Dawsons' daughter Rhoda described Wentworth Studios as the place where the couple 'camped out' together, 'having their kippers cooked on the studio stove'. The studio was emblematic of the Dawsons' early attempts to construct an artistic lifestyle together, but was also, through necessity, their sole domestic space. Edith even had to buy their bed from her savings due to Nelson's poverty. She later confided in her daughters that she had found it hard to adapt to this new rhythm of life, having to 'work all and every day, and missed very much the companionship of her cheerful girlfriends, now so far away'. Financial necessity drove the Dawsons. They stopped painting and focused on metalwork, with Nelson designing and Edith enamelling. Their shared studio home became 'a very well-staged studio hung with paintings and metalwork, beaten copper dishes, a candelabra with a sailing ship, doors with hand-wrought iron hinges … all common objects made beautifully'. By 1896, success had enabled them to move to a 'proper house', the Mulberry Tree, Manresa Road, Chelsea. The following year they moved again, this time to Swan House, Chiswick Mall, by the river in Hammersmith, centrally positioned within the artistic community, and a place where their professional and marital partnership could be nurtured.[69]

As public interest in artists grew, the homes of artistic couples attracted ever more interest. Their homes were portrayed as romanticised sites which should be celebrated by society. Journalists – across the press – stressed the historic nature of such relationships, positioning them in favourable relation to pre-industrial cottage industries where the whole family had been involved in the production process. Mary Seton Watts and G. F. Watts' homes were described as 'beautiful specimens of the artist-home. Not on the gorgeous scale of more fashionable and less ideal artists, but more consonant with the seriousness of the phase of art of which Mr. Watts is the chief exponent'.[70] Similarly to their unmarried peers, restrained taste was praised as demonstrative of suitable commitment to the artistic (and not hedonistic or overtly bohemian) lifestyle. *Hearth and Home* noted approvingly in the column 'Chats with Celebrities' that married painters Henrietta Rae and Ernest Normand lived in: 'an artist's house, like its neighbours in the Holland Park Road built for an artist and designed by an artist'. Their shared studio was simply 'a bare and workaday one. There is little in it beyond the easels and the pictures. On the one side is the husband's work ... on the other side the wife's.' The columnist suggested the studio represented 'partnership in the day's task which, since they first met at Heatherley's school both have found mutually useful'.[71] There was rarely any discussion of the complexities of everyday life in these households. The married artistic home instead functioned as an enticing visual advertisement – and also subtly represented the gradual move towards modern marital practices, where it would become increasingly expected that the wife may wish to work.

Shortly after moving to the Mulberry Tree, the Dawsons were interviewed in the *Studio*. In the piece, which this chapter began with, it quickly becomes apparent just how important the home could be in marketing the couple's work to the world, helpfully disguised as this was amidst the journalist's repeated enthusiastic outbursts about the authenticity of this hybrid artistic, domestic environment. The article discussed in opulent detail how: 'In the hall your eye is attracted by delightful and ingenious appliances in wrought copper, while the reception-rooms ... are full of most fascinating experiments in all sorts of metals.' The aesthetic appeal of the art on display at the house featured heavily, with the interviewer pointing out works which had been displayed at the New Gallery and the Royal Academy, continually emphasising objects 'which are too tempting to resist, and infect you with a covetous desire to carry them away'.[72] The home of the artistic married couple was clearly being imagined as diametrically opposed to the oppressive and restrictive world of traditional bourgeois domestic sociability, often portrayed as plagued with uninspired tastes and drab convention.

During this era, rooms in middle-class households were conceptualised in openly gendered ways: the drawing room designated for 'female' activities, the smoking room for 'male'. But in artistic households such separation does not seem to have been common. Instead, studios and workrooms constituted the axis around which household interactions oriented. In another article, this time for the *Architectural Review*, the editor reported that the Dawsons 'have chosen each a workroom – Edith Dawson for her enamelling, Nelson Dawson for his drawing – and both rooms look out and away over the garden'. Edith's room was on the top floor, 'on a level with the Mulberry Tree top that gives its name to the house'.[73] Her room had been described in the *Studio* as an 'artistic laboratory' which contained all the necessary tools for her craft, such as pestle, mortar, and furnace.[74] Nelson worked on the ground floor, sketching and designing in 'the draughtsman's workroom', supposedly 'distinguishable by the lesser neatness – a matter which is remedied from time to time by feminine incursions and alarms'. In these two rooms 'they do their own and personal work' with their workshops, operated by a group of men, in a street close by, 'surrounded by the studios of the Chelsea painters and sculptors – so close that they are able to watch the progress of their work'.[75] Presumably the feminine incursions are those of Edith (or domestic servants). Demonstrating the complexity of the mingling of artistic and home/studio life, the obligations incumbent upon the women partners in these relationships was both rhetorically obscured in the admiring press and implicitly revealed, through chance references to a silent and shadowy expectation of the intrusion of female domesticity in the home.

These workrooms can easily be viewed in gendered terms. Edith's enamelling room at the top of the house, likely to have been strategically close to the nursery, was portrayed as appropriately neat, an attribute commonly used to describe feminine traits, whilst Nelson's draughtsman's workroom was presented as chaotic and requiring cleaning. Callen has argued that contemporary articles about the Dawsons are troubling because the 'impression given is that she [Edith] furnished nothing but the manual labour while he [Nelson] was the "ideas man"'.[76] Callen's discussion of the Dawson's relationship is formed through selective quotations from these articles, but the *Architectural Review* did inform readers that a highlight of the visit was the 'dual regard and delightful co-operation in the work of the Dawsons. The collaboration is somewhat rare in national domestic life.' Admittedly, there was a continual tendency to focus on Nelson. However, the interviewer also sought to encourage public approval of their partnership: 'That they have managed to make such interdependence practical, as well as, in several ways, ideal, is, in itself, one of the grateful surprises the Mulberry Tree has under its shade.'[77] Furthermore, Edith took much pleasure in her role and saw this as a matter of collaboration rather than subordination. In her 1906 book on enamelling, which Callen does not reference, Edith proudly discussed her life as a 'worker' in the 'arts', reflecting on the 'joy and the care that all serious work brings', based in her 'little workroom which looks over the river, seated at a table spread with the implements of the enameller's craft, or standing, tongs in hand, before the furnace'. She concluded her book by asserting that 'Enamelling must be taken seriously; it entails work of both mind and body'.[78] Artist Rhoda Bickerdike, who felt Callen had misrepresented Bickerdike's mother Edith B. Dawson's role in her artistic partnership with Nelson, even wrote her own article, 'An Equal Partnership of Artists', in 1988 to correct what she saw as this historiographical misconception.[79]

The Dawsons photographed themselves working at home across their lives. One album the couple made for Edith's parents to celebrate Christmas 1895 provides a useful vantage point onto how the Dawsons themselves wished to represent their union. The album begins with a miniature photograph of the couple pasted on the first page. Below, their hand-inked initials are inscribed within illustrated leaves that link their names together on the branch of a tree, suggesting an equal partnership of artistic endeavour (Figure 3.5). Alongside shots of Edith and Nelson together and alone (Figures 3.6 and 3.7), the couple included images of Edith's mother and Nelson's sister. One closely framed shot of Edith at work in her new home (on the front cover of this book) directly contrasts with another of Edith before marriage, looking restless in her parents' drawing room in Scarborough, gripping a copy of *Century Illustrated Monthly Magazine* (Figure 3.8). Although both photographs were taken in domestic settings, Edith's life had changed profoundly with marriage, a transition she sought to depict for her peers in visual form. One photograph of the couple at home

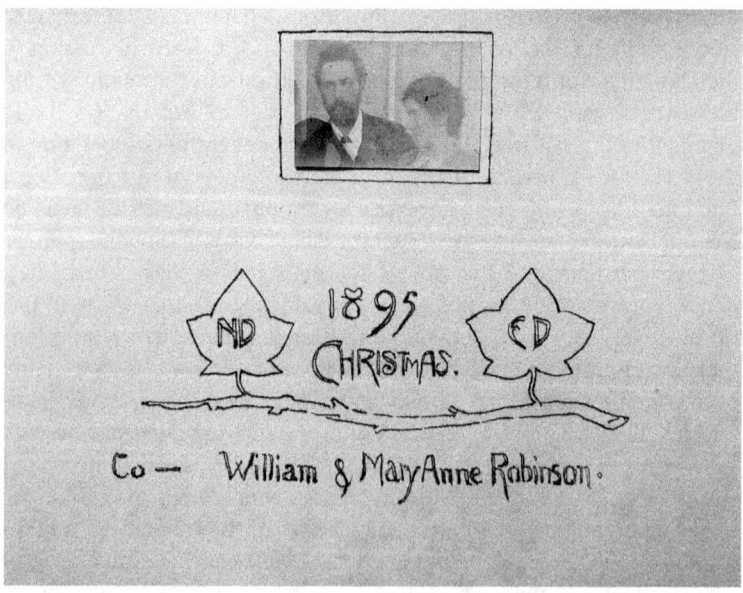

Figure 3.5 Front page of photo album made by Edith B. and Nelson Dawson for Edith's parents. Family album 1895

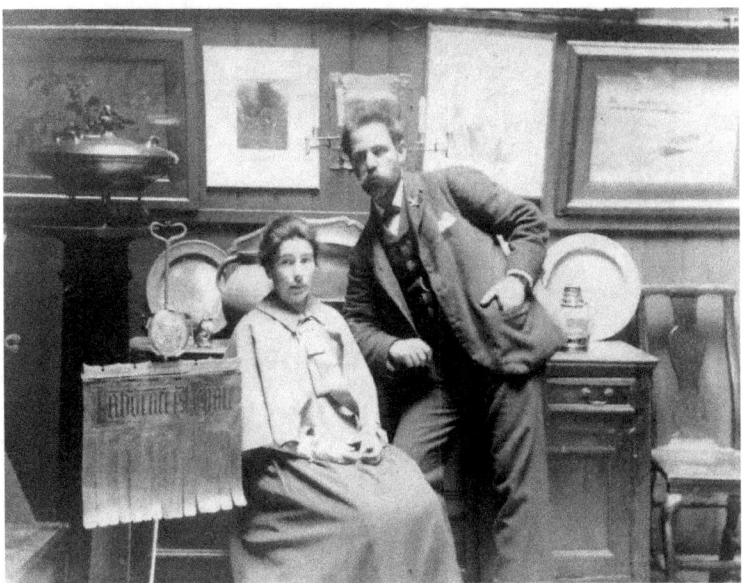

Figure 3.6 Edith B. and Nelson Dawson. The fringed sign to Edith's left says 'Laborare est orare' which means 'to work is to pray' and reflects their Quaker beliefs. Family album 1895

was published in the *Architectural Review* article, reiterating the sophisticated manner in which the Dawsons sought to market themselves and their artistic household to the world.

Clearly, artistic marriages and homes could offer new prospects for the construction of creative identities, with different models of behaviour being tolerated or even promoted, but also a diversification of opportunities. Several husbands made concerted efforts to showcase the skills of their wives. In a letter to the Victoria and Albert Museum in 1921, Alfred Powell ensured Louise Powell's work was clearly labelled, writing: 'Mrs Powell's full name to be given, viz. <u>Mrs Louise Powell</u> not Mrs Alfred Powell', and 'The ordinary title we use is as given AH and LP but if you have to mention Mrs Powell then it is Mrs Louise Powell.' In a letter touching on his wife's work in 1952, Alfred wrote further: 'I've been thinking about the vast amount of work she has done, and so well done – we are near our 6000th pot and she was always quicker than I a-doing! And then the embroidery – flower painting – illumination – a lot of work and all, as I have seen it, done right at the beginning and never

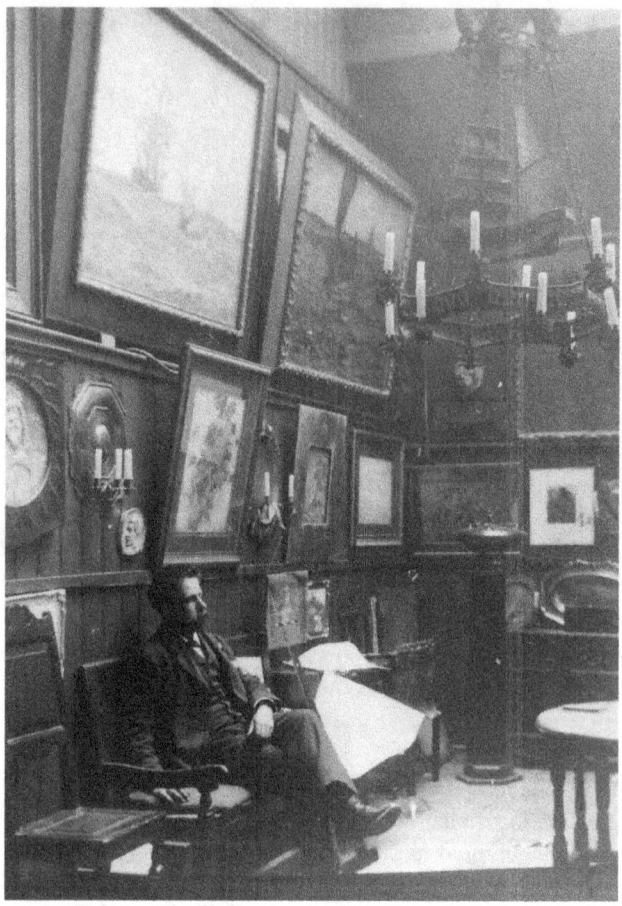

Figure 3.7 Nelson Dawson sitting below paintings by himself and his wife
Edith B. Dawson. Family album 1895

altered and very beautiful.'[80] Similar comparisons can be found with the
Dawsons. Nelson stressed his wife's involvement in interviews, crediting
her as equal, stating, 'My wife and I work together in this.'[81] A copper
bowl with cloisonné enamelled lid, bought by Queen Victoria in 1896,
was also inscribed with the lettering 'Nelson and Edith Dawson me made'
so there could be no doubt about who had been involved.[82]

Yet despite the artistic equality which husbands such as Alfred Powell
and Nelson Dawson emphasised, it remained common for the wife to be
responsible for orchestrating household tasks alongside artistic work. Edith

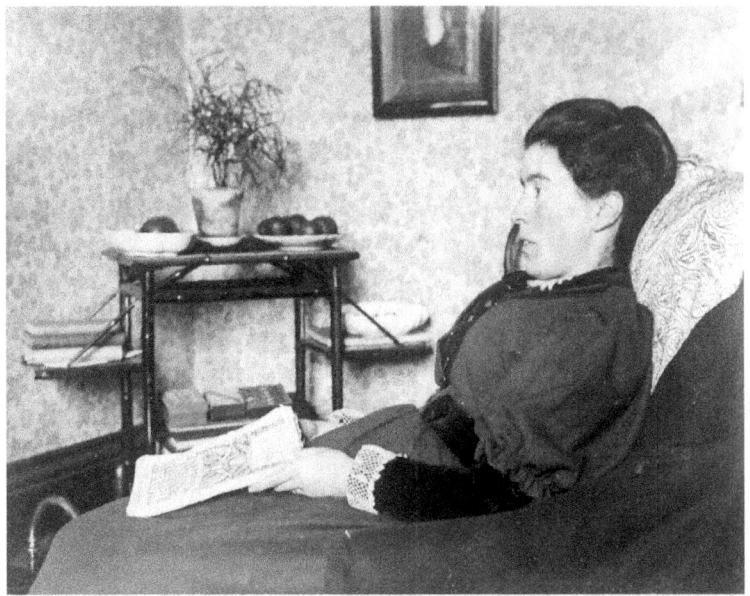

Figure 3.8 Edith B. Dawson in the parlour in Scarborough. Family album 1895

wrote to her artist friend Josephine Webb about the strains of domestic management. Josephine reminded her: 'you can't be quite equal'. They discussed Edith's extensive household duties, which Josephine knew 'must take a large share of your thoughts and energies – and you can have only a limited amount of time for Art'.[83] The prevalent model, with the wife in charge of domestic management, was therefore upheld in this aspect, regardless of how revolutionary these relationships could be in other areas. In a letter Phoebe Stabler sent to the art collector Eric Millar in 1952, from her home at 34 Upper Mall, Hammersmith, she wrote reflectively about her marriage to Harold Stabler. The letter provides a glimpse of the extensive domestic duties married women were expected to fulfil, and her anxieties people would assume her work was that of her husband:

> I found it impossible to work when my husband was in ... <u>creative</u> work one must be alone, and unworried to do fresh work, all day I was busy housekeeping and sewing. When at 5.30 H and his secretary went off teaching, I would gladly go into my studio and do <u>real</u> work. I must have been strong in those days. I could not do it all now. For a long time I have wanted to tell you this, that my work is my own, no one helped me with it, I feel I might have done something fine if I had had

help in the house, and freedom to work when I wanted to. When I have passed on, I would not like people to say 'she stole <u>her husband's work</u>.'

Underlining the words 'creative', 'real', and 'her husband's work', Phoebe Stabler added she had rewritten the letter several times, and had been uncertain about sending it, but needed Millar to know 'my work is really my own'.[84] Stabler was evidently all too aware that her own artistic production could get subsumed by her husband's in the eyes of wider society, particularly after her death.

Only very small numbers of women in the Arts and Crafts movement married non-artistic men. Here the demands of domesticity appear even more far-reaching. The case of woodcarver Julia Hilliam emphasises how extreme these changes could be. A memoir by her daughter Agatha reveals Hilliam came from a wealthy background, but her family 'ran into financial difficulties' and she was obliged to live with aunts. They moved to London and she trained in woodcarving at South Kensington Art School. She also had a brief stint studying in Paris and Brussels. Financial necessity drove her work as her aunts had burned through their capital 'with remarkable speed' and she had to support them.[85] She taught woodcarving for several county councils – teaching up to a hundred pupils a week – and spent her time 'on her bicycle rushing across Berkshire, to visit her classes'. Hilliam also rented a studio in Reading with her friend 'Miss Cromwell', c. 1897, where the public could view specimens of their work. Highly successful, designing and making furniture, lecterns, and pulpits, she was given several commissions by Princess Louise to undertake woodcarvings for the Royal Family, and in 1899 secured a position as 'Instructor in wood carving' at Reading College.

But after marrying statistician and economist Arthur Bowley in 1904, Julia's public activities were reformed around domestic life – although he had promised her, 'We will labour truly for the common weal … I propose no unequal match where you should be merged in my work'.[86] She initially continued her work at Reading College, whilst also keeping up her 'own professional wood carving at home', even when she had a baby (she had two servants). But by 1908 she had resigned, with the next baby born the following year.[87] In Agatha's view, Julia was, ultimately, '"merged in his work" while neglecting her own talents, which had not been the intention when they married'. Furthermore, she lost touch with her contacts at Reading, which 'was, I know, a great disappointment to her'.[88] Still, the home provided some limited opportunities to attempt to approach her twin roles as wife and artist holistically, running the household in such a way that enabled her to reassert her identity as both artist and homemaker.

She channelled her talents into designing the Bowleys' first family home: it had a veranda, balcony, and most importantly, 'a large studio for herself' and a separate study for her husband.[89] Clearly, it was initially intended that the home would allow both partners to pursue their chosen occupations in separate workspaces. Even in old age Julia continued to use her home for craft, with her loom taking up most of her bedroom.[90] But, unlike for some of her peers, marriage had imposed upon Julia Hilliam a painful compromise between the demands of domesticity and motherhood and those of the creative art worker.

The difficulties faced by women who married non-artists was shaped by their ability to participate in an artistic milieu, the availability of financial resources, the fields they worked in, and by the specific dynamics of each marriage. Louisa Starr provides a perfect example of how becoming a mother and wife did not have to mean one's artistic career was so overtly threatened. In contrast to Hilliam, the worst that Starr received was surprised, yet congratulatory letters from her friends when she had a baby.[91] Louisa's status as an established, wealthy bohemian woman seems to have exempted her from a wide range of societal expectations surrounding domestic life. Similarly, when Louisa suffered difficulties because she did not have sufficient space to work, painting in the drawing room of 14 Russell Square with her mother 'on guard', her wealthy husband's resources resolved the problem. As her daughter Estella recounted:

> My mother needed a better studio than her adapted drawing-room, and was always looking for a house. One night she dreamed of an ideal house, but she thought no more of the dream. When one day, driving in Kensington Palace Gardens, she saw a board up, 'House to Let', and recognized the house and the surroundings of her dream, she telegraphed to my father, who had reached Paris on his way to Italy: 'Found a house, come back', and he returned.

The couple purchased 3 Palace Green in 1886 and Starr 'built the studio' in the courtyard where she could finally 'work alone in a real studio'. Two years later Estella was born 'in this old-world corner of Kensington'.[92] For such wealthy women there was more potential to reshape the family life and home to suit their needs: the servants rose at dawn with Louisa Starr when she had painting deadlines and needed full days for painting.[93] Still, even Starr felt the obligations of household management impinged on her ability to dedicate herself to her career. She reflected in a lecture for the International Congress of Women in 1899 that: 'We women are heavily handicapped in Art, as in all else, by the fact of our womanhood and its duties. I hold that when a woman has a profession it means in most cases that she has two professions.'[94]

Married Arts and Crafts women reconfigured dominant Victorian understanding of marital domesticity through their creative pursuits, altering the culture of homes and studios and the relationships that took place within these spaces. Clearly, the demands of marriage, which brought with it expectations of adherence to conventional classed and gendered domestic practices, and sometimes children, impacted enormously on daily life and ability to pursue an artistic profession. It is often argued that after marriage women artists were subsumed into, and concealed behind, the careers of husbands. However, if we look past the narrow lens of the press to analyse marriage through a wider array of source materials which better capture these domestic situations, the extensive attempts made by women to pursue both marriage and artistic lives comes into sharper focus. The marital home provided a powerful material way to display dedication to art, functioning as a constant reminder of artistic intent. Marriage could be a site not simplistically and exclusively of marginalisation and the obscuring of women's contributions, but also one of collaboration, support, and the fashioning of intertwined artistic identities.

Building Arts and Crafts networks at home and in the studio

Where you lived mattered. It brought with it a certain amount of prestige which could reinforce social respect; attract customers, patrons, and collaborators; and obtain invitations to social events where links with networks of fellow artists could be fostered. Where possible, artists sought to immerse themselves in middle- and upper-class neighbourhoods by living in South-West London, around Kensington and Chelsea, Hammersmith, and Holland Park, and in Hampstead and St John's Wood in North-West London. Contemporary accounts are filled with descriptions of the rural and romantic aesthetic of these areas of the city. A typical 1881 portrayal of Chelsea emphasised it was: 'home of the refined arts'.[95] Another, in 1913, described St John's Wood as the place to which 'both Art and Nature may be said to have fled some decades ago from the commercial and industrial banalities of Town'.[96] Celebrated painter Frederic Leighton, who lived at 12 Holland Park Road, Kensington, and fellow painter Lawrence Alma-Tadema, at 44 Grove End Road, St John's Wood, received streams of visitors to their 'palaces of art'.

Women art workers were active participants in these cultural zones. Members of the Women's Guild of Arts who were based in the capital predominantly lived in West London in the early twentieth century. A hot-spot was Glebe Place, Chelsea, a famed area for artists. Painter Rose Barton rented a studio there, as did Emily Ford. Ford's studio was described as 'a meeting-ground for artists, suffragists, people who *did* things'. She and her neighbours held 'famous "coffee smokes"' evenings, where they wandered in and out of each other's studios, whilst figures such as William De Morgan told ghost stories.[97] Barton wrote in her book *Familiar London* that Chelsea was 'a happy hunting-ground for artists, professional and amateur', where she could carry a 'sketching stick' or even an easel and 'beyond a small crowd of interested playmates have suffered no inconvenience whatever'. She contrasted Chelsea favourably with other areas where her painting adventures attracted too much public attention.[98] Others enjoyed comparable privileges a short stroll away. Elinor Hallé worked from 8 Upper Cheyne Row and Mary Sargant Florence had a studio at 1 Smollet Studios, Cheyne Walk. She later rented 43 Glebe Place. Elsewhere in Chelsea and Kensington there was Mary Lowndes, Evelyn De Morgan, Annie Swynnerton, Estella Canziani, Feodora Gleichen, Alys Fane Trotter, Mary A. Sloane, Edith Harwood, and Alice B. and E. C. Woodward, amongst others. In Hammersmith there was May Morris, Phoebe Stabler, and Edith B. Dawson, and several more of their friends, based in a line of houses nestled on the edge of the river.

Community, reorganised along artistic lines, was a key factor in the acquisition of these houses and studios. One 1903 article detailed Alice B. Woodward's integral contribution to the Chelsea art scene, writing that she 'lives and works in Chelsea, where so many artists foregather; here as everywhere she is a general favourite'.[99] The familiar presence of friends, often a walkable distance away, helped create and sustain a spirit of comradeship. Stained-glass artist Clare Dawson represented her social network in a handmade map of the city (Figure 3.9). It depicts the homes of three Guild members who were also family members. Sculptor E. M. Rope and her niece D. A. A. Rope shared a studio. Another Rope, E. M.'s niece, stained-glass window maker M. E. A. Rope, had a studio nearby. Their homes and studios are positioned alongside historic sites of the city (Fulham Palace, Fulham Pottery, founded *c.* 1671, and the King's Road, complete with miniature drawings of Charles II), imbuing the cityscape with a sense of tradition and artistic heritage. This drawing neatly embodies an artistic conception of the space of the city, as a nexus of studios, houses of art workers, and monuments to historic tradition.

Nowhere was this network of homes and studios made so tangible as in the practice of holding regular 'At Homes', a widespread domestic ritual in the nineteenth and early twentieth centuries. Each week, on a selected day, the woman heading the household was expected to designate time away from domestic duties to entertain guests. Marion Sambourne, wife of *Punch* cartoonist Linley Sambourne, documented her extensive

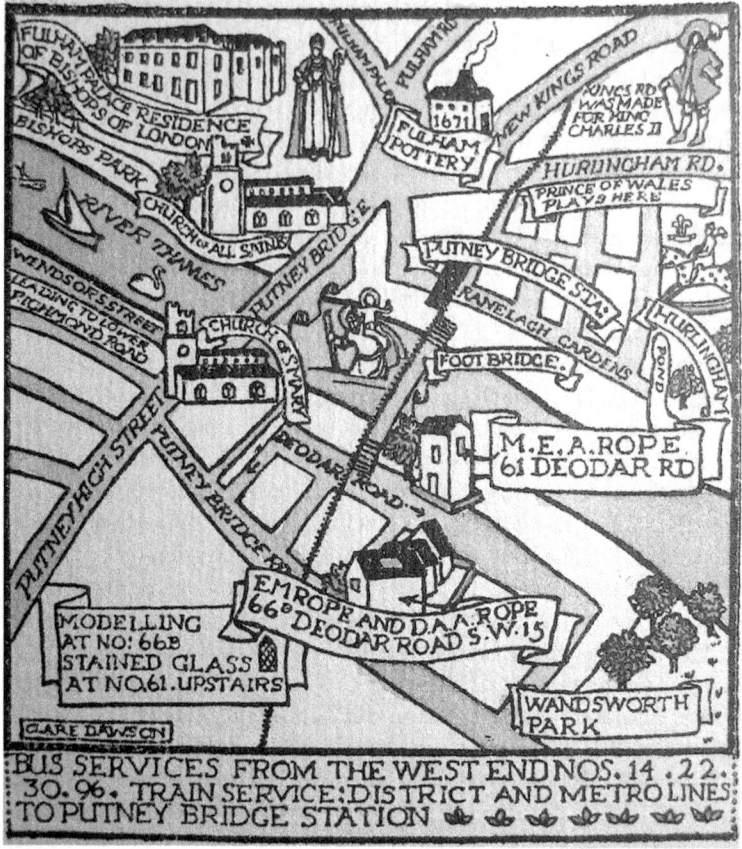

Figure 3.9 The studio network of the Rope family in London as depicted by Clare Dawson

schedule of 'At Homes' in her diary, providing testimony of their regularity within literary and artistic circles: 'Mrs. Alma-Tadema had her at home day on Monday, Mrs. Rider Haggard on Wednesday, Mrs. du Maurier on Thursday, and Mrs. Marcus Stone on Sunday.'[100] Feminist scholars have viewed etiquette practices such as 'At Homes' as forming part of a repressive social model that encouraged the trapping of women within private domestic positions. Leonore Davidoff takes a broadly negative view of such codes of gentility, in her words it was 'one of the most effective instruments for social control ever devised'.[101] Suffrage campaigner Evelyn Sharp, in her short story 'The Other Anna', written in 1897, shared this view. She portrayed her main character as being released by turning her back on her 'At Home' day, writing: 'no one who was a bit nice ever called on her At Home day' and 'the only interesting people were the people who never called on one at all ... at this point of her reflections she laughed unaccountably, and resolved to give up her At Home day'.[102] For some contemporary women, 'At Homes' were clearly representative of the restrictions inherent within a lifestyle from which they wished symbolically to break free.

But among women art workers, this seems to have been a minority view. Instead, 'At Homes' functioned as an adaptable practice which could be at once intimate and informal, and yet maintained a framework of respectability. This remained true even when the objectives of such meetings were radical or progressive. Many suffrage campaigners relied on their 'At Homes' to demonstrate class status, respectability, and simultaneously to draw upon their social networks to organise politically. Painter Emily Ford hosted an 'At Home' at 44 Glebe Place, Chelsea, where attendees could meet 'Mrs. Fawcett about Women's Suffrage' and have coffee and cigarettes.[103] The proximity of artists to suffrage campaigners in London meant women were regularly being drawn into suffrage debates due to local encounters on the street. In an environment where fostering collaborative and quasi-institutional networks was so important, the relatively low-key 'At Home' was a tool which could be exploited very actively to further an artistic career, providing a way to visit and invite new people into one's life with little questioning of motive. All adults in the middle- and upper-middle-class home tended to have calling cards; these began to function as business cards in the art world, enabling women and men greater agency in controlling how they were perceived by society. 'At Home' cards could be slipped into pockets, added to letters, and placed on hall tables when making visits. The 'At Home' became the default window into the interior life and process of self-fashioning of the artist. By the 1880s interviews with artists were increasingly framed as 'At Homes', enabling a mass audience who could not physically attend – or who had not been invited – to participate by voyeuristically imagining they too were welcomed into the hybrid space of the home studio, where the comforting respectability of middle-class domesticity blended with a heady mix of intimacy, celebrity, creativity, and authenticity.

Artistic women constructed extensive social worlds at their homes and studios which functioned as important counter-settings alongside their activities within guilds and clubs. Often refused entry to art classes, or feeling unwelcome in masculine settings, women made art together in sympathetic environments. Rose Barton enjoyed the opportunities her studio offered her to form new relaxed friendships away from the stifling demands of conventional domesticity. She wrote: 'what a delightful contrast one finds in the cosy fire in one's studio, in one's own ingle-nook, with the kettle on the hob' and that '"dish of tea with one's greatest pal"! Oh! 'tis all glorious.' She perceived all 'minor grievances' to be forgotten when:

> two or three of us, after trying to sketch on the Embankment in the short winter evenings, till one's fingers were too much numbed to hold the brush, used to get back to a cheerful fire and discuss one's failures over tea and rounds of buttered toast and muffins. Only those initiated into 'studio tea' can know to what a pitch of excellence toast and muffins can rise![104]

Many of these networks became formalised over time: the '91 Art Club was founded because of the friendships which had developed between women living in studios in Chelsea. In 1894, E. C. Woodward and her sister Alice were involved in a competition to design invitation cards for the Club. One of E. C. Woodward's cards was a striking black-and-white piece portraying an illustrated series of women's faces which invited recipients to attend a Club 'At Home' at 8 Trafalgar Studios, Chelsea (Figure 3.10). Their hair, flowing around them, connects the women, creating a harmonious representation of a united artistic 'sisterhood'. Published with several others in the *Studio*, the card is emblematic of the emergence of a widely recognised, fashionable, women-focused artistic culture. The writing on Woodward's card is presented on the back of a large framed canvas, demonstrative of the Club's artistic nature yet also suggestive of an element of secrecy, showing the sophisticated ways such women, alongside pushing for more public opportunities, continued to align their activities with an elite artistic and intellectual model where social codes of secrecy and membership status played a critical role in the establishment of reputations. The card is also demonstrative of the porous and fluid definitions of domesticity, as these women spatially – but not linguistically – began to move professional meetings out of domestic settings and into studios and workshops.

Similarly for Women's Guild of Arts members, although formal meetings took place at the Guild Hall, many 'At Homes', demonstrations, parties, and 'private' exhibitions, took place at their homes and studios.[105] Here many members felt freer, away from the formal, masculine atmosphere at the Hall, to perform their artistic roles on their own terms. They relied on buildings belonging to wealthier members such as Estella Canziani and Maud Beddington, who rented 9 St Paul's Studios, Hammersmith, which had been built in 1891 and was designed to suit the requirements of 'bachelor' artists. In 1916, several Guild members hosted a week-long 'At Home' there, giving papers, showing art, and listening to music.[106] In

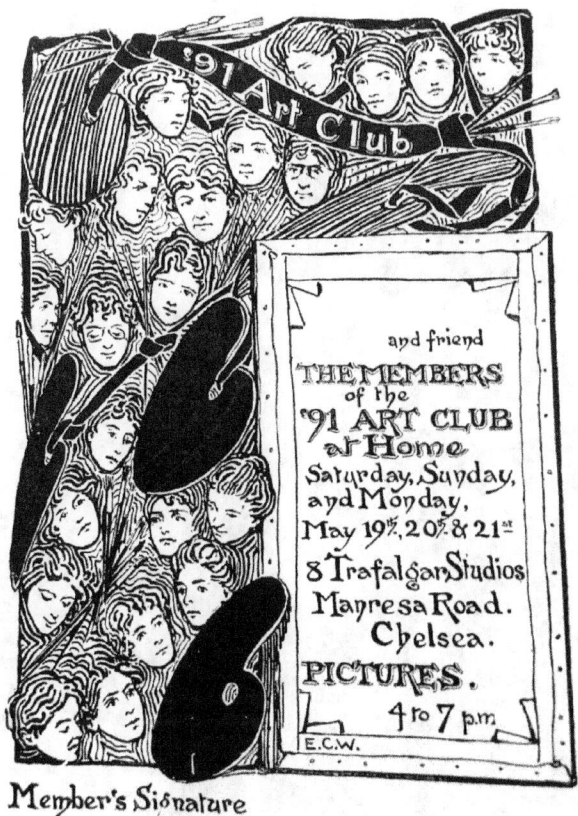

The card reads:

> '91 Art Club
>
> and friend
>
> THE MEMBERS
> of the
> '91 ART CLUB
> at Home
> Saturday, Sunday,
> and Monday,
> May 19ᵗʰ, 20ᵗʰ & 21ˢᵗ,
> 8 Trafalgar Studios
> Manresa Road.
> Chelsea.
> PICTURES.
> 4 to 7 p.m.
> E.C.W.

Member's Signature

Figure 3.10 E. C. Woodward's card for the '91 Art Club, 'The '91 Art Club at Home', *Studio*, 3 (1894), p. 96

a similar fashion to the Hall's architectural presence and austere, professional environment – which it was felt alleviated amateur or feminine connotations – 'known' studios such as St Paul's Studios were significant venues in the strategies of professionalisation implemented by women art workers. Guild member Ruby Levick had made sure to rent 5 St Paul's Studios the very decade the studios were built (Figure 3.11).[107]

Events at studios and artistic houses were not regulated in the same ways as male-only clubs, and this sense of liberation was clearly part of their appeal. Entrance was decided by those living in the household, and in these progressive environments new mixed-sex networks flourished. Mary A. Sloane visited Edward Burne-Jones's studio on Sunday afternoons

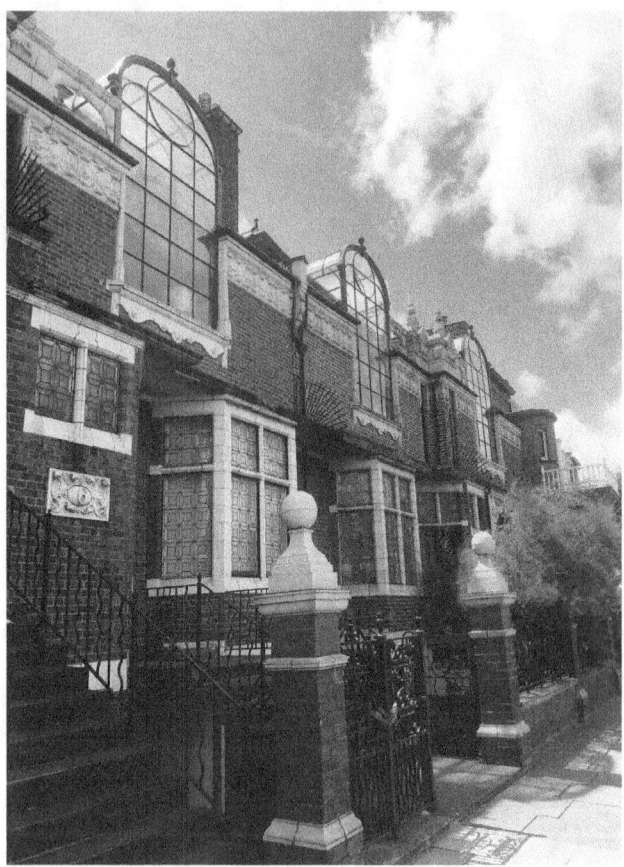

Figure 3.11 St Paul's Studios, Talgarth Road, London, 2019

when it was open for visitors to peer in and see the paintings on display.[108] One of Edith Robinson's friends wrote to her in delight in 1892 about a literary evening at Nelson Dawson's studio:

> We went, and enjoyed it immensely, it was most delightfully informal and sociable, it is so nice to go amongst people who don't try to be 'genteel' if you know what I mean. Four of us Slade girls went, and Win, so they must have been rather overdone I am afraid with aspiring female students.[109]

The erosion of societal restrictions in the 'At Home' even allowed unmarried women to invite men to attend events in a domestic setting. In one 1896 letter, Margaret M. Jenkin invited Mary A. Sloane to attend a lecture at the home of E. M. Rope:

> Would you care to hear a lecture on 5th century Greek sculpture by Mr Hill of British Museum? – it will be held on Wednesday next at 8 in Miss Rope's rooms 107 Marylebone Rd. I am going ... I shall be arriving at Baker St Station at 7.48 ... if you can meet me there.[110]

These women were at ease with a male speaker talking in the private rooms of Rope – who was unmarried – and were confident about travelling the city at night by public transport. Artistic sociability based in studios and homes evidently provided a less rigidly structured, and more permissive, environment for women's professional and intellectual activities. Furthermore, not all of the potential deconstructions of conventional restrictions were relating to gender. Estella Canziani, who took over her mother's home studio and entertained 'artists, scholars, scientists and visitors of many nationalities' recalled one potentially fraught meeting in 1914 where 'members of nine nations, including Germans, met in friendliness for tea in my studio. The barriers were forgotten in mutual admiration of one another's work.'[111] Taking tea together at Canziani's studio helped forge a sense of group identity focused on art, which temporarily minimised other identity markers.

The social practice of the 'At Home', while linked to the traditionally feminised sphere of middle-class domesticity, was not as absolutely delineated by gender as it would first appear. This is true in two senses: firstly, male artists seem to have used 'At Homes' in roughly analogous ways to those adopted by women, although, of course, they did not face the same pressures to carve out an alternative space for artistic self-fashioning as a result of institutional and associational exclusion. In 1901, the *Art Record* stated that 'Studio At Homes were general all over London last Sunday', and referenced mostly men.[112] The page detailed that certain male artists had refused to admit 'the casual visitors' of 'Show Sunday', portraying greater male concern about appropriate etiquette in artistic sociability than normally admitted in the scholarship. Secondly, the presentation of women-led artistic 'At Homes' to the outside world did not usually adopt any trace of the 'feminine', spurning this for a purely professional aspect. The cards used to invite participants simply stated the name and field the artist was working in. They were also by no means all held within private homes. By the early twentieth century E. C. Woodward was hosting 'At Homes' at her Notting Hill workshop (Figure 3.12). 'At Homes', in some ways at least, provided an opportunity to constitute a space where gendered division was not so omnipresent.

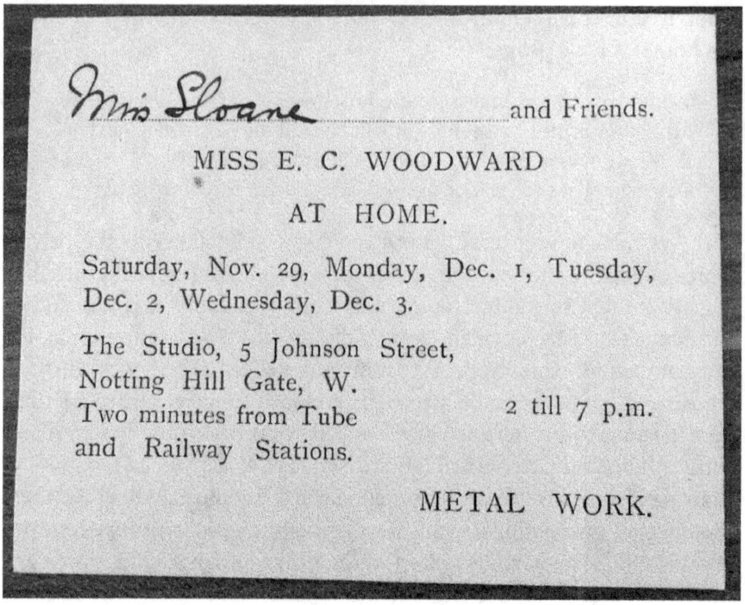

Figure 3.12 E. C. Woodward, 'At Home', 1913

This is not to say, however, that women in artistic marriages were not obligated to take on the practical arrangements for the planning and execution of these events, while often being portrayed as 'the artist's wife'. Writer Arthur Ransome discussed in *Bohemia in London* (1907), his popular book about artistic life in the capital, an evening at Pamela Colman Smith's studio where he had made friends with 'Benn' (likely the painter, etcher, and engraver Alphaeus Cole), who asked Ransome to visit his studio, upon which 'he gave me a card with his address upon it, for which he had to ask his wife'. Social etiquette was viewed as a task for his wife Peggotty, who was also an artist. At the event, Benn got overexcited about a 'gigantic two-edged sword' hanging on the wall and tried to swing for it; his wife calmly and 'instantly brought him to sense and saved the place from devastation. Instead, he described the picture he was painting.'[113] Ransome also detailed a time when Peggotty:

> who was strong on the social side of a painter's life, gave an 'at home' in their studio for the benefit of some American visitor who was likely to buy a picture … I used to go round and do my part in making the buyer feel that he was lucky to get it.[114]

Conversely, some artistic couples issued invitations for 'At Homes' which acknowledged their existence as a partnership of artists, such as Phoebe and Harold Stabler, who jointly invited the Women's Guild of Arts to their Hammersmith home to view 'the mace for Westminster cathedral'.[115] Even in the phenomenon of the organisation of 'At Homes', marriage could result in a diversity of outcomes, ranging from productive partnership to unequal distribution of domestic labour.

This chapter has shown that outside of the segregated world of institutions and associations, women were able to take a more central role in mixed-sex artistic sociability within the quasi-deregulated space of the home and studio, utilising the 'acceptable' model of the creative soirée of the 'At Home'. While many journalists and writers continued to conceptualise the artist par excellence as a lone man working in his studio, women art workers' contributions to the social scene could position them at the heart of the artistic cityscape. One final example illuminates these contradictions and also demonstrates how far abstracted from the conventional model of *petit bourgeois* domesticity such practices could be. Ransome's *Bohemia in London* exemplifies the opportunities for artistic sociability to be oriented around a female-led studio evening. A chapter titled 'In the Studios' first situates the studio as a site for the performance of artistic masculinity. The imagined artist is male, 'his coat off ready for work, strolling up and down with a cigarette between his lips', absorbed by painting his model during the day – 'slashing in the rough work' – before heading to one of London's male-only artistic clubs for an evening of revelry.[116] However, in another chapter titled 'A Chelsea Evening', where Ransome details a characteristically bohemian night in the city, he situates discussions around the studio of Pamela Colman Smith, who is given the pseudonym of 'Gypsy'. Without modifying the archetype of the artist, Ransome nevertheless portrays an idealised artistic social culture as taking place within a woman's studio, demonstrating the efficacy of sociability as a tactic for women art workers seeking to infiltrate these networks. Colman Smith's studio, 'a mad room out of a fairytale', was where people went to 'meet the best poets and painters and men and women of spirit in the town'. Ransome lingered over his descriptions, seeking to convey to readers that this studio was authentic, with its dark green walls adorned with 'brilliant-coloured' drawings, etchings, and pastel sketches, and tables cluttered with bottles of painting inks. The room contained various symbols of the sophisticated taste and individuality of its inhabitant: cigarette boxes, burning incense, and a 'broadly whiskered picture-dealer' poring over a book of Japanese prints. There was even a 'woolly monkey perched ridiculously on a pile of portfolios', which appeared to grin 'at the cast of a woman's head'.[117]

Such studio evenings were not a mere archetype disseminated by Ransome but were a popular and fashionable fixture in London artistic life. Colman Smith entertained friends and potential customers at least once a week, even keeping a guest book to record and show off famous attendees. Regular visitors included poets William Butler Yeats and John Masefield, alongside Ransome and Cole.[118] It was not just within her own studio that Colman Smith positioned herself at the heart of networks of artistic culture and intellectual sociability. She travelled back and forth across the Atlantic, telling folklore stories in private houses and clubs across London and New York. The *Brooklyn Daily Eagle* entertained readers in 1904 with stories of how: 'In London drawing rooms the enthusiasm and the fashion of the hour is Pamela Coleman [sic] Smith' who, 'in a brilliant frock of orange with a red turban', would sit on a board with lit candles around her and tell 'crowds of delighted people weird and strange folklore tales of Jamaica'.[119] Colman Smith took advantage of the networks available to her to construct a transatlantic world of artistic socialisation, framed around her diverse creative interests.

These bohemian studio parties are suggestive of a world far removed from staid meetings in drawing rooms, but in fact many artistic figures were more concerned about the dictates of etiquette than often assumed. Scholars tend to frame artists as 'outsiders, foreign to normal society', who did not adhere to commonly accepted conventions of social inter-action.[120] Yet an examination of the lives of art workers has revealed ongoing engagement in numerous etiquette models for both women and men. There was often an *adaption* rather than a *rejection* of middle-class codes of conduct, even whilst these individuals sought to assert their authenticity, exceptionality, and unique artistic lifestyles. This was especially important for those in the applied arts (rather than the fine), where there was greater suspicion about class status. The 'At Home', far from being a blunt mechanism for social control and the limitation of women's professional and social lives, could be a tool for the creation of new artistic roles, linked to a vibrant network of home and studio spaces, constantly alive with the assertion of cultural authority.

The breadth of situations experienced by this group of women, unmarried and married, reveals the importance of homes, studios, and family life in facilitating and – at times – severely restricting the development of an artistic, professional self. Gendered attitudes about domesticity, marriage, and respectability altered women's choices in ways which continued to be potentially detrimental for artistic aspirations across the period spanning the 1870s to the 1930s. Yet for many of these women, rooms at home were key spaces in which they could try to mitigate the effects of social restrictions. The studio and the artistic home could be employed by women as a means to represent themselves as expert art workers. By the early twentieth century, 'At Homes' – which merged professional endeavours within the rhythm and structure of domestic daily life – were deeply entrenched practices and provided the central framework for a busy world of socialisation across London and England. Such lives contradict the conception of women as lone outliers, held at a distance from a masculine network of male bachelor artists: on an informal level, artistic women and men interacted in a series of intermeshing communities. By piecing together rapturous depictions in the press, literary writings, photographs, fragmentary archival materials, and memoirs, the efforts of women across the Arts and Crafts to turn their homes into workspaces, and to – jointly – use these homes and studios to create an extensive nexus of artistic sociability, becomes clear. The next chapter analyses several of these women who went even further: turning studios into workshops and setting up small businesses spread across the capital.

Notes

1 E. B. S., 'Interview with Mr. and Mrs. Nelson Dawson', *Studio*, 6 (1896), pp. 173–178 (p. 173). Italics in original.

2 For women's studios, with particular focus on painters and illustrators, see: Deborah Cherry, *Painting Women: Victorian Women Artists* (London: Routledge, 1993); Deborah Cherry and Janice Helland (eds), *Local/Global, Women Artists in the Nineteenth Century* (Farnham: Ashgate, 2006); Lynne Walker, 'Vistas of Pleasure: Women Consumers of Urban Space in the West End of London, 1850–1900', in *Women in the Victorian Art World* (ed.) Clarissa Campbell Orr (Manchester: Manchester University Press, 1995), pp. 70–85; Lynne Walker, 'Women Patron-Builders in Britain: Identity, Difference and Memory in Spatial and Material Culture', in *Local/Global, Women Artists in the Nineteenth Century* (eds) Deborah Cherry and Janice Helland (Farnham: Ashgate, 2006), pp. 121–136. More generally see Caroline Dakers, *The Holland Park Circle: Artists and Victorian Society* (New Haven: Yale University Press, 1999); Charlotte Gere, *Artistic Circles: Design and Decoration in the Aesthetic Movement* (London: Victoria and Albert Museum, 2010); Giles Walkley, *Artists' Houses in London, 1764–1914* (Aldershot: Scolar, 1994).

3 Virginia Woolf, *A Room of One's Own* (Oxford: Blackwell, 1929).

4 A small cluster did attend school. For example, May Morris went to Notting Hill High School, London.

5 Bertha E. Mahony and Elinor Whitney, *Contemporary Illustrators of Children's Books* (Boston: Bookshop for Boys and Girls, Women's Educational and Industrial Union, 1930), p. 80.

6 'Interview', *Women's Penny Paper* (18 January 1890), p. 145.

7   Helena Gleichen, *Contacts and Contrasts* (London: Murray, 1940), p. 21.

8   Anthea Callen, *Angel in the Studio: Women in the Arts and Crafts Movement, 1870–1914* (London: Astragal, 1979), p. 219.

9   Rhoda Bickerdike, 'The Dawsons: An Equal Partnership of Artists', *Apollo*, 128 (November 1988), pp. 320–325 (p. 320).

10 Mahony and Whitney, *Contemporary Illustrators*, p. 80.

11 University of Reading, Special Collections, Bell papers, 329/260, Alice B. Woodward to 'Mr Bell', 16 September 1908.

12 Estella Canziani, *Round about Three Palace Green* (London: Methuen, 1939); 'Interview', *Woman's Herald* (12 November 1892), p. 9.

13 Gleichen, *Contacts and Contrasts*, pp. 21–22.

14 A. M. W. Stirling, *William De Morgan and His Wife* (New York: Holt, 1922), pp. 173, 174, 177.

15 Canziani, *Round about Three Palace Green*, pp. 53, 72–81.

16 Gleichen, *Contacts and Contrasts*, p. 8.

17 Jan Marsh, *Jane and May Morris: A Biographical Story, 1839–1938* (London: Pandora, 1986), pp. 98, 102.

18 In 1851, just under one quarter of all women younger than thirty were unmarried. Rebecca Jennings, *A Lesbian History of Britain: Love and Sex Between Women since 1500* (Oxford: Greenwood, 2007), p. 61.

19 Gordon and Nair have rejected the argument that nineteenth-century single, unsupported women were 'fettered by an all-powerful ideology which decreed that they languish in the home of a male relative'. Eleanor Gordon and Gwyneth Nair, *Public Lives: Women, Family and Society in Victorian Britain* (New Haven: Yale University Press, 2003), p. 64. Holden has, however, recently asserted that the 'shadow of marriage' had a major influence on unmarried singles in the twentieth century. Katherine Holden, *The Shadow of Marriage: Singleness in England, 1914–1960* (Manchester: Manchester University Press, 2007).

20 Ian Hamerton, 'W. A. S. Benson: "Gentleman Architect"', in *W. A. S. Benson: Arts and Crafts Luminary and Pioneer of Modern Design* (ed.) Ian Hamerton (Suffolk: Antique Collectors' Club, 2005), pp. 181–236 (p. 210).

21 For more on Lobb and Morris's relationship see Simon Evans, 'The Eclectic Collection of Miss M. F. V. Lobb' (unpublished paper, National Library of Wales, 2017).

22 'Exhibition: Paintings and Sculpture at Lord's Wood', *Country Life* (17 June 2009), p. 98.

23 WGAA, unknown author to Mary A. Sloane, undated.

24 Christiana Herringham and Agnes Garrett were amongst the founding Directors of the Ladies' Associated Dwellings Company in 1888. Elizabeth Crawford, *Enterprising Women: The Garretts and Their Circle* (London: Boutle, 2002), p. 207.

25 'Notes', *Women's Trades Union Review* (1 April 1891), p. 12.

26 'Lectures', *Woman's Signal* (20 December 1894), p. 395; Edith Harwood, 'Studies from Pictures of Women in the National Gallery', *Woman's Signal* (4 July 1895), p. 6.

27 1901 census. The others were William P. Dickson and Mary and Charles J. Preetorius [sic].

28 Emily Hobhouse, 'Women Workers: How They Live, How They Wish to Live', *Nineteenth-Century Magazine*, 47 (1900), p. 473.

29 Stella Panayotova, *I Turned it into a Palace: Sydney Cockerell and the Fitzwilliam Museum* (Cambridge: Fitzwilliam Museum, 2008), p. 41; Pamela Colman Smith often called publishers 'pigs' as they routinely failed to pay her on time, fairly, or give her royalties. Huntington Library, AP 1677, Colman Smith to Albert Bigelow Paine, 17 March 1901.

30 See Katharine Adams's advertisement for 'Bookbinding', *Cheltenham Looker-On* (24 November 1906), p. 21 or Julia Hilliam's advertisement offering 'Wood Carving and Modelling' classes in the *Windsor and Eton Express* (6 February 1897), p. 1.

31 'An Artist at Home: An Interview with Mr. W. P. Frith, R. A.', *Pall Mall Gazette* (22 May 1885), p. 1; 'Afternoons in Studios. A Chat with Mr. George Frampton, A. R. A.', *Studio*, 6 (1896), p. 205.

32 'Interview', *Woman's Herald* (6 June 1891), p. 515; 'People, Places, and Things', *Hearth and Home* (7 April 1898), p. 878.

33 'Interview', *Women's Penny Paper* (13 September 1890), p. 1.

34 Elizabeth Butler, *An Autobiography* (London: Constable, 1922), p. 184.

35 Mary Lowndes, 'Dr Faustus', *Englishwoman*, 13/38 (1912), pp. 206–220 (p. 206).

36 Melinda Boyd Parsons, *To All Believers: The Art of Pamela Colman Smith* (Delaware: University of Delaware, 1975), unpaginated.

37 Joseph Hone, *J. B. Yeats: Letters to His Son W. B. Yeats and Others, 1869–1922* (London: Secker & Warburg, 1983), p. 162.

38 Parsons, unpaginated.

39 Marianne Tidcombe, *Women Bookbinders, 1880–1920* (New Castle: Oak Knoll, 1996), p. 104.

40 WGAA, 'Cecilia' to Mary A. Sloane, 1922.

41 Annabel Robinson, *The Life and Work of Jane Ellen Harrison* (Oxford: Oxford University Press, 2002), p. 70.

42 Gleichen, *Contacts and Contrasts*, p. 31.

43 Kate Orme, *Artists' Studios Supplementary Planning Guidance* (London: Planning Information Office, 2002), p. 20.

44 Rose Barton, *Familiar London* (London: Adam and Charles Black, 1904), p. 87.

45 WGAA, Julia Alsop to Mary A. Sloane, 27 February 1923.

46 'Miss Ida Ashworth Taylor', *The Times* (22 October 1929), p. 18.

47 University of Reading, Special Collections, Bell papers, 353/237, Alice B. Woodward to 'Mr Bell', 24 May 1920.

48 Sculptor Ruby Levick wrote to Mary A. Sloane asking if she knew anyone who would 'like to share a studio, either to work in or to hold classes' at Edwardes Square. Levick was 'anxious to let half of mine if possible'. It was: 'A nice bright one with a very good north light. I think it would do excellently for black and white or etching etc.' WGAA, Ruby Levick to Mary A. Sloane, 19 February 1902.

49 Sharon Marcus, *Between Women: Friendship, Desire, and Marriage in Victorian England* (Princeton: Princeton University Press, 2007); Laura Doan and Jane Garrity (eds), *Sapphic Modernities: Sexuality, Women and National Culture* (London: Palgrave Macmillan, 2006); Martha Vicinus, *Intimate Friends: Women Who Loved Women, 1778–1928* (Chicago: University of Chicago Press, 2004).

50 1911 census.

51 Lowndes, 'Dr Faustus', p. 220.

52 WGAA, Membership List, 1911.
53 Joan Perkin, *Victorian Women* (London: John Murray, 1993), p. 237.
54 Callen, *Angel in the Studio*, p. 156.
55 Melanie Unwin, 'Significant Other: Art and Craft in the Career and Marriage of Mary Watts', *Journal of Design History*, 17/3 (2004), pp. 237–250 (p. 237); Lucy Ella Rose, *Suffragist Artists in Partnership: Gender, Word and Image* (Edinburgh: Edinburgh University Press, 2018).
56 Cherry, *Painting Women*, pp. 32–44.
57 Florence Marryat, 'For Ever and Ever', *Myra's Journal* (1 May 1891), p. 17.
58 Dorothy Chips, 'Miss Chips' Chatter', *Illustrated Chips* (16 March 1895), p. 7.
59 Alice King, 'Higher Thoughts on Housekeeping', *Girl's Own Paper* (12 January 1884), p. 235.
60 Arthur L. Schwarz (ed.), *Dear Mr. Cockerell, Dear Mr. Peirce: An Annotated Description of the Correspondence of Sydney C. Cockerell and Harold Peirce in the Grolier Club Archive* (High Wycombe: Rivendale Press, 2006), p. 31.
61 Canziani, *Round about Three Palace Green*, pp. 27–28.
62 Ibid., pp. 29–32.
63 Cherry, *Painting Women*, p. 37.
64 Bickerdike, 'The Dawsons', p. 321.
65 Private archive, Dawson papers, Nelson Dawson to Edith Robinson, 24 March 1892.
66 Private archive, Dawson papers, Nelson Dawson to Edith Robinson, 1892.
67 Cheryl Buckley, *Potters and Paintresses: Women Designers in the Pottery Industry, 1870–1955* (London: Women's Press, 1990), p. 77.
68 Cheltenham Art Gallery and Museum, 'Eve Simmonds: A Personal Account Compiled from Conversations and Letters to Heather and Robin Tanner', 1971, and 'A Taped Conversation with John Gwynne, of Quenington, Gloucestershire on the Subject of William and Eve Simmonds', 1980.
69 Bickerdike, 'The Dawsons', p. 322.
70 Kineton Parkes, 'Modern Artists and Their Methods', *Atalanta* (1 April 1896), p. 460.
71 'Chats with Celebrities', *Hearth and Home* (13 August 1891), p. 405.
72 'Interview with Mr. and Mrs. Nelson Dawson', *Studio*, pp. 173, 177.
73 'Nelson and Edith Dawson', *Architectural Review* (1 December 1896), pp. 35–45 (p. 35).
74 'Interview with Mr. and Mrs. Nelson Dawson', *Studio*, p. 175.
75 'Nelson and Edith Dawson', *Architectural Review*, p. 35.
76 Callen, *Angel in the Studio*, p. 156.
77 'Nelson and Edith Dawson', *Architectural Review*, p. 42.
78 Edith B. Dawson, *Enamels* (London: Methuen, 1906), pp. 1–3, 197.
79 Bickerdike, 'The Dawsons', p. 324.
80 Aberystwyth University, Ceramic Collection, Kathy Talbot, 'Alfred and Louise Powell', unpublished paper, undated; Annette Carruthers and Mary Greensted (eds), *Simplicity or Splendour: Arts and Crafts Living – Objects from the Cheltenham Collection* (Cheltenham: Cheltenham Art Gallery and Museums, 1999), p. 116.
81 'Interview with Mr. and Mrs. Nelson Dawson', *Studio*, p. 175.
82 Bickerdike, 'The Dawsons', p. 323.
83 Private archive, Dawson papers, Josephine Webb to Edith B. Dawson, 24 January 1897.

84 Huntington Library, Eric Millar papers, Phoebe Stabler to Eric Millar, 1 January 1952.

85 Agatha Bowley, *A Memoir of Professor Sir Arthur Bowley (1869-1957) and his Family* (Britain: self-published, 1972), pp. 49-54.

86 Ibid., pp. 52-55.

87 Ibid., p. 61.

88 Ibid., p. 68.

89 Ibid., p. 60.

90 Ibid., p. 74.

91 Canziani, *Round about Three Palace Green*, p. 47.

92 Ibid., pp. 35, 60, 61.

93 Birmingham Museum and Art Gallery, Estella Canziani papers, handwritten document by Louisa Starr depicting 'A Day in the Life of a Woman Artist'.

94 Huntington Library, Sanford and Helen Berger Collection, 608188, Louisa Starr, 'The Spirit of Purity in Art', paper read at the Art Session of the Women's International Congress, London, 1899.

95 William Spencer Clarke, *The Suburban Homes of London: A Residential Guide to Favourite London Localities, their Society, Celebrities, and Associations, with Notes on their Rental, Rates, and House Accommodation* (London: Chatto and Windus, 1881), p. 90. Although suitable sites became scarcer as the price of developments continued to rise, Chelsea's status was confirmed in the 1921 census. This noted the area had the greatest concentration of male artists in the capital, at nine per 1,000 men. The next highest was Hampstead with six per 1,000 men. Census records for 1921.

96 Alan Montgomery Eyre, *Saint John's Wood: Its History, its Houses, its Haunts and its Celebrities* (London: Chapman and Hall, 1913), p. v.

97 Dora Meeson Coates, *George Coates: His Art and His Life* (London: Dent, 1937), pp. 40-41. Italics in original.

98 Barton, *Familiar London*, pp. 85-86, 118-119.

99 E. M. Evors, 'Some Women Illustrators of Children's Books', *Girls' Realm*, 5 (1903), pp. 455-463.

100 Shirley Nicholson, *A Victorian Household* (Gloucestershire: Sutton, 1994), p. 53.

101 Leonore Davidoff, *The Best Circles: Society, the Season and Etiquette* (London: Croom Helm, 1973), p. 36.

102 Evelyn Sharp, 'The Other Anna (1897)', in *Nineteenth-Century Short Stories by Women* (ed.) Harriet Devine Jump (London: Routledge, 1998), pp. 383-397 (p. 387).

103 WGAA, 'At Home' card for Emily Ford, 1907.

104 Barton, *Familiar London*, pp. 87-88, 196.

105 Zoë Thomas, 'At Home with the Women's Guild of Arts: Gender and Professional Identity in London Studios, c. 1880-1925', *Women's History Review*, 24/6 (2015), pp. 938-964.

106 WGAA, card for 9 St Paul's Studios, 26 June to 3 July 1916. The main members involved were Mary A. Sloane, Ethel Everett, Mabel Esplin, and Letty Graham. There are numerous other examples.

107 Algernon Graves, *The Royal Academy of Arts: A Complete Dictionary of Contributors and Their Work*, 5 (London: George Bell, 1906), p. 48.

108 WGAA, Georgiana Burne-Jones to Mary A. Sloane, 19 January 1890.

109 Private archive, Dawson papers, 'Sophia' to Edith B. Dawson, 12 January 1892, underlining in original.

110 WGAA, Margaret M. Jenkin to Mary A. Sloane, 5 December 1896.

111 Canziani, *Round about Three Palace Green*, p. 4.

112 'The Editor's Studio', *Art Record: A Weekly Illustrated Review of the Arts and Crafts* (6 April 1901), p. 104.

113 Arthur Ransome, *Bohemia in London* (New York: Dodd and Mead, 1907), p. 59.

114 Rupert Hart-Davis (ed.), *The Autobiography of Arthur Ransome* (London: Cape, 1976), p. 89.

115 WGAA, Phoebe and Harold Stabler 'At Home' card for Guild members, undated.

116 Ransome, *Bohemia in London*, pp. 69, 71, 79.

117 Ibid., pp. 54, 57–58.

118 Parsons, *To All Believers*, unpaginated.

119 'Winsome Witchery in London Drawing Rooms', *Brooklyn Daily Eagle* (1 November 1904), p. 9.

120 Davidoff, *The Best Circles*, p. 78.

4

'Artistic' businesses and 'medieval' workshops

I n an 1895 interview titled 'A Lady Goldsmith', the goldsmith in question, Charlotte Newman, detailed her approach to managing her jewellery business at 18 Clifford Street in central London for readers of the *Woman's Signal*. Newman informed them:

> I took these premises four years ago, and set up my own workshops. I have a competent set of workmen, and take apprentices. I am my own foreman, and never have any trouble with my *employés* – indeed, I fancy that they like a lady 'boss.' I alloy all the gold myself, and tell the men what is to be done.[1]

The *Woman's Signal* was a publication keen to promote the new opportunities available for middle-class women wishing to work in the 1890s and clearly hoped to align Newman's business with this politicised objective. But the interview also provides a rare glimpse of an unexplored world of women's entrepreneurship in the arts, which deviates greatly from the dominant narrative of the English Arts and Crafts movement as revolving around the workshops of a small cluster of male designers such as William Morris. Most importantly, Newman was part of an active group of women who pursued new artistic and professional opportunities through small-scale entrepreneurship during this era. By independently establishing their own businesses they augmented their positions in the Arts and Crafts movement and in wider society.

This chapter reframes understanding across multiple fields of scholarly inquiry by providing the first account of the network of women such as Newman who established 'artistic' businesses where they independently designed, made, and sold their work during the era spanning the 1870s to the 1930s. Across the capital, this network spread through the West End and into 'artistic' Kensington, Chelsea, and Hammersmith. Business owners included: Newman; M. V. Wheelhouse and Louise Jacobs at Pomona

Toys toyshop; E. C. Woodward and Agnes Withers of the metalwork workshop Woodward and Withers; Pamela Colman Smith of the Green Sheaf Press, alongside many other owners of metal, stained-glass, bookbinding, needlework, leather, and weaving shops and workshops. Women also set up businesses in urban and rural locations across the country, such as Annie Garnett's hand-spinning and weaving business, the Spinnery, in the Lake District. My focus is the activities of business owners who were members of professional groups such as the Women's Guild of Arts and the Lyceum Club – women who were committed to workshop cultures, skilled design, and historic methods of production.[2] The social and cultural contexts in which figures such as Newman, Wheelhouse, and Woodward positioned themselves – just as much as the objects they designed and made – were central in connecting them to contemporary understanding of the Arts and Crafts.

'Professionals' and 'entrepreneurs' are often portrayed as fixed, separate categories: a distinctive identity people either historically did or did not manage to gain access to and 'become'.[3] Furthermore, art historians have understandably tended to emphasise artworks or the designer's creative process instead of considering 'artistic' entrepreneurship, due to the implied focus on commercialism and profit. This has, however, truncated understanding of how 'artistic' business owners carved out new positions in society. Throughout, I foreground self-representation and contemporary discourse rather than relying on late twentieth-century modes of categorisation. Overt rejection of one's commercial, entrepreneurial intent, and even professional aspirations, was a central strategy used by many contemporaries, in particular those associated with the Arts and Crafts. But in actuality these individuals still relied upon numerous – cleverly disguised – professional and entrepreneurial methods to claim cultural capital.

Uniting these traditionally separated categories of work culture enables a richer account of the processes these historical actors were involved in, the reputations they upheld, and the ways gender hierarchies were independently reworked – away from institutional cultures – at a critical moment in the making of the modern art world. Central to the performance of 'authentic' artistic masculinities in the late nineteenth and early twentieth centuries was the idea of the 'medieval' workshop. Male Arts and Crafts figures persistently portrayed 'artistic' business ownership as an essentially masculine pursuit, foregrounding the dirty, busy, and intimate authenticity of male-only workshop cultures. The range of workshops and businesses women established, and the breadth of local, national, and international interest, is delineated in the second part of this chapter. The most important negotiation which permitted the establishment of such businesses concerned the creation of a respectable identity in the face of competing demands, and this topic is addressed in the final section. Women continually had to legitimise their positions as business owners and professional art workers, as well as maintain positions as middle-class women. They faced extensive domestic and familial expectations, financial hardship, and had to maintain respectability through constant navigation of the 'social borderland' between public and private.[4] The *fin de siècle* was a moment when there were extensive discussions in the press about the emergence of a little-studied cultural figure: the 'lady shopkeeper', eager to sell her fashionable stock. Women art workers sought to differentiate themselves from this wider feminised hinterland by instead portraying their premises as spaces of 'serious' 'artistic' work, stressing factors such as the allure of having a 'medieval' workshop on site. I trace how these women benefited from propinquity and asserted expertise, respectability, and historic methods of artistic production through print culture, photography, quotidian encounters, and established middle- and upper-class networks.

Throughout, engrained narratives which position elite male cultural production as the nexus around which interest in the Arts and Crafts, design, urban modernity, medievalism, and England's artistic reputation coalesced are challenged. The artworks these women designed and made were bought and sold internationally. Many of these objects have disappeared without trace, undoubtedly due to the gendered acquisition choices of museums and galleries in the mid- to late twentieth century, but also because such items have been eagerly purchased to be placed in private households and collections. Still, in their day, these businesses became crucial spaces which enabled a network of women to play an influential part in disseminating the ethos of the Arts and Crafts across an array of new local, national, and international spheres of influence.

Arts and Crafts masculinities: combating the commercial at the 'medieval' workshop

The Arts and Crafts movement blossomed in the final third of the nineteenth century in direct response to the growth in industrialisation, urbanisation, and mass consumption. This stoked great public and artistic interest in an idealised world of the simplicity and beauty of medieval workshops, part of an acute social nostalgia for a romanticised pre-industrial past. A desire to engage more fully in the small-scale workshop model of design and making was central to William Morris's strategies when he started the celebrated firm Morris, Marshall, Faulkner & Co. with a number of his peers in 1861 (it became Morris & Co. in 1875, with Morris as sole manager). The first headquarters were at 8 Red Lion Square, Bloomsbury, where the 'Firm' – as they called themselves – had an office, showroom, and most importantly workshops in which they could design and make handcrafted objects, ranging from metalwork and carpets to stained glass.[5] The 1880s saw many more Arts and Crafts workshops and businesses being established across the city, one of the most famous being C. R. Ashbee's Guild and School of Handicraft, which was established in the East End of London in 1888, and later moved to the village of Chipping Campden in Gloucestershire.

By the turn of the century, the word 'art' was increasingly – as argued by art historian Alan Crawford – being 'attached to anything from a tea tray with a couple of peacock's feathers painted on it to radical craftsmanship of the most Ruskinian kind'.[6] Suspicion was ever growing about the commercial aspirations of artists, part of a wider anxiety about the profit-driven, entrepreneurial fervour of capitalist society, which we saw permeating the exhibition scene in Chapter 2. There was a widely held view in society that artists should be guided by an innate calling to their craft, and across print culture readers were repeatedly told that 'the artist is a simple creature, devoid of business instincts'.[7] But for all this public avoidance of profit, the outputs of the Arts and Crafts movement fed into a booming international art market, something the vast majority of artists quietly encouraged.

Workshops were always at the heart of the strategies of early adherents but as the movement became more popular the workshop became critical in signifying 'serious' and 'artistic' commitment, alleviating anxieties, and engendering a sense of authenticity, for artists, journalists, and customers alike. Ashbee argued in 1917 that although the movement had not managed to revolutionise modern industry it had made the 'great social discovery' of recovering 'the small workshop'.[8] His earlier *Craftsmanship in Competitive Industry* provides an extensive history of the Guild of Handicraft, including several sketches and photographs of unnamed labouring men in flat caps and aprons, portrayed in the setting of the workshop, hard at work, surrounded by the dirty authenticity of wood chippings, offcuts of their work, and the smut of coal.[9]

Gustav Stickley, who established the Arts and Crafts inspired Craftsman Workshops in North America, stated that the purpose of the workshop was 'not the work itself, so much as the making of the man; the soul-stuff of a man is the product of work, and it is as good, indifferent or bad, as is his work'.[10] A great many of his peers felt similarly: that the workshop represented the very 'making of the man', imbuing his work with irresistible credibility. Positioned in these workshops, figures such as Stickley and

Ashbee held up their sites of work on both sides of the Atlantic as material examples of dedication to the movement. Here, different men could form close bonds of solidarity and commitment to a world that seemed to be slipping away. Ashbee's interview process for employing working-class men supposedly consisted of 'a steady gaze into their eyes and a firm grasp of the hand', an approach intended to judge character rather than measure skill. Indeed, Ashbee's biographer even stressed that Ashbee 'probably did not prize his designs in themselves', instead prioritising processes of making and interpersonal interactions between men, which it was believed would make the world a better place.[11]

Ashbee's vision of the workshop was framed around the need for this to be a space for male labour and he appears considerably frustrated at the repeated attempts by women to encroach on this. Although small numbers of women were involved in the Guild of Handicraft – often aristocratic women who paid to watch the men work – his published writings reveal the considerable concerns about female participation circulating at his business:

> In the Guild's workshops our fellows are rightly nervous of this competi-
> tion of the amateur, especially the lady amateur, and albeit with the
> utmost consideration they speak of her generically as 'dear Emily.' I
> have seen a great deal of her work in the last ten years, she is very
> versatile, she makes jewellery, she binds books, she enamels, she carves,
> she does leatherwork, a hundred different graceful and delicate crafts.
> She is very modest and does not profess to any high standard, nor
> does she compete in any lines of work where physique or great experience
> are desired, but she is perpetually tingling to sell her work before she
> half knows how to make it, and she does compete because her name
> is legion and because, being supported by her parents she is prepared
> to sell her labour for 2d. an hour, where the skilled workman has to
> sell his for 1s. in order to keep up standard and support his family.

Ashbee claimed to keep his own album of letters from different 'Society ladies' who had written to him, desperate for him to give 'dear Emily' a chance. His diatribe appears to be a rallying call against female participation by the early twentieth century, positioning the involvement of women on par with the horrors of industrialisation. Ultimately, he declared: 'It is difficult to see how this is to be stopped, especially as there is so much that is good in "dear Emily." But it must be stopped somehow.'[12] Just before the book's publication in 1908 Ashbee was so incensed by this intrusion that he added a further section where he discussed how: 'As these sheets are going to press I am informed of another case of a wealthy lady … who has some skill in enamelling. She devotes the proceeds of her craftsmanship … to the maintenance of cripple homes … I also happen to know the craftsmen whose livelihood she is destroying and whose Standard she is bringing down.'[13] Deliberately positioning women as having either charitable or amateur interests, in contrast to the 'authentic' male designers and workers at his workshops, he sought to deny understanding of women as engaged participants in Arts and Crafts workshop cultures, a perspective which has remained remarkably consistent ever since.

Setting up shop and finding a market: women and Arts and Crafts entrepreneurship

At the heart of Anthea Callen's argument that the Arts and Crafts movement strengthened prevalent nineteenth-century gender hierarchies was the perspective that 'Because of family ties or of the need for chaperoning, many craftswomen … tended to avoid production-oriented tightly-knit workshops.'[14] Stella Tillyard has argued that for women, 'The common denominator of all of these pursuits, and the "feminine" crafts, was that they were all small scale, they did not use cumbersome and expensive equipment, they were "clean" and they could be carried on in the home. They did not require a studio or workshop.'[15] Others, such as Jan Marsh, have discussed the open hostility to women in workshops and small industries managed by male designers such as Ashbee, although Marsh did point out the opportunities for women in needlework: the Royal School of Art Needlework and the Morris & Co. embroidery department were both staffed and managed by women.[16] Since this point, scholars have emphasised the philanthropic opportunities middle-class women forged through craft revival schemes such as the Home Arts and Industries Association, an institution with a didactic, working-class focus. There was concern about the taint of amateurism often seen as inherent in such organisations, but here women more easily carved out new opportunities by espousing a moral duty to educate those less fortunate about the social benefits of craft work.[17]

Although women were undoubtedly often excluded from workshop settings by their male peers, and by societal concerns about 'dirty' work and troubling independence, scholars have largely adopted a narrative of women's alienation from the authentic Arts and Crafts workshop which is lifted straight from Ashbee's discourse. The substantial network of women who positioned themselves as authoritative spokespersons through their own businesses, where they had greater freedom to design work, pick materials and commissions, employ staff, and make a name for themselves, have received little attention.[18] From the 1870s onwards, a number of women began to establish independent businesses to augment their commitment to the Arts and Crafts, assert expertise on their own terms, and also often due to a need to sustain a steadier income.[19] Business ownership offered an attractive route for women hoping to carve out new independent roles outside of the exclusionary mechanisms of the male-dominated art world or of work cultures more generally. As Alison Kay has emphasised, the traditional, narrow definition of the term 'entrepreneur' needs to be overturned. The activities of the many women who historically provided for themselves and their families 'need to be examined as businesses, rather than as minor extensions of their domestic lives. Anything less would be to ignore the economic evidence and diminish the achievements of female proprietors.'[20] This model, which prioritised business ownership, was also, in many instances, inherently a professionalising strategy.

The second half of the nineteenth century marked a formative moment in the making of modern cities around the world as populations swelled, transport links grew, and urban culture offered entertainments to suit all in society. Positioning themselves as authoritative consumers, middle- and upper-class women redefined shopping as the quintessential leisure activity for women and formed extensive female-focused networks and spaces at department stores, clubhouses, and exhibitions. Pioneering business-minded 'artistic' women, aware of such developments, rented targeted rooms to tap into this market. Several Women's Guild of Arts members moved from across the country to 'set up shop' in the capital. After the cousins Rhoda and Agnes Garrett had trained for three years: 'calling themselves simply house decorators, and taking a small flat, they commenced business upon a small scale' and were celebrated as the first interior decoration firm registered by women.[21] Charlotte Newman worked for the jeweller John Brogden in Covent Garden, but set up her own business when he died in 1884, publicising widely she had learned her craft from a male jeweller, an astute strategy which indicated her ability to use 'the old traditions by herself' now and to retain Brogden's workmen, models, references, and recipes.[22] She established her business at 18 Clifford Street, off Bond Street, an area well known as a 'symbol of elite associations and activities, a spatial representative of metropolitan female Society', as Jessica P. Clark's research into the female beauty entrepreneurs working in these same streets has shown.[23] In 1897, Newman moved to 10 Savile Row where she worked at the heart of the men's tailoring district.[24] During a period when the jewellery trade was dominated by men, Newman deliberately marketed herself as a woman to distinguish herself from her competition, naming her business 'Mrs Newman'. This was a rare decision amongst her female artistic peers (although it was a tactic used by several women in the beauty trade). Newman clearly felt her marital status would reassure the public as married women were not thought to need chaperoning in the same ways as single women. Newman was praised in the national and international press for feats such as designing and making a diamond tiara in a week, which was said to be an achievement 'unparalleled in goldsmiths' annals', alongside manufacturing popular items such as heraldic designs and badges.[25]

At the dawn of the twentieth century, this network of women-owned Arts and Crafts businesses was well established. Stained-glass designer Mary Lowndes had co-founded Lowndes and Drury with Alfred Drury in Chelsea. As briefly discussed in Chapter 2, in 1906 she and Drury also set up the Glass House at Lettice Street, Fulham, a series of purpose-built stained-glass workshops for independent artists, many female.[26] Unlike Lowndes, the vast majority of women circumvented prohibitive financial outlays by going into partnership with a female friend. Metalworker E. C. Woodward ran Woodward and Withers with Agnes Withers at 5 and 7 Johnson Street, Notting Hill Gate c. 1905–1913.[27] One of their 'principal departments' was dedicated to 'reconstructing jewellery'. Here 'Bracelets are melted down and turned into necklaces' whilst brooches or earrings were 'converted into rings'. Apparently, 'whole piles of old-fashioned jewellery' were brought to Woodward and her team, 'who melts the metal, takes out the gems, and creates beautiful and completely new designs'.[28] M. V. Wheelhouse established Pomona Toys close by with Louise Jacobs c. 1915. In 1924, the guidebook *London Discoveries in Shops and Restaurants* described Pomona Toys as the place 'where you may be sure of getting the real thing'.[29] The toy shop supplied Harrods, Fortnum and Mason, Liberty, designed items for the Royal Family (such as a 'gipsy caravan' for Princess Elizabeth), and even produced nursery school bricks for the London County Council.[30]

London provided a fertile environment, but business owners promoting an Arts and Crafts ethos appeared across the country. In Leeds in the 1890s, Violet Banfield established a studio and showrooms where, alongside her own work, she sourced items to sell by renowned male designers, such as wallpaper and tapestry designs by William Morris and Walter Crane's illustrations of the Seven Ages of Man.[31] For some, the countryside offered an amenable location: bookbinder Katharine Adams began by taking a room in Lechlade in the Cotswolds above a saddler's shop. With second-hand equipment, she 'worked very hard, alone, for a year' before she had enough commissions to form her own bindery in a cottage near her home, the Eadburgha Bindery, and to train pupils.[32] Annie Garnett meanwhile had a thriving business in the Lake District, the Spinnery, which produced fabrics, from linen and silk, to embroideries.[33] After the war E. C. Woodward gave up her Notting Hill workshop and moved with family to Bushey, Hertfordshire. She quickly acquired a workshop there, but regularly travelled back to London to meet clients at the Halcyon Club for professional women. The Club provided rooms where women could meet clients by appointment. One 1925 meeting led to Woodward being commissioned to make a pendant and repair an agate brooch for £2 15s.[34] Yet a move away from the city was not always a productive endeavour, as it could abstract the woman art worker from her potential market. Pamela Colman Smith, who established the short-lived Green Sheaf Press *c.* 1904 with a Mrs Fortescue at 3 Park Mansions Arcade, Knightsbridge, part of an 'artistic little group of lady shop-keepers' in the area, found little success after moving to Cornwall.[35] She wrote to her friend, theatre director Edith Craig, in 1928 offering prints and drawings of Edith's mother, the actress Ellen Terry, with a price list and mentioned she had turned a room at home into a shop to sell her illustrations – but had sold nothing that year.[36] Her home had become the only space available to exhibit her artistic skills and make money, but she experienced little success away from the capital.

These examples are just a few of the many women who established 'artistic' businesses during this period. A survey of advertisements and directories reveals the extent of this phenomenon by the 1920s. The 'Handicraft Productions' column in *The Times* in 1924 reveals the extreme growth in female artistic entrepreneurship: out of thirty-two advertisements listed on an average day that year, at least fifteen can be identified as managed by women. Similarly, the 1924 *Notable Londoners* included twenty-two individuals under the category 'Art (Industrial)'. The editor offered profiles of eighteen women (and only four men), in contrast to other categories of work, which were dominated by male figures. The majority of these women had their own businesses in desirable locations in the city.[37]

Customers quickly responded to this new market, spreading the reach of the movement far beyond local and national lines. Many women stated they made items available to a wide set of price brackets: Pomona Toys advertised 'artistically designed and carefully executed toys appeal to all classes' and 'Wooden Toys, large and small, to suit all purses'.[38] Newman stressed she sold 'at moderate prices, a selection of the most Artistic Jewelry'.[39] But wealthy customers were extremely desirable, as they were for their male peers. Elsewhere, Newman's customers were described as 'grand dames'. Her jewellery gave them 'a certain satisfaction in the knowledge that they will not see similar designs in catalogues or shop windows' or being worn by friends.[40] The *Architectural Review* similarly informed readers that Edith B. and Nelson Dawson have 'given the *cachet* of Craft to no inconsiderable number of … homes', and because 'No design of theirs is repeated … you have the satisfaction of knowing you possess something that is yours alone, not to be found in the houses of Mrs. Afternoon-Tea or Mr. Heavymeal.'[41] Jeweller Amy Sandheim was described as working for 'a very distinguished circle of patrons' from her studio at 130 Notting Hill Gate; wealthy sculptor Feodora Gleichen being 'one of the most constant'.[42] Erika Rappaport's research has demonstrated that female shoppers fuelled consumerism by the late nineteenth century, keeping department stores in business.[43] Women, particularly those focused on procuring unique pieces redolent of their cultural sophistication, just as actively supported small shops and workshops established by artistic women, spreading word through friends, family members, professional acquaintances, suffrage networks, and the wider women's movement.

Women art workers engaged in running artistic businesses utilised an international reputation of cultural authority, promoted by professional and social connections, to sell their work both in Britain and overseas. Katharine Adams was described by the curator of the Fitzwilliam Museum, Sydney Cockerell, in 1952 as having been 'one of the leading English craftswomen of this century'. Her bindery was 'much visited by English and American tourists' and 'the most prominent book collectors in the country'.[44] Adams found a steady stream of work from 'William Morris's old associates' whilst also binding prayer books and back numbers of *Country Life* for the local gentry.[45] American customers were particularly keen to purchase art which portrayed them as taste makers at home across the Atlantic. Annie Garnett told interviewers in 1898, 'The Americans are good customers.' She sent out 'parcels of embroideries every day' from the Lake District, and 'the sale of them last season was extremely large'.[46] Roberta Mills proudly informed *Penrose's Pictorial Annual* in 1913 about the American interest in her work, drawing on an anecdote about an unnamed 'American gentleman' who described it as the 'dandiest' he had seen, telling her 'his friends on the other side would be interested'. He commissioned a cabinet with leather panels, requiring the wood to be as old as possible to please his taste.[47] Charlotte Newman was even commissioned to design diplomatic gifts to encourage bonds between nations; in 1899 the French government paid her to design twelve gold medallions for the Empress of Russia, each bearing the portrait of a celebrated French woman, beginning with the first Christian Queen of France and ending prior to the French Revolution.[48] Clearly then, the size of these businesses did not mean societal interest was small, nor that the customer base was limited geographically. Far from being excluded from the business opera-tions of the Arts and Crafts movement, women-led endeavours accounted for a large proportion of the artistic production associated with the movement, and had a wide-reaching impact on the social conception of the artisan.

Performing expertise at women's Arts and Crafts businesses

This final section assesses the strategies artistic women used to balance their tripartite statuses as art workers, middle-class women, and business owners. Gillian Sutherland has recently suggested, when analysing female writers, that public visibility brought about 'fierce and sometimes con-demnatory scrutiny', limiting the genres women worked in and 'never cost-free in social terms'.[49] Yet in debates about the Arts and Crafts there appears little of the ferocious discussions about the 'unsexed' female journalists that circulated during the same era.[50] Although art journals dedicated little time to the businesses of female art workers in England, a growing transatlantic print culture of women's magazines, newspapers, suffrage papers, and travel guides all generated substantial interest.

From the 1880s, articles avidly described the potential for women to establish small-scale businesses, many of which fit within the nebulous category of 'artistic'. Newspaper magnate Alfred C. Harmsworth, in the *Young Folks' Paper*, wrote of the supposed winning combination of those with 'capital and artistic tastes' who could 'make a very good income by starting a business'.[51] The artistic 'lady shopkeeper' even featured in New Woman literature: Amy Levy's 1888 *The Romance of a Shop* centred on the poverty-stricken Lorimer sisters who established a photography business after their father's death. There had clearly been some overemphasis of the opportunities for women to achieve quick success in the press, and there were notes of caution in subsequent publications. By 1894 *Myra's Journal*, for instance, advised a woman named simply as Ethel (who was considering setting up a dressmaking business) to proceed with care: 'Don't, pray don't, think of setting up a shop of your own on such insufficient capital and slender knowledge … you want capital to lock up in material, to pay away in rent, wages, and food. You must find your customers, and when they are found you must wait for their money'.[52] Constance Smedley similarly detailed the difficulties facing 'the worker with no capital' who could not 'tie up all her money in material for work, which if it does not sell at once may leave her with no further capital to expend on the metal and gems she requires for the pursuit of her craft'. Such women with limited means often had to buy cheaper artistic materials as a consequence.

Smedley also advised 'the genuine wage-earner' to consider that alongside materials, and 'the great wear and tear of her tools', one had to pay for rent and extra servants 'for if the artist works all day she has no time for housework'.[53]

Despite practical difficulties being raised, there was a palpable shift taking place in the acceptability of certain models of female entrepreneurship being repositioned as alternatives to domesticity. At the turn of the century, women's 'artistic' businesses were rarely perceived as morally dubious and those closely associated with the Arts and Crafts movement were seen to be exemplary examples of the working woman who had maintained integrity. Some publications even produced alternative, female-oriented shopping routes for readers to visit these 'artistic' and fashionable businesses at the heart of the capital. In 1910, feminist paper the *English-woman* encouraged readers to journey across the West End, providing insight into the wide range of women now working in their independently run 'artistic' shops and workshops. Readers were encouraged to visit such individuals as 'Mrs Wright' at 49 Old Bond Street, and her 'beautiful hand-pierced and embossed silver casement teapots', the artistic dresses and 'purely hand-embroidery of the best craftsmanship' at the Studio, 31 York Place, Baker Street, and finally to see the 'Artistic leatherwork' of Roberta Mills.[54] Mills crafted ties, bags, belts, and cushions out of leather, and advertised in *Votes for Women* that there was 'Nothing like leather for suffragettes' wear'.[55] In this urban milieu, artistic, suffrage, and feminist networks flourished and became entangled. Female-centred shopping routes were still being discussed in 1930 when Thelma Hilda Benjamin, editor of the 'Woman's Page' for the *Daily Mail*, published *A Shopping Guide to London* for American visitors. Benjamin included a chapter on 'Arts, Crafts, and Exhibitions that Matter', where she discussed her thirty-four favourite 'artist craftsmen'. At least twenty-seven of these were women, such as Sybil Dunlop who made hand-wrought jewellery and 'stamps her work with the seal of originality'.[56] Although not explicitly political – in contrast to earlier suffrage papers – Benjamin's detailed discussions still encouraged a woman-centred approach to shopping and artistic culture.

Print culture provides a vantage point onto the strategies women business owners in the Arts and Crafts movement used to perform professional status and gain customers, whilst also maintaining a reputation within artistic networks. Journalists played a crucial role in spreading knowledge about their expertise, linking it explicitly to a form of artistic cultural authority (and authenticity) which transcended that of the conventional businessperson or the commercialist entrepreneur. The *Magazine of Art* praised Newman for her 'far larger view' of the role of art in public life 'than a merely selfish one', 'looking to a future that must be beyond her time' whilst *Homes and Gardens* described Pomona Toys as 'truly representative of the taste of the modern child, and truly British in idea and execution'.[57]

Those that could afford to advertised in high-profile publications such as the *Studio*, the *Saturday Review*, *The Times*, and across the women's press. The unique, handcrafted nature of this work was always stressed, like in the advertisements placed by their male peers. Newman's regular advertisements in *The Times* (ironically) proclaimed her 'Artistic jewelry designs are not published in trade catalogues'. Readers were informed she 'employs her own skilled workmen, alloys her own gold, and selects the finest precious stones'.[58] The *Englishwoman* regularly included advertisements by Lowndes and Drury and Woodward and Withers, their metalwork competitors Florence M. Rimmington, Alice S. Kinkead, Beth Amoore, and needlework artist Ruth Cross, amongst others (Figure 4.1). These advertisements all stressed cultural signifiers such as West London addresses, workshops, apprentices, and commitment to skilled, handcrafted work. Others, such as Pamela Colman Smith – perhaps unable to afford press advertisements – instead provided detailed, hand-printed versions (Figure 4.2). This array of 'artistic' advertisements, so quotidian they have escaped the interest of researchers, depicts the importance of demonstrating authenticity through the use of fine materials and methods, and the adoption of the model of the 'medieval' workshop and 'handcrafted' work which was so essential to navigating the expectations placed upon entrepreneurial women art workers.

Training provided another way to assert status and attract customers. Although many women received little or no formal training, a cluster of pioneers took care to advertise this as testament of their perseverance and hard-won learned knowledge. The difficulties of gaining access to these opportunities, and the tendency for women to be placed in segregated rooms at 'male' businesses, meant most women hired female staff once they had progressed in their own careers, creating an expanding network of women's workshops.[59] Katharine Adams had two to three assistants, 'artistically-dressed ladies organized and paid in the conventional way' whilst E. C. Woodward's apprentices were bound for three years, worked five days a week, from nine to five, and had six weeks' holiday each year. Furthermore, 'she teaches them all that she knows, and arranges for them to have expert lessons and lessons in designing in addition'.[60] The hiring of women enabled a younger generation to bypass some of the gendered restrictions faced by pioneers.[61] Woodward was committed to encouraging women to enjoy the physicality of workshop life, an approach which

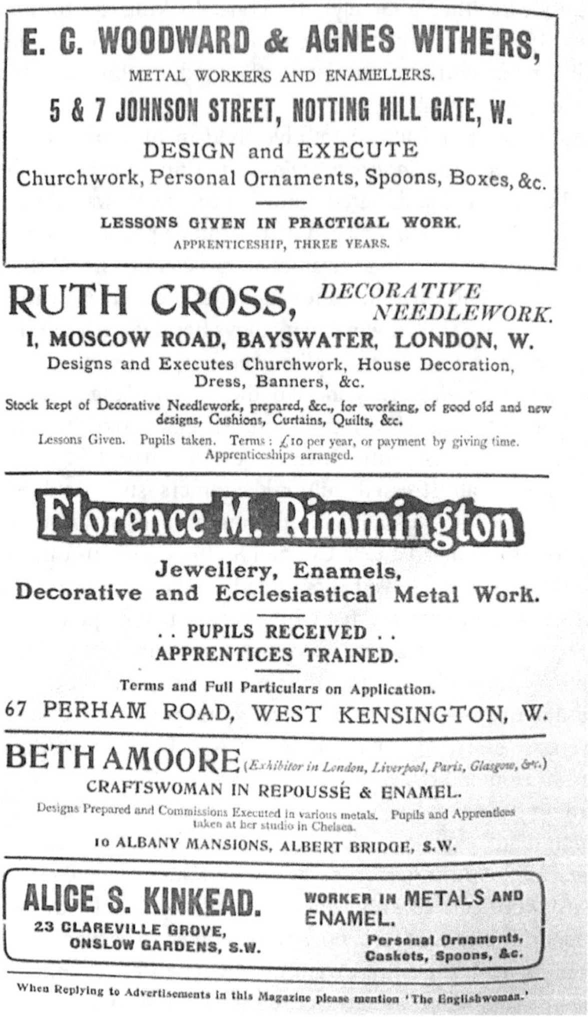

Figure 4.1 'Advertisements', *Englishwoman*, 60/25 (1911), p. xii

simultaneously reasserted her own status as an authentic disciple of the idealised Arts and Crafts workshop espoused by Ashbee and others. Her employees were 'engaged in the practical making of all sorts of articles: every sort of work, big and small, passes through their hands'. They could feel 'that the professional credit of the workshop rests to some extent in their hands' as she taught them how 'to hammer with a poker-head, to

MISS PAMELA COLMAN SMITH begs to inform the *Green Sheaf* subscribers, and other friends and customers, that she, in conjunction with MRS. FORTESCUE, has opened a shop for the sale of Hand-Coloured Prints and other Engravings, Drawings and Pictures, Books, &c., at the foregoing address. ❦ ❦ ❦ ❦

Orders taken and promptly executed for Christmas and Invitation Cards, Menus, Ball Programmes, Book Labels, and every kind of Decorative Printing and Hand-colouring. ❦

❦ ❦ ❦

SIGN BOARDS PAINTED, and the Decoration of Rooms and Illustration of Books undertaken. ❦

Figure 4.2 Advertisement for the Green Sheaf, *c.* 1904

use the tool at hand'.[62] Employing women was beneficial for numerous other reasons: women could be paid less; journalists often stressed that these businesses offered a solution to national anxieties about the 'surplus' of impoverished women; and, finally, managing female staff in these specialised sites helped avoid being seen to 'take' male jobs, a circulating anxiety which reached its zenith after the First World War.

In contrast to figures such as Ashbee, whose commitment to employing working-class men was central to his vision of the radical potential of the arts, female employers had less to gain from promoting cross-class interactions – at least publicly. When pressed, there was even emphasis that working-class women were not popular. Annie Garnett told one interviewer that such women were too 'hemmed in by tradition'. She instead preferred to employ 'village girls and tradesmen's daughters'.[63] Newman expressed similar anxieties, equating 'educated women' with 'reliability and carefulness', as people who could be trusted with her expensive materials, and were more 'teachable than those in the classes below'.[64] Garnett and Newman were unusual as they did employ men, a fact which they used to garner interest and enhance their own statuses. Using these figures as unnamed ciphers, they constructed a heightened sense of the tradition of the workshop and the male craft worker, emblematic of a long-lost culture. Garnett told *Atalanta* her male weaver was a 'delightful old Welshman, at work the year round, and he is able to weave all the yarns the spinsters bring in.'[65] Despite claiming to receive many letters from women seeking work, Charlotte Newman, whose memorable evocation of her male employees liking 'a lady boss' began this chapter, employed only one woman: a pearl stringer, hired to prepare necklaces due to her perceived competency at this dainty task, because she did not have 'a separate room for training girls'. Even though many girls had applied to be apprentices, Newman instead favoured male apprentices with family connections to the craft, proudly discussing one apprentice who was 'fifth in direct line who has followed the trade, and the others are sons or grandsons of goldsmiths'.[66] Intent on forging their own reputations, Newman and Garnett promoted this model of male craftsmanship handed down over the generations, and although subverting social norms to promote the power they now held over their male employees, still upheld gender and class hierarchies in the management of their own staff. Similarly, a striking photographic depiction (c. 1906) of Lowndes and Drury, which Mary Lowndes co-owned with Alfred Drury, shows large numbers of working-class men in flat caps waiting outside their workplace. Although the business was supportive of women's endeavours, this photograph represents the ease with which female-owned businesses continued to exploit traditional models of workshop employment (Figure 4.3).

Curation of access to, and promotion of, the rarefied authentic spaces of the art worker were the key means of differentiation that women had to distance themselves from societal disapproval or accusations of problematic mercantilism. Taking a similar approach to that of discerning gallery owners, a shopfront was often avoided to enable a non-commercial atmosphere to be established even whilst visitors stood outside on the street.[67] This tactic conveniently allowed women to play with gendered ideas about appropriate 'public' and 'private' spheres, as they worked behind closed doors in upmarket environments. The Garrett cousins advertised their establishment simply by placing 'A neat brass plate upon the dark green door of No. 2 Gower Street'.[68] Charlotte Newman, at this point based just off Bond Street, implemented the same approach. When Sarah Tooley visited in 1895 she had initially been puzzled because Newman had 'nothing to indicate her occupation but her name simply inscribed across the window'. Participating in a competitive male-dominated jewellery trade, where lavish shopfronts were increasingly expected, Newman kept her shopfront intriguingly bare. She boasted, 'I do not have a shop-window' because her customers 'come to me without advertisement; and, as a designer, I have no wish to exhibit my things in a window and run the risk of having them copied'. Only once inside could visitors gain access to her showrooms of 'dazzling beauty'. 'Mrs Newman' could be found

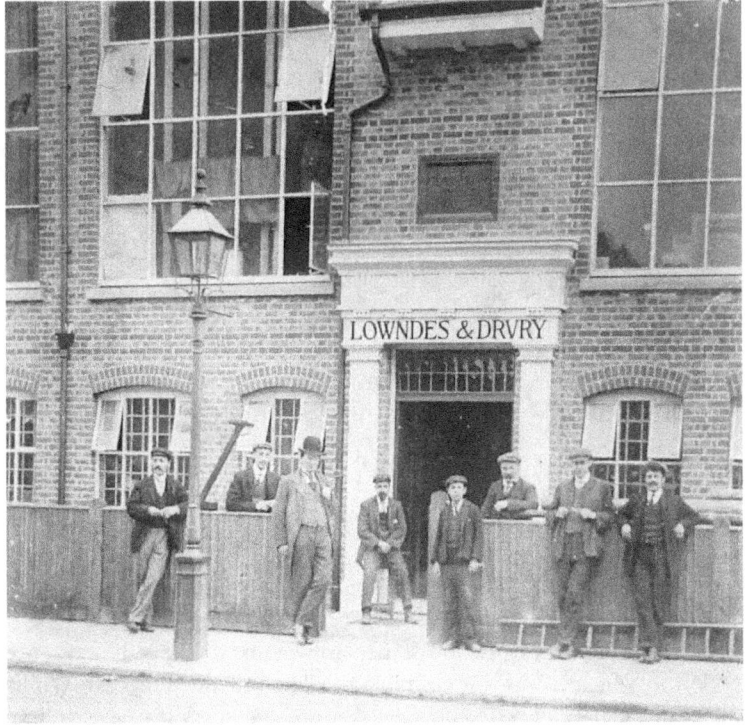

Figure 4.3 Lowndes and Drury, London, *c.* 1906

seated behind glass cases filled with 'specimens of her craft' lamenting that 'Machinery is answerable for the decadence of special design'.[69]

Yet for others, the shopfront provided a frame through which design skills could be curated for the curious customer, although discretion, and the display of refined taste, remained key. Focus was always on the work rather than gaudy or excessive ornamentation. A surviving postcard photograph (itself a testament of sophisticated marketing) advertising Pomona Toys in the 1920s provides a glimpse of the approach taken at this business (Figure 4.4). The shop has an enticingly open door, and handcrafted giraffes and a horse-drawn carriage are balanced on the windows to attract families shopping in the area. Displays of objects were acceptable, but had to be carefully controlled and limited to the 'tasteful'.

The workshop, with its potential to invoke ideas of rough male labour and dangerous transgression of gendered roles, at the same time as embodying the idealistic radicalism of the Arts and Crafts ideal, was a

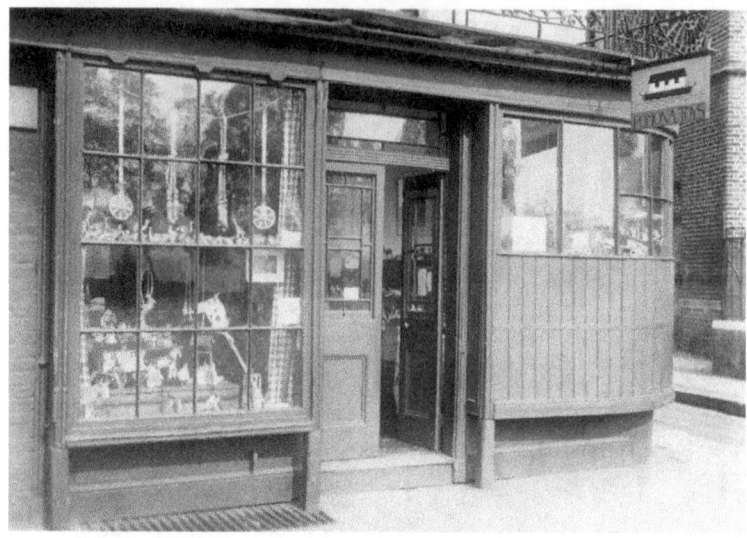

Figure 4.4 Postcard for Pomona Toys

site which was very helpful for women art workers to imply the existence of, but to which it was not desirable to allow unfettered access. Whilst the vast majority of Arts and Crafts business owners claimed to have workshops 'on site', or at least on a street close by, numerous techniques were introduced to market these spaces, regardless of their inaccessibility. Depicting them to the customer had obvious implications for their respectability and authenticity as art workers. For women, the grubby reality of the actual workshop was rarely discussed or depicted in detail in the press: here the need to maintain gender and class status was heightened. In contrast to C. R. Ashbee's socio-realist snapshots photographing life at the Guild of Handicraft, women tended not to use images of the gritty reality of these spaces to build their reputations. Photographs provide insight into the ways women instead carefully sought to position themselves. One image of Pamela Colman Smith in *Cassell's Magazine* exemplifies a common approach used by women art workers: she is removed from the business context, instead portrayed as the height of feminine sophistication, with pristine white lace collar and embroidered shawl, neatly braided hair, and clasped hands (Figure 4.5). As explained in Chapter 3, Colman Smith in fact marketed herself amongst numerous different environments; she looks far less composed in a photograph captured by *Brooklyn Life*, depicting her at one of her story-telling evenings. Here she

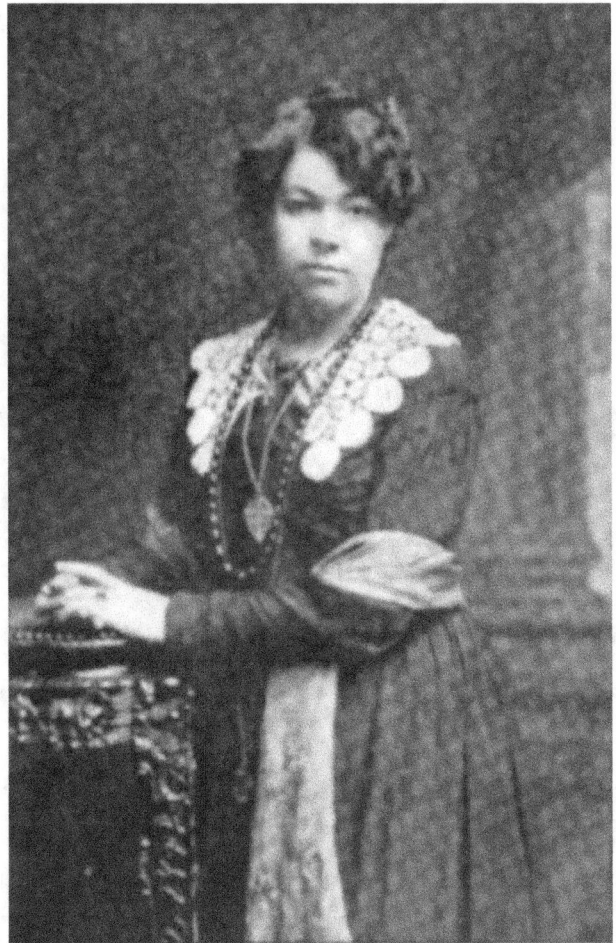

MISS PAMELA COLEMAN SMITH (*THE GREEN SHEAF*).
(*Photo: Russell & Sons, Baker Street, W.*)

Figure 4.5 'The Woman Editors of London – Miss Pamela Colman Smith',
Cassell's Magazine (December 1902 to May 1903), p. 685

is relaxed, in crumpled dress, with a visionary expression; surrounded
by lit candles she personifies Edwardian bohemianism (Figure 4.6). Colman
Smith's markedly different presentation as a business owner was evidently
designed to allay fears about the respectability of women when they became
associated with commerce and industry.

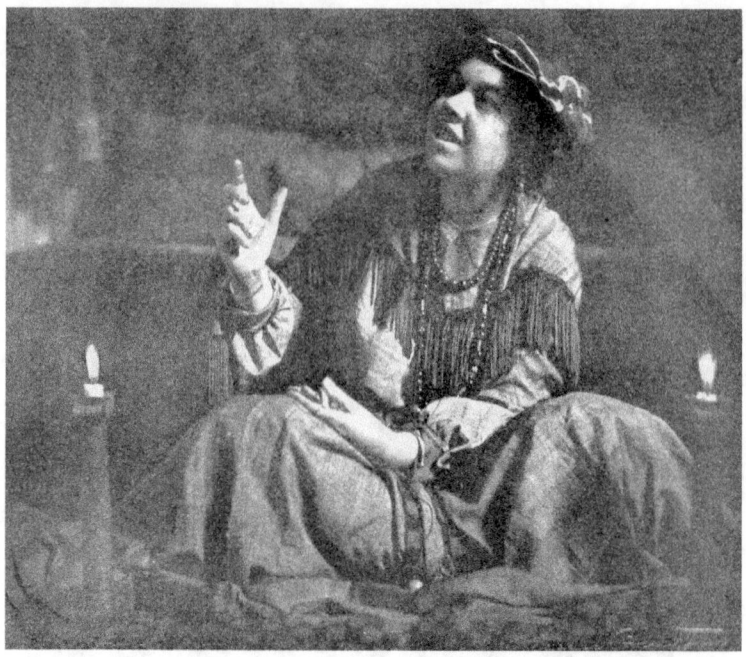

Figure 4.6 'Pamela Colman Smith', *Brooklyn Life* (12 January 1907), p. 9

Refusing entry to the workshop could function as a way of heightening public curiosity. 'Retiring' Agnes Wilson, producer of 'painted mirrors, quaint boxes, and a hundred and one other bibelots' was described as working alongside her 'clever artists' in a 'mysterious workshop up aloft on the other side of thick concealing curtain' in 1924.[70] Similarly, Newman refused entry to her workshops, stating her 'skilled workers do not care to be shown off to visitors'. In her interview for the *Woman's Signal* she instead beckoned for an apprentice to bring out a diamond tiara he was working on, at this stage a 'grimy, smutty-looking object'. Newman stressed she was predominantly the designer rather than the maker, although she admitted that 'The hands get as black as possible from the action of the flames', something which prompted Tooley to inform readers that – although she had not liked to admit this to Newman – she felt sure 'lady goldsmiths of the future' would solve 'the difficulty of the "hands" as the lady gardeners have done', through wearing gloves.[71] At the heart of this comment is a journalistic renegotiation of the divide – thought as desirable – between the front of Newman's business (clean, amenable to the presence of women) and the heart of her artistic credibility (manual, authentic, and associated with the creativity of male workers).

Despite the benefits of upholding the workshop as a secret and private space, considerable advantages in publicity were available to those women who did find ways to represent its atmosphere to an eager public, who saw it as an emblem of authenticity. Middle-class reputations relied on engaging with the *right* sort of art, making the business premises of heightened importance in convincing visitors of authentic design skills. Access to the workshop had to be painstakingly curated, to avoid implications of transgression. Photography could provide just such an easily controlled glimpse into the fertile creative hub of the artistic business. In the late nineteenth century, Annie Garnett decided to have a series of photographs taken of the Spinnery to market her business. The women appear as ghosts, all facing away from the camera, or positioned behind the different tools of their craft, as though determined not to break the spell. The viewers are instead encouraged to focus on the austere yet aesthetically charming rooms, lit with natural sunlight and filled with handcrafted fabrics, spinning wheels, sturdy wooden furniture, within a pleasing setting at the heart of the English countryside (Figures 4.7–9).

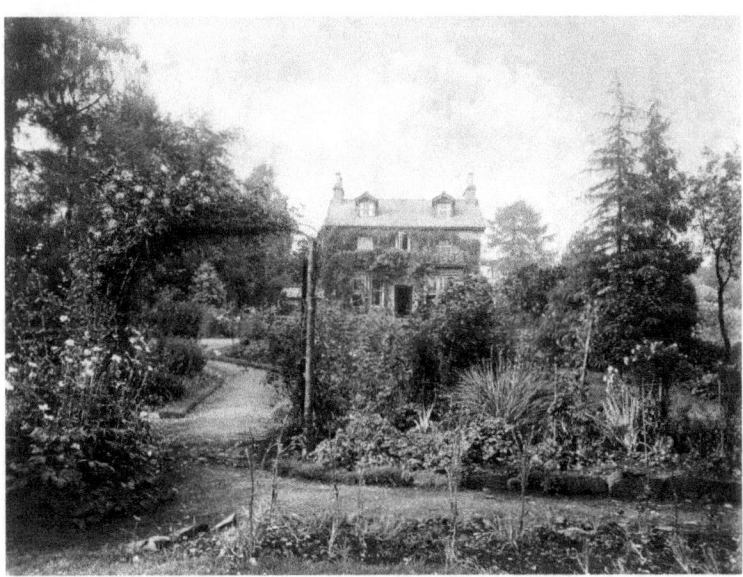

Figure 4.7 Annie Garnett's the Spinnery, undated but *c*. 1890s

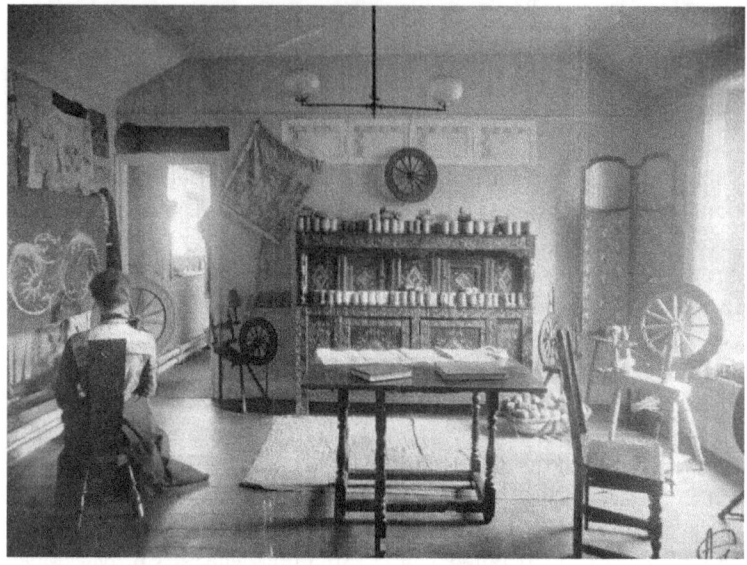

Figure 4.8 Inside the Spinnery, undated but *c.* 1890s

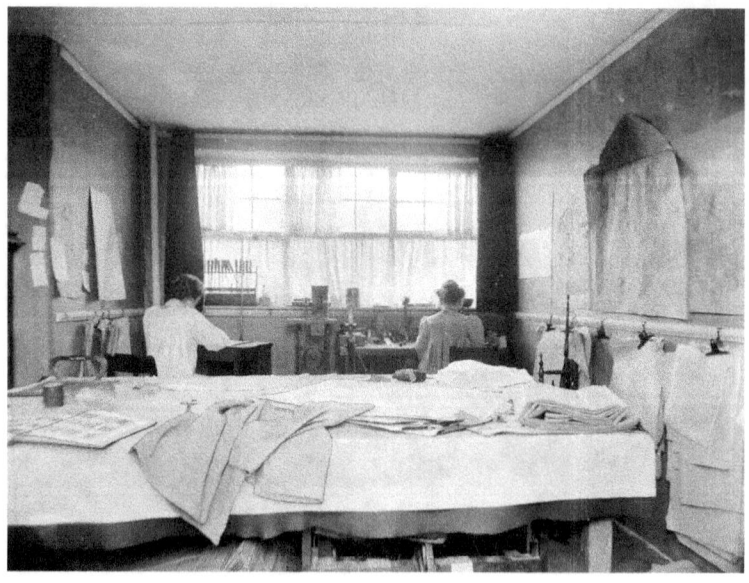

Figure 4.9 Inside the Spinnery, undated but *c.* 1890s

Photography which was produced for the women's press tended to be more upfront about women's direct involvement, but still promoted a model of women's participation in these spaces as emblematic of artistic credibility and virtuous labour. In 1921, *Mrs Strang's Annual for Girls* marketed Woodward as the modern working woman in several staged photographs depicting her at work in her workshop, with labels describing the activities she was undertaking. Dressed in a white smock, she employed the tools of her craft such as footbellows for 'big work' (Figure 4.10). She was one of many women to mention the plethora of expert tools needed,

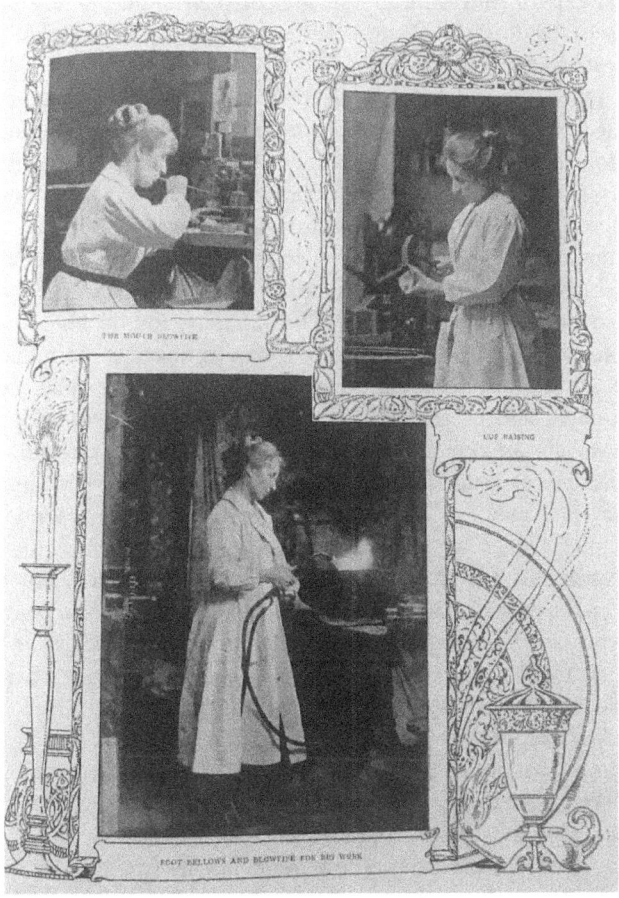

Figure 4.10 E. C. Woodward, 'Jewellery and Metalwork', *Mrs Strang's Annual for Girls* (Oxford, 1921), p. 51

in this instance ranging from saws, hammers, through to a mouth blowpipe. These items were particularly necessary for serious workers like herself, who were involved in making 'bigger and heavier branches of metal work' for churches such as altar furniture and processional crosses. 'Such are the most important of the hundred and one things that go to make up the fittings of a workshop,' Woodward lamented, asserting her need for an 'isolated' workshop 'as neighbours often object to hammering'. She reassured readers simply wanting to make jewellery that they could do this in an 'ordinary room, where the light is good and where gas is available for the blowpipe'. However, she also took care to stress they ought to have 'at least experimented' in all branches of their craft, because 'when a worker is able to make his own designs such designs are almost always the most satisfactory'.[72]

A more drastic but highly effective tactic in attracting customers to a rarefied, culturally sophisticated environment was opening the workshop to visitors. Again, imposing a sense of control, restriction, and exclusivity was key so as to avoid accusations that such a tactic was a self-interested commercial gambit. Allowing visitors to browse and socialise in the workshop came to be an important part of validating one's artistic reputation. Craftworker Gordon Russell approvingly noted that when visiting Katharine Adams he had been 'free to wander round the bindery at any time I liked'.[73] Adams's credentials were directly linked to the authenticity of her workrooms, and their accessibility to a refined public. Cultural cachet could also be enhanced through ensuring the workshop had a 'medieval' atmosphere. Edith B. and Nelson Dawson's 'workshop party' was described as 'delightful and mediaeval!' in one letter, whilst Constance Smedley informed readers of the *World's Work* that E. C. Woodward's workshop provided 'a good example of what the mediaeval workshop of a craftsman must have been'.[74] This pseudo-medieval interior environment captured the public imagination and situated such owners in contrast to the plethora of shopkeepers selling cheap, mass-produced goods.

Visits to the workshop were not just intended for elite artistic networks, or curious journalists. Public engagement was greatly encouraged – particularly at women's workshops. Constance Smedley found it encouraging 'how greatly people are patronising such workshops'. In her view, women art workers were the most involved in beginning 'to regard their studios more and more as workshops, and keeping them always open and accessible'. The art worker 'must learn not to mind being interrupted' and to:

> encourage friendly relationships with the public, and encourage patrons
> to get used to the idea of dropping into the studio to see what new

things are being made, and of bringing their friends to see the interesting processes. Even if the people come and do not buy, one never knows when they may recommend one's work: and for those master craftswomen who have large workshops, who regard their work as a serious profession, and are always engaged in creating new objects for sale and exhibition, it is of the greatest importance that this work should be readily accessible.[75]

This approach was evidently widespread as publications frequently discussed women welcoming visitors to their places of work. The *Ladies' Treasury* provides a typical example, when it encouraged readers hunting for Christmas presents to visit bookbinder Johanna Birkenruth on Cromwell Road in 1895. Her workshop was 'a thoroughly artistic abode' where 'purchasers, and visitors merely desirous of inspecting, are equally welcome'.[76] Such events could command large numbers: E. C. Woodward held metalwork shows at her workshop and one in 1907 had over 500 visitors in a few days.[77] *Art Workers' Quarterly* informed readers that 'Visitors are always welcome' at Garnett's Spinnery and that 'things are mostly for sale', although the usual caveat was given that 'selling is not by any means the chief motive in displaying them'.[78] Such distancing from the idea of commercial advertisement might at first appear like a mere rhetorical tactic, but in a sense these workshop events were not directly intended to whip up sales. What they instead sought to promote was an image of the woman art worker as a figure of cultural and artistic authority, embodying the appropriate balance of gendered respectability and creative authenticity.

The establishment of national institutions such as the South Kensington Museum in 1857 (later the Victoria and Albert Museum), and municipal museums across the country, enabled a wider sector of society to begin to familiarise themselves with artistic culture.[79] But workshops and businesses offered an alternative 'hands-on' way for people to learn about the transformative potential of the Arts and Crafts. Here women had far greater independence, curatorial control, and opportunities to open up the movement's social and cultural potential. Paid lessons could be offered within workshops (which helped supplement costs of running the business), ranging from short courses to long-term apprenticeships, alongside free, regular 'demonstration days' where people could visit and see women 'in action' hammering with tools, weaving, and sketching – in the process engraining the centrality of such women to an Arts and Crafts culture to contemporaries.

The artistic business also provided a base from which women could then seek out further recognition by travelling locally, nationally, and internationally, and by sending their work to be judged at the exhibitions discussed in Chapter 2. Annie Garnett was awarded the gold cross, 'the highest award of the Association' for an embroidered linen and silk piece she exhibited at the Home Arts and Industries Exhibition at the Albert Hall.[80] Pomona Toys similarly received 'much favourable attention at the several Exhibitions of Arts and Handicrafts' spread across England.[81] Women were deeply aware of the role of the workshop, and the tasteful business, in authenticating their credibility at exhibitions and in wider society. They exploited the model established by their male peers, and adeptly shaped the portrayal of their workspaces in wider society, negotiating societal anxieties surrounding gendered transgression and inauthenticity, to represent themselves as figures of cultural authority, laudable entrepreneurship, and respectable art workers on the same footing as their male peers.

Anxieties about artistic authenticity fundamentally shaped the ways people in the late nineteenth and early twentieth centuries understood and discussed the world of Arts and Crafts. Although there was evidently a substantial growth in opportunities for women to establish 'artistic' businesses from the late nineteenth century onwards, as 'lady' art workers grew in number, concerns about amateurism and the 'wrong' sort of art continued to grow, far beyond the movement, and across artistic culture.[82] Pioneering 'professional' women art workers had deeply felt concerns about the need for high-quality artwork. They asserted their exceptionality in opposition to the hinterland of feminine and amateur interest in craft, which was rapidly increasing at the very point they too were seeking to construct professional lives and entrepreneurial opportunities. Hoping to make their mark on society through industrious self-fashioning, the lives of Arts and Crafts women and men demonstrate that terms such as 'artists', 'professionals', and 'entrepreneurs' should not be assumed to be separate categories or used to signify a fixed, stable identity. For women, in particular, the ability to navigate between these different categories offered them radical new opportunities to participate in the arts and in society. The approach taken by women such as Mary Lowndes, Annie Garnett, and Charlotte Newman continued to be influenced by their gender throughout their lives: this influenced staff, the size of the enterprise, and daily navigation of different hybrid spaces (rural, urban, commercial, professional, artistic). But such women rhetorically laid claim to the language of artists, and not that of commerce. Through consistent promotion of historical methods of production, permitting exclusive glimpses into the 'private' workshop, they asserted the authenticity of their businesses. Entrepreneurship could be short lived, and required start-up capital, but collectively these businesses, shops, and workshops helped democratise Arts and Crafts ideals and carve space for women to forge expert reputations within professional, artistic, and commercial environments.

Notes

1 Sarah A. Tooley, 'A Lady Goldsmith: An Interview with Mrs Philip Newman', *Woman's Signal* (9 May 1895), p. 289.

2 In the Women's Guild of Arts, out of approximately sixty members, at least a third had workshops or businesses. Some women artists, such as jewellers, had owned businesses since the eighteenth century. Toni Lesser Wolf, 'Women Jewelers of the British Arts and Crafts Movement', *Journal of Decorative and Propoganda Arts*, 14 (Autumn 1989), pp. 28–45 (p. 28).

3 It is important to note that even though many of these women would have defined themselves as 'professionals', they would have rejected the term 'entrepreneurs'. As F. M. L. Thompson has observed: 'enterprise culture is a very recent ideological and managerial construct ... Victorians themselves never used such an expression.' F. M. L. Thompson, *Gentrification and the Enterprise Culture* (Oxford: Oxford University Press, 2003), p. 75.

4 Anne Digby, 'Victorian Values and Women in Public and Private', *Proceedings of the British Academy*, 78 (1992), pp. 195–215.

5 Rosalind P. Blakesley, *The Arts and Crafts Movement* (London: Phaidon, 2006), p. 35.

6 Alan Crawford (ed.), *By Hammer and Hand: The Arts and Crafts Movement in Birmingham* (Birmingham: Birmingham Museums and Art Gallery, 1984), p. 8. Crawford's dichotomy between 'radical' art and decorative objects creates a hierarchy which itself contributes to the marginalisation of the contributions of artists outside a central Morris–Ashbee circle and misrepresents the potential for the radical creation of new artistic identities built around craft production.

7 'Social Studies', *Judy* (17 October 1900), p. 495.

8 C. R. Ashbee, *Where the Great City Stands: A Study in the New Civics* (London: Essex House and B. T. Batsford, 1917), p. 11.

9 C. R. Ashbee, *Craftsmanship in Competitive Industry* (Campden: Essex House Press, 1908).

10 Gustav Stickley, 'Art True and False', *Craftsman: An Illustrated Monthly Magazine for the Simplification of Life*, 8 (April–September 1905), p. 686.

11 Alan Crawford, 'The Object is Not the Object: C. R. Ashbee and the Guild of Handicraft', in *Pioneers of Modern Craft: Twelve Essays Profiling Key Figures in the History of Twentieth-Century Craft* (ed.) Margot Coatts (Manchester: Manchester University Press, 1997), pp. 1–11 (pp. 2, 10).

12 Ashbee, *Craftsmanship in Competitive Industry*, pp. 37–38.

13 Ibid., p. 88.

14 Anthea Callen, 'Sexual Division of Labour in the Arts and Crafts Movement', in *A View from the Interior: Feminism, Women and Design* (eds) Judy Attfield and Pat Kirkham (London: Women's Press, 1989), pp. 151–164 (p. 160).

15 Stella Tillyard, *The Impact of Modernism, 1900–1920: Early Modernism and the Arts and Crafts Movement in Edwardian England* (London: Routledge, 1988), p. 9.

16 Jan Marsh, 'May Morris: Ubiquitous, Invisible Arts and Crafts-Woman', in *Women Artists and the Decorative Arts, 1880–1935: The Gender of Ornament* (eds) Bridget Elliott and Janice Helland (Farnham: Ashgate, 2002), pp. 35–52 (p. 37).

17 Alla Myzelev, 'Craft Revival in Haslemere: She, Who Weaves ...', *Women's History Review*, 18/4 (2009), pp. 597–618; Janice Helland, *British and Irish Home Arts and Industries, 1880–1914: Marketing Craft, Making Fashion* (Dublin: Irish Academic Press, 2007).

18 A small number of 'exceptional' women have been the subject of scholarship, as have specific artistic fields, such as bookbinding, interior decoration, and pottery. Marianne Tidcombe, *Women Bookbinders, 1880–1920* (New Castle: Oak Knoll, 1996); Cheryl Buckley, *Potters and Paintresses: Women Designers in the Pottery Industry, 1870–1955* (London: Women's Press, 1990); Deborah Cohen, *Household Gods: The British and Their Possessions* (New Haven: Yale University Press, 2006). Cohen has stressed the role played by 'lady art advisors', the female house decorators and writers who were 'foot soldiers' and played an influential role in linking the 'spheres of high art, home decoration, and the shops', p. 65. Elizabeth Crawford, Emma Ferry, and Miranda Garrett have researched Agnes Garrett and her cousin Rhoda, who set up what is thought to have been the first interior design company by women *c.* 1872 called A. & R. Garrett House Decorators. Elizabeth Crawford, *Enterprising Women: The Garretts and Their Circle* (London: Boutle, 2002); Emma Ferry, '"Decorators May be Compared to Doctors": An Analysis of Rhoda and Agnes Garrett's Suggestion for House Decoration in Painting, Woodwork and Furniture (1876)', *Journal of Design History*, 16/1 (2003), pp. 15–33; Miranda Garrett, 'Window Smashing and Window Draping: Suffrage and Interior Design', in *Suffrage and the Arts: Visual Culture, Politics and Enterprise* (eds) Miranda Garrett and Zoë Thomas (London: Bloomsbury, 2018), pp. 93–116; Miranda Garrett, 'Professional Women Interior Decorators in Britain, 1874–1899' (Unpublished PhD thesis, Central St Martin's, 2018). The same can be said for the entrepreneurial efforts of artistic women in Glasgow. See Jude Burkhauser, *Glasgow Girls: Women in Art and Design, 1880–1920* (Edinburgh: Canongate, 1990).

19 Newman openly told the *Woman's Signal* about her reduced economic circumstances which made it necessary for her to find an occupation during youth. Tooley, 'A Lady Goldsmith', p. 289. In comparison, bookbinder Katharine Adams only started work in her thirties when, due to financial insecurity, it became necessary for her to work to make money. Tidcombe, *Women Bookbinders*, p. 132.

20 Alison Kay, *The Foundations of Female Entrepreneurship: Enterprise, Home, and Household in London, c. 1800–1870* (London: Routledge, 2009), p. 5.

21 'Interview', *Women's Penny Paper* (18 January 1890), p. 145.

22 Alfred Whitman, 'The Jewellery of Mrs Philip Newman', *Magazine of Art* (London, 1902), p. 466.

23 Jessica P. Clark, 'Pomeroy v. Pomeroy: Beauty, Modernity, and the Female Entrepreneur in *Fin-de-siècle* London', *Women's History Review*, 22/6 (2013), pp. 877–903 (p. 885).

24 'Classified Advertising', *The Times* (26 March 1897), p. 1.

25 'Untitled', *Le Follet: Journal du Grand Monde, Fashion, Polite Literature, Beaux Arts, &c.* (1 May 1896), p. 13.

26 Initially, Lowndes and Drury contributed £30 each of the needed capital of £60, but this was later supplemented by further substantial loans from Lowndes, her partner

Barbara Forbes, her aunt Alice Vivian Kaye, and a Miss J. F. Pearson. Peter Cormack, *Arts and Crafts Stained Glass* (New Haven: Yale University Press, 2015), p. 96.

27 John Culme, *The Directory of Gold and Silversmiths, Jewellers and Allied Traders 1838–1914, From the London Assay Office Registers* (Woodbridge: Antique Collectors' Club, 1987), p. 497; 'Notice of Dissolution of Partnership', *London Gazette* (5 December 1913), p. 9023.

28 Constance Smedley, 'A Guild of Craftswomen', *World's Work: An Illustrated Magazine of National Efficiency and Social Progress*, 9 (December 1906–May 1907), pp. 314–322 (p. 319). The article revealed that trowels 'range from any price from fifteen guineas' whilst the silver christening bowl and spoon 'were made specially for the donor for six guineas'.

29 Elizabeth Montizambert, *London Discoveries in Shops and Restaurants* (London: Women Publishers, 1924), p. 53.

30 Several Pomona Toys are mentioned and photographed in A. C. Benson and Lawrence Weaver, *Everybody's Book of the Queen's Doll's House* (London: Methuen, 1924), p. 74. Also 'Modern Toys', *Homes and Gardens* (December 1931), p. 34.

31 'People, Places, and Things', *Hearth and Home* (25 January 1894), p. 349.

32 Tidcombe, *Women Bookbinders*, p. 132.

33 Jennie Brunton, *The Arts and Crafts Movement in the Lake District: A Social History* (Lancaster: University of Lancaster, 2001).

34 Bushey Museum, Woodward file, receipt signed by E. C. Woodward, 28 August 1925.

35 *Olivia's Shopping and How She Does It: A Prejudiced Guide to the London Shops* (London: Gay and Bird, 1906), p. 59.

36 British Library, Edith Craig papers, Add. MS EC-Z3, 149, Pamela Colman Smith to Edith Craig, 29 October 1928.

37 'Handicraft Productions', *The Times* (1 November 1924), p. 1; *Notable Londoners*, pp. 55–60.

38 *Notable Londoners*, p. 59; 'Advertisements', *English-Speaking World*, 19 (1937), p. 286. A surviving 1919 Pomona Toys price list (with illustrations by Louise Jacobs) lists prices ranging from a Noah's Ark for £3 15s to small wooden animals for 2s. Special Collections, University of Sheffield, Sheffield Educational Settlement Papers, MS91.

39 'Classified Advertising: Mrs Newman, Goldsmith', *The Times* (9 July 1892), p. 1.

40 Whitman, 'The Jewellery of Mrs Philip Newman', p. 467.

41 'Nelson and Edith Dawson', *Architectural Review* (1 December 1896), pp. 35–45 (pp. 35, 45).

42 *Notable Londoners*, p. 59.

43 Erika Rappaport, *Shopping for Pleasure: Women in the Making of London's West End* (Princeton: Princeton University Press, 2001); Lise Shapiro Sanders, *Consuming Fantasies: Labor, Leisure, and the London Shopgirl, 1880–1920* (Columbus: Ohio State University Press, 2006).

44 Sydney Cockerell, 'Obituary: Mrs Edmund Webb', *The Times* (20 October 1952), p. 8.

45 Alan Crawford, 'Broadway, Worcestershire-II', *Country Life* (31 January 1980), p. 309.

46 Winifred M. Jones, 'The Revival of an Old World Industry', *Atalanta* (1 June 1898), p. 497.

47 Roberta Mills, 'Leather Craft', in *Penrose's Pictorial Annual: The Process Year Book for 1912–13* (ed.) William Gamble (London: Lund, Humphries, 1913), pp. 71–72.

48 'An Interesting Commission', *Illustrated London News* (15 July 1899), p. 72.

49 Gillian Sutherland, *In Search of the New Woman: Middle-Class Women and Work in Britain, 1870–1914* (Cambridge: Cambridge University Press, 2015), p. 160.

50 Seth Koven, *Slumming: Sexual and Social Politics in Victorian London* (Princeton: Princeton University Press, 2004), p. 153.

51 Alfred C. Harmsworth, 'What Shall I Be?', *Young Folks' Paper: Literary Olympic and Tournament* (24 September 1887), p. 203.

52 'Answers to Correspondents', *Myra's Journal* (1 January 1894), p. 23.

53 Smedley, 'A Guild of Craftswomen', pp. 320–321.

54 'Notes by the Way', *Englishwoman*, 16/6 (May 1910), p. 121.

55 'Nothing Like Leather for Suffragettes Wear', *Votes for Women* (15 October 1909), p. 48.

56 Thelma Hilda Benjamin, *A Shopping Guide to London* (New York: R. M. McBride, 1930), pp. 136–153. It was evidently popular as four years later she published Thelma Hilda Benjamin, *London Shops and Shopping* (London: Herbert Joseph, 1934). See also the chapter on 'Artistic Shops' in Montizambert, *London Discoveries*.

57 Whitman, 'The Jewellery of Mrs Philip Newman', p. 466; 'Modern Toys', *Homes and Gardens*, p. 34.

58 'Classified Advertising', *The Times* (9 January 1895), p. 1.

59 Newman went to the South Kensington Schools, where she was encouraged by Henry Cole to become a designer. Later, she worked for John Brogden, 'a manufacturing jeweller and a most artistic man'. Although she was initially seated away from the main business, upstairs: 'sitting in my little room, out of sight, designing', she was slowly 'drawn more into the business, and eventually became the manager' because her 'design gave satisfaction' when dealing with Princess Louise, the sculptor, who visited the shop wanting a locket to be made. Tooley, 'A Lady Goldsmith', p. 289. Similarly, in a short story, which very likely reflected her own experiences, Lowndes discussed how the two female protagonists, 'James' and 'Kit-cat', were initially segregated at a stained-glass firm 'in the slums near King's Cross', in a room by themselves which was 'very dirty and queer, containing two long benches and some rickety chairs; and on the bench along the windows were two table-easels for the glass'. Here the women made designs for stained glass although 'Nobody would tell us anything, and we struggled along.' Over time, they were, similarly to Newman, absorbed into the business, in this instance because men began to be placed in their room due to the lack of separate space, and the two women started to interact with them. Mary Lowndes, 'Their Training', *Englishwoman*, 82/28 (1915), pp. 73–74.

60 Fiona MacCarthy, *The Simple Life: C. R. Ashbee in the Cotswolds* (Berkeley: University of California Press, 1992), p. 105; Smedley, 'A Guild of Craftswomen', p. 319.

61 The women's press provides a wealth of information about the growing range of opportunities for women to work at decorative art businesses from around the 1880s onwards. One such article in 1887 advised readers to contact: Agnes Garrett, who offered three years' training (the premium was a prohibitive £300) from ten to four; a Miss Collingridge of 9 Beaumont Street, Portland Place, who received pupils daily from half-past nine to four; 'Messrs. Simpson' of 100 St Martin's Lane, who 'employ many ladies in various kinds of decorative work' with salaries beginning at £40 a year working from nine to six, or Louisa Avant at 13 Queen's Mansions, who had a centre for producing 'every kind of decorative work' and employed 'ladies for all the orders

she undertakes, and keeps a register of workers in all departments'. Harmsworth, 'What Shall I Be?' *Young Folks' Paper* (24 September 1887), p. 203. The British Library holds a rare surviving 'Indenture of Apprenticeship' to Mary Lowndes signed by Gertrude Esther Young from 1900. British Library Add. MS 72833 fol. 47^r.

62 Smedley, 'A Guild of Craftswomen', p. 319.
63 Linda Cluckie, *The Rise and Fall of Art Needlework: Its Socio-Economic and Cultural Aspects* (Bury St Edmunds: Arena, 2008), p. 154.
64 Tooley, 'A Lady Goldsmith', p. 289.
65 Jones, 'The Revival of an Old World Industry', p. 497.
66 Tooley, 'A Lady Goldsmith', p. 289. Artist Katherine Everett also claimed that her working-class male employees preferred a 'lady boss': Mo Moulton, 'Bricks and Flowers: Unconventionality and Queerness in Katherine Everett's Life Writing', in *British Queer History: New Approaches and Perspectives* (ed.) Brian Lewis (Manchester: Manchester University Press, 2013), pp. 63–86 (p. 77).
67 Samuel Shaw, '"The New Ideal Shop": Founding the Carfax Gallery, *c.* 1898–1902', *British Art Journal*, 13/2 (2012), pp. 35–43.
68 'Interview', *Women's Penny Paper*, p. 145.
69 Tooley, 'A Lady Goldsmith', p. 289.
70 Montizambert, *London Discoveries*, p. 51.
71 Tooley, 'A Lady Goldsmith', p. 289.
72 E. C. Woodward, 'Jewellery and Metal Work', in *Mrs Strang's Annual for Girls* (Oxford: Oxford University Press, 1921), pp. 47–53 (pp. 47–48).
73 Gordon Russell, 'Mrs Edmund Webb', *The Times* (14 November 1952), p. 8.
74 Private collection, Dawson papers, Josephine Webb to Edith B. Dawson, 20 July 1904; Smedley, 'A Guild of Craftswomen', p. 318.
75 Ibid., pp. 319–320.
76 'What One Hears at Afternoon Tea', *Ladies' Treasury* (1 December 1895), p. 849.
77 University of Reading Special Collections, Bell papers, 330/238, Alice B. Woodward (sister of E. C. Woodward) to 'Mr Bell', 6 November 1907.
78 'Windermere Industry', *Art Workers' Quarterly*, 13/4 (January 1905), pp. 56–57.
79 Giles Waterfield, *The People's Galleries: Art Museums and Exhibitions in Britain, 1800–1914* (New Haven: Yale University Press, 2015); Kate Hill, *Women and Museums, 1850–1914: Modernity and the Gendering of Knowledge* (Manchester: Manchester University Press, 2016); Amy Woodson-Boulton, *Transformative Beauty: Art Museums in Industrial Britain* (Stanford: Stanford University Press, 2012).
80 Jones, 'The Revival of an Old World Industry', p. 497.
81 *Notable Londoners*, p. 59.
82 Octave Uzanne declared in *The Modern Parisienne* that 'The twentieth century will witness the emancipation of women in art and letter. We are at the dawn of a new era, which will give facilities to women for the development as far as possible of their intellectual facilities … One may even say that they are too much in favour, too much encouraged by the pride and ambition of their families, for they threaten to become a veritable plague, a fearful confusion, and a terrifying stream of mediocrity'. Octave Uzanne, *The Modern Parisienne* (London: Heinemann, 1912), p. 129.

5

Out of the guild hall and into the city

For the 1916 Arts and Crafts Exhibition Society exhibition, held at the height of the First World War, the Women's Guild of Arts was asked to decorate a room with the work of members, to represent the Guild to the public. The exhibition was held at Burlington House, home of the Royal Academy. This was an intriguing turn of events for the Society, its exhibitors, and the public, symbolising the acceptance of the Arts and Crafts by 'the establishment' to an unprecedented extent.[1] The letter sent by the Society to members seeking their involvement was rooted in a nationalistic framing which had become increasingly common during the war: 'place, circumstance, and time combine to make the decision one of capital importance, not only to the Society but also to the Nation'.[2] Masterminded by architect Henry Wilson, the Society transformed the Academy's 'old conventional galleries, with their gilded frames' into a series of rooms dedicated to a display of the cultural, restorative, and commemorative significance of the arts in war-torn society.[3] Rooms included a 'hall of heroes', a municipal hall, a weaving room, and a 'treasury for jewels and silver work', amongst others. The Women's Guild of Arts displayed the work of members as a 'Lady's Bedroom'. By choosing to decorate the room in this way – at an exhibition seeking to showcase the heights of Arts and Crafts creativity at one of the premier exhibition venues in the country – members publicly proclaimed their special feminine expertise in the decoration of the ideal bedroom for a woman. Although a popular exhibition style for women's art groups at the time, the Guild's decision is puzzling. It contradicts both its institutional policy towards exhibitions, discussed in Chapter 2, and the personal views of many members who had sought to avoid overtly feminised modes of artistic expression.

So far, *Women Art Workers* has surveyed the artistic, professional world these women constructed through strategies relating to the use of space and the built environment. This final chapter considers how women's professional engagement in the Arts and Crafts movement was influenced by the changing context of early twentieth-century society: of the suffrage campaigns, a world at war, and the build-up of frustrations at the lack of opportunities at the Guild Hall. After the early years, the majority of members increasingly focused their artistic energies – on an individual and collaborative level – away from the Hall, and on the public life of the city, by using their art and artistic skills to engage in political debates, reform civil society, and contribute to the war effort. Many acted as key figures in the construction of suffrage spectacle, both in their art and by campaigning. But the opportunities the suffrage campaigns presented publicly to assert political views and professional status radically deviated from the approach being taken at the Guild at an institutional level. Disagreements about precisely *how* women should be performing their professional roles in the arts had been raging across society since the late nineteenth century, but debates reached a head in 1913. Minutes of meetings at the Guild Hall and letters between members reveal in precise detail the rupture in opinions between different women art workers about their strategic priorities for the maintenance of artistic reputations: about the appropriateness of women-only professional spaces, strategies of public and private representation, the meaning of artistic equality, and the implications of suffrage militancy on gender relations. Situating the campaigns amidst the wider historical landscape provides a productive window onto the intersecting political and professional allegiances which shaped women's priorities and responses to suffrage and feminism in twentieth-century England.

In the second half of the chapter, I turn to discuss the seismic effect of war in further reshaping the focus and priorities of women in the Arts and Crafts movement. The First World War brought about a surprising range of new professional, commercial, medical, and philanthropic opportunities for art workers, but also ushered in an ever more nationalistic and traditional framing to the Arts and Crafts. This simultaneously encouraged a resurgence of essentialised understanding of gendered difference, as exemplified by the 1916 exhibition. Ultimately, the combined effects of suffrage and war led to an irrevocable shift in the mind-sets of many women art workers, as they increasingly focused their energies on promoting an Arts and Crafts movement envisaged on their own terms. This took them ever further away from the Hall and into the city, to the exhibitions, events, and spaces which were more receptive to their social, political, and cultural agendas.

Suffrage politics and the splintering of strategies of professionalisation

The highly politicised nineteenth-century socialist circles of William Morris and C. R. Ashbee remain iconic today, but for many artistic women – who could still be active in socialist networks – the political potential of the Arts and Crafts lay in the new opportunities it offered to find creative fulfilment and financial independence. For women, this process of professionalisation was a challenge to prevalent gender hierarchies, situating them amidst the expansive orbit of the women's movement. As such, many women art workers identified as supporters of women's enfranchisement, feeling the quest for artistic equality to be deeply connected to the fight for political emancipation.

Women have long used art to make politicised statements about society, but it was in the early twentieth century that the contributions of different Arts and Crafts women *made* the visual spectacle of the campaigns.[4] Art workers designed and made banners, posters, postcards, and other ephemera, and were important political campaigners in their own right: marching in parades, petitioning the press, and establishing societies and journals. Some, such as Julia Chance, even resigned from groups such as the Women's Guild of Arts because suffrage began to take up all her 'time and interest'.[5] Guild member Emily Ford was in the Manchester Society for Women's Suffrage, the London Society for Women's Suffrage, was a Vice President of the Leeds Suffrage Society, and was Vice Chairman of the Artists' Suffrage League. She designed striking posters such as 'Factory Acts', which sought to emphasise the problematic legal control men had over women's working lives. Mary Sargant Florence was a founding member and on the Committee of the Tax Resistance League, subscribed to various suffrage groups – militant and non-militant – and designed banners and posters such as 'Dare to be Free' for the Women's Freedom League (Figure 5.1).[6] Surviving material contributions situate several other members as supporters when textual evidence of commitment is difficult to find. Pamela Colman Smith, Ada Ridley, and Alice B. Woodward all contributed stencils to the collaborative 1911 *An Anti-Suffrage Alphabet* designed by Laurence Housman and edited by Leonora Tyson (organiser for the Women's Social and Political Union), which sardonically depicted the prevalence of sexist attitudes in society. Louise Jacobs, who was a member of the Suffrage Atelier, designed the famed 1912 'The Appeal of Womanhood' poster, which provides clear insight into her views about the wider ramifications of enfranchisement: it featured a woman in classical robes holding a scroll emblazoned with the words,

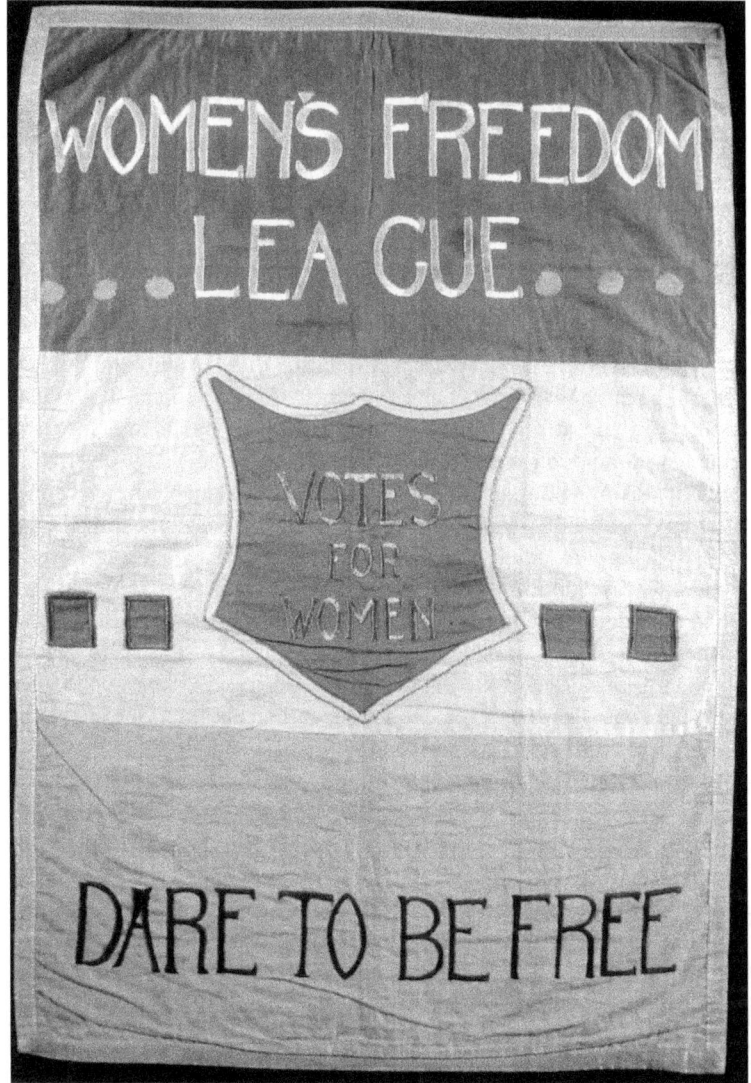

Figure 5.1 'Dare to be Free' designed by Mary Sargant Florence, *c.* 1908–1914

'We want the vote to stop the white slave traffic, sweated labour, and to save the children'.[7]

Mary Lowndes wrote a stream of articles for newspapers and the suffrage press and designed an astonishing numbers of banners. She was instrumental in founding the Artists' Suffrage League in 1907 – the year the Guild was formed. Members of both groups included Lowndes, Christiana Herringham, Emily Ford, Mary Sargant Florence, the Woodward sisters (Alice B. and E. C.), and M. V. Wheelhouse. Unlike the Guild, the League focused on providing a forum for professional artists to channel their creative skills into publicising the campaign and was associated with the constitutional National Union of Women's Suffrage Societies. Still, both groups advocated for collaboration between the sexes; the League's banner was embroidered with the words 'Alliance Not Defiance', which Herringham assisted in stitching.[8]

Chapter 2 discussed the participation of several women art workers in suffrage art exhibitions: perhaps exhibiting there to show support for the campaign, but also using these supportive environments to establish reputations and at times to make money. The compassionate, inclusive milieu at these public spaces presented certain ideological problems for women seeking to be considered on strictly professional terms, yet could also provide an empowering and charged atmosphere where politics, art, and working life could temporarily coincide. Many suffrage events functioned as important processes of professionalisation in their own right, offering women unique opportunities to make their statuses known to the world in busy public settings in the capital. For the 1909 Pageant of Women's Trades and Professions at the Albert Hall, *Votes for Women* reported that 'For over half an hour, contingents, carrying emblems symbolic of their work, marched round the hall, and took their places in the arena. From the women doctors in their blazing scarlet hoods, to the pitbrow women, in their shawls, every branch of women's work was represented.'[9] One photograph, by Christina Broom, shows painter Louise Jopling (wearing the light coat) standing on the streets next to her fellow campaigners, holding signs whilst flanked by sober-faced policemen (Figure 5.2). At other events, banners were used to inspire the crowds by depicting inspirational professional women from across history, fluttering with the names of writers Charlotte and Emily Brontë, and painter Mary Moser. For Moser's banner, care was taken to stitch 'RA', the signifier which reminded knowledgeable spectators that women artists had been Academicians in the eighteenth century but were no longer involved.

Yet, although many Arts and Crafts women supported the vote, they tended to prioritise their working lives. Only a few – most notably Sylvia Pankhurst – ultimately gave up their professions for the cause. May Morris exemplifies the tendency of women art workers to, at times, show considerable support, but at other points appear uninterested, instead focusing on their artistic careers. Morris designed, and provided materials,

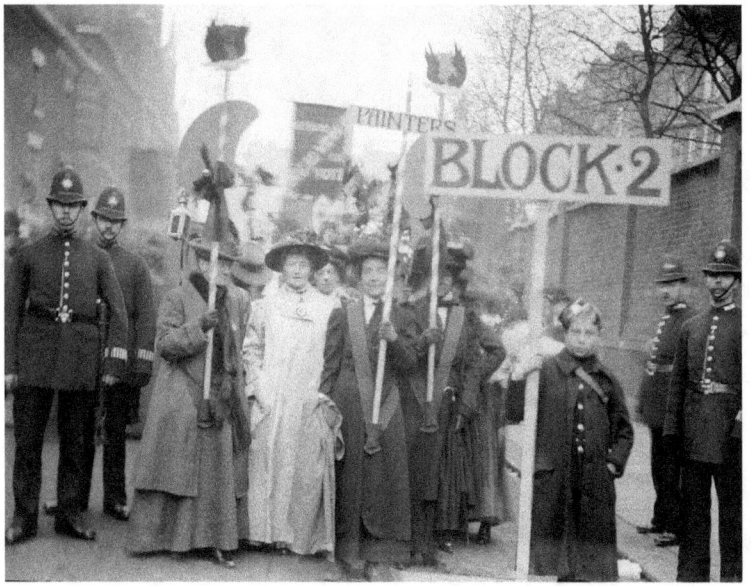

Figure 5.2 Pageant of Women's Trades and Professions, 1909

for a Fabian Society banner in 1908 intended for a National Union of Women's Suffrage Societies' procession. The banner is noticeably plain, simply stating 'Fabian Women, Equal Opportunities for Men and Women' (Figure 5.3).[10] Although clearly influenced by a need to use a simple slogan that could be read from afar, the banner exemplifies the views of Morris and many of her fellow women art workers who sought to avoid maternalistic, feminised language. A similar approach can be seen in Sargant Florence's 'Dare to be Free' banner. Justifications for artistic and political equality were instead framed around a long-established approach of liberty and universal justice. Morris also consented to having her name included in a list of contributors to the *Coming Citizen*, although she was reluctant to join in any work to which she could only lend occasional aid. She wrote that she hoped the paper would bring about women's suffrage, so people could give place to other important matters.[11] During a 1909–1910 lecture tour of North America, audiences assumed Morris would be immersed in campaigning, and were surprised when she 'shrank into herself as a snail into its shell as she was bombarded with questions about woman suffrage and such topics of the hour'. When pushed to present her perspective, she replied simply that her 'interest in suffrage is linked with the guild workers in the arts and crafts'.[12]

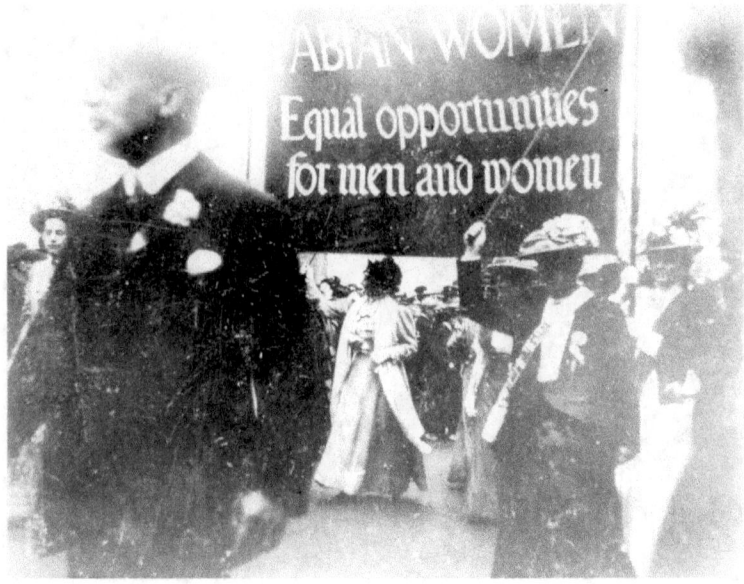

Figure 5.3 Photograph showing 'Fabian Women, Equal Opportunities for Men and Women' banner, *c.* 1908

Jan Marsh has argued that this reluctance to support suffrage activism wholeheartedly was a result of Morris's socialist beliefs, which prioritised class hierarchies as the major issue within society.[13] Alongside this, Morris evidently wished to focus on artistic unity and professional mixed-sex collaborations, which she saw as being at odds with the separatist strategies prevalent in the suffrage campaigns. Instead, she preferred to focus her energies on the Women's Guild of Arts, whilst also finding ways to familiarise contemporaries with the rich tradition of women's involvement in the guild system. She gave a lecture in New York on 'Mediaeval Embroidery', and the *New York Times* reported she offered a detailed account of the 'first woman's trade union league of which historic record remains', educating her audience about 'the long roll of embroidery mistresses' in thirteenth-century Paris.[14] Morris's international drive to encourage knowledge about the extensive history of women in the arts helped build her own sense of legitimacy and sphere of influence as a modern embroidery designer, and bolstered the validity of the Women's Guild of Arts, of which she continued to be Honorary Secretary.

Many other professional women grew increasingly alienated by the violent tactics of groups like the Women's Social and Political Union, considering them counterproductive. In 1908, Christiana Herringham and the painter Bertha Newcombe sent a petition to *The Times*, pointing out that the signatures collected were from 'leading women' and not as 'the act of a party or society'. Those who signed included May Morris, and other prominent figures such as Beatrice Webb and Millicent Garrett Fawcett. The cause of this petition was that the Chancellor of the Exchequer David Lloyd George had promised to speak at a meeting at the Albert Hall for the Women's Liberal Federation, which had 'aroused a great interest and expectation among women of all shades of political opinion who desire the Parliamentary vote'. The Women's Social and Political Union planned to break up the meeting and prevent Lloyd George from speaking, something Herringham and Newcombe cuttingly described as 'part of their usual tactics'. Clearly a number of prominent professional women, including those linked to institutions such as the Women's Guild of Arts, were keen to distance themselves from radical suffrage activism in the eyes of wider society. Even so, they were adamant that their policy should be considered as individual rather than related to their status as leading lights of women's organisations.[15]

Other artistic women felt increasingly pulled between their professional commitments and the needs of the campaign. In a letter from the suffrage organiser Philippa Strachey to Millicent Garrett Fawcett in 1908, Strachey worried about the impact of Mary Lowndes's commitment to the campaign on her stained-glass business: 'Her organising capacities are ... remarkable. She got the banners made & she worked out every detail in connection with them without letting me have the smallest trouble about them from first to last ... She really did an immense amount of work for us & I shudder to think of what was happening to her own trade.'[16] The following year Lowndes's partner Barbara Forbes wrote to Strachey lamenting, 'we have a lot of work, and as she spends all her time on suffrage I must do what little I can for the despised customer'.[17] Lowndes herself commented on these difficulties in 1911. When asked to be involved in the Women's Coronation Procession she wrote to Strachey that 'Miss Forbes and I are both absolutely unable to give the time required for organising such a thing at this moment; and I do not know anyone else in the Artists' League who will give up their home and all their work for some weeks'.[18] The campaign was increasingly demanding full-time commitment, something women who needed to make money, and had established professional lives, found impossible to juggle.

Amidst the wealth of empowering opportunities engendered by campaigning, and the political obligations evidently felt by certain art workers, were seeds of anxiety about the impact of feminist politics on strategies of professionalisation. As many chapters of this book have foregrounded, there was an underlying feeling of dissatisfaction with segregated spaces: although women's professional groups could be empowering spaces and provide occasions for women-centred curation and peer support, remaining embedded within a feminised associational culture simultaneously strengthened perceptions of the supposedly differentiated persona of the 'lady artist', which alienated women from a masculine world of prestigious professional opportunities. Helen McCarthy has noted that throughout the first half of the twentieth century, women across the professions could be ambivalent to feminist ideologies, wanting 'to claim for themselves an identity that was not solely defined by gendered political struggle'.[19] Such feeling was intensified in professional single-sex group settings, and despite being institutions seeking to improve women's artistic lives, the committees of many major women's art organisations, such as the Glasgow Society of Women Artists, the Women's International Art Club, and the Women's Guild of Arts avoided putting forward a united, formal perspective on the topic, despite the fact that clusters of members were ardent suffrage campaigners.[20] This approach was mirrored by many other major organisations, such as the International Congress of Women, which, in its early years, avoided taking a stance on the issue of suffrage in order to appeal to the broadest possible array of women.[21] Furthermore, to date, it has been difficult for researchers to assess the institutional perspectives of the networks of women who made up these organisations due to a lack of detailed surviving archival materials, which reiterates the significance of the archive for the Women's Guild of Arts in providing unprecedented insight into the breadth of views of women art workers during this era.[22]

The Guild was formed at the precise moment that concerns about gender segregation were reaching a breaking point within the arts. Now in middle age, with prominent, established careers, founding members were determined to be recognised in a manner not shaped by problematic assumptions relating to their gender. In one letter from Feodora Gleichen to May Morris, Gleichen wrote:

> I have always been dead against any women's societies of Art, because there ought to be no such thing as distinction of sexes in Art, and if this society is going to become one of the many woman's society things, I shall certainly leave it. I only joined because I understood it to be on a totally different basis to these other narrow societies.[23]

Morris continually battled with her feelings about socialising with groups of artistic women. In a letter to the art collector John Quinn in 1910,

Morris wrote, 'You know, theoretically I don't seek out the society of women.' However, contemplating an evening she had just spent with Guild members at her home she went on to say:

> I must say, it was as fine a little knot of women with an all-round, not self-centered, view of the arts as you could meet anywhere; all comely well-grown creatures, bubbling with vitality and good-humour. Anyway, it is a pleasure to meet women who know their work and are not playing at art.[24]

While Morris was evidently supportive of her own particular network of women, the hint towards the existence of another category of women art workers whom she saw as merely 'playing' indicates the conditional nature of such camaraderie. For those such as Morris and Gleichen, although members of the Art Workers' Guild revelled in calling each other 'Brothers', the Guild was never intended to be a 'sisterhood', which would have held problematical connotations of domesticity endemic to their status as women. They sought merely to be considered as 'professionals', pushing for a field of work where gendered difference had been negated to the maximum possible amount. This was not always compatible with the cause of women's political enfranchisement.

This sense of breaking point was not just happening in the arts: the Women's Social and Political Union were increasingly engaging in militant strategies, from planting bombs to committing arson, out of frustration at the government's failure to give women the vote. The year before the Guild was established, the Union had even strategically moved its head-quarters a five-minute walk from Clifford's Inn Hall at 3 and 4 Clement's Inn. Close to the law courts, it provided the ideal hub for frenetic campaigning. Despite the very different aims of these groups, both were now poised at the heart of the capital, asserting their right to occupy 'male' space. Gender segregation as a phenomenon was a battleground in both political and professional spheres.

Reflecting these anxieties about the purpose and implications of gender-segregated spaces, Women's Guild of Arts' materials reveal ongoing debates about the conflict between its role as a network for artistic sociability and its status as an institution dedicated to the transfer of 'ungendered' cultural authority. Some members evidently thought that the latter conception, with activities focused around lectures by members, was less likely to lead to its ghettoisation as a 'women's group'. As early as 1908, May Morris had addressed the need for more opportunities for 'business and social intercourse'; for her there seemed to be no separation between the two. She encouraged members to attend future meetings, 'eager to give out some of your own mental activity and to absorb that of your fellows'.[25] One annual report from 1910, which was not written in May Morris's hand (it was likely either written by Mary Lowndes, who had become Vice Chairman, replacing Christiana Herringham, or Honorary Secretary Mary A. Sloane) lamented the Guild's inability to have their own 'permanent home' where they could meet 'in the social way desired, as the men art workers do'. Instead they were reliant on occasional use of the Art Workers' Guild's rooms, and:

> Six or seven meetings in the year are not enough to keep the Guild going according to the scheme as originally thought out. We want to see more of each other's work, know more of each other's outlook: I might almost say if it does not seem too sentimental, we want the opportunity of an occasional glimpse at the dreams that lie at the back of our creative work: we have to change views on theory and practice in our various subjects – and listening to lectures at such long intervals will severely affect this.

Despite Morris's view that the Hall was 'so friendly and familiar' (scribbled on the Annual Report referenced above), the Committee was having difficulties in finding women who would speak there. This suggests that other women did not find the atmosphere at the Hall so conducive to artistic sociability.[26] The Annual Report for 1911 had a crossed-out section which originally stated, 'while the secretaries have found quick response to their invitations to lecture from friends from outside, it is quite difficult to coax the members of the Guild to accept', and the lecture lists each year 'represent more effort and persuasion on our part than you would imagine'.[27] A Sub-Committee was even established to encourage women to speak, but had 'not any report to make except that members asked were reluctant to engage themselves to demonstrate'.[28] Some members were evidently anxious about speaking at the Hall. Both Clifford's Inn and later 6 Queen Square were fraught with established and ongoing processes of masculine institution-building which could be isolating for women. Others simply did not wish to speak publicly at all. Although small numbers of women did give public lectures during this period, it was still unusual.[29] At the Guild, a list was written documenting everyone who had refused. This sample shows the range of responses received:

Bedford – refused once in committee
Bowerley – very delicate
Bowley – country
Canziani – relatives implored me not to <u>allow</u> her to do anything additional. Not strong

Christie – (we have had 2 lectures and one extra meeting on her subject)
embroidery
Garnett – refused twice firmly. Will let us know if she changes
Gleichen – 'would certainly never be able'
Hallé – (abroad). Twice asked to give lecture. No reply to that point
Harwood – complained of being asked by a private member. Refused
(abroad)
Prideaux – failed. Refused to help find sub
Sandell – can't lecture she says.[30]

Those who did speak were firm about how the meeting was to be organised. Mary Sargant Florence stated she was 'quite willing to open a Discussion on Wall painting, which ought to prove a very prolific subject' but wanted it to be framed as a 'discussion rather than a debate' and to be held 'in a studio', an environment she felt more conducive to open discussion.[31] A second letter reveals she had been compromised into giving a debate at the Hall but she remained determined to adapt this to her wishes, underlining points she felt strongly about:

> Please particularly avoid word 'Debate'. I asked Miss Sloane to put it down as 'Discussion' and refuse to debate on anything. It is a discussion – informal discussion is the best term. I want to bring out other people's knowledge on the subject. Could we not arrange Clifford's Inn Hall leaving out the platform business? Shall refuse to speak unless one can do so without … Please also name … printed as above – no Mrs.[32]

The microscopic detail with which these women planned such meetings shows the imposition such events represented to them and elucidates the stress they entailed. Much discussion focused on the Hall, which elicited strong views about established cultural rituals such as standing on the platform. Ultimately, it is clear the gendered realities for women art workers were considerable. Facing institutional exclusion from the Art Workers' Guild, in their determination they had managed to position themselves at the very same Hall. However, entering this established site of masculine artistic performativity, from which they continued to be barred during official 'male' Guild meetings, must have created a discomforting environment. This was compounded by the societal disapproval towards public lectures given by women, and the growing tensions around the perceived politicisation of women in English society. The idea (held by several dominant members) that the Guild was, first and foremost, to be dedicated to the exchange of cultural authority through lectures, debates, and discussions, was leading to the alienation of members who merely sought to foster an environment of supportive artistic sociability and institutional coherence in the face of their exclusion from male-led associations and exhibition societies.

By the 1910s, the need to avoid separatism was being reiterated to members with ever greater urgency: if the Guild was to learn from expertise (regardless of the gender of its practitioner), what possible objections could there be to the idea of male speakers? At one 1911 meeting, May Morris stressed they were not to be 'self-supporting' (meaning to be reliant on female members) for lectures. Instead, the Guild was to encourage 'stimulating intercourse with ... other workers outside'. Morris regularly asked men, often from the Art Workers' Guild, to lecture, telling members that 'one of our traditions which from the first included men in the invitations to attend our meetings and to lecture before us, is really one of our strong points as a body of artists preoccupied solely with questions of art'.[33] In 1912, Morris went even further, writing in a handwritten version of the Secretary's Report, 'I believe too we are agreed that we are not banded together to show what we can do <u>alone</u> – an isolated society in the community bound together by sex rather than by Art'. The Guild instead was to mirror the Art Workers' Guild, 'men already having their organisation' and simply 'to do what they are doing, i.e. to keep at the highest level the arts by which and for which we live'.[34] However, the gendered realities inherent in early twentieth-century society, which had but a few years earlier forced women to create a segregated group, meant they were never to achieve the degree of formal mixed-sex Arts and Crafts networking that women such as Morris desired.

That year, tensions reached breaking point, in the campaign and in the Guild. The Women's Social and Political Union had become increasingly isolated in outlook, and other campaigners became disillusioned and looked for alternatives.[35] Single-sex organisations were increasingly being viewed as inherently political by wider society, and women's groups, by virtue of their membership, were prone to being associated implicitly with the divisive campaigns of contemporary feminists. By this stage, the annual programme of speakers at the Women's Guild of Arts mostly constituted male speakers, in contrast to the nearly exclusively female roster in its first few years.[36] At the Guild's 1912 annual meeting, Alys Fane Trotter proposed that more needed to be done to encourage mixed-sex sociability. She suggested the creation of Honorary Associates, so they could formally invite eminent figures such as Una Taylor to join, but also, crucially, members of the Art Workers' Guild. A cluster of women, including known suffragists such as Mary Lowndes and Emily Ford, felt differently. They wrote a joint letter of complaint arguing men should not be allowed to join as Honorary Associates, as it created a gendered hierarchy, worsened because it was a free position, while members had to pay an annual sum. In addition, it 'endors[ed] a policy which has of late limited the functions of the Guild almost entirely to listening to lectures' – the majority of which were by male speakers.[37]

The increasing prevalence of male speakers appears in stark contrast to the direction being taken simultaneously by organisations such as the Lyceum Club, which by this point, had become 'well known for an assured supply of women speakers … requests continually flowed in to the Club, as a unit, to furnish speakers for all sorts of public entertaining'. Many members of the Club had initially been concerned about giving public speeches, but in response Constance Smedley had established a private 'Debating Society' in her office where those interested could practise the art of public speaking. Smedley personally went on to speak at many prestigious events: she commanded the stage with suffragette Christabel Pankhurst to discuss 'Women's Suffrage'; she spoke at the annual Banquet of the International Society of Sculptors, Painters, and Gravers (where she claimed to be the first woman 'allowed to be audible … in the history of public dinners'); and she played a central role at a Ladies' Banquet for the London Chamber of Commerce event where, with figures such as Walter Crane, she led a discussion on 'The Relations of Art to Commerce'.[38]

Yet at the Guild, in early 1913, over thirty members wrote a formal letter to their Chair, Mary Seton Watts, disagreeing with those who wanted to limit male participation. They stated:

> We welcome any means of widening the scope of the Guild, such as stimulating and interesting lectures, not only from our own members but from men and women outside. Such lectures we have been in the custom of having and they help to keep our body in touch with the work and thought of the world in a way perhaps not otherwise possible for many women whose time is much occupied.[39]

This letter marked a turning point in the institutional policy of the Guild towards gender segregation. Many members believed that making their institution porous to 'outside' artists – which appears to have mostly symbolised men – would embed it within a wider cultural and professional world and distance themselves from politically charged debates about women's enfranchisement. These members who welcomed male participation in the form of Honorary Associates were seeking to balance a need for empowerment through networking with other women with their wish to be considered as professionals on a level footing with their male peers. Far from being abstract and external threats to the coherency of their organisation, these men were often co-workers, husbands, family members, and champions of their work.

Alongside this, a flurry of individual letters was sent. All the surviving letters are from women in favour of male involvement; it is impossible to determine whether it was decided to keep only those letters, or whether these supporting letters were the only ones sent. Illuminator Ethel Sandell thought the concerns about male Honorary Associates 'excessively silly and feminine'. She had recently been asked to scribe the Guild Roll, but warned she had stopped as she did not want 'to go down to posterity in the roll of a Guild of man-eaters!'[40] A letter from decorative painter Ethel K. Martyn revealed she had worried about the Guild's motives for a long time: 'the strong movement against it seemed to me to be from a purely anti-man tendency and to go towards weakening the Guild altogether ... I have felt rather doubtful whether I ought to remain in the Guild if it stood at all for the possibly political or above tendency for years ... I'll resign if the Guild is evidently going to be an anti-man affair.'[41] Similarly, illustrator Ethel Everett felt that 'our great art should be ideally human and neither man nor woman should be excluded from anything connected to it'. Everett's decision to underline the word 'human' elucidates her belief that artistic culture should foreground human endeavour rather than divide it into gendered categories of cultural worth. Everett, who personally contributed several illustrations to suffrage papers, worked through her justifications as to why her Guild was separated from the Art Workers' Guild, ultimately reconciling this by writing: 'tho' of course it's necessary sometimes to have clubs and societies for one and other, but to get a feminine element into art is a mistake which must be unless there is somewhere an interchange of ideas'.[42] One unnamed member even wrote:

> Personally, I do not feel strongly about it, except that I loathe the thought of suffrage sex wars being brought into it and warmly welcome new lecturers who have studied their subject instead of ... little papers by half-baked people who think it their duty to stand on their legs because they are members.[43]

This belief in the equal artistic potentials of men and women at an ideal, theoretical level was frequently adapted by women art workers to fit the specific material conditions they found themselves facing in everyday life.

The fact so many women signed the group letter, alongside the others who wrote special letters to further detail their personal perspectives, is emblematic of the weight members placed on this matter. There was no other occasion in the history of the Guild which resulted in so much interest. There was a general consensus, articulated most fully by Feodora Gleichen to May Morris, that to

> reject any form of external help, such as lectures by outsiders whether men or women is narrowing it all down to a silly sort of childish game. There can be no possible question of politics in such a society and the sort of retaliation about not admitting men as Associates, because they do not admit us to their Guild seems to me unutterably small and petty.[44]

Going on, she added in a note to Mary A. Sloane, 'The letter looks to me as if it was only a cloak for their real reason … their objection to admitting men at all. However of course this is only my <u>private</u> opinion!'[45] But Gleichen did also write that if having Honorary Associates 'causes such dismay amongst certain members of the Guild, that it is not of sufficient importance to allow it to make a permanent split in the Society'.[46] Pamela Colman Smith similarly confided to Mary A. Sloane that she felt members were 'old enough' to know their own minds, but to her, limiting male involvement meant going against the founding principles, as it would 'make this Guild into a purely woman's affair – which it was never originally started on'.[47]

At the Extraordinary Meeting on 28 February 1913, Mary Sargant Florence, backed by Mary Batten, proposed it be reconsidered whether men could join. However, this was lost by a vote of sixteen to twenty-one and the principle of admitting male Honorary Associates was reaffirmed.[48] This caused considerable frustrations and at a Committee Meeting later that year, Mary Sargant Florence said she was 'dissatisfied with the way the Guild was managed', and resigned from the Committee.[49] Others followed her, dramatically leaving mid-meeting, and later resigning.[50] The ripple effects of this decision were still being felt at the next Committee Meeting, when Mary Batten told the Guild she would not be standing for re-election as Honorary Treasurer, and that she 'entirely agreed with the protest that had been made' and 'entirely disagreed' with the way in which it had been addressed by the Guild.[51] Invitations to join the Guild as Honorary Associates were quickly sent to Una Taylor, Laurence Binyon, W. R. Lethaby, and Emery Walker, who all accepted. That year the 1913 Annual Report finished by stating:

> Now, the Art Workers' Guild for reasons of their own are unable to admit women, but as far as our Guild is concerned, there is no principle involved in keeping men at a distance. It is undeniable that the principal workers in most crafts are men, and from the first our Guild has felt that the best authorities in every branch of Arts and Crafts should, regardless of sex or distinction, be encouraged to come into our midst

and talk to us in the intimate and comrade-like way that is so stimulating to an artist's work capacity.[52]

The dilemmas and disagreements which played out at the Women's Guild of Arts speak fundamentally of the diversity of approaches to professional and artistic equality held by members. Some women, who otherwise appear to have supported the aims of women's emancipation, permitted their political ideologies to be subsumed to the demands of their professional aspirations, seeking to collaborate with men in the hope of being considered artistic equals. Others could not see the encroachment of men on women-only groups as anything other than an affront to their previous structural renegotiation of hierarchies which excluded them from male artistic circles.

An important comparator here is the Women's International Art Club. Both groups already shared several members but after the spate of Guild resignations many former members immersed themselves in the Club instead.[53] M. V. Wheelhouse became Chair of the Club's Committee from 1914 to 1917, while E. C. Woodward hosted several Club meetings at her workshop. Others who had resigned, such as Edith B. Dawson and Mary Sargant Florence, exhibited with the Club. The ease with which these women forged new formal ties amply demonstrates the sophisticated, multi-layered kinship and professional networks women artists had developed by this point, moving between groups they felt to be the most beneficial to them. But there was to be no respite from debates about separatism. In 1917, whilst war raged, the Club hosted a special meeting to discuss its 'Character', an event reminiscent of the Guild's meeting four years earlier. With Wheelhouse in the chair, painter and etcher Elsie Druce asked members to 'make their feelings known about changing the Club and making it a mixed society'. The meeting minute book diplomatically notes that 'Several arguments were brought forwards'. The first viewpoint was that 'the Club had attained a certain reputation, which it could not afford to lose', as a women's group. Another argument, perhaps put forward by those knowledgeable about the Guild – now dominated by invited male speakers – suggested 'it would be better to disband altogether than to be submerged into the men's societies'. The final decision was to remain women-only. They felt that 'after the war it would be easier to maintain the international element for which the club was formed'.[54]

Arts and Crafts during the First World War

War transformed the suffrage campaigns, as it transformed the Arts and Crafts. Alongside the decline in militant activism there was an outpouring of fervent patriotism from many suffrage groups, although several campaigners rejected this and became embedded in pacifist networks.[55] In the context of war, the anti-commercial ethos of the Arts and Crafts was aligned with an austere reassertion of art as an indication of the nation's social probity: the language used to describe artworks now frequently focused on the 'useful' and 'long lasting' nature of these durable handmade items. The movement became a source of national pride, representative of 'a bit of old England'.[56] Art workers and the press stressed the many opportunities offered by handcrafted cultures to remake the country – for the better – after the guns fell silent. Carolyn Malone has evidenced the centrality of Arts and Crafts men in efforts to commemorate the dead and to help reconstruct society after the war.[57] The role played by women in spearheading the promotion of Arts and Crafts during the war, and in the aftermath, has, however, been ignored, as have the ramifications of war in refracting gender hierarchies in the applied arts.[58] This is indicative of the ongoing failure to incorporate women's experiences adequately in cultural histories of war.

The war ushered in a challenging time for artists, as schools and workshops closed, and materials became more expensive. The art world was initially viewed with suspicion, a luxury peripheral to the concerns of ordinary citizens. Mary Lowndes lamented in a short story in the *Englishwoman* in 1915 about the problems facing women artists. Although there were now opportunities to do 'crayon portraits of handsome young men in khaki, with delicately pencilled melancholy eyes', these had to be done for 'war-prices', and:

> War-prices means working for almost nothing if you have anything to sell, and paying a frightful price if you have to buy anything ... How girls who pay their way are going to keep their heads above water I can't think, for the newspapers do nothing but say that nobody must buy the things women make, because they are luxuries.[59]

War also inevitably meant many artists had far less time. One illustration by M. E. A. Rope shows her battle to coordinate her work for the Land Army with her stained-glass work, conceptualised as *The Arts of Peace/ of War* (Figure 5.4).

In response to these challenges, women art workers strategically adapted their tactics, using their creativity and professional skills in numerous new philanthropic, commercial, cultural, and medical spheres. War shifted the creative focus of a great many women at the Women's Guild of Arts. Alys Fane Trotter, whose son died during the war, turned from sketching to writing poetry: *Nigel and Other Verses* in 1918, followed

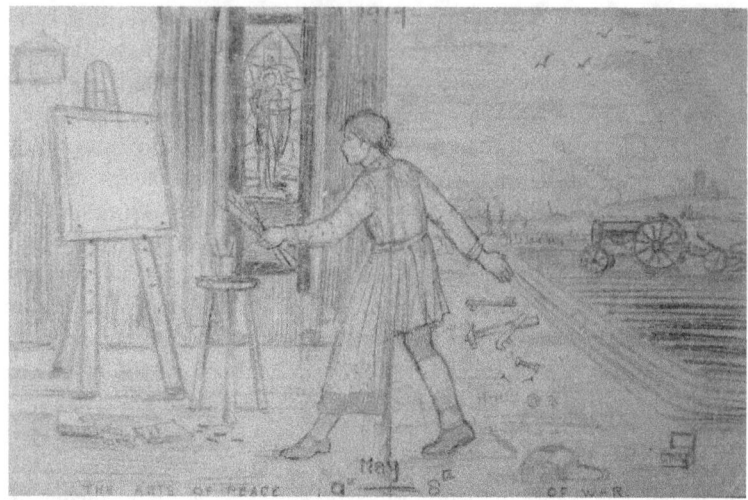

Figure 5.4 *The Arts of Peace/of War* by stained-glass window designer, M. E. A. Rope, 1919

by *Houses and Dreams* in 1924. She also contributed to a poetry anthology reflecting on the devastating ramifications of war.[60] Estella Canziani painted the dreamy watercolour *The Piper of Dreams* in 1914, a calming fantasy utopia depicting a boy playing a pipe to a robin, seated at the foot of a tree and surrounded by fairies and primroses. The image became phenomenally popular. Alongside Holman Hunt's *The Light of the World*, it was one of the most popular prints published by the Medici Society, selling 250,000 reproductions in the first year. Distributed across France, Egypt, and India, it became a talisman for trench-bound combatants.[61] Feodora Gleichen chose to tackle military life directly in her memorial to the fallen of the 37th (British) Division at Monchy-le-Preux, France, a division commanded by her brother Lord Edward Gleichen. For this piece Gleichen was admitted to the Légion d'Honneur. Similarly, Edith B. and Nelson Dawson designed and made commemorative plaques for those lost in the war, such as the poet Rupert Brooke.[62]

By 1917, rather than lamenting the difficulties, Lowndes was instead writing about the generative potential of warfare in facilitating new opportunities for women which they 'might have vainly sought through decades of peace; they have established in the face of the world an economic position and capacity which have astonished our statesmen'.[63] In her writings, Lowndes regularly used the accomplishments of E. C. Woodward as emblematic of the pioneering efforts of artistic women on the home front. Woodward turned her metalwork business at 5 and 7 Johnson Street, Notting Hill Gate, into the first oxyacetylene school and workshop dedicated to training women in September 1915.[64] It was organised under the aegis of the Women's Service Bureau of the London Society for Women's Suffrage, which was set up in the first week of war.[65] The work of the Bureau was vast, involved in recruiting and training women in a wide range of fields, from the industrial to the domestic and medical. The Bureau worked with established employment organisations such as the Labour Exchange and the Board of Trade to find positions for women seeking to contribute to the war effort, providing, for instance, the London General Omnibus Company with its first women conductors.[66] Investigations by the Bureau had revealed that although oxyacetylene welders were sorely needed in factories – as the demand for aeroplanes had increased enormously, and many male welders had enlisted – the technical schools were not open to women. Taking time away from her own busy working life, Woodward learned how to do oxyacetylene welding herself, with the aid of a 'stiff text book', 'picturesque experiments in her workshop', lessons from 'friendly workmen and technical advisors', and by simply 'working it out for herself'.[67] She then began to instruct other women how to weld flat plates, sockets, and tubes.[68] An adjoining workshop, with a power lathe and drilling machine were installed, and lessons were given in topics such as metal-fitting and filing for shells and hand grenades and mechanical drawings.[69] By 1916, over a hundred women welders had been trained and sent out across the country.[70]

Woodward's workshop quickly received extensive press interest. Replicating the long-established approach of the nineteenth-century women's press, such women were portrayed as inspirational pioneers, although the scrutiny they faced was evoked: 'On their shoulders rested the responsibility of proving to the manufacturing world that women could, and would, make first class welders.'[71] Several articles included photographs of the workshop with women *in situ*, which appealed to readers eager to see the uniforms women were wearing (a topic of great debate) and how they were dealing with the dirty physicality of workshop life (Figure 5.5). Lowndes and the Women's Service Bureau actively encouraged such publicity. At one event, the Queen visited and the *Common Cause* discussed in lavish detail how she had supportively 'spent nearly half-an-hour at the Welding Workshop, watching the flames through coloured glasses' whilst Woodward explained the process to her. Later, Woodward and the Queen, alongside others such as Mary Lowndes, who

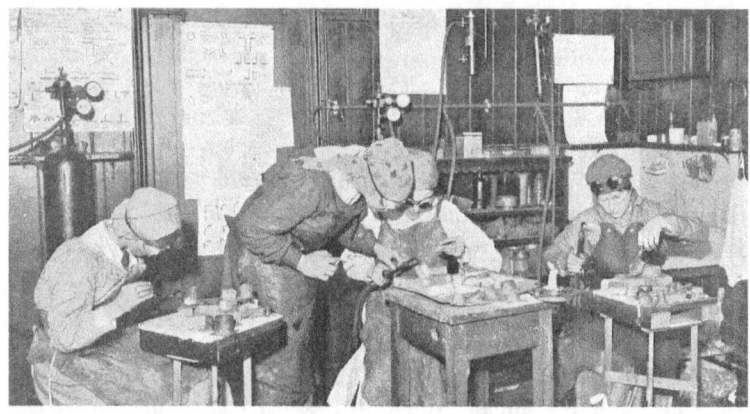

Figure 5.5 'Women Welders at Work on Pieces of Metal – In the Centre a Beginner Receiving Instruction', at E. C. Woodward's workshops at 5 and 7 Johnson Street, Notting Hill Gate, *Sphere* (11 March 1916), p. 278

was centrally involved in the scheme, all had a 'workshop tea' together, using a teapot without a handle and a packing case for a table.[72]

The war stimulated many other small women-led enterprises, particularly in industries previously dominated by German industries. The English toy industry became infiltrated by women toy makers, who often employed a nationalistic rhetoric to encourage consumers to support the country by only buying 'English' toys.[73] Pomona Toys repeatedly advertised 'English Toys for English children, designed and made in Chelsea, from 2d. to £5' during the war and in the interwar era.[74] Others, such as the Bee Toymakers, whose headquarters were 58 Victoria Street, Westminster, were established with the aim of providing work for 'highly skilled women workers'. The Committee was composed of wealthy women including Feodora Gleichen and was presided over by Sylvia Brett, the Ranee of Sarawak.[75]

In Chelsea, two more art workers – the sculptors Elinor Hallé and Anne Acheson – redirected their creative energies into supporting the war effort by drawing from the technical knowledge, anatomical expertise, and manual dexterity they had obtained as a result of their artistic professions. They both became heavily involved with the Surgical Requisites Association at 17 Mulberry Walk, Chelsea, a branch of the charity, Queen Mary's Needlework Guild. Hallé was widely lauded in the press as producing work that was 'exquisitely artistic'. Having studied at the Slade, she had made the collar for the Royal Victorian Order, the insignia of the Order of the British Empire and Companions of Honour, and numerous medals. At the Surgical Requisites Association she used papier-mâché to make innovative arm cradles and a light boot for men with drop foot, which were used across Britain, France, Italy, and India.[76] Acheson had a similar reputation; having studied at the Royal University of Ireland and the Royal College of Art, she had exhibited in Toronto, Stockholm, Brussels, Rome, and at the Paris Salon and the Royal Academy. At the Surgical Requisites Association she worked with Hallé designing papier-mâché splints made from sugar bags, developing a bath for bathing injured limbs and specialist shoulder, arm, and adjustable splints.[77] Hallé and Acheson visited various military hospitals sharing their expertise. In one photograph for the press, Hallé shows off her skills surrounded by splints (Figure 5.6). After the war, both women were awarded CBEs for their work. In a similar manner, Estella Canziani also sought to use her artistic skills to encourage medical innovations. She detailed in a chapter of her memoir

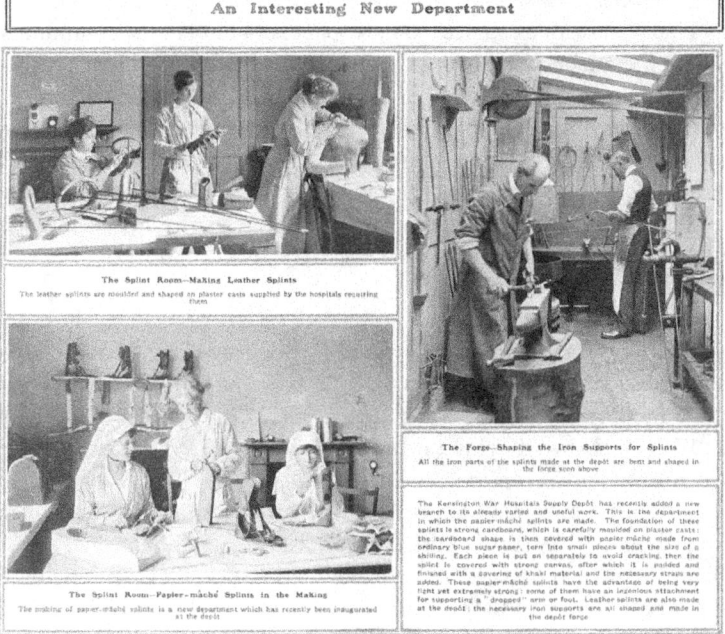

Figure 5.6 'The Kensington War Hospital Supply Depot', *Sphere* (13 January 1917), p. 38

titled 'Painting Wounds', her extensive work for twenty-two different hospitals and twenty-six surgeons during the war, making plaster of Paris casts and papier-mâché splints, painting on nerve injuries in different colours, and creating extensive sketches and notes to aid doctors.[78] Hallé, Acheson, and Canziani, along with the analogous example of Alice B. Woodward and Phyllis Gardner, who employed their drafting skills to make military maps for the Naval Intelligence Bureau, demonstrate that many women art workers took pragmatic steps to utilise their creative skills for the benefit of wartime society.[79]

During the war, concerns about separatism seem to have dissipated. At the Women's Guild of Arts, members dedicated far more energy towards asserting their group presence in public life. There was an abrupt shift in tactics away from the privacy of the Guild Hall towards the public-facing concepts of service and dissemination of artistic ideals, accompanied by a subsiding of anxiety about their gendered positions, although this was in part clearly due to the departure of many prominent suffrage campaigners the previous year. In the winter of 1914 May Morris instructed members on the narrative arc of the Arts and Crafts, positioning the movement as ever growing in reputation. She portrayed the years leading up to the war as a 'new phase of existence – a new sphere of utility to the community', which had made her 'hope great things for the future of the Arts and Crafts movement to which all of us here present belong'. Having asserted the involvement of Guild members in the movement, she stressed that although members did not 'court public attention', it was imperative now that war had broken out that they all dedicated themselves to promoting projects 'more frugal in material comforts, more generous in communal life, more eager for the advancement of the arts' to 'show our belief in the Beauty of Life'.[80]

A professional framing continued to be threaded throughout the Guild's activities – membership was still strictly regulated – but the focus was transferred towards charitable endeavours and the need to support the war effort. Members invited men to speak on pertinent topics, such as W. R. Lethaby on 'Tidy up London' and Henry Wilson on 'History, Civilisation and Reconstruction'.[81] An exhibition was hosted at 9 St Paul's Studios in 1915 to 'make known' the extensive contribution of members to the built environment, 'work done or designed for public buildings … Banners, stained-glass, designs, cartoons, photographs of memorials and other works'.[82] Furthermore, the Guild started to collaborate with women's art groups across the country, interacting with Ethel Spiller, Honorary Secretary of the Art Teachers' Guild, an association for women teachers which proclaimed, 'If art is to be national its ethical value must become a social part of the fabric of our life.'[83] Spiller had given a presentation to Prime Minister H. H. Asquith on 'Art and Education' and the Guild urged her to speak at the Hall.[84] They targeted young women artists, sending information, cards advertising lectures, and free tickets to Guild meetings for students from art schools such as the Royal College of Art and Goldsmiths College. In return, they received invitations to art events hosted by these schools.[85] The Guild also worked with Rachel Kay Shuttleworth, who established the Gawthorpe Textile Collection in Lancashire. Shuttleworth sent particulars of a new society for 'helping arts and crafts', and there were discussions about hosting an 'informal guild show' in support.[86] The Guild was clearly seeking to link its activities to a national network, largely composed of middle-class women, all dedicated to promoting the moral and educational potential of the Arts and Crafts in twentieth-century society.

Public events, conferences, and philanthropic schemes were organised. In 1915, members created an '83 feet by 5 ft' frieze for the Women's Recreation Room at the Belgium War Refugees Camp, Earl's Court, at the request of the authorities. Estella Canziani, May Morris, Pamela Colman Smith, Ethel Everett, Lola Frampton, and Eleanor Rowe were involved.[87] It is not known what the frieze depicted, but *The Times History of the War* declared how the 'painted friezes round the walls bespoke the wish of a guild of women artists to give pleasure to their eyes.'[88] That the Guild were specially requested to design this frieze shows it was felt women would have particular aptitude in the task. War provided a way for members to publicise their collaborative activities acceptably, taking focus away from their status as a segregated art group for women, although in other ways this reaffirmed tropes that artistic practices should be divided by gender: while male pictorial artists were suitable for portraying the horrors of war through documentary painting, women in the applied arts took on commissions associated with domesticity, nurturing care, and philanthropy. This did not stop the Guild putting on an exhibition of work by wounded soldiers at 155 Brompton Road in 1918, in collaboration with several members of the Art Workers' Guild such as Henry Wilson, Selwyn Image, W. R. Lethaby, and Emery Walker.[89]

War and artistic culture could be fully integrated in the exact same spaces that had served before the war as the nodes of a nexus of sociability among women art workers. In 1917, Mary A. Sloane held an 'At Home' at 9 St Paul's Studios where Serbian handicrafts were exhibited by the Serbian Relief Fund alongside other crafts. Each day, 'Miss Radford', organiser of the Serbian Relief Fund's workrooms in Serbia, gave talks on 'Serbian Handicraft and Design'.[90] Charitable relief for those affected by war extended to their activities at the Bethnal Green Military Hospital, where the Guild became involved in training disabled and discharged soldiers how to dye materials and weave by hand, with the intention this would offer them creative satisfaction and the potential for remunerative work.[91] Later, after the war, the Guild received a grant to help veterans take up art.[92] Schemes such as these constituted a sustained attempt to contribute to the moral and cultural reconstruction of modern society.

In addition to these altruistic projects, members began publicly to assert their importance as taste makers. A 1916 conference titled 'Art and the Public' at 6 Queen Square was organised jointly by May Morris, W. R. Lethaby, and a sub-committee of members of the Women's Guild of Arts. A flyer asserted:

> We wish that those who write about the Arts and those who work at them should meet and talk together, and consider the need of laying stress on the wide and natural aspect of Art, so that the public may come to view it familiarly and as part of the practical everyday life of the City.[93]

A letter Morris read to fellow members repeated this need to widen the scope of the arts, and turn 'some part of its activities into productive channels for the welfare of the nation'. Although the Arts and Crafts had always been framed around collaboration, Morris clearly envisaged the wartime atmosphere of nationalism and civic action as a critical moment to push further for social reforms through art, and to ensure the Guild was centrally involved. The conference brought together many well-known figures such as George Bernard Shaw, Laurence Binyon, and William Rothenstein.[94] In Morris's opinion, war had 'awakened a sense of citizenship throughout the country' and a crucial opportunity to 'develop demands of [a] less material nature'. Art workers needed, in her view, 'to raise their voices and assert themselves, not as a sheltered clan of artists, but as practical members of a community who felt it their duty and their right to take part in the ordering of the life of the city'.[95] Morris was the most eloquent and forthright spokesperson of a tendency to move into the public sphere and embody civic values shared by many artistic women during this period.

The most striking indication of the Guild's complete *volte face* in their approach to public representation was the 'Lady's Bedroom' they put together for the Arts and Crafts Exhibition Society's 1916 exhibition which this chapter opened with. In stark contradiction to their pre-war refusal to contribute to 'feminised' or gendered 'women's sections' at exhibitions, by 1916 they not only did so, but adopted a rhetorically problematic label which associated their work with the domestic, the feminine, and the bourgeois. Being invited to be involved in the Society's exhibition was evidently an enticing prospect for members such as Morris. Her dominance in the Guild now patent, she sent a letter to other members stating she hoped that, 'whether exhibiting or not', they would 'share in the prestige of this special room … an unprecedented opportunity of which we should avail ourselves to the utmost'.[96] Although it is tempting to frame this as a capitulation of the Guild's earlier principled refusal to segregate their work in exhibitions, the precise context, in the heightened wartime atmosphere which encouraged the publicising of institutional artistic virtue for moral and nationalistic reasons, accompanied by the novel nature of the request – the Guild had been invited as a body, to curate an entire room – evidently meant that the offer was difficult to turn down.

The works of a large number of women were shown. Contributions ranged from silver combs to a painted silk fan and a tempera crucifix. A wardrobe showed embroidered clothes, a collection of books, and the Guild Roll. But overall, the room was predominantly organised around a series of embroidered hangings and bedspreads which adorned furniture by designer Ernest Gimson. He contributed a painted cabinet (executed by Fred Davidson), a chestnut wood chest painted with vermilion (decorated by May Morris), and a bedstead (decorated by May Morris, Ethel F. Everett, Alfred Powell, and A. E. Swinny). Lola Frampton provided an embroidered bedspread executed by her, 'W. Edelstein', and 'Miss Veasay'. May Morris contributed two embroidered bedstead hangings executed by her, Mary Newill, and Birmingham School of Art students. The hangings were later exhibited at the Detroit Society Exhibition of British Arts and Crafts before being purchased by newspaper magnate George Booth and Ellen Scripps Booth for their Detroit home.

The layout of the exhibit, foregrounding the traditionally feminine craft of embroidery, exacerbated the sense of gendered division between different strands of art work. The needlework was arranged to adorn the 'masculine' craft of woodwork – for which they used furniture by a male designer, despite the Guild having woodworkers as members. Louise Powell, although primarily a potter, contributed an ebony and walnut cabinet to another room at the very same exhibition. Furthermore, in the catalogue, there was an extra layer of deferential focus to the exceptionality of male designers: a note emphasised the wools used in the hangings were 'dyed under William Morris's direction'. Elsewhere, a special 'Retrospective Room: From William Morris, 1834–1896, to Walter Crane, 1845–1915' was set up to celebrate the movement, and the Society's first exhibition in 1888, which was framed as 'literally the birth of the Arts and Crafts movement.[97] The room had been proposed by May Morris, ever keen to assert the centrality of her father.[98]

In some senses, the 'Lady's Bedroom' depicted a Guild now increasingly complicit in its own marginalisation. Yet it cannot be denied that the exhibit offered an occasion to celebrate the expertise and skill of members. Positioning needlework solely as a feminised craft flattens its subversive potential, and the pleasure and skill inherent in its design and making, as a collaborative endeavour between different women, was still very much on display. The inclusion of the Roll functioned as a further powerful symbol of comradeship; listing the names of all the members who worked across the crafts, it provided the audience with a sense of the coherence and unity of the Guild.

Admiring private letters about the exhibition were subsequently received, but the room was little discussed in the press (although the *Daily Mail* did delightedly frame it as the ultimate expression of youthful femininity: 'No more dainty bedroom for a child princess can be conceived than that which Miss May Morris has arranged.'[99]) The most detailed report was by critic W. T. Whitley, who favourably reviewed the whole exhibition for the *Studio*, but specifically used the 'Lady's Bedroom' to lament the high prices: although some objects were not priced, those costed added up to around £500. Admittedly, the costs contrast noticeably with the Woman's Kingdom exhibition in 1914 which demonstrated how to furnish a 'woman worker's bed-sitting room' for 'a £5 note'.[100] For Whitley, it was another room, designed by Ernest Gimson and May Morris, which he felt to be far more 'successful, sober and reserved in its general scheme'. He concluded that 'There should be hope indeed for the revival of village industries when work like this is the result' although he cautioned that 'a master craftsman' would be 'essential … and while villages are many master craftsmen are few'.[101] Here, he did not stop to add up the costs, which were of a similarly grand price to the 'Lady's Bedroom', totalling over £400.

Taking a step back from the 'Lady's Bedroom' and surveying the exhibition as a whole reveals the extensive growth of women's engagement in the Society at this point. With many men away at war, the work Guild members had individually designed and made was everywhere. Louise Powell had her very own ante room – Room No. 4 – which she designed, and was painted by her and her husband Alfred Powell. Another member, Grace Christie, designed and arranged Room No. 7 with her husband Archibald Christie and F. W. Troup as another bedroom, this time for a 'small Country House', filled with oak furniture, painted chairs, samplers, and embroidered hangings.[102] As such, the exhibition exemplifies the growth of opportunities for women on an individual level, but also draws attention to the perceptions that ensued (and criticism faced, for pricing their work at the same comparative level as their male peers, for example) when women tried to make their collaborative and institutional presence known.

The Guild's shift from private to public was particularly pronounced, but these activities were emblematic of a wider shift in women's art groups during the war. Pre-war women designating themselves as professionals had been anxious to situate themselves in a different context to the established role of women's engagement in philanthropy, charity bazaars, and 'amateur' crafting. But during the war there was a sharp transfer of activities towards the philanthropic and nationalistic. At the 1917 Women's International Art Club exhibition, for instance, 20 per cent from all sales was given to the British Prisoners of War Fund.[103] But it was at the Englishwoman Exhibition to which the press most readily thronged: here the activities of women art workers were described in rapturous detail. The suffrage press repositioned the exhibition for a wartime audience, notifying potentially suspicious readers that women art workers had already shown 'their readiness to serve the nation in any capacity in which their training would make them of value' by entering their names on the Women's War Register.[104] Having established this, the exhibition was described as of critical importance in 'cultivating a sounder taste' and educating the 'general public' so that 'German substitutes, made to look like much more expensive articles, will never again win such a place in our markets as they held before the war.' There was an overt positioning of the exhibition as 'refreshingly genuine; some simple and quite moderate in price, others of fine and elaborate workmanship, but none pretending to be what they are not.'[105]

The Englishwoman Exhibition, too, exemplified the shift towards a philanthropic, patriotic, charitable, and more overtly commercial focus. It started to include stalls by disabled soldiers such as the popular Sir Arthur Pearson's 'blinded soldiers and sailors' making baskets.[106] Specimens of Armenian needlecraft were sold to help survivors of the 'recent Turkish savagery in Armenia.'[107] At the 1917 exhibition a 'Guard of Honour' of wounded soldiers in 'hospital blue' even lined the route to the platform, whilst women police officers patrolled around the rooms.[108] An increasing number of popular interest stands were included to attract as wide an array of participants as possible. A section was devoted to demonstrations of bread making at home which attracted 'eager crowds' and, when written about in the press, focused on the maternal responsibilities of women as mothers and housewives. Such an approach would have seemed out of place at the exhibition only a few years earlier.[109] Furthermore, a range of novel commercial projects were displayed: heraldic embroideries by Helen Hall, coloured woodcuts by 'Captain Gibbings', and 'Mr Aumonier's tiny war-shrines'.[110] This continued into the 1920s: at the 1922 exhibition, one newspaper reported that it had 'got about that moderate-priced and unusual presents could be acquired', and so 'Quite a number went', where, alongside 'sacred subjects for church decoration', people could buy plaster relief 'heads of soldiers'. One commissioned piece, 'Sir Galahad', made for a grieving mother, had the head of a 'warrior lad who was killed in action' but the 'body of a kneeling knight holding a great two-edged sword'.[111] These examples of new ventures make explicit the connection between the influence of war, growing commercialism, and the broadening appeal of Arts and Crafts work to a wider sector of society.

Still, reviews continued to reiterate that only professional work was accepted for the art stalls. Lowndes and her Committee cannily realised that appealing to a wartime (and interwar) appetite for a nationalistic, consumer-friendly, leisure space would enable the Englishwoman to become one of the most famous annual exhibitions in the capital. People could wander around the exhibits feeling they were showing patriotic support through their very presence, whilst simultaneously absorbing the Arts and Crafts ethos of respect for materials, collaborative endeavours, and the work of professional art workers, the majority of whom were women. Art workers such as E. C. Woodward did exactly this: she used multiple exhibitions to further showcase her contributions to the war effort. At both the Women's International Art Club and the Englishwoman's Exhibitions, Woodward showed specimens of the oxyacetylene welding she and her peers had executed for aircrafts, to demonstrate women's skills in the field as 'the life of the airman depends on the welding being absolutely flawless'.[112] At other exhibitions, photographs of the welding classes were even enlarged and displayed on the walls.[113] Exhibitions such as this enabled women's artistic and moral contributions to society to be, both literally and figuratively, writ large upon the public consciousness.

The move towards the public sphere, philanthropy, and civic contributions was not permanent, nor was it immune from being renegotiated in future years. Throughout the decades following the end of the war and the partial emancipation of women in 1918, we catch only glimpses of the institutional involvement of women art workers in the Arts and Crafts movement as the documentary record becomes patchier. In 1923–1924, the *Woman's Year Book* stated that the Guild 'rarely holds exhibitions of women's work', suggesting that after the war the Guild reverted to its more separatist stance on exhibitions, as in earlier years.[114] Yet members also apparently submitted work to the vast 1922 Women's Art Exhibition organised at Olympia by the *Daily Express*.[115] The *Woman's Year Book* noted, however, that the Guild was largely directed towards bringing together artists and interested parties by this point. The Guild formally ran until at least 1963, although it slowly began to function as a meeting point for a number of older founding members to relive earlier memories of the movement, particularly after the Second World War.[116] Attempts to collaborate with their male peers continued across the early to mid-century. For instance, an Art Workers' Guild's Ladies' Night was held at the Hall in October 1926 where member Phyllis Gardner, Noel Rooke, and C. R. Ashbee, gave a paper on 'Wood Engraving and Wood Cuts'. A list of meetings for 1937 reveals all of the talks at the Women's Guild of Arts that year were given by men.[117] On the 15 November 1946 a record number of attendees turned up at a special event at the Art Worker's Guild to commemorate the fiftieth anniversary since the death of William Morris. Mary A. Sloane, of the Women's Guild of Arts, chaired the event.[118] Despite the evident contraction of women art workers' institutional presence, debates about the interrelation between the Women's Guild and their male peers, and the gendered separation of members' artwork from that of their contemporaries, remained at the heart of the Women's Guild of Art's existence to the very end.

Ultimately, the decline in vibrancy of the Women's Guild of Arts by the interwar era was not necessarily concomitant with a perceived abandonment of the values of the Arts and Crafts movement, nor did it represent the cessation of the political, artistic, and civic activities of members. In the interwar period, women art workers continued to disseminate ideas about cultural authority and the centrality of art work to moral virtue. Many promoted single-sex networks as a route to professional enfranchisement, by exhibiting with the Women's International Art Club and the Society of Women Artists. Some continued to focus their energies on political efforts: 'pioneer worker' Mary Lowndes sat on the Gallery bench with Millicent Garrett Fawcett and Eleanor Rathbone during the debates which brought about the Equal Franchise Act in 1928, whilst others, such as May Morris, Mary A. Sloane, and Freda Derrick, instead channelled their efforts into providing a strong female presence in Arts and Crafts ventures like the Kelmscott Fellowship, an organisation which aimed 'To extend the knowledge of the Life, Work, and Teaching of William Morris'.[119] Several chapters in this book have shown how the activities of women art workers continued to thrive long after the First World War had ended. If anything, the move from private, closely guarded institutional space – protected by mechanisms of exclusion – to a more patent, publicly minded engagement with wider society was so successful among women art workers by this later era that it caused their efforts to be spread across multiple fields in a manner which has unfortunately contributed to their later historiographical obscurity.

This final chapter has shown how the broadening of the activities of Arts and Crafts women into the public sphere was rooted primarily in two catalytic processes: suffrage and war. The strategies of professionalisation and priorities of women art workers were deeply shaped by the rapidly changing world around them. The suffrage campaign offered professional women tantalising new opportunities to self-actualise and perform their roles across a range of empowering, political, and commercial spheres. Some women, however, increasingly felt that suffrage politics threatened to tear apart the monopolisation of cultural authority and the hard-won respect of the art world being consolidated at the Women's Guild of Arts. Many members stressed – in words and actions – the need for artistic equality throughout their lives, and their professional roles meant they could be apathetic to women-only spaces, particularly at a moment of anxieties surrounding heightened suffrage militancy. Exploring the existential crisis that ensued when women, on a collaborative level – already battling against unshifting structural inequalities – sought to navigate the different views of members about strategies of professionalisation through the choppy waters of contemporary political debates demonstrates how discussions about suffrage, gender, and citizenship played out in the wider sphere of women's working lives.

Shortly afterwards, war profoundly altered the cultural production of many different Arts and Crafts women and engendered a surprising range of new commercial and philanthropic opportunities to claim cultural authority and attract a consumer market keen to show support for 'English' crafts. Again, the lives of suffrage campaigners and certain women art workers were interwoven. Mary Lowndes was one of many campaigners to write hopefully about how war would finally bring recognition and equality to the field of women's contributions to the labour market: 'in a happier future, when aircrafts, no longer needed as engines of destruction, shall be developed in many directions as yet only dreamed of, the work of women welders should be of service to the country'.[120] War work was seen as a starting point for a future renegotiation of women's relationship with work: it was never the end goal, nor was the labour viewed as a temporary exigency. Yet, as a result of the 1919 Restoration of Pre-War Practices Act, by 1920 many women welders were unemployed, or having to accept unskilled jobs. On a collaborative level, war marked a sharp move away from the Guild's unease with itself as a segregated organisation for women and a decision to begin to embrace the public possibilities in the city. This new arena of civic, philanthropic, and profoundly public activity which suffrage and war encouraged women art workers into pursuing, was a space for the manifestation of artistic, professional careers like any other. Taking control of the cityscape, which as a function of the softening of gendered exclusion during wartime offered greater opportunities for women to exhibit respectable nationalistic civic roles, women artists showed off their expertise to a receptive public who lauded their activities. Political engagement brought new markets, drove commercial interest, and added to the prestige of the 'authentic' artist, conceptualised as an engaged intellectual contributing to societal debates through their work. Like the artistic self-fashioning in the secluded institutional Hall, the rarefied exhibition, the sophisticated 'At Home', and the 'medieval' workshop, the lives of women art workers of the Arts and Crafts movement were dominated by the concept of spatial semiotics. Over time, while consistently negotiating the use of public and private space in such hybrid sites, they progressed towards having a prominent role in public life during and after the First World War, seeking to familiarise the public with the Arts and Crafts movement in the twentieth century. These spaces – homes, studios, workshops, businesses, and exhibitions – were all critical sites where ideas about gender, Arts and Crafts, expertise, and professional status were reworked. They collectively constituted the crucible for the forging of a new artistic identity, beaten into shape under the hammer blows of exclusion and marginalisation.

Notes

1 Traditional accounts have portrayed the Royal Academy as 'an institution of privilege and limited scope' in the late nineteenth century. Linda Parry has argued that the failure of the Academy to change 'led to such drastic outside reform that within ten years the attention of practicing artists and the general public had been so forcefully turned away from the Academy that it never regained its prestigious place as the ultimate exhibiting institution for the arts in Britain'. Linda Parry, *Textiles of the Arts and Crafts Movement* (London: Thames and Hudson, 1988), p. 9. In reality, despite the growth of competing exhibition venues, the Academy was still considered one of the most important exhibitions for many early twentieth-century artists and the public alike.

2 WGAA, Henry Wilson and Edward S. Prior to the Guild, 15 May 1916.

3 C. R. Ashbee, 'The English Arts and Crafts Exhibition at the Royal Academy: An Open Letter from C. R. Ashbee', *American Magazine of Art* (February 1917), p. 137.

4 A small number of artistic men were also involved, but this was unusual. Australian artist and suffragist Dora Meeson Coates wrote that 'Chelsea men artists – always

conservative – were not partisans of the women's suffrage movement. In this they did not differ from the average male … It was the women-artists, not the men, who welcomed us as new-comers to Chelsea.' Dora Meeson Coates, *George Coates: His Art and His Life* (London: Dent, 1937), p. 43. See also Joseph McBrinn, 'The Spectacle of Masculinity: Men and the Visual Culture of the Suffrage Campaign', in *Suffrage and the Arts: Visual Culture, Politics and Enterprise* (eds) Miranda Garrett and Zoë Thomas (London: Bloomsbury, 2018), pp. 205–230.

5 WGAA, Handwritten Annual Report, 1911.

6 Elizabeth Crawford, *The Women's Suffrage Movement: A Reference Guide, 1866–1928* (London: UCL Press, 1999), pp. 223–226.

7 The artworks discussed in this paragraph can all be located in the Museum of London and the WL.

8 Mary Lago, *Christiana Herringham and the Edwardian Art Scene* (Columbia: University of Missouri Press, 1996), p. 173.

9 'The Pageant', *Votes for Women* (30 April 1909), p. 606.

10 Sally Alexander (ed.), *Women's Fabian Tracts* (London: Routledge, 1988), p. 147.

11 WL, 9/01/0457, May Morris to 'Miss Ward', 3 January 1909.

12 Natasha Thoreson, 'The Reluctant Reformer: May Morris' United States Lecture Tour of 1909–1910', *Textile Society of America Symposium Proceedings* (2012), pp. 1–9 (pp. 3, 8).

13 Jan Marsh, *Jane and May Morris: A Biographical Story, 1839–1938* (London: Pandora, 1986), p. 258.

14 'First Trades Union of Women Workers', *New York Times* (19 December 1909), p. 16.

15 'Woman Suffrage', *The Times* (3 December 1908), p. 10.

16 WL, 9/01/0417, Philippa Strachey to Millicent Garrett Fawcett, 22 June 1908.

17 Lisa Tickner, *The Spectacle of Women: Imagery of the Suffrage Campaign, 1907–1914* (London: Chatto and Windus, 1987), p. 20.

18 Ibid., pp. 123–124.

19 Helen McCarthy, 'Service Clubs, Citizenship and Equality: Gender Relations and Middle-Class Associations in Britain Between the Wars', *Historical Research*, 81/213 (2008), pp. 531–552 (p. 545).

20 Liz Arthur's work has shown that although the Committee of the Glasgow Society of Women Artists sought to portray itself as officially non-political and rejected the request of a member to gather signatures in support of the vote at the Club's premises, they still invited prominent suffrage campaigner Lady Frances Balfour to lecture. Liz Arthur, 'The Artistic, Social, and Suffrage Networks of Glasgow School of Art's Women Artists and Designers', in *Suffrage and the Arts: Visual Culture, Politics, and Enterprise* (eds) Miranda Garrett and Zoë Thomas (London: Bloomsbury, 2018), pp. 43–64 (pp. 58–59). Other groups, such as the Society of Women Artists, did place advertisements for the National Union of Women's Suffrage Societies in their catalogues. The suffrage press also supportively reviewed these exhibitions and those of the Women's International Art Club.

21 Leila J. Rupp, 'Constructing Internationalism: The Case of Transnational Women's Organisations, 1888–1945', *American Historical Review*, 99/5 (1994), pp. 1571–1600 (p. 1574).

22 For instance, the main archive covering the Society of Women Artists' early years is thought to have been destroyed in the Second World War.

23 WGAA, Feodora Gleichen to May Morris, February 1913.

24 Janis Londraville, *On Poetry, Painting, and Politics: The Letters of May Morris and John Quinn* (London: Associated University Presses, 1997), p. 69.

25 WGAA, Handwritten Secretary Report, 1908.

26 WGAA, Handwritten Annual Report, 1910.

27 WGAA, Handwritten Annual Report, 1911.

28 WGAA, Committee Meeting 24 October 1913, Meeting Minutes Book 1913–1917.

29 Georgie Gaskin wrote 'regretting her inability to lecture or demonstrate in public'. WGAA, Committee Meeting 24 October 1913, Meeting Minutes Book 1913–1917. May Morris wrote privately to the American pianist Richard Buhlig that she was glad he had not attended a lecture she had given as 'the audience was cold which hindered me very much, and I was tired, and it was not one's best, by any means. Besides which, my chairman (chairwoman) went away in the middle, leaving me to wind up the meeting all by my tired self, which did not help to make things go'. Huntington Library, MOR 295, May Morris to Richard Buhlig, 27 May 1908.

30 WGAA, list of requested speakers for meetings, undated but *c.* 1912. Underlining in original.

31 WGAA, Mary Sargant Florence to the Guild, 22 September 1912.

32 Before the meeting Sargant Florence announced she would sit below the platform, not on the platform, although she was willing to lay out illustrations on the platform itself. She also wished to arrive two hours early to 'set the hall into shape'. See the letters in the WGAA between Mary Sargant Florence and Mary A. Sloane, March 1913. Underlining in original.

33 WGAA, Handwritten Annual Report, 1911.

34 WGAA, Handwritten Secretary Report, 1912. Underlining in original.

35 Lucy Delap, *The Feminist Avant-Garde: Transatlantic Encounters of the Early Twentieth Century* (Cambridge: Cambridge University Press, 2007), p. 17.

36 In 1912 there were four talks by men and three by women, in 1916 five by men and one by a woman, and in 1919 there were five by men and one by a woman. WGAA, meeting cards.

37 WGAA, letter from Ruby W. Bailey (presumed to be Ruby Gervase Bailey), Mary Batten, Helen Bedford, A. G. I. Christie, Edith B. Dawson, Mary Sargant Florence, Emily Ford, Mary Lowndes, Phoebe Stabler, M. V. Wheelhouse, Alice B. Woodward, E. C. Woodward, 22 February 1913.

38 Constance Smedley, *Crusaders: Reminiscences of Constance Smedley / Mrs Maxwell Armfield* (London: Duckworth, 1929), pp. 94–96.

39 WGAA, letter 'To be read out at the Extraordinary General Meeting'. The names were: Elinor Hallé, Katharine Adams, Marianne Stokes, Feodora Gleichen, Julia Bowley, Eleanor Rowe, May Morris, Ethel K. Martyn, Mary A. Sloane, M. D. Spooner, Ethel Sandell, E. M. Rope, Maud Beddington, Alys Fane Trotter, Pamela Colman Smith, Amelia M. Bowerley, Kate E. Bunce, Estella Canziani, Evelyn De Morgan, Mabel Esplin, Ethel F. Everett, Lola Frampton, Georgie Cave Gaskin, Edith Goodman, Letty Graham, Camilla Edith Harwood, Margaret Kemp Welch, Esther M. Moore, Ella L. Moore, Jane Morris, Clara Tustain, Mary Newill, Violet G. M. Ramsay, Anna Simons, Marie Stillman, H. Mabel White.

40 WGAA, Ethel Sandell to Ethel K. Martyn, 9 March 1913.

41 WGAA, Ethel K. Martyn to Mary A. Sloane, 22 January 1913.

42 WGAA, copy of letter from Ethel Everett, 1913. Underlining in original.
43 WGAA, copy of anonymous letter. Note attached stating 'From a member who had not quite understood'.
44 WGAA, Feodora Gleichen to May Morris, 25 February 1913.
45 WGAA, Feodora Gleichen to Mary A. Sloane, 25 February 1913, underlining by Gleichen.
46 WGAA, Feodora Gleichen to May Morris, 25 February 1913.
47 WGAA, Pamela Colman Smith to May Morris, 22 January 1913.
48 WGAA, Extraordinary Meeting 28 February 1913, Meeting Minutes Book 1913–1917.
49 WGAA, Committee Meeting 24 October 1913, Meeting Minutes Book 1913–1917.
50 WGAA, Committee Meeting 27 November 1913, Meeting Minutes Book 1913–1917. Their names were: Mary Sargant Florence, Emily Ford, Ruby Gervase Bailey, Margaret M. Jenkin, Edith B. Dawson, Alice B. Woodward, E. C. Woodward, and M. V. Wheelhouse.
51 WGAA, Committee Meeting 27 November 1913, Meeting Minutes Book 1913–1917.
52 WGAA, Printed Annual Report, 1913.
53 There were at least twenty-two members involved in both. The actual number may have been higher as the Guild's membership lists only go to the mid-1920s. See Women's Art Library, Goldsmiths, University of London (hereafter WAL), Women's International Art Club membership list, and the WGAA membership list.
54 WAL, Women's International Art Club, Meeting Minutes Book 29 November 1917.
55 Mary Sargant Florence made an important contribution to early feminist pacifist debates in *Militarism Versus Feminism* (1915), which argued warfare helped keep women in subjugation.
56 Tanya Harrod, *The Crafts in Britain in the Twentieth Century* (New Haven: Yale University Press, 1999), p. 22.
57 Carolyn Malone, 'The Art of Remembrance: The Arts and Crafts Movement and the Commemoration of the British War Dead, 1916–1920', *Contemporary British History*, 26/1 (2012), pp. 1–23; Carolyn Malone, 'A Job Fit for Heroes? Disabled Veterans, the Arts and Crafts Movement and Social Reconstruction in Post-World War I Britain', *First World War Studies*, 4/2 (2013), pp. 201–217.
58 For women in the fine arts see Caroline Speck, *Beyond the Battlefield: Women Artists of the Two World Wars* (London: Reaktion, 2014).
59 Mary Lowndes, 'Their Training', *Englishwoman*, 82/28 (October 1915), pp. 69–78 (p. 69).
60 See Jacqueline T. Trotter (ed.), *Valour and Vision: Poems of the War, 1914–1918* (London: Longmans, 1920).
61 Estella Canziani, *Round about Three Palace Green* (London: Methuen, 1939), pp. 204–205; Jeremy Maas and Jane Martineau, *Victorian Fairy Painting* (London: Merrell Holberton, 1997), p. 21.
62 Victoria and Albert Museum, Archive of Art and Design, Dawson papers.
63 'The Master Key', *Common Cause* (27 April 1917), p. 26.
64 'The Society of Women Welders', *Common Cause* (27 April 1917), p. 27.
65 Helen Fraser, *Women and War Work* (New York: G. A. Shaw, 1918), p. 95.

66 Angela K. Smith, *Suffrage Discourse in Britain During the First World War* (Aldershot: Ashgate, 2005), pp. 72–75.

67 'The Society of Women Welders', *Common Cause*, p. 27.

68 'Acetylene Welding for Women', *Sphere* (11 March 1916), p. 278.

69 'Aircraft and Munition Work for Women', *Common Cause* (5 November 1915), p. 377.

70 'The Munitions Department of the Women's Service Bureau', *Common Cause* (8 December 1916), p. 459.

71 'Technical Training for Women', *Common Cause* (11 February 1916), p. 582.

72 'The Queen and Training for Women', *Common Cause* (31 March 1916), p. 1.

73 The *Studio* discussed how the toy trade had previously been 'practically a German monopoly' but the war had offered 'scope for invention and realization for artists, especially lady artists'. 'Studio-Talk', *Studio*, 72 (1918), p. 80.

74 'Classified Advertising', *The Times* (4 December 1928), p. 29.

75 'The Bee Toymakers', *Pall Mall Gazette* (24 November 1914), p. 6.

76 'Place aux dames', *Graphic* (5 May 1906), p. 17; 'Elinor Jessie Marie Hallé', www.sculpture.gla.ac.uk/view/person.php?id=msib5_1207150652, accessed 24 September 2019.

77 'Anne Crawford Acheson', www.sculpture.gla.ac.uk/view/person.php?id=msib7_120 5418483, accessed 24 September 2019.

78 Canziani, *Round about Three Palace Green*, p. 295.

79 Bertha E. Mahony and Elinor Whitney, *Contemporary Illustrators of Children's Books* (Boston: Bookshop for Boys and Girls, Women's Educational and Industrial Union, 1930), p. 80.

80 WGAA, Printed Version, Annual Report, 1914.

81 WGAA, cards for 1917 and 1918.

82 The exhibition resulted in sales of £44 5s. WGAA, Printed Version, Annual Report, 1915.

83 WGAA, Committee Meeting 15 May 1914, Meeting Minutes Book 1913–1917. Michael Saler, *The Avant-Garde in Interwar England: Medieval Modernism and the London Underground* (Oxford: Oxford University Press, 2001), p. 88.

84 WGAA, Committee Meeting 7 November 1916, Meeting Minutes Book 1913–1917.

85 WGAA, letter from the Royal College of Art, 31 January 1913; Committee Meeting January 1916, Meeting Minutes Book 1913–1917; Handwritten Annual Report, 1911.

86 WGAA, Committee Meeting 4 May 1915, Meeting Minutes Book 1913–1917.

87 WGAA, Annual Meeting 11 December 1914, Meeting Minutes Book 1913–1917; Committee Meeting 23 January 1915, Meeting Minutes Book 1913–1917.

88 *The Times History of the War*, 4 (London: The Times, 1915), p. 466. Elizabeth Masterman's notes suggest part of the design was originally kept at Kelmscott Manor. Masterman mentions the frieze was listed in a Hobbs and Chambers sales catalogue in July 1939 after Morris's death. WL, KM: 319 7/YYY7/2.

89 'Arrangements for Today: Women's Guild of Arts Exhibition', *The Times* (11 May 1918), p. 9. See also the WGAA flyer for 'The Women's Guild of Arts Exhibition of Soldiers' Work'.

90 WGAA, 'At Home' card, 9 St Paul's Studios, 1917.

91 WGAA, undated flyer, post 1914.

92 WGAA, Annual Report, 1920.

93 WGAA, Committee Meeting 31 January 1916, Meeting Minutes Book 1913–1917; and 1916 flyer.

94 WGAA, Printed Version, Annual Report, 1916.

95 WGAA, May Morris to the Guild, 1916.

96 WGAA, letter from the Guild to all members, July 1916.

97 Arts and Crafts Exhibition Society, *Catalogue of the Eleventh Exhibition* (London: Chiswick Press, 1916), pp. 33, 214.

98 Peter Rose, '"It Must be Done Now": The Arts and Crafts Exhibition at Burlington House, 1916', *Journal of the Decorative Arts Society 1850–the Present*, 17 (1993), pp. 3–12 (p. 4).

99 For instance, a 'Mrs McDowall' had very much admired the 'Lady's Bedroom', and was now 'desiring advice on the furnishing of a small flat'. May Morris herself replied to the letter, offering advice. WGAA, Committee Meeting 7 November 1916, Meeting Minutes Book 1913–1917. T. M. W., 'British Arts and Crafts', *Daily Mail* (9 October 1916), p. 3. It is hard to imagine members of the Guild before the war – or even during the war – would have been pleased with such comments.

100 'Notes and Comments', *Mid Sussex Times* (10 February 1914), p. 4.

101 W. T. Whitley, 'The Arts and Crafts Exhibition', *Studio*, 69/285 (December 1916), pp. 126–128.

102 Arts and Crafts Exhibition Society, *Catalogue of the Eleventh Exhibition*.

103 'Advertisement', *Common Cause* (9 March 1917), p. 638.

104 'The "Englishwoman" Exhibition', *Common Cause* (17 September 1915), p. 295.

105 'The Englishwoman Exhibition', *Common Cause* (24 November 1916), p. 423.

106 'For Town and Country', *Country Life* (24 November 1917), p. 22.

107 '"The Englishwoman" Exhibition', *Common Cause* (22 October 1915), p. 353.

108 'The Englishwoman Exhibition', *Common Cause* (23 November 1917), p. 400.

109 'War Bread Made at Home', *Newcastle Daily Journal* (1 December 1915), p. 5.

110 'The Englishwoman Exhibition', *Common Cause* (7 November 1919), p. 384.

111 'The World of Women', *Illustrated London News* (2 December 1922), p. 908.

112 'Items of Interest', *Common Cause* (9 March 1917), p. 639; 'The "Englishwoman" Exhibition', *Common Cause* (26 November 1915), p. 444.

113 'The London Society', *Common Cause* (10 December 1915), p. 475.

114 G. Evelyn Gates, *Woman's Year Book, 1923–1924* (London: Women Publishers, 1924), p. 52.

115 An advertisement in *Colour* magazine said the exhibition would focus on 'the stupendous business and social activities of the twentieth-century woman. It will be the outstanding feminine event of the year.' 'Advertisements', *Colour*, 16 (1922), p. i.

116 Katharine Adams, who became President of the Guild, gave two reflective talks about the lives of eminent members during this later era: one on S. T. Prideaux in 1936 and one on May Morris in 1940. Katharine Adams papers, University of Berkeley, Bancroft Library. Mary A. Sloane's obituary in *The Times* listed her as President of the Guild between 1953 and 1961. 'Obituary', *The Times* (7 December 1961), p. 21. D. A. A. Rope (Co-Honorary Secretary) wrote a letter to the Curator of the William Morris Gallery in 1962 asking about organising a Guild trip to see items bequeathed by Mary A. Sloane. William Morris Gallery, London. Furthermore, there was a Women's Guild

of Arts talk in October 1963 about St Paul's Cathedral during the Second World War. London Metropolitan Archives, CLC/521/MS38567.

117 A small number of surviving cards give details about Guild meetings across the interwar era. Private collection.

118 AWGA, Annual Report, 1946.

119 'History Repeats Itself', *Woman's Leader* (1 June 1928), p. 135; William Morris Society, Kelmscott Fellowship materials show Morris as President and Derrick and Sloane on the Committee.

120 'Women as Acetylene-Welders', *Common Cause* (3 December 1915), p. 454.

Epilogue

In the summer of 1964, after a great many discussions and a process of 'careful study' by different Brothers at the Art Workers' Guild – which had been ongoing since at least the 1950s – women finally became eligible to join. In the preceding years, the men deliberating the matter had formed themselves into two opposing camps, although others stated they did not feel strongly either way.[1] Those against having women as members urged their peers to consider the 'far-reaching' impact of 'so revolutionary a proposal', which could disrupt the 'great tradition' and 'happy atmosphere' that existed between those men who had gained entry, who were all 'distinguished in diverse arts and crafts'.[2] Some were anxious women could potentially 'lower the qualifications of scholarship'.[3] Others raised concerns the Guild would become 'social, rather than professional or technical in character, and would be less congenial to the male members', although this final point was later deleted from formally circulated documents.[4] Further insight into this carefully guarded, long-established 'happy atmosphere' can be gleaned through a 1932 work by Hugh de Poix titled *Nunc est Sherryendum* ('Now is the time to drink sherry'), which still hangs at 6 Queen Square today (Figure 6.1). Designed to represent a stained-glass window, the work depicts the Brothers, in middle to old age, loitering in a close, companionable circle around Master Basil Oliver, festooned in his red cape. A Past-Master rests a supportive hand on his shoulder. Smoking pipes and swilling sherry, their expressions range from the jovial and the imperious to the suspicious. Some Brothers even gaze directly back at the viewer – the outsider – reminiscent of their long-held concerns about publicity.[5] Although clearly intended to be satirical, in this painting we are still confronted with the elite, secretive, multi-generational model of masculinity so often associated with artistic excellence across the modern era. The list of members' names at the bottom of the piece, and their roles as 'Bro', 'Master', or 'Past-Master', reiterates their significance as important members of an exclusive, bohemian, male-only world.

Those in favour of allowing women to join focused instead on the need to be meritocratic, and sought to chide members into action by arguing the Guild had lost respect with 'the men who count in the art world'. In their view, this was, 'justly or unjustly', because it was commonly believed the Guild had 'become a stronghold of artistic conservativism'.[6] Some felt (although these comments were also deleted from the final document sent to all members) that 'as long as the Guild excludes women, it will fail to win the respect of the general public'.[7] Across the first half of the twentieth

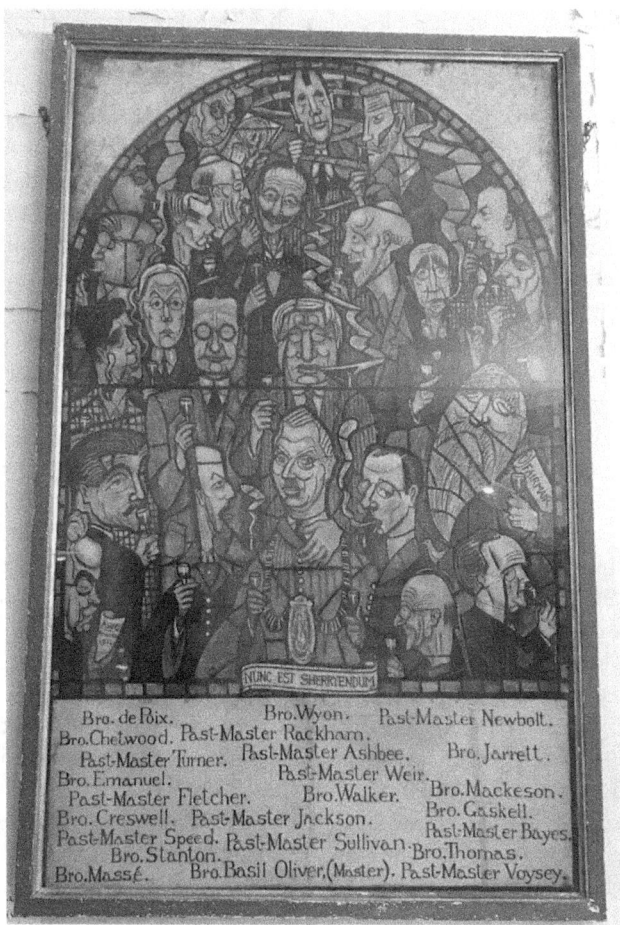

Figure 6.1 Hugh de Poix, *Nunc est Sherryendum*, 1932

century, at various moments, different Brothers had periodically raised their concerns about the Art Workers' Guild's relevance to wider society, and the need to do more to assert their reputations as cultural arbiters. Such views undoubtedly influenced the debates about women members: it was clearly hoped this would demonstrate to the world that the Guild was becoming more progressive in its aims. By 1964, enough members had finally been won over to this perspective – or perhaps simply felt discussions had gone on long enough – and it was decided by a vote of a 'decisive majority' that women should be allowed to join. That year sculptor Marjorie Crossley, wood engraver Joan Hassall, calligrapher Dorothy Hutton, silk weaver Ursula Brock, and potter and stained-glass worker Moira Forsyth took their places as members of the Art Workers' Guild. Today, paintings of prominent women members occupy a sizeable portion of one of the four walls of the Hall, disrupting the display of solely men's creativity on the other three.

This moment, which initially appears to symbolise a fundamental shift in attitudes about gender and expertise in the arts, functions as a useful heuristic device to probe simplistic narratives of the steady progress of women's opportunities across the twentieth century in England. The earlier period spanning the 1870s to the 1930s was an era of profound change, as increasing numbers of women gained access to the professional art world and, in certain circumstances, received considerable acclaim. In the interwar period, a prominent network of women can be found working across the Arts and Crafts, and in craft more generally; this flourishing culture was directly influenced by the energies of the individuals and groups who had constructed this landscape over the preceding sixty years. But in other regards, the twentieth century continued to be an ongoing battle. Deeply engrained views about gender difference, and persistent informal and structural hierarchies, had to be repeatedly addressed by different generations, in the arts and in wider society.[8] There were various backlashes, as shown in the post-First World War era, when essentialised ideas recalibrated understanding of gender difference. Although women's political enfranchisement (partially in 1918 and fully in 1928) is often heralded as a sign of clear progress, women did not gain formal access to groups such as the Art Workers' Guild until several decades later. Additionally, women only gained access when it was deemed to have become too embarrassing to maintain such segregated social networks, rather than out of any deeply felt commitment towards promoting gender equality or systematic change across the art world.

The Art Workers' Guild's reticence towards women's participation has been mirrored across various professional, public, and 'private' cultures in the twentieth and twenty-first centuries. Although, slowly, doors began to open, women were routinely granted privileges only later in life – or after their death: long after they had established artistic reputations. Such individuals were then heralded as evidencing a fundamental shift in the culture of these establishments. Painter Annie Swynnerton, who had been a Women's Guild of Arts member, gained entry to the hallowed echelons of the Royal Academy in 1922 when she became the first woman Associate, aged seventy-eight, although she never became a full Royal Academician. Laura Knight was then the first woman to be elected as an Academician in 1936, and was the first woman to be given a solo retrospective there in 1965.[9] Still, Knight had to wait until she was eighty-four before she received an invitation to the Annual Dinner. As Annette Wickham's research has shown, it was only after Gertrude Hermes – the Academy's first woman engraver – realised at a General Assembly meeting in 1966 that she and the other women were not to be invited to the dinner that evening, and wrote to them taking issue with this, that the following year, four women Academicians were finally invited to dine with the men. *The Times* reported that after dinner that night Hermes enjoyed a 'thoroughly masculine cigar'.[10] Looking at this now from the distance of the twenty-first century it is sobering that the election of the first female President was only announced in December 2019 (painter and printmaker Rebecca Salter).

In 1972, Joan Hassall became Master of the Art Workers' Guild, in her late sixties. Her experiences present remarkable similarities with those of the network of women art workers who came before her. One article in the *Sphere* from 1956 would not have been out of place in Chapter 3. The interview was framed around the journalist's visit to her 'comfortable, porticoed house, with its roomy studio' on Kensington Park Road, where her father, 'Hassall senior', 'still looks down on his studio', his 'moustached and pensive face with a singularly intent gaze' (Figure 6.2).[11] She lived in this vast West London house for the majority of her life, surrounded by the tools of her craft, and symbols of her privileged, artistic life, such as a harp and antique chaise longue. Perhaps she knew Estella Canziani, who lived and worked close by at 3 Palace Green until her death in 1964, the very year Hassall joined the Art Workers' Guild. Mirroring Evelyn De Morgan's battles in the 1870s, Joan Hassall's mother and father were 'firmly opposed to so un-orthodox a calling' as art in the interwar period. This conservatism is perhaps unsurprising: although described as a 'carefree Bohemian' in the *Sphere*, her father had also been a famous anti-suffrage poster artist.[12] Instead, Hassall trained as a teacher, then took up secretarial work for her father. Finally, after managing to save £60, and presumably convincing her parents, she 'presented herself' to Walter Russell, Keeper of the Royal Academy Schools, and began her artistic training. In 1936, Heinemann commissioned her to engrave the title page of a book of poems by her brother Christopher – although she later found out they had deducted her pay from his royalties.[13] But after this she carved out an illustrious career. Her work included bookplates, letterheads, booklets for British Transport films, illustrations for editions of *Cranford* by Elizabeth Gaskell, *Our Village* by Mary Russell Mitford, a seven-volume edition of the novels of Jane Austen for the Folio Society, a postage stamp issued in commemoration of the Silver Wedding of King George VI and Queen Elizabeth, and invitation cards for the Queen's Coronation guests.

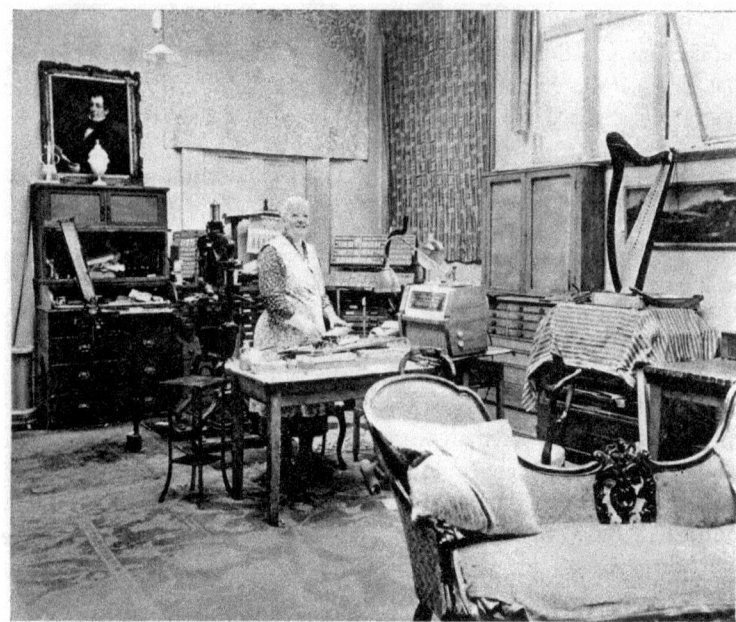

A STUDIO WITH A FAMILY TRADITION : The room in Kensington in which Miss Hassall is standing was previously the studio of her father, the late John Hassall, R.I., who died in 1948. Over the mantelpiece is a portrait of her great-grandfather, an architect. Miss Hassall has lived almost all her life in this house.

Figure 6.2 'Joan Hassall – The Charm of Wood Engraving', *Sphere* (23 June 1956), p. 450

Hassall interests me because of her beautiful woodcuts, but also because she is not the sort of person who is usually written about by feminist scholars. None of her artworks is overtly 'political' or has the allure of being considered avant-garde. Instead they evoke a romanticised, timeless, and rather conservative version of English history: of thatched cottages, woodland animals, and women with ringlets in Regency dresses. These woodcuts do not fit neatly within any specific twentieth-century artistic movement, but their ability to conjure a nostalgic sentimentalism for a pre-industrial world made them popular with a very large sector of the public. I have also found no evidence to situate Joan Hassall amongst the feminist artistic currents which began to spring up across the country with the dawn of the Women's Liberation Movement from the late 1960s. Hassall instead simply stated she was driven by the freedoms her wood engravings gave her to make 'my own statement of my own ideas'.[14] Clearly, she faced some of the same gendered battles encountered by earlier generations, but like many of the core network of women in the Arts and Crafts movement, she constructed a life filled with achievements.

Her experiences as an artist are a reminder of the central role class privilege has consistently played in enabling certain women to conceptualise and pursue lives as artists. When the journalist at the *Sphere* visited Hassall's studio on Kensington Park Road, he felt the need to tell readers how he had 'discovered' to his joy that their 'early childhood memories coincided' because they had lived close to each other in the same wealthy district of West London when they were growing up. Although Hassall in fact struggled to maintain this large house, the privileged cultural milieu she was immersed in, alongside the artistic lineage of her family, played a central role in helping her to maintain her reputation and connections. When she became Master of the Art Workers' Guild in 1972 she discussed these benefits in a rare interview for the BBC's *Woman's Hour*. Despite the Guild's anxieties about its traditional, rather than radical or fashionable, reputation by this point, Hassall's responses are testament to the ongoing strength of such upper-middle-class groups, which together created a series of interlocking networks which constituted the heart of the artistic establishment in England. She discussed the many 'distinguished people' associated with the Guild, the benefits of the 'private patrons' supporting her and other craft workers, and the generosity of members, working in at least twenty-six different categories, to whom you could always go with 'any problem you might have.'[15]

As such, when women gained formal entry to the Art Workers' Guild in 1964 it *was* a significant moment, but it was also a moment which formalised already established elite mixed-sex artistic networks. Hassall had spoken there some years earlier and was a 'beloved friend' of curator and collector Sydney Cockerell, amongst other members.[16] The small coterie of elite, predominantly older, women who slowly intertwined themselves in the life of the Guild at this point helped to dissipate the Brothers' wider anxieties about the gendered difference inherent in 'women artists', because these specific women were already often long-established friends, committed to maintaining the same artistic world in the capital.

This is not to suggest that Hassall did not feel deeply her gendered status: we simply cannot know either way, as she rarely discussed the topic. Even during her interview for *Woman's Hour*, although she began by conveying her surprise at being nominated to become Master of the Art Workers' Guild – 'well it never crossed my mind that they would ask a woman' – she quickly moved on to talk about the historical prestige of the group, 'founded in 1884 by a group of young architects.'[17] Clearly feeling a sense of loyalty towards the Guild of Brothers of whom she was now Master, Hassall was also likely influenced by a desire not to be pigeonholed. One of the most persistent statements made by women in the arts across the modern era has been an express determination to move beyond being understood as 'women artists'. Many have felt that engagement in topics or spaces deemed overtly 'political' would hinder serious engagement in their work or with them as individuals.

Artistic women (and professional women more generally) have repeatedly had to negotiate a balance between holding individually respected positions and their wish to belong to a collaborative network of likeminded figures. Many formed and joined women's art groups in an attempt to empower themselves and to exert greater influence on the world: the Women's Guild of Arts and the Lyceum Club provide two key early twentieth-century examples. Writing in one 1908 letter to May Morris, Edith B. Dawson discussed her hope for a future where 'we may grow into a strong and influential Guild, whose voice will be a real power in the land'.[18] Yet although such groups were forced into existence by the exclusivity of men's artistic networks, they repeatedly came under criticism for tribalism and separatism, attracting suspicion that they inherently represented a lower standard of work. This was a clear double standard; segregated groups consisting solely of artistic men faced no comparable distrust. Women were compelled – and compelled themselves – to give up these carefully carved-out spaces. Considerable pressure was placed upon them to abandon single-sex institutions by a powerful rhetoric promising equal consideration and apolitical neutrality, portraying such associations as unnecessary in a modern, supposedly meritocratic, society. After the First World War in particular, professional women often preferred to position such groups as part of an associational backdrop to their lives, rather than a key strategy through which to fight for societal change.[19] Reminiscent of comparable battles across the professions, women art workers pursued absorption into existing networks where masculinity was intrinsically valued, but bolstered this by quietly continuing to draw strength from partially separatist strategies.

In 1950, the painter Margaret Geddes, Chair of the Women's International Art Club, wrote about the history of the Club for the *Studio*. The caveat with which she begins the piece reiterates the ongoing suspicions about women's alternative networks, which can be traced back to the nineteenth century.[20] She informed readers that:

> There is a good deal of prejudice, both amongst the lay public and amongst artists themselves, against any society which exists exclusively for women artists, and the Women's International Art Club has come in for its share of criticism on that account. Whatever may have been

the case in the past, it is said, nowadays there is surely no reason for women to segregate themselves in this way? It is apparently necessary, therefore, when writing of a women's club, that one should start with an apology for its existence!

Geddes then proclaimed that she refused to 'get involved in an argument about women' and instead wanted to focus on the 'interesting' and 'outstanding work' at the Club's exhibitions. She did, however, reassure readers the group was 'entirely non-political'.[21] Although scholars have tended to be more interested in telling the histories of workplace activism or retracing the lives and works of radical artists, many contemporary figures, historians and artists alike, repeatedly portrayed themselves as in pursuit of objective truths, devoid of any political agendas, across the nineteenth and twentieth centuries. Members of the Art Workers' Guild, for instance, firmly believed in the 1950s that they had no 'artistic "politics"' and were instead focused purely on 'what is good and enduring'.[22]

But the twentieth century was not simply a period when women persistently fought to gain access to male-only networks; many women were equally concerned about surrendering their own separatist strategies. Although the Women's Guild of Arts opened its doors to the participation of men (and lost several members in the process), elsewhere there tended to be a strong desire to keep these spaces framed around the needs of women. A history of the Glasgow Society of Women Artists – which continues to meet today – noted with certain pride in 1950 that the 'proposal to permit men guests into the Club has been many times defeated'. At this point, rules remained strict and spaces were still carefully segregated. Men could now be invited 'any day, within certain hours, to the Dining-room, Smoke-room and Gallery' but they were still not allowed to enter the drawing room.[23] Despite concerns about status, alongside disapproval from the outside world, women's formal and informal networks have played a vital, often little-recognised role, across the twentieth century. Such groups were not necessarily always sites of 'sisterhood', and tensions could run high, but these spaces did consistently offer women licence to behave in a wide variety of ways with each other, and to perform and assert their competing strategies of professionalisation.

The feminist 'wave' paradigm can function as useful intellectual shorthand but is largely inadequate in capturing the breadth of ways professional women have sought empowerment through collaborative endeavours across the twentieth century. In the arts, the Women's Guild of Arts and Women's International Art Club, amongst others, continued to function as supportive, women-focused sites through the mid-century, and – whether they liked this or not – did constitute a politically charged presence in society, because of their encouragement of artistic opportunities for women. In contrast to many other women-focused, mid-century organisations, they avoided a maternal or overtly feminised framing.[24]

But the advent of 'second-wave feminism' and the Women's Liberation Movement from the late 1960s, and across the 1970s and 1980s, did bring a shift in tactics for many artistic women. Taking a very different approach to those such as Joan Hassall, a younger generation became far more overt in their arguments of the need to carve out separatist feminist art groups and spaces. This younger generation included activists such as Anthea Callen, Mary Crockett, Wendy Holmes, and Linda Newington, who collectively declared in one co-written piece that they had become awakened by the still 'rife … sexist notion of art as a "hobby" for females, a profession for men; a woman artist has to struggle for respect and appear tougher than her female counterpart to survive'.[25] The same concerns echoed across generations, muddling notions of progress and periodisation. Stained-glass designer Mary Lowndes had lamented in the *Common Cause* in 1914 the question of 'Genius, and Women Painters'; American art historian Linda Nochlin asked in 1971 in her now-legendary piece, 'Why Have There Been No Great Women Artists?'[26] Feminist artists and art historians began to organise exhibitions and establish groups, conferences, journals, and bookshops. Many different artists dedicated considerable energies to these feminist projects, using a whole range of methods (installations, paintings, craftworks) to encourage diverse audiences, often in community spaces such as libraries, to reflect on the prevalence of patriarchal structures in modern capitalist society. Groups such as the Women's Workshop, founded as part of the Artists' Union, began to use their homes and studios as meeting spaces for feminist discussions. Across this network of spaces, artistic women again critically examined the hierarchical processes inherent in societal understanding of professionals and amateurs, public and private, and the fine arts and the crafts. Many questioned whether women should even 'seek to establish themselves as professionals, or should the trappings of professionalism be rejected in favour of the wholesale recognition as art of whatever women make'.[27]

Much like their forebears in the Arts and Crafts movement, the artistic women tangled in these diverse creative networks and spaces ever looked to balance their artistic, political, individual, and collaborative needs. Art historian Katy Deepwell has discussed the tensions that arose in the 1970s and 1980s because it was felt artistic women ought to be providing 'service to pre-existing causes' being fostered on the left, which 'proved very unsatisfactory to many professional women artists who, even though they did occasionally contribute in this way, wanted to find other forms of expression in and through art and sought other venues and audiences for their art practice.[28] Ultimately, with notable similarities to the suffrage campaigns, there were ongoing tensions between the explicitly political, artistic think-pieces women produced to assert their feminist aspirations to the world, and their desires to focus on creative needs as individual artists, which could lead them in directions beyond their espoused identities amidst these political collectivities.

As Joan Wallach Scott has recently argued, there are no easy solutions to 'questions of equality and difference, of individual rights and group identities': 'To pose them as opposites misses the point of their interconnection. It is, rather, in recognizing and maintaining a necessary tension ... that we achieve the best and most democratic results.'[29] Different women, and different generations, have engaged in a constant process of strategising, so as to balance professional and creative aspirations most usefully, and move towards a greater sense of equality at various historical junctures. These approaches have fluctuated between a variety of, often conflicting, perspectives about whether it is best to maintain women's separatist spaces, and a sense of a 'women's culture', or whether separate spaces exacerbate notions of gendered difference, and focus should instead be invested into integrating women's voices amidst 'mainstream' culture. In 2013, Kathryn Gleadle reflected on the rhizomatic developments in the field of women's history since the 1970s and made an argument that is remarkably applicable to discussions of art, professional cultures, and feminist politics. She suggested that this diversity of approaches is critically important: 'It is these multiple and repeated points of convergence which will enable yet further advances in the acceptance of feminist history and the weakening of those barriers to it which remain. Modest shifts and mutations in historical practice can cumulatively be more effective than single grand strategies.'[30]

For women art workers in the Arts and Crafts movement it was the range of women-focused and mixed-sex methods and spaces – from the feminist and the intellectual to the openly commercial – which together enabled them to carve out expert roles and to interest a diverse public in their vision of the movement. Such a process, as today, required constant reassertion in the face of dominant hierarchies, structural inequality, and institutional ambivalence. Arranging the chapters around the principal spaces within which key figures such as E. C. Woodward, Mary Lowndes, Charlotte Newman, Edith B. Dawson, and M. V. Wheelhouse individually and collaboratively interacted has revealed the fissures between ideals and praxis and the complexities inherent in being an art worker and a woman during this era. Paying close attention to what may be seen to be the minutiae of daily practices – such as tea parties in the studio and the endless flow of letters between these women and their friends who also functioned as customers – more fully unveils just how central women art workers were to the movement and the contemporary cultural milieu. Throughout, they continued to cultivate extensive middle-class networks of sociability to uphold these new working lives, often whilst seemingly in the very act of compliance with gendered and classed expectations. In many ways, the special high status of the artistic genius continued to be reserved for the male designer or painter. But to anchor discussions around this framework would be missing the point: few of these women wanted to be celebrated in this way. Instead they positioned themselves amidst a network of expert disciples all dedicated to democratising the arts, spreading ideas about the power of collaboration, alternative patterns of labour, the social potential of the Arts and Crafts, and the intellectual and creative capabilities of women in modern life, across society.

The artistic model of professionalisation this network of women maintained was reliant on their constant presence and ability to commit their whole lives to the movement, endlessly reasserting their authority through rhetoric, action, and labour. Staunchly middle and upper middle class, they travelled across the country and internationally, showing off their skills and combating prevalent discourses through their own writings and by cultivating a method of presentation which encouraged a portrayal in line with their own self-conception. Drawing on the myriad of other strategies discussed in the preceding pages, and reacting to the wider changing fabric of English society (urbanisation, developments in print culture, the women's movement), this privileged group of individuals managed to establish and defend these expert new positions in society during their lifetimes.

In many ways, the real issues began when the Arts and Crafts movement started to be understood in the past tense. Reliant on asserting their artistic status through a range of, often transitory, strategies, knowledge of these women faded fast. Formal histories began to be written by men involved in the Art Workers' Guild, who painted a picture of the movement as neatly framed around their own activities. In his 1935 history, Brother H. J. L. J. Massé described the Art Workers' Guild as the 'parent guild', and positioned the Women's Guild of Arts as a minor 'offshoot' – a perspective feminist art historian Anthea Callen then adopted wholeheartedly in her own work in the 1970s.[31] A steady stream of books also began to tell the history of the movement through biographies of leading men from the mid-century. They have shown little sign of stopping ever since.[32] Women have consistently been omitted from these histories, their work deemed 'arty crafty' rather than part of the radical male craftsmanship constituting the 'Arts and Crafts Movement'. This has been compounded further by the high status and curatorial focus repeatedly reserved for the historic designs, objects, buildings, institutions, and writings pertaining to 'exceptional' male figures. While they were still alive, women art workers tried to correct this portrayal; Estella Canziani firmly positioned the Women's Guild of Arts as 'the counterpart of the Art Workers' Guild' in her 1939 memoir.[33] But by the 1970s women had been almost entirely effaced from the movement. Even feminist art historians Ann Sutherland Harris and Linda Nochlin unfortunately began to claim from this point that 'women as a group were not prominent in the English Arts and Crafts Movement'.[34] The Women's Guild of Arts had still been meeting in the 1960s, which makes this statement even more surprising.

As I write this Epilogue, the Women's Guild of Arts archive is in the process of being catalogued and digitised at the William Morris Society, and there continues to be widespread national and international interest in the Arts and Crafts movement. Most recently, the 2014 'Anarchy & Beauty: William Morris and His Legacy, 1860–1960' exhibition at the National Portrait Gallery was immensely popular and did attempt to include women's voices and expand the chronological breadth of the movement. Yet despite this, the exhibition still framed the movement around Morris, the exceptional genius. In this book, I have taken a rather different approach, instead telling the history of the movement by positioning a wide network of women at the heart of the research. But whether interest will turn away from the singular celebrated male (and occasionally female) designer, and whether women's artworks will be brought out of storage, their private papers seen as worthy of saving and cataloguing, only the following decades will tell. In a hyper-competitive market, ever looking for the next big artistic name, I have offered a reflection on the alternative model of creativity proposed by women working across the arts in the late nineteenth and early twentieth centuries. It is striking that their battles to democratise the arts, balance married life and work, fight for a living wage, and tussle with the appropriateness of women-only spaces, continue to be such major topics of discussion today.

Notes

1 See for instance, the letter from Hamilton T. Smith to Arthur Llewellyn Smith: 'Ladies. My instinct is against this proposal but I don't know that I should feel strongly enough to fight it very hard'. AWGA, Smith to Llewellyn Smith, 18 November 1958.

2 The 1959 Annual Report stated the topic of women members was: 'discussed at length but not put to the vote, it being felt that so revolutionary a proposal needed further

careful study'. AWGA, Annual Report, 1959. Discussions continued over the next few years; the 1960 Annual Report pointed out that 'women now take their place beside men in the arts as in many other walks of life'. AWGA, Annual Report, 1960. At a meeting of the Committee in 1962 Past-Master Brian Thomas asked, 'whether there was evidence that women wished to join the Guild', to which Brother Llewellyn Smith said that this was 'hardly relevant; as a principle was at stake'. AWGA, Meeting of the Committee, 13 June 1962. The Guild finally decided to admit women at a Special General Meeting on the 27 May 1964. This was reported in the Minutes of a Meeting of the Committee of the Guild held on 8 July 1964.

3   AWGA, undated document but *c.* 16 February 1954.

4   AWGA, 'Alteration of the Rules by Referendum', undated document.

5   In 1970, members were still discussing how their activities were not 'heralded with trumpets nor ostentatiously advertised'. AWGA, Master's Foreword, Annual Report, 1970.

6   AWGA, undated document but *c.* 16 February 1954.

7   AWGA, 'Alteration of the Rules by Referendum', undated document.

8   One key example here is the introduction of marriage bars across several professional fields in the interwar era. See Helen Glew, *Gender, Rhetoric and Regulation: Women's Work in the Civil Service and the London County Council, 1900–55* (Manchester: Manchester University Press, 2016), pp. 178–235.

9   Two of the founder members of the Royal Academy in 1768 were women, Mary Moser and Angelica Kauffman, but they were invited, not elected like Knight.

10   Annette Wickham, 'A "Female Invasion", 250 Years in the Making', www.royalacademy.org.uk/article/magazine-ra250-female-invasion-women-at-the-ra, accessed 25 September 2018.

11   Nevile Wallis, 'Joan Hassall – The Charm of Wood Engraving', *Sphere* (23 June 1956), p. 450.

12   John Hassall designed posters such as 'A Suffragette's Home' which portrays a man coming home after 'a hard day's work' to find his children distressed and alone, the house a mess, and his wife having left a note, pinned on a 'Votes for Women' poster, saying she had gone out.

13   Joan Hassall, 'Introduction', in *Joan Hassall: Engravings and Drawings* (ed.) David Chambers (London: Private Libraries, 1985), pp. vii–xii (p. x).

14   Joan Hassall, Master of the Art Workers' Guild, *Woman's Hour*, BBC Radio 2, 7 May 1972, British Library Sound Archive.

15   Hassall, *Woman's Hour*.

16   Brian North Lee (ed.), *Dearest Sydney: Joan Hassall's Letters to Sydney Cockerell from Italy and France, April–May 1950* (Wakefield: Fleece Press, 1991), p. 5. Cockerell was Master of the Guild in 1961.

17   Hassall, *Woman's Hour*.

18   WGAA, Edith B. Dawson to May Morris, 5 February 1908.

19   Catherine Clay, *British Women Writers, 1914–1945: Professional Work and Friendship* (Farnham: Ashgate, 2006).

20   As the century wore on, journalists informed readers with increasing urgency about their disapproval at such segregation. One typical press report in 1958 discussed, 'though I do not approve of the segregation of the sexes, I must admit that I found

the Women's International Art Club Exhibition at the Whitechapel Gallery ... well worth a visit'. 'A Season of Art Exhibitions', *Sketch* (22 October 1958), p. 378.

21 Margaret Geddes, 'The Women's International Art Club', *Studio*, 139 (January–June 1950), pp. 65–70 (p. 65).

22 AWGA, leaflet from 16 February 1954. For similar beliefs in the male historian's ability to provide a direct mirror onto the past see the Introduction to Bonnie G. Smith, *The Gender of History: Men, Women, and Historical Practice* (Cambridge, Mass: Harvard University Press, 1998).

23 DeCourcy Lewthwaite Dewar, *History of the Glasgow Society of Lady Artists' Club* (Glasgow: Robert Maclehose, University Press, 1950), pp. 36–37.

24 Caitriona Beaumont, *Housewives and Citizens: Domesticity and the Women's Movement in England, 1928–1964* (Manchester: Manchester University Press, 2013).

25 Anthea Callen and others, 'A Beginning', in *Framing Feminism: Art and the Women's Movement, 1970–1985* (eds) Rozsika Parker and Griselda Pollock (London: Pandora, 1987), pp. 149–151 (p. 150).

26 Mary Lowndes, 'Genius, and Women Painters', *Common Cause* (17 April 1914), p. 31. One of the first places the chapter was published was as Linda Nochlin, 'Why Are There No Great Women Artists?', in *Woman in Sexist Society: Studies in Power and Powerlessness* (eds) Vivian Gornick and Barbara Moran (New York: Basic Books, 1971), pp. 344–366. It has been published numerous times since, most commonly as 'Why Have There Been No Great Women Artists'.

27 Rozsika Parker and Griselda Pollock, 'Fifteen Years of Feminist Action: From Practical Strategies to Strategic Practices', in *Framing Feminism*, pp. 3–78 (p. 13).

28 Katy Deepwell, 'Feminist Collaborative Projects in the UK in the 1970s', in *All-Women Art Spaces in Europe in the Long 1970s* (eds) Agata Jakubowska and Katy Deepwell (Liverpool: Liverpool University Press, 2018), pp. 71–95 (p. 83).

29 Joan Wallach Scott, 'The Conundrum of Equality', in *Gender and the Politics of History, Thirtieth Anniversary Edition* (ed.) Joan Wallach Scott (New York: Columbia University Press, 2018), pp. 199–215 (p. 199). See also Joan Wallach Scott, *Only Paradoxes to Offer: French Feminists and the Rights of Man* (Cambridge, MA: Harvard University Press, 1997).

30 Kathryn Gleadle, 'The Imagined Communities of Women's History: Current Debates and Emerging Themes, a Rhizomatic Approach', *Women's History Review*, 22/4 (2013), pp. 524–540 (p. 535).

31 H. J. L. J. Massé, *The Art Workers' Guild, 1884–1934* (London: Shakespeare Head, 1935), p. 28; Anthea Callen, *Angel in the Studio: Women in the Arts and Crafts Movement, 1870–1914* (London: Astragal, 1979), p. 9. Callen similarly called it a 'minor offshoot'.

32 The most famous example is Nikolaus Pevsner, *Pioneers of Modern Design: From William Morris to Walter Gropius* (London: Faber and Faber, 1936). The book has been republished many times. For more recent examples taking this approach see the Introduction of this book.

33 Estella Canziani, *Round about Three Palace Green* (London: Methuen, 1939), p. 177.

34 Ann Sutherland Harris and Linda Nochlin, *Women Artists: 1550–1950* (New York: Knopf, 1976), p. 60.

Select bibliography

Primary sources

Manuscript papers
Katharine Adams papers, Bancroft Library, University of Berkeley
Arts and Crafts Exhibition Society papers, Archive of Art and Design, Victoria and Albert Museum
Art Workers' Guild papers, Art Workers' Guild
Bell papers, Special Collections, University of Reading
Sanford and Helen Berger Collection, Huntington Library
Estella Canziani papers, Birmingham Museum and Art Gallery
Edith Craig papers, British Library
Edith B. and Nelson Dawson papers, Archive of Art and Design, Victoria and Albert Museum
Edith B. and Nelson Dawson papers, private archive
Englishwoman Exhibition papers, Women's Library, London School of Economics
Phyllis and Delphis Gardner papers, British Library
Kelmscott Fellowship papers, William Morris Society
Mary Lowndes, 'Indenture of Apprenticeship' signed by Gertrude Esther Young from 1900, Add. MS 72833 fol. 47^r, British Library
Lowndes and Drury papers, Archive of Art and Design, Victoria and Albert Museum
Elizabeth Masterman papers, Women's Library, London School of Economics
Eric Millar papers, Huntington Library
May Morris papers and uncatalogued papers relating to Women's Guild of Arts members, William Morris Gallery
Ethel Sandell papers, Wiltshire Museum and Archive
Sheffield Educational Settlement papers, Special Collections, University of Sheffield
Mary A. Sloane papers, William Morris Society
Alys Fane Trotter papers, University of Cape Town Library
Women's Guild of Arts lecture, 1963, CLC/521/MS38567, London Metropolitan Archives
Women's Guild of Arts papers, William Morris Society
Women's Guild of Arts papers, Duke University, North Carolina
Women's Guild of Arts papers, private archive
Women's International Art Club, Women's Art Library, Goldsmiths, University of London
Alice B. and E. C. Woodward file, Bushey Museum
'91 Art Club, Clifford's Gallery Exhibition Pamphlet, 1896, National Art Library, Victoria and Albert Museum

Published authored works

Ashbee, C. R., 'The English Arts and Crafts Exhibition at the Royal Academy: An Open Letter from C. R. Ashbee', *American Magazine of Art* (February 1917), pp. 137–145

Ashbee, C. R., *Where the Great City Stands: A Study in the New Civics* (London: Essex House and B. T. Batsford, 1917)

Ashbee, C. R., *Craftsmanship in Competitive Industry* (Campden: Essex House, 1908)

Atherton, Gertrude, 'The Greatest Woman's Club in the World', *Bookman: An Illustrated Magazine of Literature and Life*, 27 (March–August 1908), pp. 250–261

Barton, Rose, *Familiar London* (London: Adam and Charles Black, 1904)

Benjamin, Hilda Thelma, *London Shops and Shopping* (London: Herbert Joseph, 1934)

Benjamin, Hilda Thelma, *A Shopping Guide to London* (New York: R. M. McBride, 1930)

Benson, A. C., and Lawrence Weaver, *Everybody's Book of the Queen's Doll's House* (London: Methuen, 1924)

Bickerdike, Rhoda, 'The Dawsons: An Equal Partnership of Artists', *Apollo*, 128 (November 1988), pp. 320–325

Blomfield, A. W., and others, 'Architecture – A Profession or an Art?', *The Times* (3 March 1891), p. 9

Bowley, Agatha, *A Memoir of Professor Sir Arthur Bowley (1869–1957) and his Family* (Britain: self-published, 1972)

Brittain, Vera, *Women's Work in Modern England* (London: Noel Douglas, 1928)

Butler, Elizabeth, *An Autobiography* (London: Constable, 1922)

Canziani, Estella, *Round about Three Palace Green* (London: Methuen, 1939)

Carter, Elizabeth Ellin, *Artistic Leather Work* (London: E. and F. N. Spon, 1921)

Chips, Dorothy, 'Miss Chips' Chatter', *Illustrated Chips* (16 March 1895), p. 7

Clarke, William Spencer, *The Suburban Homes of London: A Residential Guide to Favourite London Localities, their Society, Celebrities, and Associations, with Notes on their Rental, Rates, and House Accommodation* (London: Chatto and Windus, 1881)

Coates, Dora Meeson, *George Coates: His Art and His Life* (London: Dent, 1937)

Cockerell, Sydney, 'Obituary: Mrs Edmund Webb', *The Times* (20 October 1952), p. 8

Crane, Walter, *An Artist's Reminiscences* (London: Methuen, 1907)

Dawson, Edith B., *Enamels* (London: Methuen, 1906)

Dewar, DeCourcy Lewthwaite, *History of the Glasgow Society of Lady Artists' Club* (Glasgow: University Press, 1950)

Evors, E. M., 'Some Women Illustrators of Children's Books', *Girls' Realm*, 5 (1903), pp. 455–463

Eyre, Alan Montgomery, *Saint John's Wood: Its History, its Houses, its Haunts and its Celebrities* (London: Chapman and Hall, 1913), p. v

Faithfull, Emily, 'Ladies as Shopkeepers', *Pall Mall Gazette* (23 December 1887), p. 11

Fincham, Ernest C., *Women as Bookbinders* (London: Guild of Women Binders, 1901)

Francis-Lewis, Cécile, *The Art and Craft of Leatherwork* (London: Seeley, 1928)

Fraser, Helen, *Women and War Work* (New York: G. A. Shaw, 1918)

Garnett, Annie, *Notes on Hand-Spinning* (London: Dulau, 1896)

Gates, G. Evelyn, *Woman's Year Book, 1923–1924* (London: Women Publishers, 1924)

Geddes, Margaret, 'The Women's International Art Club', *Studio*, 139 (January–June 1950), pp. 65–70

Gleichen, Helena, *Contacts and Contrasts* (London: Murray, 1940)

Graves, Algernon, *The Royal Academy of Arts: A Complete Dictionary of Contributors and Their Work*, 5 (London: George Bell, 1906)

Hadaway, Jean, 'Developments in the Art of Jewellery', *Journal of the Royal Society of Arts*, 56 (1908), pp. 287–297

Hamilton-Gordon, Ishbel Maria (ed.), *Women in Professions: Being the Professional Section of the International Congress of Women, London, July 1899* (London: Fisher Unwin, 1900)

Harmsworth, Alfred C., 'What Shall I Be?', *Young Folks' Paper: Literary Olympic and Tournament* (24 September 1887), p. 203

Harwood, Edith, 'Studies from Pictures of Women in the National Gallery', *Woman's Signal* (4 July 1895), p. 6

Hay-Edwards, C. M., *A History of Clifford's Inn, with a Chapter on its Present Owners by Willoughby Bullock* (London: Thomas Werner Laurie, 1912)

Hobhouse, Emily, 'Women Workers: How They Live, How They Wish to Live', *Nineteenth-Century Magazine*, 47 (1900), p. 473

Jones, Winifred M., 'The Revival of an Old World Industry', *Atalanta* (1 June 1898), p. 497

Jopling, Louise, 'Occupations for Gentlewomen', *Atalanta* (January 1895), p. 221

King, Alice, 'Higher Thoughts on Housekeeping', *Girl's Own Paper* (12 January 1884), p. 235

Krout, Mary H., *A Looker on in London* (New York: Dodd and Mead, 1899)

Leslie, Marion, 'Women's Work at the Victorian Era Exhibition', *Lady's Realm: An Illustrated Monthly Magazine* (May–October 1897), pp. 58–65

Lowndes, Mary, 'Their Training', *Englishwoman*, 82/28 (1915), pp. 73–74

Lowndes, Mary, 'Genius, and Women Painters', *Common Cause* (17 April 1914), p. 31

Lowndes, Mary, 'Dr Faustus', *Englishwoman*, 13/38 (1912), pp. 206–220

Lowndes, Mary, *Banners and Banner Making* (London: Artists' Suffrage League, 1909)

Mahony, Bertha E. and Elinor Whitney, *Contemporary Illustrators of Children's Books* (Boston: Bookshop for Boys and Girls, Women's Educational and Industrial Union, 1930)

Massé, H. J. L. J., *The Art Workers' Guild, 1884-1934* (London: Shakespeare Head, 1935)

Mills, Roberta, 'Leather Craft', in *Penrose's Pictorial Annual, The Process Year Book for 1912-13* (ed.) William Gamble (London: Lund, Humphries, 1913), pp. 71-72

Montizambert, Elizabeth, *London Discoveries in Shops and Restaurants* (London: Women Publishers, 1924)

Morris, May, *Decorative Needlework* (London: Hughes, 1893)

Parkes, Kineton, 'Modern Artists and Their Methods', *Atalanta* (1 April 1896), p. 460

Prideaux, S. T., *Modern Bookbindings: Their Design and Decoration* (London: Archibald Constable, 1906)

Prideaux, S. T., *Bookbinders and their Craft* (London: Zaehnsdorf, 1903)

Prideaux, S. T., *An Historical Sketch of Bookbinding* (London: Lawrence and Bullen, 1893)

Ransome, Arthur, *Bohemia in London* (New York: Dodd and Mead, 1907)

Rowe, Eleanor, *Practical Wood-Carving: A Book for the Student, Carver, Teacher, Designer, and Architect* (London: Batsford, 1907)

Rowe, Eleanor, *Hints on Wood-Carving: Recreative Classes and Modelling for Beginners* (London: City and Guilds Institute, 1891)

Russell, Gordon, 'Mrs Edmund Webb', *The Times* (14 November 1952), p. 8

S., E. B., 'Interview with Mr. and Mrs. Nelson Dawson', *Studio*, 6 (1896), pp. 173-178

Smedley, Constance, *Crusaders: Reminiscences of Constance Smedley / Mrs Maxwell Armfield* (London: Duckworth, 1929)

Smedley, Constance, 'A Guild of Craftswomen', *World's Work: An Illustrated Magazine of National Efficiency and Social Progress*, 9 (December 1906-1907), pp. 314-322

Stickley, Gustav, 'Art True and False', *Craftsman: An Illustrated Monthly Magazine for the Simplification of Life*, 8 (April-September 1905), pp. 684-693

Stirling, A. M. W., *William De Morgan and His Wife* (New York: Holt, 1922)

Tooley, Sarah A., 'A Lady Goldsmith', *Woman's Signal* (9 May 1895), p. 289

Trotter, Jacqueline T. (ed.), *Valour and Vision: Poems of the War, 1914-1918* (London, 1920)

Uzanne, Octave, *The Modern Parisienne* (London: Heinemann, 1912)

Various authors, *Some Arts and Crafts* (London: Chapman and Hall, 1903)

Wallis, Nevile, 'Joan Hassall – The Charm of Wood Engraving', *Sphere* (23 June 1956), p. 450

Watts, Mary Seton, *The Word in the Pattern* (London: Astolat, 1905)

Weeks, Charlotte J., 'Women at Work: The Slade Girls', *Magazine of Art* (January 1883), pp. 324-329

Whitley, W. T., 'The Arts and Crafts Exhibition', *Studio*, 69/285 (December 1916), pp. 126-128

Whitman, Alfred, 'The Jewellery of Mrs Philip Newman', *Magazine of Art* (London, 1902), pp. 465–467

Woodward, E. C., 'Enamelling and Hall-marking', in *Mrs Strang's Annual for Girls* (Oxford: Oxford University Press, 1922), pp. 82–87

Woodward, E. C., 'Jewellery and Metal Work', in *Mrs Strang's Annual for Girls* (Oxford: Oxford University Press, 1921), pp. 47–53

Woolf, Virginia, *A Room of One's Own* (Oxford: Blackwell, 1929)

Anonymous articles have been cited from the following publications
Architectural Review
Artist: An Illustrated Monthly Record of Arts, Crafts, and Industries
Art Record: A Weekly Illustrated Review of the Arts and Crafts
Art Workers' Quarterly
Belfast Weekly News
Birmingham Daily Gazette
Brooklyn Daily Eagle
Builder
Cheltenham Examiner
Common Cause
Country Life
Daily Mail
Darlington and Stockton Times, Ripon and Richmond Chronicle
Englishwoman's Review
Girl's Own Paper
Graphic
Hearth and Home
Homes and Gardens
Illustrated London News
Illustrated Sporting and Dramatic News
Journal of the Royal Society of Arts
Journal of the Society of Arts
Judy
Ladies' Treasury
Lancashire Evening Post
Le Follet: Journal du Grand Monde, Fashion, Polite Literature, Beaux Arts, &c.
Lloyd's Weekly Newspaper
London Daily News
London Gazette
Magazine of Art
Manchester Guardian
Midland Daily Telegraph
Mid Sussex Times
Morning Post
Myra's Journal
Newcastle Daily Journal

New York Times
Pall Mall Gazette
Pottery Gazette
Punch
Sanitation Record
Scotsman
Sheffield Daily Telegraph
Sketch
Sphere
Studio
The Times
Votes for Women
Western Gazette
Woman's Herald
Woman's Leader
Woman's Signal
Women's Penny Paper
Women's Trades Union Review
Yorkshire Post and Leeds Intelligencer

Advertisements
'Bookbinding', *Cheltenham Looker-On* (24 November 1906), p. 21
Colour, 16 (1922), p. i
Common Cause (9 March 1917), p. 638
English-Speaking World, 19 (1937), p. 286
Studio Year-Book of Decorative Art (1925), p. iv
The Times (4 December 1928), p. 29
— (9 January 1895), p. 1
— (9 July 1892), p. 1
'Wood Carving and Modelling', *Windsor and Eton Express* (6 February 1897),
    p. 1

Catalogues and guides
Arts and Crafts Exhibition Society Catalogues (various)
Notable Londoners: An Illustrated Who's Who of Professional and Business Men
    (London, 1924)
Official Catalogue of Exhibitors, Universal Exposition St. Louis, USA (St Louis:
    Catalogue Company, 1904)
Official Catalogue of the British Section, Royal Commission for the Chicago Exhibition,
    1893 (London: William Clowes, 1893)
Olivia's Shopping and How She Does It: A Prejudiced Guide to the London Shops
    (London: Gay and Bird, 1906)
The Times History of the War, 4 (London: The Times, 1915)
Victorian Era Exhibition Guide (London: Riddle and Couchman, 1897)

Woman's Exhibition, 1900, Fine Art, Historical, and General Catalogue (London: Spottiswoode, 1900)
Woman's Exhibition, 1900, Official Guide (London: Spottiswoode, 1900)

Transcripts of oral interviews
'A Taped Conversation with John Gwynne, of Quenington, Gloucestershire on the Subject of William and Eve Simmonds', 1980, Cheltenham Art Gallery and Museum
Joan Hassall, Master of the Art Workers' Guild, *Woman's Hour*, BBC Radio 2, 7 May 1972, British Library Sound Archive
'Eve Simmonds: A Personal Account Compiled from Conversations and Letters to Heather and Robin Tanner', 1971, Cheltenham Art Gallery and Museum

Secondary literature

Aston, Jennifer, *Female Entrepreneurship in Nineteenth-Century England: Engagement in the Urban Economy* (London: Palgrave Macmillan, 2016)
Barker, Hannah, *The Business of Women: Female Enterprise and Urban Development in Northern England, 1760–1830* (Oxford: Oxford University Press, 2006)
Barker, Hannah, and Jane Hamlett, 'Living Above the Shop: Home, Business, and Family in the English "Industrial Revolution"', *Journal of Family History*, 35/4 (2010), pp. 311–328
Barter, Judith A. (ed.), *Apostles of Beauty: Arts and Crafts from Britain to Chicago* (New Haven: Yale University Press, 2009)
Beachy, Robert, Béatrice Craig, and Alastair Owens (eds), *Women, Business and Finance in Nineteenth-Century Europe: Rethinking Separate Spheres* (London: Berg, 2005)
Beaumont, Caitriona, *Housewives and Citizens: Domesticity and the Women's Movement in England, 1928–1964* (Manchester: Manchester University Press, 2013)
Beebe, Kathryne, Angela Davis, and Kathryn Gleadle, 'Introduction: Space, Place and Gendered Identities: Feminist History and the Spatial Turn', *Women's History Review*, 21/4 (2012), pp. 523–532
Black, Barbara J., *A Room of His Own: A Literary-Cultural Study of Victorian Clubland* (Athens: Ohio University Press, 2012)
Blakesley, Rosalind P., *The Arts and Crafts Movement* (London: Phaidon, 2006)
Boisseau, T. J., 'White Queens at the Chicago World's Fair, 1893: New Womanhood in the Service of Class, Race, and Nation', *Gender and History*, 12/1 (2000), pp. 33–81
Boisseau, T. J., and Abigail M. Markwyn (eds), *Gendering the Fair: Histories of Women and Gender at World's Fairs* (Urbana: University of Illinois Press, 2010)
Bounia, Alexandra, 'Exhibiting Women's Handicrafts: Arts and Crafts Exhibitions in Greece at the Dawn of the Twentieth Century', *Gender and History*, 26/2 (2014), pp. 287–312

Brockington, Grace, *Above the Battlefield: Modernism and the Peace Movement in Britain, 1900–1918* (London: Yale University Press, 2010)

Brockington, Grace, "'A World Fellowship": The Founding of the International Lyceum Club', *Transnational Associations*, 1 (2005), pp. 15–22

Brunton, Jennie, 'Annie Garnett: The Arts and Crafts Movement and the Business of Textile Manufacture', *Textile History*, 32/2 (2001), pp. 217–238

Brunton, Jennie, *The Arts and Crafts Movement in the Lake District: A Social History* (Lancaster: University of Lancaster, 2001)

Buckley, Cheryl, *Designing Modern Britain* (London: Reaktion, 2007)

Buckley, Cheryl, *Potters and Paintresses: Women Designers in the Pottery Industry, 1870–1955* (London: Women's Press, 1990)

Buckley, Cheryl, 'Made in Patriarchy: Towards a Feminist Analysis of Women and Design', *Design Issues*, 3/2 (1986), pp. 3–14

Burkhauser, Jude (ed.), *Glasgow Girls: Women in Art and Design, 1880–1920* (Edinburgh: Canongate, 1990)

Burton, Antoinette, *Burdens of History: British Feminists, Indian Women, and Imperial Culture, 1865–1915* (Chapel Hill: University of North Carolina Press, 1994)

Callen, Anthea, 'Sexual Division of Labour in the Arts and Crafts Movement', in *A View from the Interior: Feminism, Women and Design* (eds) Judy Attfield and Pat Kirkham (London: Women's Press, 1989), pp. 151–164

Callen, Anthea, 'Sexual Division of Labor in the Arts and Crafts Movement', *Woman's Art Journal*, 5/2 (1984–1985), pp. 1–6

Callen, Anthea, *Angel in the Studio: Women in the Arts and Crafts Movement, 1870–1914* (London: Astragal, 1979)

Callen, Anthea and others, 'A Beginning', in *Framing Feminism: Art and the Women's Movement, 1970–1985* (eds) Rozsika Parker and Griselda Pollock (London: Pandora, 1987), pp. 149–151

Campbell Orr, Clarissa (ed.), *Women in the Victorian Art World* (Manchester: Manchester University Press, 1995)

Carruthers, Annette, *The Arts and Crafts Movement in Scotland: A History* (New Haven: Yale University Press, 2013)

Carruthers, Annette, *Edward Barnsley and his Workshop: Arts and Crafts in the Twentieth Century* (Oxford: White Cockade, 1992)

Carruthers, Annette, and Mary Greensted (eds), *Simplicity or Splendour: Arts and Crafts Living – Objects from the Cheltenham Collection* (Cheltenham: Cheltenham Art Gallery and Museums, 1999)

Cheasley Paterson, Elaine, 'Decoration and Desire in the Watts Chapel, Compton: Narratives of Gender, Class and Colonialism', *Gender and History*, 17/3 (2005), pp. 714–736

Cheasley Paterson, Elaine, 'Crafting a National Identity: The Dun Emer Guild, 1902–1908', in *The Irish Revival Reappraised* (eds) Betsey Taylor FitzSimon and James H. Murphy (Dublin: Four Courts, 2004), pp. 106–118

Cherry, Deborah, *Beyond the Frame: Feminism and Visual Culture, Britain 1850–1900* (London: Routledge, 2000)

Cherry, Deborah, *Painting Women: Victorian Women Artists* (London: Routledge, 1993)

Cherry, Deborah, and Janice Helland (eds), *Local/Global, Women Artists in the Nineteenth Century* (Farnham: Ashgate, 2006)

Cinamon, Gerald, 'Alice B. Woodward', *Private Library*, 2/4 (1989), pp. 148–177

Clark, Jessica P., 'Pomeroy v. Pomeroy: Beauty, Modernity, and the Female Entrepreneur in *Fin-de-siècle* London', *Women's History Review*, 22/6 (2013), pp. 877–903

Clay, Catherine, *British Women Writers, 1914–1945: Professional Work and Friendship* (Farnham: Ashgate, 2006)

Coatsworth, Elizabeth, '"A Formidable Undertaking": Mrs. A. G. I. Christie and English Medieval Embroidery', in *Medieval Clothing and Textiles*, 10 (eds) Robin Netherton and Gale R. Owen-Crocker (Woodbridge: Boydell and Brewer, 2014), pp. 165–194

Cockroft, Irene, *New Dawn Women, Women in the Arts and Crafts and Suffrage Movements at the Dawn of the 20th Century* (Guildford: Watts Gallery, 2005)

Cockroft, Irene, and Susan Croft, *Art, Theatre and Women's Suffrage* (Twickenham: Aurora Metro, 2010)

Cohen, Deborah, *Household Gods: The British and Their Possessions* (New Haven: Yale University Press, 2006)

Corfield, Penelope J., *Power and the Professions in Britain, 1700–1850* (London: Routledge, 1995)

Cormack, Peter, 'The Glass House: A Great Feminist Enterprise', *Journal of Stained Glass*, 41 (2017), pp. 6–14

Cormack, Peter, *Arts and Crafts Stained Glass* (New Haven: Yale University Press, 2015)

Cormack, Peter, 'A Truly British Movement', *Apollo: The International Magazine of the Arts*, 161 (April 2005), pp. 48–53

Cowman, Krista, and Louise A. Jackson, 'Introduction: Middle-Class Women and Professional Identity', *Women's History Review*, 14/2 (2005), pp. 165–180

Cowman, Krista, and Louise A. Jackson (eds), *Women and Work Culture: Britain c. 1850–1950* (Farnham: Ashgate, 2005)

Crawford, Alan, 'The Object is Not the Object: C. R. Ashbee and the Guild of Handicraft', in *Pioneers of Modern Craft: Twelve Essays Profiling Key Figures in the History of Twentieth-Century Craft* (ed.) Margot Coatts (Manchester: Manchester University Press, 1997), pp. 1–11

Crawford, Alan, *C. R. Ashbee: Architect, Designer and Romantic Socialist* (New Haven: Yale University Press, 1985)

Crawford, Alan (ed.), *By Hammer and Hand: The Arts and Crafts Movement in Birmingham* (Birmingham: Birmingham Museums and Art Gallery, 1984)

Crawford, Alan, and Wendy Kaplan, *The Arts and Crafts Movement in Europe and America: Design for the Modern World, 1880–1920* (London: Thames and Hudson, 2004)

Crawford, Elizabeth, *Art and Suffrage: A Biographical Dictionary of Suffrage Artists* (London: Francis Boutle, 2018)

Crawford, Elizabeth, *Enterprising Women: The Garretts and Their Circle* (London: Boutle, 2002)

Crawford, Elizabeth, *The Women's Suffrage Movement: A Reference Guide, 1866–1928* (London: UCL Press, 1999)

Crinson, Mark, and Jules Lubbock, *Architecture, Art or Profession? Three Hundred Years of Architectural Education in Britain* (Manchester: Manchester University Press, 1994)

Crook, David, 'Some Historical Perspectives on Professionalism', in *Exploring Professionalism* (ed.) Bryan Cunningham (London: Institute of Education, 2008), pp. 10–27

Crook, Tom, 'Craft and the Dialogics of Modernity: The Arts and Crafts Movement in Late-Victorian and Edwardian England', *Journal of Modern Craft*, 2/1 (2009), pp. 17–32

Cumming, Elizabeth, *Hand, Heart and Soul: The Arts and Crafts Movement in Scotland* (Edinburgh: Birlinn, 2006)

Cumming, Elizabeth, and Nicola Gordon Bowe, *The Arts and Crafts Movement in Dublin and Edinburgh, 1885–1930* (Dublin: Irish Academic Press, 1998)

Cumming, Elizabeth, and Wendy Kaplan, *The Arts and Crafts Movement* (London: Thames and Hudson, 1991)

Dakers, Caroline, *The Holland Park Circle: Artists and Victorian Society* (New Haven: Yale University Press, 1999)

Danahay, Martin, 'Arts and Crafts as a Transatlantic Movement: C. R. Ashbee in the United States, 1896–1915', *Journal of Victorian Culture*, 20/1 (2015), pp. 65–86

Darling, Elizabeth, and Lynne Walker, *AA Women in Architecture,1917–2017* (London: Architectural Association, 2017)

Darling, Elizabeth, and Lesley Whitworth (eds), *Women and the Making of Built Space in England, 1870–1950* (London: Ashgate, 2007)

Davidoff, Leonore, *The Best Circles: Society, the Season and Etiquette* (London: Croom Helm, 1973)

Davidoff, Leonore, and Catherine Hall, *Family Fortunes: Men and Women of the English Middle Class, 1780–1850*, 2nd edition (London: Routledge, 2002)

Deepwell, Katy, *Women Artists Between the Wars: 'A Fair Field and No Favour'* (Manchester: Manchester University Press, 2010)

Delap, Lucy, *The Feminist Avant-Garde: Transatlantic Encounters of the Early Twentieth Century* (Cambridge: Cambridge University Press, 2007)

Delap, Lucy, Maria DiCenzo, and Leila Ryan, *Feminist Media History: Suffrage, Periodicals and the Public Sphere* (London: Palgrave Macmillan, 2010)

Delap, Lucy, Ben Griffin, and Abigail Wills (eds), *The Politics of Domestic Authority in Britain since 1800* (Basingstoke: Palgrave Macmillan, 2009)

Digby, Anne, 'Victorian Values and Women in Public and Private', *Proceedings of the British Academy*, 78 (1992), pp. 195–215

Doan, Laura, and Jane Garrity (eds), *Sapphic Modernities: Sexuality, Women and National Culture* (London: Palgrave Macmillan, 2006)

Elliott, Bridget, and Janice Helland (eds), *Women Artists and the Decorative Arts, 1880–1935: The Gender of Ornament* (Farnham: Ashgate, 2002)

Ferry, Emma, "'A Novelty among Exhibitions": The Loan Exhibition of Women's Industries, Bristol, 1885', in *Women and the Making of Built Space in England, 1870–1950* (eds) Elizabeth Darling and Lesley Whitworth (Farnham: Ashgate, 2007), pp. 51–68

Ferry, Emma, "'Decorators May be Compared to Doctors": An Analysis of Rhoda and Agnes Garrett's Suggestion for House Decoration in Painting, Woodwork and Furniture (1876)', *Journal of Design History*, 16/1 (2003), pp. 15–33

Fletcher, Pamela, and Anne Helmreich (eds), *The Rise of the Modern Art Market in London, 1850–1939* (Manchester: Manchester University Press, 2011)

Fraser, Hilary, *Women Writing Art History in the Nineteenth Century* (Cambridge: Cambridge University Press, 2014)

Freedman, Estelle, 'Separatism as Strategy: Female Institution Building and American Feminism, 1870–1930', *Feminist Studies*, 5/3 (1979), pp. 512–529

Garrett, Miranda, 'Professional Women Interior Decorators in Britain, 1874–1899' (Unpublished PhD thesis, Central St Martins, 2018)

Garrett, Miranda, 'Window Smashing and Window Draping: Suffrage and Interior Design', in *Suffrage and the Arts: Visual Culture, Politics and Enterprise* (eds) Miranda Garrett and Zoë Thomas (London: Bloomsbury, 2018), pp. 93–116

Garrett, Miranda, and Zoë Thomas (eds), *Suffrage and the Arts: Visual Culture, Politics and Enterprise* (London: Bloomsbury, 2018)

Gee, Emily, 'Where Shall She Live? The History and Designation of Housing for Working Women in London, 1880–1925', *Journal of Architectural Conservation*, 15/2 (2009), pp. 27–46

Gere, Charlotte, *Artistic Circles: Design and Decoration in the Aesthetic Movement* (London: V&A, 2010)

Gere, Charlotte, and Geoffrey C. Munn, *Pre-Raphaelite to Arts and Crafts Jewellery* (Woodbridge: Antique Collectors' Club, 1989)

Gergits, Julia M., 'Women Artists at Home', in *Keeping the Victorian House: A Collection of Essays* (ed.) Vanessa D. Dickerson (New York: Garland, 1995), pp. 105–130

Gerrish Nunn, Pamela, *Victorian Women Artists* (London: Women's Press, 1987)

Gerrish Nunn, Pamela, *Canvassing: Recollections by Six Victorian Women Artists* (London: Camden Press, 1986)

Giles, Judy, *The Parlour and the Suburb: Domestic Identities, Class, Femininity and Modernity* (Oxford: Berg, 2004)

Girouard, Mark, *Sweetness and Light: The Queen Anne Movement, 1860–1900* (New Haven: Yale University Press, 1984)

Gleadle, Kathryn, 'The Imagined Communities of Women's History: Current Debates and Emerging Themes, a Rhizomatic Approach', *Women's History Review*, 22/4 (2013), pp. 524–540

Gleadle, Kathryn, "'The Riches and Treasures of Other Countries": Women, Empire and Maritime Expertise in Early Victorian London', *Gender and History*, 25/1 (2013), pp. 7–26

Gordon, Eleanor, and Gwyneth Nair, *Public Lives: Women, Family and Society in Victorian Britain* (New Haven: Yale University Press, 2003)

Gordon Bowe, Nicola, *Wilhelmina Geddes: Life and Work* (Dublin: Four Courts, 2015)

Gordon Bowe, Nicola, 'The Irish Arts and Crafts Movement (1866–1925)', *Irish Arts Review Yearbook* (1990–1991), pp. 172–185

Gordon Bowe, Nicola, 'Women and the Arts and Crafts Revival in Ireland, c. 1886–1930', in *Irish Women Artists From the Eighteenth Century to the Present Day* (eds) Wanda Ryan-Smolin and others (Dublin: National Gallery of Ireland/Douglas Hyde Gallery, 1987), pp. 22–27

Gotsi, Chariklia-Glafki, 'Towards the Formation of a Professional Identity: Women Artists in Greece at the Beginning of the Twentieth Century', *Women's History Review*, 14/2 (2005), pp. 285–300

Gowrley, Freya, and Katie Faulkner, 'Making Masculinity: Craft, Gender, and Material Production in the Long Nineteenth Century', *Nineteenth-Century Gender Studies*, 14/2 (2018), pp. 1–10

Greensted, Mary, *The Arts and Crafts Movement in Britain* (Oxford: Shire, 2010)

Greensted, Mary (ed.), *An Anthology of the Arts and Crafts Movement: Writings by Ashbee, Lethaby, Gimson and their Contemporaries* (London: Lund Humphries, 2005)

Hadjiafxendi, Kyriaki, and Patricia Zakreski (eds), *Crafting the Woman Professional in the Long Nineteenth Century: Artistry and Industry in Britain* (Burlington: Ashgate, 2013)

Hamlett, Jane, *Material Relations: Domestic Interiors and Middle-Class Families in England, 1850–1910* (Manchester: Manchester University Press, 2010)

Hamlett, Jane, and Lesley Hoskins (eds), 'Special Issue: Home and Work', *Home Cultures* (2011)

Hannam, June, and Karen Hunt, *Socialist Women: Britain, 1880s to 1920s* (London: Routledge, 2001)

Harrod, Tanya, *The Crafts in Britain in the Twentieth Century* (New Haven: Yale University Press, 1999)

Hart, Imogen, 'On the Arts and Crafts Exhibition Society', www.branchcollective .org/?ps_articles=imogen-hart-on-the-first-arts-and-crafts-exhibition), accessed 19 September 2019

Hart, Imogen, *Arts and Crafts Objects* (Manchester: Manchester University Press, 2010)

Haskins, Heather, 'Now You See Them, Now You Don't: The Critical Reception of Women's Work at the Arts and Crafts Exhibition Society, 1888–1916' (Unpublished PhD thesis, Concordia University, 2005)

Helland, Janice, '"Good Work and Clever Design": Early Exhibitions of the Home Arts and Industries Association', *Journal of Modern Craft*, 5/3 (2012), pp. 275–293

Helland, Janice, *British and Irish Home Arts and Industries, 1880–1914: Marketing Craft, Making Fashion* (Dublin: Irish Academic Press, 2007)

Helland, Janice, *Professional Women Painters in Nineteenth-Century Scotland: Commitment, Friendship, Pleasure* (Farnham: Ashgate, 2000)

Helland, Janice, *The Studios of Frances and Margaret MacDonald* (Manchester: Manchester University Press, 1996)

Helland, Janice, and Beverley Lemire (eds), *Craft, Community and the Material Culture of Place and Politics, 19th–20th Century* (Farnham: Ashgate, 2014)

Hill, Kate, *Women and Museums, 1850–1914: Modernity and the Gendering of Knowledge* (Manchester: Manchester University Press, 2016)

Hobsbawm, Eric, and Terence Ranger (eds), *The Invention of Tradition* (Cambridge: Cambridge University Press, 1983)

Hulse, Lynne (ed.), *May Morris: Art and Life, New Perspectives* (London: Friends of the William Morris Gallery, 2017)

Jakubowska, Agata, and Katy Deepwell (eds), *All-Women Art Spaces in Europe in the Long 1970s* (Liverpool: Liverpool University Press, 2018)

Jennings, Rebecca, *A Lesbian History of Britain: Love and Sex Between Women Since 1500* (Oxford: Greenwood, 2007)

Kaplan, Stuart R., and others, *Pamela Colman Smith: The Untold Story* (Stamford: US Games, 2018)

Karlin Zorn, Elyse, *Maker and Muse: Women and Early Twentieth Century Art Jewellery* (New York: Monacelli, 2015)

Karlin Zorn, Elyse, *Jewelry and Metalwork in the Arts and Crafts Tradition* (Pennyslvania: Schiffer, 1993)

Kay, Alison, *The Foundations of Female Entrepreneurship: Enterprise, Home, and Household in London, c. 1800–1870* (London: Routledge, 2009)

Kay, Alison, 'Retailing, Respectability and the Independent Woman in Nineteenth Century London', in *Women, Business and Finance in Nineteenth-Century Europe: Rethinking Separate Spheres* (eds) Robert Beachy and others (Oxford: Berg, 2006), pp. 152–166

Kay, Alison, 'Small Business, Self-Employment and Women's Work-Life Choices in Nineteenth-Century London', in *Origins of the Modern Career* (eds) John Brown and others (Aldershot: Ashgate, 2004), pp. 191–206

Kimmel, Michael S., 'Review: The Arts and Crafts Movement: Handmade Socialism or Elite Consumerism?', *Contemporary Sociology*, 16/3 (1987), pp. 388–390

Kinchin, Juliet, 'Interiors: Nineteenth-Century Essays on the "Masculine" and the "Feminine" Room', in *The Gendered Object* (ed.) Pat Kirkham (Manchester: Manchester University Press, 1996), pp. 12–29

Kreilkamp, Vera (ed.), *The Arts and Crafts Movement: Making it Irish* (Chestnut Hill: McMullen Museum, 2016)

Lago, Mary, *Christiana Herringham and the Edwardian Art Scene* (Columbia: University of Missouri Press, 1996)

Larmour, Paul, *The Arts and Crafts Movement in Ireland* (Belfast: Friar's Bush, 1992)

Laucks Walter, Hilary, 'Another Stitch to the Legacy of William Morris: May Morris's Designs and Writings on Embroidery', in *William Morris in the*

Twenty-First Century (eds) Philippa Bennett and Rosie Miles (Bern: Lang, 2010), pp. 73–90

Levine, Philippa, *The Amateur and the Professional: Antiquarians, Historians and Archaeologists in Victorian England, 1838-1886* (Cambridge: Cambridge University Press, 2003)

Livingstone, Karen, and Linda Parry, *International Arts and Crafts* (London: V&A, 2005)

Londraville, Janis, *On Poetry, Painting, and Politics: The Letters of May Morris and John Quinn* (London: Associated University Presses, 1997)

MacCarthy, Fiona, *William Morris: A Life for Our Time* (London: Faber and Faber, 1995)

MacCarthy, Fiona, *The Simple Life: C. R. Ashbee in the Cotswolds* (Berkeley: University of California Press, 1992)

Malone, Carolyn, 'A Job Fit for Heroes? Disabled Veterans, the Arts and Crafts Movement and Social Reconstruction in Post-World War I Britain', *First World War Studies*, 4/2 (2013), pp. 201–217

Malone, Carolyn, 'The Art of Remembrance: The Arts and Crafts Movement and the Commemoration of the British War Dead, 1916-1920', *Contemporary British History*, 26/1 (2012), pp. 1–23

Mandler, Peter (ed.), *Liberty and Authority in Victorian Britain* (Oxford: Oxford University Press, 2006)

Marcus, Sharon, *Between Women: Friendship, Desire, and Marriage in Victorian England* (Princeton: Princeton University Press, 2007)

Marsh, Jan, 'May Morris: Ubiquitous, Invisible Arts and Crafts-Woman', in *Women Artists and the Decorative Arts, 1880-1935: The Gender of Ornament* (eds) Bridget Elliott and Janice Helland (Farnham: Ashgate, 2002), pp. 35–52

Marsh, Jan, *Jane and May Morris: A Biographical Story, 1839-1938* (London: Pandora, 1986)

Mason, Anna, and others, *May Morris: Arts and Crafts Designer* (London: Thames and Hudson, 2017)

Massey, Doreen, *Space, Place and Gender* (Cambridge: Polity, 1994)

McBrinn, Joseph, 'The Spectacle of Masculinity: Men and the Visual Culture of the Suffrage Campaign', in *Suffrage and the Arts: Visual Culture, Politics and Enterprise* (eds) Miranda Garrett and Zoë Thomas (London: Bloomsbury, 2018), pp. 205–230

McBrinn, Joseph, '"The Work of Masculine Fingers": The Disabled Soldiers' Embroidery Industry, 1918-1955', *Journal of Design History*, 31/1 (2018), pp. 1–23

McBrinn, Joseph, '"A Populous Solitude": The Life and Art of Sophia Rosamond Praeger, 1867-1954', *Women's History Review*, 18/4 (2009), pp. 577–596

McLeod, Ellen Easton, *In Good Hands: The Women of the Canadian Handicrafts Guild* (London: Routledge, 1999)

Melman, Billie, *The Culture of History: English Uses of the Past, 1800-1953* (Oxford: Oxford University Press, 2006)

Melman, Billie, 'Gender, History and Memory: The Invention of Women's Past in the Nineteenth and Early Twentieth Centuries', *History and Memory*, 5/1 (1993), pp. 5–41

Mesplède, Sophie, and Charlotte Gould (eds), *Marketing Art in the British Isles, 1700 to the Present: A Cultural History* (Farnham: Ashgate, 2012)

Milne-Smith, Amy, *London Clubland: A Cultural History of Gender and Class in Late-Victorian Britain* (London: Palgrave Macmillan, 2011)

Mitchell, Rosemary, 'A Stitch in Time? Women, Needlework, and the Making of History in Victorian Britain', *Journal of Victorian Culture*, 1/2 (1996), pp. 185–202

Morowitz, Laura, and William Vaughan (eds), *Artistic Brotherhoods in the Nineteenth Century* (Farnham: Ashgate, 2000)

Morton, Tara, '"An Arts and Crafts Society, Working for the Enfranchisement of Women": Unpicking the Political Threads of the Suffrage Atelier, 1909–1914', in *Suffrage and the Arts: Visual Culture, Politics and Enterprise* (eds) Miranda Garrett and Zoë Thomas (London: Bloomsbury, 2018), pp. 65–89

Morton, Tara, 'Changing Spaces: Art, Politics, and Identity in the Home Studios of the Suffrage Atelier', *Women's History Review*, 21/4 (2012), pp. 623–637

Myzelev, Alla, 'Craft Revival in Haslemere: She, Who Weaves …', *Women's History Review*, 18/4 (2009), pp. 597–618

Neiswander, Judith A., *The Cosmopolitan Interior: Liberalism and the British Home, 1870–1914* (New Haven: Yale University Press, 2008)

Nicholson, Shirley, *A Victorian Household* (Stroud: Sutton, 1994)

Nochlin, Linda, 'Why Are There No Great Women Artists?', in *Woman in Sexist Society: Studies in Power and Powerlessness* (eds) Vivian Gornick and Barbara Moran (New York: Basic Books, 1971), pp. 344–366

O'Neill, Morna, 'Rhetorics of Display: Arts and Crafts and Art Nouveau at the Turin Exhibition of 1902', *Journal of Design History*, 20/3 (2007), pp. 205–225

Palmer, Amy, 'Radical Conservatism and International Nationalism: The Peasant Arts Movement and its Search for the Country Heart of England', *Journal of the Social History Society*, 15/5 (2018), pp. 663–680

Parker, Rozsika, *The Subversive Stitch: Embroidery and the Making of the Feminine* (London: Women's Press, 1984)

Parker, Rozsika, and Griselda Pollock (eds), *Framing Feminism: Art and the Women's Movement, 1970–1985* (London: Pandora, 1987)

Parry, Linda, *Textiles of the Arts and Crafts Movement* (London: Thames and Hudson, 2005)

Parsons, Melinda Boyd, *To All Believers: The Art of Pamela Colman Smith* (Wilmington: Delaware Art Museum, 1975)

Pedersen, Joyce Senders, 'Victorian Liberal Feminism and the "Idea" of Work', in *Women and Work Culture: Britain, c. 1850–1950* (eds) Krista Cowman and Louise A. Jackson (Farnham: Ashgate, 2005), pp. 27–47

Perkin, Harold, *The Rise of Professional Society: England since 1880* (London: Routledge, 1989)

Peterson, M. Jeanne, *Family, Love, and Work in the Lives of Victorian Gentlewomen* (Bloomington: Indiana University Press, 1989)

Platman, Lara, *Art Workers Guild: 125 Years* (Norwich: Unicorn, 2009)

Pollock, Griselda, *Vision and Difference: Feminism, Femininity and the Histories of Art* (London: Routledge, 1988)

Pomeroy, Jordana (ed.), *Intrepid Women: Victorian Artists Travel* (Farnham: Ashgate, 2005)

Potvin, John, *Material and Visual Cultures Beyond Male Bonding, 1870–1914: Bodies, Boundaries and Intimacy* (Aldershot: Ashgate, 2008)

Prieto, Laura R., *At Home in the Studio: The Professionalization of Women Artists in America* (Cambridge, MA: Harvard University Press, 2001)

Quirk, Maria, 'Portraiture and Patronage: Women, Reputation, and the Business of Selling Art, 1880–1914', *Visual Culture in Britain*, 17/2 (2016), pp. 181–199

Quirk, Maria, 'Stitching Professionalism: Female-Run Embroidery Agencies and the Provision of Artistic Work for Women, 1870–1900', *Journal of Victorian Culture*, 21/2 (2016), pp. 184–204

Quirk, Maria, 'Reconsidering Professionalism: Women, Space and Art in England, 1880–1914' (Unpublished PhD thesis, University of Queensland, 2015)

Quirk, Maria, 'An Art School of Their Own: Women's Ateliers in England, 1880–1920', *Woman's Art Journal*, 34/2 (2013), pp. 39–44

Rappaport, Erika, 'Art, Commerce, or Empire? The Rebuilding of Regent Street, 1880–1927', *History Workshop Journal*, 53/1 (2002), pp. 94–117

Rappaport, Erika, *Shopping for Pleasure: Women in the Making of London's West End* (Princeton: Princeton University Press, 2001)

Readman, Paul, 'The Place of the Past in English Culture, c. 1890–1914', *Past and Present*, 186/1 (2005), pp. 147–199

Reed, Christopher, *Bloomsbury Rooms: Modernism, Subculture, and Domesticity* (New Haven: Yale University Press, 2004)

Rogers, Rebecca, and Myriam Boussahba-Bravard (eds), *Women in International and Universal Exhibitions, 1876–1937* (London: Routledge, 2017)

Roscoe, Barley, 'Artist Craftswomen Between the Wars', in *Women and Craft* (eds) Gillian Elinor and others (London: Virago, 1987), pp. 139–149

Rose, Gillian, *Feminism and Geography: The Limits of Geographical Knowledge* (Cambridge: Polity, 1993)

Rose, Lucy Ella, *Suffragist Artists in Partnership: Gender, Word and Image* (Edinburgh: Edinburgh University Press, 2018)

Rose, Lucy Ella, 'A Feminist Network in an Artists' Home: Mary and George Watts, George Meredith, and Josephine Butler', *Journal of Victorian Culture*, 21/1 (2016), pp. 74–91

Rose, Peter, '"It Must be Done Now": The Arts and Crafts Exhibition at Burlington House, 1916', *Journal of the Decorative Arts Society 1850–the Present*, 17 (1993), pp. 3–12

Saler, Michael, *The Avant-Garde in Interwar England: Medieval Modernism and the London Underground* (Oxford: Oxford University Press, 2001)

Schaffer, Talia, *Novel Craft: Victorian Domestic Handicraft and Nineteenth-Century Fiction* (New York: Oxford University Press, 2011)

Seddon, Jill, and Suzette Worden (eds), *Women Designing: Redefining Design in Britain Between the Wars* (Brighton: University of Brighton, 1994)

Shapiro Sanders, Lise, *Consuming Fantasies: Labor, Leisure, and the London Shopgirl, 1880–1920* (Columbus: Ohio State University Press, 2006)

Speck, Caroline, *Beyond the Battlefield: Women Artists of the Two World Wars* (London: Reaktion, 2014)

Stamp, Gavin, *Beauty's Awakening: The Centenary Exhibition of the Art Workers' Guild, 1884–1984* (Brighton: Brighton Museum, 1984)

Stansky, Peter, *Redesigning the World: William Morris, the 1880s, and the Arts and Crafts* (Princeton: Princeton University Press, 1985)

Stratigakos, Despina, *A Women's Berlin: Building the Modern City* (Minneapolis: University of Minnesota Press, 2008)

Sugg Ryan, Deborah, *Ideal Homes, 1918–1939: Domestic Design and Suburban Modernism* (Manchester: Manchester University Press, 2018)

Sutherland, Gillian, *In Search of the New Woman: Middle-Class Women and Work in Britain, 1870–1914* (Cambridge: Cambridge University Press, 2015)

Swinth, Kirsten, *Painting Professionals: Women Artists and the Development of Modern American Art, 1870–1930* (Chapel Hill: University of North Carolina Press, 2001)

Thomas, Zoë, "'I Loathe the Thought of Suffrage Sex Wars Coming into It": Institutional Conservatism in Early Twentieth-Century Women's Art Organizations', in *Suffrage and the Arts: Visual Culture, Politics and Enterprise* (eds) Miranda Garrett and Zoë Thomas (London: Bloomsbury, 2018), pp. 23–42

Thomas, Zoë, *Founding Members of the Women's Guild of Arts (act. 1907–c. 1939)*, Oxford Dictionary of National Biography, 2018

Thomas, Zoë, 'The Women's Guild of Arts: Gender, Space, and Professional Identity in London, 1870–1930' (Unpublished PhD thesis, Royal Holloway, University of London, 2016)

Thomas, Zoë, 'At Home with the Women's Guild of Arts: Gender and Professional Identity in London Studios, c. 1880–1925', *Women's History Review*, 24/6 (2015), pp. 938–964

Thoreson, Natasha, 'The Reluctant Reformer: May Morris' United States Lecture Tour of 1909–1910', *Textile Society of America Symposium Proceedings* (2012), pp. 1–9

Tickner, Lisa, 'Men's Work? Masculinity and Modernism', in *Visual Culture: Images and Interpretations* (ed.) Norman Bryson and others (Middletown: Wesleyan University Press, 1994), pp. 42–82

Tickner, Lisa, *The Spectacle of Women: Imagery of the Suffrage Campaign, 1907–1914* (London: Chatto and Windus, 1987)

Tidcombe, Marianne, *Women Bookbinders, 1880–1920* (New Castle: Oak Knoll, 1996)

Tillyard, Stella, *The Impact of Modernism, 1900–1920: Early Modernism and the Arts and Crafts Movement in Edwardian England* (London: Routledge, 1988)

Todd, Pamela, *William Morris and the Arts and Crafts Home* (London: Thames and Hudson, 2012)

Todd, Pamela, *The Pre-Raphaelites at Home* (London: Pavilion, 2001)

Tusan, Michelle Elizabeth, *Women Making News: Gender and Journalism in Modern Britain* (Champaign: University of Illinois Press, 2005)

Unwin, Melanie, 'Significant Other: Art and Craft in the Career and Marriage of Mary Watts', *Journal of Design History*, 17/3 (2004), pp. 237–250

Vicinus, Martha, *Intimate Friends: Women Who Loved Women, 1778–1928* (Chicago: University of Chicago Press, 2004)

Vicinus, Martha, *Independent Women: Work and Community for Single Women, 1850–1920* (Chicago: University of Chicago Press, 1985)

Walker, Lynne, 'Women and Church Art', *Studies in Victorian Architecture and Design*, 3 (2010), pp. 121–143

Walker, Lynne, 'Locating the Global/Rethinking the Local: Suffrage Politics, Architecture and Space', *Women's Studies Quarterly*, 34/1&2 (2006), pp. 174–196

Walker, Lynne, 'Women Patron-Builders in Britain: Identity, Difference and Memory in Spatial and Material Culture', in *Local/Global: Women Artists in the Nineteenth Century* (eds) Deborah Cherry and Janice Helland (Farnham: Ashgate, 2006), pp. 121–136

Walker, Lynne, 'Home and Away: The Feminist Remapping of Public and Private Space in Victorian London', in *The Unknown City: Contesting Architecture and Social Space* (eds) Iain Borden and others (Cambridge: MIT Press, 2001), pp. 296–311

Walker, Lynne, 'Vistas of Pleasure: Women Consumers of Urban Space in the West End of London, 1850–1900', in *Women in the Victorian Art World* (ed.) Clarissa Campbell Orr (Manchester: Manchester University Press, 1995), pp. 70–85

Walker, Lynne, 'The Arts and Crafts Alternative', in *A View from the Interior: Feminism, Women and Design* (eds) Judy Attfield and Pat Kirkham (London: Women's Press, 1989), pp. 165–173

Walkley, Giles, *Artists' Houses in London, 1764–1914* (Aldershot: Scolar, 1994)

Walkowitz, Judith R., *City of Dreadful Delight: Narratives of Sexual Danger in Late-Victorian Britain* (London: Virago, 1992)

Wallach Scott, Joan, 'The Conundrum of Equality', in *Gender and the Politics of History, Thirtieth Anniversary Edition* (ed.) Joan Wallach Scott (New York: Columbia University Press, 2018), pp. 199–215

Wallach Scott, Joan, *Only Paradoxes to Offer: French Feminists and the Rights of Man* (Cambridge, MA: Harvard University Press, 1997)

Waterfield, Giles, *The People's Galleries: Art Museums and Exhibitions in Britain, 1800–1914* (New Haven: Yale University Press, 2015)

Whyte, William, *Founding Members of the Art Workers' Guild (act. 1884–1899)*, Oxford Dictionary of National Biography, 2007

Whyte, William, 'The Intellectual Aristocracy Revisited', *Journal of Victorian Culture*, 10/1 (2005), pp. 15–45

Witz, Anne, *Professions and Patriarchy* (London: Routledge, 1992)

Wolf, Toni Lesser, 'Women Jewelers of the British Arts and Crafts Movement', *Journal of Decorative and Propoganda Arts*, 14 (Autumn 1989), pp. 28–45

Woollacott, Angela, *To Try Her Fortune in London: Australian Women, Colonialism, and Modernity* (Oxford: Oxford University Press, 2001)

Yeates, Amelia, and Serena Trowbridge (eds), *Pre-Raphaelite Masculinities: Constructions of Masculinity in Art and Literature* (Farnham: Ashgate, 2014)

Yeldham, Charlotte, *Women Artists in Nineteenth-Century France and England* (London: Garland, 1984)

Zakreski, Patricia, *Representing Female Artistic Labour, 1848–1890: Refining Work for the Middle-Class Woman* (Farnham: Ashgate, 2006)

Zipf, Catherine W., *Professional Pursuits: Women and the American Arts and Crafts Movement* (Knoxville: University of Tennessee Press, 2007)

Index

EU authorised representative for GPSR:
Easy Access System Europe, Mustamäe tee 50,
10621 Tallinn, Estonia
gpsr.requests@easproject.com